FROM FIGHTERS TO S
HOW THE ISRAELI DEFENSE

From Fighters to Soldiers

How the Israeli Defense Forces Began

———

Yaacov N. Goldstein

With a Foreword by
Professor Yoav Gelber
Lt. Colonel (Res.),
Israel Defense Forces (IDF)

sussex
ACADEMIC
PRESS

2 4 6 8 10 9 7 5 3 1

First published 1998 in Great Britain by
SUSSEX ACADEMIC PRESS
Box 2950
Brighton BN2 5SP

and in the United States of America by
SUSSEX ACADEMIC PRESS
5804 N.E. Hassalo St.
Portland, Oregon 97213–3644

British Library Cataloguing in Publication Data
A CIP catalogue record for this book is available from the British Library.

Library of Congress Cataloging-in Publication Data
From fighters to soldiers : how the Israeli defense forces began / Yaacov N.
Goldstein : with a foreword by Yoav Gelber
p   cm.
Includes bibliographical references and index.
ISBN 1–902210–01–8 (hardcover : alk. paper). — ISBN 1–902210–02–6
(pbk. : alk. paper)
1. Israel—Armed Forces—History   2. Israel. Tseva haganah le-Yisra'el—History.
I. Title.
UA853.I8G65 1998
355'.009694—dc21   98–115252
CIP

Printed by Biddles Ltd, Guildford and King's Lynn
This book is printed on acid-free paper

Contents

Foreword by Yoav Gelber

For centuries Jews and militarism/combat were concepts alien to each other. Only with the progress of emancipation in the nineteenth century did Jews join the armies of their countries in ever-growing numbers and take part in national liberation movements. Jewish officers, other ranks, militia combatants and revolutionaries served among gentiles and fought for general goals, but not for their people's sake. In the wake of the pogroms which befell East European Jewry following the Russian revolutions of 1905 and 1917, Jewish self-defense organizations emerged across the Russian Pale. This was the first example of a Jewish paramilitary organization for a Jewish cause.

Veterans of the early self-defense groups, as well as members of clandestine revolutionary cells, immigrated to Palestine in the decade that preceded the First World War. They transferred the idea of Jews defending themselves against hostile surroundings, and brought the characteristics of revolutionary conspirative cells from Eastern Europe to the Middle East. Embodying these concepts in the Bar Giora and Hashomer organizations, which they founded in 1907 and 1909, they laid the foundations for a succession of Jewish paramilitary bodies that were active throughout the Ottoman and the British Mandate periods. Hashomer's vision of an independent Jewish force employed for purely Jewish national missions was the first conceptual breakthrough which culminated, forty years later, in 1948, in the formation of the Israel Defense Force (IDF).

In this original and innovative book, Yaacov Goldstein describes the interesting history of this small but pioneering organization. Penetrating into the ideological and social world of these fighters, he perceptively analyses Hashomer's unique role in the long process of changing the Jew's traditional non-combatant image. Particularly and correctly, Goldstein underscores the group's foresight of building a national Jewish army which has made it the forerunner of the IDF.

Lt. Colonel (Res.) Prof. Yoav Gelber
Director of the Herzl Institute for Research of Zionism
Haifa, April 1998

Acknowledgments

I would like to acknowledge my grateful thanks to the following institutions for their generous support, which has assisted in the publication of this book:

The Faculty of Humanities, University of Haifa and The Research Authority, University of Haifa.

Cover picture: Meir Hazanovitch is the horserider; from left to right in the group picture – Mendel Portugali, Yisrael Shohat and Yisrael Gil'adi. This trio led Hashomer between 1909 and 1914.

Introduction

If you long to inherit the land of your birth,
Buckle on the sword and take up the bow,
And go in the footsteps of your fathers.
With weeping and tearful pleadings
Zion will not be won.
With sword and bow-hark ye!
Jerusalem will be rebuilt.

Naftali Hertz Imber

THE IDEA of armed self-defense, as distinct from spiritual self-defense involving martyrdom, was never foreign to the Jews throughout their long years of exile in the diaspora. This was so despite the absence of fundamental elements possessed by all nations that underlie and encourage the use of force in passive or active self-defense. In the diaspora the Jews had no territorial, demographic or historical center. Their political and religious-cultural center in the Land of Israel was desolate, with no possibility, it seemed, of restoration. The people themselves were dispersed among the nations like unwanted intruders, in conditions of discrimination and persecution, and with no viable, stable foundation for their physical and economic existence. These facts predetermined that in most cases armed self-defense, even if momentarily successful, was in the end doomed to failure. Being in exile, the fighting Jew lacked the driving force of any self-defense, namely, the hope of survival. For him, armed struggle, fierce and courageous as it may be, was bound to end cruelly, in his death. In its outcome armed defense was no different from the supreme form of spiritual and religious protest – martyrdom. The means differed but the result was the same. The effect of this was undoubtedly to weaken the resolve of the Jewish communities to engage in defense by resorting to arms.

The hope of renewing the spiritual, cultural, and perhaps political center in Palestine was entangled in a web of messianic aspirations. These aspirations generally did not necessitate activism or any concrete economic or political measures. Except at times of the short-lived appearances of false messiahs, the return to the Land of Israel remained a fond but forlorn hope, requiring a miracle for its realization. In this setting it is surprising that the evidence of courage in individual Jews and in whole communities, not just through martyrdom but through armed defense, is so manifest throughout the ages of the diaspora.

Political and military conflict were inherent in the various national movements that arose in nineteenth-century Europe. Sustained by the ideas of the French Revolution and the post-Napoleonic period, these struggles were for liberation and political independence. The uprisings of oppressed peoples (Greeks, Poles, Italians and others) and the wars that restored sovereignty to ancient states and created new ones (Greece, Italy, the Balkan countries) highlighted the need for the generation and organization of military power as an integral part of national aspirations and national movements.

Moreover, modern nationalism fostered self-awareness and the formulation of the unique history of each nation, with its sagas of valor of bygone days. National romance, nurtured on the past, fired a readiness for struggle in the present.[1] These characteristics of the European national movements did not bypass modern Jewish nationalism in the nineteenth century which, while drawing on religious messianic hopes already rooted in the people, also breathed the political and ideological air of Europe in that age.[2] From the start, this twofold influence inseparably joined thoughts about the need for some kind of military force to ideas of a return to the homeland and the restoration of the Jewish national concept.

Bar Giora and Hashomer constitute one of the most enthralling subjects in the history of the Yishuv. The manifestation of the new Jew, who met force with force, was jealous of his honor and defended the national interest with weapon in hand, well suited the Zionist and Yishuv ethos that was seeking to shape a new Jewish man and society in the ancient and renascent homeland. To this was added the aura of mystery and daring of the underground, which actually engaged in combat and in external appearance struck a romantic chord in the youth of the *Second Aliya* and the periods that followed. Bar Giora and Hashomer also fashioned a bond between the Jewish present and the long-gone golden age of the First and Second Temples and its heroic figures. In this sense the two organizations remade the historic tie replete with bravery that had been severed by millennia of exile, and they heralded a different and better future.

The Bar Giora and Hashomer associations were the first organized and consistent expression on a national Yishuv scale of the combination of the norm of force *with* the Zionist ethos for the purpose of realizing national goals in Palestine. The fascination of Bar Giora and Hashomer is, among other things, that for all their dedication and concentration on the dimension of force, they understood that to attain Zionist and social aims they had to actualize other norms too. These included the norm of Jewish labor, return to the land, rural demographic expansion, understanding of Arab culture and mentality, and fostering friendship with the Arab population. In their belief in all these they were the true sons of the *Second Aliya* and the Palestinian labor movement.

In light of all this, it is not surprising that the historiography of the Zionist movement, the Yishuv, the Palestinian labor movement and obviously of the development of Jewish defense forces, has treated Bar Giora and Hashomer insofar as they affect each of the areas listed. Many historians have discussed Hashomer, including Yosef Gorney, Elkana Margalit, Matityahu Mintz, Jonathan Frankel, Yisrael Kollat, Anita Shapira, and others. Each has contributed a share to the subject of Hashomer, even though this organization was not the focus of their scholarship.

Mention must be made of the foundation stones of the research into Hashomer, such as documentary evidence in various archives and also the recollections, testimony, and writings of the personages themselves: Yisrael and Manya Shohat, Zvi Nadav, Pinhas Shneorson, Alexander Zayd, Mordechai Yigael, Yitzhak Ben Zvi and Rahel Yanait Ben Zvi, and many others, whose works have been published as books or are included in *Second Aliya Volume, Hashomer Anthology* and *Hashomer Volume*. Elements of this material also served the earliest studies on the Palestinian labor movement, which refer to Hashomer, such as Zvi Even-Shoshan's book *History of the Palestine Workers' Movement* and Moshe Baraslavsky's *The Palestinian Worker's Movement*.

Above all, note should be made of the far-ranging work of Yehuda Slutzky and his associate in producing *History of the Hagana*. With this great composition Slutzky laid the foundation and masterfully portrayed the history of the Bar Giora and Hashomer associations. Slutzky regarded them as the basis upon which the Hagana was built, namely, the fighting arm of the Zionist movement and the organized Yishuv. Not surprisingly, previous and ongoing scholarship on the history of the Yishuv has had recourse, directly or indirectly, to the wealth of material gathered by Slutzky.

Such is my indebtedness.

The innovations of the present research are the following. This is the first comprehensive book on Bar Giora and Hashomer and Hashomer veterans and former members. To date, all studies and publications have covered the history of the association until its dissolution in May 1920. Studies do exist relating in one way or another to the Hashomer veterans, but only marginally to their treatment of other matters. Such are Anita Shapira's essay and Elkana Margalit's book on the Joseph Trumpeldor Labor Battalion. By contrast, this book concentrates on Hashomer and the fate of its veterans and former members as the focus of the research. It traces the first glimmer of ideas on the creation of a Jewish defensive force prior to the *First Aliya*, the beginnings of individual self-defense and the defensive organizations in the *First Aliya*, the founding of Bar Giora and Hashomer in the *Second Aliya,* and their history until the disbanding of Hashomer in the spring of 1920. The text then follows the activity of the Hashomer veterans and former members in the framework of the Hagana and as the separate Hakibbutz organization with the Joseph Trumpeldor Labor Battalion until the latter broke up at the end of 1926. The integration and contribution of former Hashomer members in the defense of the Yishuv is also described. The work concludes with a chapter on the involvement and input of the Hashomer veterans in the Hapoel association, where they laid the foundation on which they aspired to create a human reservoir for defense and also a Palestinian *Schutzbung*. The book ends with the departure of the Hashomer veterans from Hapoel in 1934. This step was the swan-song of their activity as a group. Henceforth they were pushed aside, as a collective entity and as individuals, from the stage of public activity and only a few of them remained even on its margins. The silken thread of human perseverance, ideological and organizational, in the sphere of defense activity is the legitimization of telling a story that continued to 1934, and did not terminate, as commonly thought, in 1920.

The work critically examines Yehuda Slutzky's comprehensive research, which has exerted a major effect on existing positions in the writing of the history of Bar Giora and Hashomer. The stances and assumptions in *History of the Hagana* primarily reflect the victorious school in the Hagana, that of Eliahu Golomb and his adherents. Slutzky established the view of Bar Giora and Hashomer as the foundation tier and the forebears of the Jewish defense movement, out of which sprang the Hagana and the Israel Defense Forces. In this Slutzky recognized the status and the historic contribution of Hashomer. But *History of the Hagana* asserts that historical development necessitated the demise of Hashomer, which indeed suited the conditions of Ottoman times but was not organizationally or ideologically constructed to contend with the new reality of the Mandatory period. To meet the new circumstances, with its special problems, a different organization was needed – one based on different premises and ideological concepts, and this found expression in the creation of the Hagana. Moreover, Slutzky unilaterally expresses the Golomb school's wholly and unswervingly negative attitude to the defensive activity of the Hashomer veterans after the disbanding of Hashomer.

This was decisive in the discrediting and delegitimization of this group and in the distortion of its historical positions on the ideology of national defense in the period before the dissolution of Hashomer and after.

This book presents the reader with the real defensive concept of the defeated school of the Hashomer veterans and their handful of allies, with its positive and negative qualities alike. An attempt is made to reveal the historical truth, which until now has been buried under a mass of inaccurate and incorrect interpretation. The need for revision and meticulous re-examination of the versions presented in *History of the Hagana* has been recognized for some time. This book addresses that need.

Like Hashomer, Hakibbutz too has been mentioned in various studies, but not as a central theme. The exception is Yehuda Slutzky, who considered the subject more broadly within the overall research into the history of the Hagana, although he too was obliged to impose limits. Slutzky's study is inaccurate and incomplete. My concern is to make a comprehensive contribution to the question. The research into Hakibbutz is likewise innovatory with respect to the place and date of its foundation, the illumination of its political and ideological views, and the political location of this body in the social and political turbulence of these days. In the research as a whole, and on Hakibbutz in particular, the author has been helped by a wide variety of material, including new documents.

The chapter on the Hapoel and Hasadran associations is the first thorough study of a subject barely touched so far in the historiography. This section attempts to shed light on the special role that the group of Hashomer veterans was called to fulfill in the Hapoel framework as a result of the political and defensive changes that took place between the 1920s and 1930s in the Zionist movement and in the Yishuv.

Four specific questions are raised:

1   The existing historiography argues a pro-Ottoman orientation in the Poaley Zion party and Hashomer during the First World War until 1917, when the south of the country was conquered by the British. This attitude was the continuation of the ideological outlook that characterized the two bodies before the war. An attempt is made to investigate the truth of this concept.

2   The chapter on the transition of Hashomer into the Hagana describes the process very differently from what is usually accepted. The relevant historiography, drawing on *History of the Hagana*, states that:

(a) In terms of its concepts, organization and human resources Hashomer did not fit the new conditions of the Mandatory period; therefore it had to be replaced by a different organizational framework suited to them.

(b) Hashomer, as a closed *avant-garde* selective organization, had to make way for a mass security organization.

(c) Hashomer was an independent organization that did not submit to the powers of the Yishuv institutions. It thereby adopted an anti-democratic stance because it did not accept the authority of the organized Yishuv over the security arm. This book takes issue with these underlying assumptions.

3   What was the status of women in Bar Giora and Hashomer?

4   What was Hashomer's policy toward the Arabs, ideologically and in daily life, until its dismemberment?

1

The First Aliya: *Defense and Guarding*

On the Jordan and in the Sharon,
where Arabs encamp –
That will be our land!
We too are among the builders!
One day the standard-bearers will arise –
Betray them not.
To your weapons with valor,
For we use them well!
Sha'ul Tchernichovsky

A S EARLY AS the first half of the nineteenth century Rabbi Yehuda Bibas, the spiritual head of the Jewish community of Corfu, wrote that the Jews must once again learn to wield arms. It was no accident that the words were written at the time of Greek liberation from the Turks. In Bibas's view the Jews should follow in the Greek path, and take Palestine from the Turks by force.[1] Similarly, Bibas's pupil, R. Yehuda Alkalai, who lived and worked in Serbia in the mid-nineteenth century, was influenced by the Balkan national movements and became a standard-bearer of the Jewish national idea, the first of a series of "forerunners of Zionism." Alkalai's many ideas, formulated in great detail, included the notion that the Christian kings should send their Jewish soldiers to Palestine to protect the renascent Jewish settlement there.[2] R. Zvi Kalisher, Alkalai's contemporary and also a forerunner of Zionism, in his book *Derishat Tsiyon* (Zion's Demand) (1862) called on the wealthy among the Jews to contribute whatever they could to the upbuilding of the land. In his detailed design for the restoration of Palestine, Kalisher held that it was necessary "to prepare guards there (in Palestine) proficient in warfare, so that Arabs do not come to offer tents to the robbers or ruin the seedlings and the vines, and they (the settlers) should establish a police force to destroy them."[3]

In the second half of the nineteenth century Perets Smolenskin, editor of the journal *Ha-shahar*, published in Vienna, also dealt with the subject,[4] as did David Gordon, the editor of the journal *Ha-maggid*.[5] These two belonged to the young generation of "enlightened" Jewish scholars, some of them secular, who were in search of a new foundation for continued Jewish identity, and arrived at the concept of nationalism.

Noteworthy among the immigrants to Palestine was Akiva Yosef Schlesinger, who came from Hungary in 1870 and later became one of the founders of Petah Tikva. Schlesinger first settled in Jerusalem, where he established the "Society of Restorers of Pristine Glory," whose goal was the return of Jews to working the land and to Hebrew speech. Schlesinger also published a booklet in which he detailed the Society's settlement plan. He held that together with settlement itself there had to be a defense force to protect the settlers. This would be based on the farmers, each of whom would be expected to carry arms and be able to use them. Schlesinger also calculated the percentage of guards required from the settlers, and divided them into foot patrols and mounted patrols. To the former group he gave the name *Shomriel* (God's Guards), to the latter *Lohmie'l* (God's Fighters).[6] These concepts, born together with the idea of the return to the soil of Palestine and national revival, were of course also held by the people of the *First Aliya*.

The term *First Aliya* (literally "ascent") was given to the wave of immigration that entered Palestine between 1882 and 1904. This influx changed the Jewish community there in size and in nature, and laid the foundations for a national home. This Aliya was a spur of the huge migration of Jews from Eastern Europe, particularly Russia, which began after the assassination of Tsar Alexander II, in consequence of which pogroms were unleashed against hundreds of Jewish communities in Russia. While some of the migrants set out for central and western Europe, for most the goal was across the seas – America. Only a tiny percentage, some 20,000 persons, made their way to Palestine, where they created the infrastructure for the new (or renewed) Jewish settlement, known by its Hebrew name, the Yishuv. The immigration raised the total Jewish population of Palestine from about 25,000 at the start of the *First Aliya* to about 55,000 at its end (including natural increase).

In its composition the *First Aliya* was heterogeneous, but three main streams could be distinguished among the new arrivals: (1) orthodox Jews, who continued to migrate to the Holy Land out of religious motives as they had for generations; (2) Jews with nationalist motivation, who settled in the existing cities, Jerusalem, Jaffa and Haifa, where they laid the foundations for new urban Jewish settlement; (3) Jews with a nationalist consciousness who wished to settle the land, and so founded a string of *moshavot* (singular *moshava*: village), which paved the way for rural

Jewish settlement in Palestine. The two latter streams also consisted of religious Jews. In fact, except for the few dozen members of the Bilu (a pre-Zionist "Zionist" movement, the name being the Hebrew acronym for *Beit ya'akov lekhu venelekha:* "House of Jacob, come, let us go" – Isaiah 2: 5), the *First Aliya* was wholly a religious immigration, although made up primarily of those with a nationalist consciousness.

Three phases characterized the founding of the *moshavot,* the great enterprise of the third of these streams. The first was from 1882 to 1884, when the following villages were established: Rishon le-Tsiyon, Zikhron Ya'akov Rosh Pina, Yesud ha-Ma'ala, 'Ekron (Mazkeret Batya), and Gedera; Petah Tikva was resuscitated during this period, and the first budding of Nes Tsiyona began. The second phase was primarily 1890–1 and then subsequent years, when two large settlements were founded: Rehovot and Hadera. Several others were also established: Bat Shelomo and Meir Shefaya in the Shomron (Samaria), 'Ein Zeitim not far from Tsefat, and Mishmar ha-Yarden in the Upper Galilee. The third phase covered the last years of this immigration, 1900 to 1904, and produced the settlements Havat Sejera, Sejera, Kefar Tabor, Yavneel and Beit Gan in the Lower Galilee, and Menahamiya (Milhamiya) in the Jordan Valley.

In addition to the development of European ideas, the situation in Ottoman Palestine obliged the Jewish settlement at the time of the *First Aliya* to acquire means of guarding and defense. In the second half of the nineteenth century some improvement had indeed taken place regarding safety of property and life, but Turkish rule, in force since 1516, was still remote from what was by then the norm in Europe, whence the settlers came. The latter had to contend with a hostile environment marked by several underlying features: (a) As stated, security conditions were poor. The Jewish settlers could expect no protection or help from the government because of corruption, inefficiency and outright antagonism toward them; (b) the European consuls and their deputies in Jaffa and Acre were far away and not always accessible; (c) the primitive means of communication inside the country, and between Palestine and government posts outside, blocked any chance of swift action; (d) cultural dissimilarity, strange and foreign ways, ignorance of language and differences in mentality generally greatly exacerbated the tensions and hostility between the Jews and their neighbors, which resulted in many clashes, including those overgrazing. The local inhabitants used to pasture their beasts on any open space that was not under the plow, regardless of ownership, whereas the Jews in their countries of origin had been accustomed to land being the exclusive domain of its owner at all times, including fallow. Lastly (e), the irregular landownership regime, the vague boundaries of title and "holdings," and tortuous land-registry laws that permitted a variety of interpretations, delays in judgment and miscarriage of justice, sometimes caused serious strife between the settlers and their neighbors over land. The history of the *moshavot* of the *First Aliya* is replete with tales of these quarrels, of which the most famous is that between the Metulla settlers and the Druze.[7] This poor state of security necessitated sound organization by the settlers who had arrived before 1882 and by the founders of the *moshavot* in the *First Aliya*. In terms of security, three phases may be distinguished in the *First Aliya* period: the heroic phase, the protection by Baron Edmond de Rothschild of Paris (1882–1900) and the crisis associated with the transfer to the Jewish Colonization Association (JCA) (1900).

The Heroic Phase

This phase immediately followed the founding of each *moshava*. The settlers were obliged to demonstrate to their neighbors their capacity to safeguard their rights. In the first place this naturally meant defending their property and their lives. With the founding of a *moshava*, which was a new and foreign body in the existing fabric, the inhabitants round about began to apply pressure to test the strength, or weakness, of the infant settlement. The outcome of this probing might be acceptance or at times amity and even efforts to strike a bargain on common defense; or there were attempts to gain control. The duration of this phase differed for each *moshava*, depending on its size, its determination to defend its rights, and its ability to protect itself. The large *moshavot*, Petah Tikva (founded in 1878, then abandoned, and revitalized in 1883), Rishon le-Tsiyon, Zikhron Ya'akov, Rehovot, passed through this stage fairly rapidly and successfully, while small villages like Kastina (later Beer Toviya) and Gedera could not withstand the test, or it was fairly prolonged.[8] In this difficult period, when the settlers were mostly forced to rely on themselves, Jews of remarkable spiritual and physical resources came to the fore, displaying extraordinary courage in the defense of their settlement. Their deeds served as a model, and swept other settlers along with them, and in several instances they thereby saved the new village. Among these personalities were Sandor Haddad of Petah Tikva, Ya'akov Ben-Maimon (Zirmati) of Jaffa, who was one of the Petah Tikva guards, Yosef Kastel of Hebron who guarded in Hadera, "Horseback Horowitz" of Hadera, Berele (Dov) Rosenblum, the blacksmith of Rehovot; these and their like became figures in the folklore that grew up around the *moshavot* of the *First Aliya*.[9] Others, no less impressive, such as Yehuda Raab, Yisrael Feinberg, Yehoshua Hankin, Yehoshua Stamper.[10] and their comrades, entered into Yishuv history.

Protection by Baron Rothschild

Responsibility for the defense of the *moshavot* under the aegis of the Baron, like other aspects of life, was transferred from the settlers to the Baron's officials. This body of functionaries was not ideologically geared to foster Jewish self-defense, and just as they mistrusted the settlers in all other matters, they had no confidence in them here either. The officials' way was different, and generally they relied on connections with the Turkish authorities and invocation of the Baron's name and the powers of the European consuls, or alternatively handing out bribes – that is, the stick-and-carrot method. In addition, they bribed, intimidated or "bought" the local Arab chiefs. This protective umbrella of the Baron defended and brought a degree of quiet to the *moshavot*, although it did not eliminate theft and damage to property, which made real defensive measures necessary. In most cases the guards were not Jews. In some places a Jewish security contractor operated, using Bedouin, Arab, Circassian (see below), and other guards; one such broker was Avraham Shapira in Petah Tikva. The transfer of responsibility for protection of life and property from the settlers themselves to the Baron's staff and Jewish and non-Jewish contractors caused a decline and attenuation of personal initiative, spontaneous response and the mental and physical capacity of the farmers to defend themselves – precisely the factors that had begun to bud in the previous phase. "Respect for the farmers is dwindling among their neighbors, but the Baron's name and money serve as their rampart."[11]

A typical story concerns the relations that developed in 1891 between Petah Tikva, most of whose territory then enjoyed the Baron's protection, and one of the neighboring Arab shaykhs, Shaykh Abu Rabah, with whom there was much trouble. In 1891 the Baron's men reached an interesting understanding with him, "and Abu Rabah undertook to 'protect' the *moshava* for a certain yearly sum. He frequently took, on loan, various items, such as a wagon, harnesses, wood, and tools, which he 'forgot' to return. The officials likewise good-naturedly conceded to him a 200-dunam tract of land, which was also plowed by tractor at his request."[12]

This episode actually reflects submission to the partial protection of a local Arab chief, what is more, by so large a *moshava* as Petah Tikva which had a tradition of self-defense and renowned Jewish guards. In some places the situation was even worse. In Yesud ha-Ma'ala, for example, after Yehoshua Osvitsky was dismissed from his position as the Baron's chief official in the Galilee (1897), "fear of the neighboring Arabs once more fell upon the villagers of Yesud ha-Ma'ala," and they hired non-Jewish guards, who in fact took over the place. Not only did they rob, they also despised the settlers who gave them their food and frequently humiliated them personally.[13]

The Transition to the JCA (1900)

In 1900 Baron Rothschild transferred *moshavot* that had been under his sponsorship and management to the aegis of the JCA, a company set up in 1891 by Baron Maurice Hirsch with the aim of giving succor to persecuted Jews, particularly from Eastern Europe. This step resulted in a general deterioration of the security situation. The Baron's protection had defended the *moshavot*, including those not under his sponsorship, from depredations by the Turkish government and wholesale attack by the surrounding Arabs; this ceased to exist. The *moshavot*, their lands already wide open and their prestige waning, now additionally became prey to constant danger at the hands of the authorities and the local chiefs. The settlers were unable to recapture the spirit that had guided and spurred them to intrepid acts in the beginning. Guarding in the *moshavot*, the large ones included, fell entirely into the hands of local Arab chiefs, Mughrabis (see below), Bedouin, Circassians and others. Here and there, as in the case of Petah Tikva, Jewish security contractors existed, but the guards themselves were not Jews. The JCA, ever loyal to its method, was unwilling to provide protection as the Baron had, and required the farmers to be profitable and self-supporting.[14]

In general, Moshe Smilansky's description fits the situation that developed in the subject under review toward the end of the *First Aliya*:

> The glorious days of the first guards in Petah Tikva had passed. In Petah Tikva the Jews were still in charge of the guards, and Avraham Shapira kept strict discipline over the Arabs under him and his name commanded respect among the Arabs generally. But in all the other *moshavot*, in the Galilee, in Samaria and Judea, guarding was handed over entirely to Mughrabis, Bedouin, Circassians, and the like. Guarding throughout the land, in towns and villages, was placed in their hands, and the Jewish farmers confined themselves to planting, plowing and sowing; they yielded the right of guarding to their neighbors.[15]

The consequence was that the Jewish agricultural settlement became subject to the mercies of its "protectors." In Metulla (founded 1896) they paid a tax to the Metuali beys (Shi'ite Muslims who lived in southern Lebanon); in Yesud Ha-Ma'ala, Mughrabis (Muslims who had fled from Algeria after its conquest by the French in 1830) and Circassians (Muslims who had fled from the Caucasus after the region was occupied by Russia and had made their way to Palestine in 1878) fought each other over the right to guard the *moshava*; Sejera was in a state of lawlessness; Rosh Pina was riddled with thievery. Even Zikhron Ya'akov paid money to the local chiefs. In Hadera outlying land was left unsown and guarding was in the hands of strangers. Rishon le-Tsiyon and Rehovot too feared any alteration in the guarding arrangements by the outsiders, because any such change undermined whatever security there was, and ended in forfeiture of property.

Yet despite the deterioration during the Rothschild and JCA phases in guarding property and protecting life, the ideas of re-educating the Yishuv Jews to take up arms and of creating a military defense body to assume responsibility for the two interlinked objectives never disappeared. These stemmed from the constant inflow of national concepts from the diaspora, and from the incessant ferment of similar notions within the young Yishuv. The first element found expression in nationalist literature, which gave voice to the longed-for goals. Naftali Hertz Imber, later to write *Hatikva,* which became the anthem of the Zionist movement and then of the state of Israel, wrote:

> If you long to inherit the land of your birth,
> Buckle on the sword and take up the bow,
> And go in the footsteps of your fathers.
> With weeping and tearful pleadings
> Zion will not be won.
> With sword and bow – hark ye!
> Jerusalem will be rebuilt.

A similar spirit informs Sha'ul Tchernichovsky's poem written in 1897:

> On the Jordan and in the Sharon,
> where Arabs encamp –
> That will be our land!
> We too are among the builders!
> One day the standard-bearers will arise –
> Betray them not.
> To your weapons with valor,
> For we use them well![16]

At the threshold of the *Second Aliya* Ya'akov Cohen wrote:

> We have arisen, we have returned!
> The restorers of might, the young men of strength
> It is we who have arisen, we returned, rebels!
> Come to redeem our land with the clamor of war –
> We claim this birthright with hand upraised!
> Judah fell in blood and fire –
> In blood and fire Judah shall arise![17]

It is well to recall that astonishing company of young people, the Bilu, mentioned above, who reached Palestine in August 1882. In their proposed charter a clause was formulated that expressly dealt with the need to train Jews to wage war. Describing the large settlement they planned to establish in Palestine and the education in it, they stated:

> The way of life that people will be taught in the land, whose every inch, every handful of dust reminds us of the great deeds and events in the lives of our forefathers in olden times . . . is to enlighten within them and ignite them with God-given passion to fill their spirit with boldness and glory and their hearts with the desire to labor faithfully on the mountains of Zion, and also to teach the sons of Judah the craft of war. There they will learn to be proficient in shooting arrows and drawing the bow, arts that are most expedient for the dwellers of the ancient land . . . [18]

Ze'ev Dubnow, one of the Bilu, wrote that weapons training should provide the basis for some future opportunity to gain control of the land,[19] a thought that was shared by a considerable number of people of the *First Aliya*. They were imbued with a still-undefined sense that somehow, when the day came, the land would be freed from the corrupt and rotten Turkish rule, and in it Jewish independence would be rebuilt.

A fascinating figure at the time was the great dreamer Michael Halperin. Halperin first reached Palestine in 1885, at which time he concluded that the country had to be conquered from the Turks by armed force. After a short stay he returned to the diaspora and began propagating his ideas. Halperin arrived in Palestine again in 1887 and became a leader of the Workers' Association in Rishon le-Tsiyon and a leader of the rebellion that broke out in the *moshava* against Yehoshua Osvitsky, mentioned above. Halperin was driven out of the village, and left the country once more. He returned yet again in the late summer of 1890, going to Rehovot where he became a leader of the Federation of the Tens. At the time of the Al-Arish idea of 1902–3 he proposed the establishment of a Jewish Legion to conquer the land. Halperin was a dreamer, not a man of action, and so failed to realize his ambitions. But he was able to influence people, whom he inspired with his vision of a resort to arms, the development of an independent capability for self-defense, and the creation of a Jewish security force. Some of the founders of Bar Giora and Hashomer were his disciples and adherents.[20] Halperin was also involved in the establishment of a short-lived organization called The Sword for Our People and Our Land (Hebrew acronym *Halul*), whose goal was to plot insurrection against the Turks.[21]

The Federation of the Tens, mentioned above, was established in Rehovot after the founding of this *moshava* in 1890. Its leaders were Aharon Eisenberg, Efrayim Harlap, Yitshak Hayutman, Natan Shapira and Michael Halperin. The Federation was clandestine, and constructed as separate cells in the best underground tradition. It undertook the tasks of a present-day trade union, that is, concern for workers and their living conditions, but at the same time it set itself a national political goal, which required "all members to engage in propaganda and military training, so that they may be able to fulfill their future role: to serve as the core of 'The Hebrew Army'."[22]

In sum, the idea of establishing some form of military defense force, being an integral part of the movement of return to the soil and of the national idea, was held by a considerable number in the nationalist segment of the *First Aliya*. In circumstances of the collapse of the Ottoman Empire and the gains of the national movements in Europe and the Balkans, it was only natural that those who had migrated to Palestine on the strength of the national concept would nurture within them ideas, dreams and aspirations for the revival of the Jewish people in its land and the restoration of its independence. A consequence of such thinking was the formation of the idea of a military security force. The *First Aliya* evinces manifestations of bravery, daring and solidarity among the *moshavot*, expressed in mutual support in cases of attack against one of them or within the *moshavot*. The *First Aliya* was influenced not only by ideas of weapons handling, defense, military training and the creation of a military force, but even reached the point of a general national outlook in these matters, as expressed in the program of the Federation of the Tens and in the very formation of this organization, with its national ambitions.

But the *First Aliya* could not get beyond the stage of ideas. The only organizational framework with a national orientation that formed was short lived and left no trace in the Yishuv. Even in guarding property or protecting life, activities concomitant with the very beginnings of this Aliya, principles and methods were not elaborated. Usually, each settlement looked to itself, and common concern or more comprehensive action were not in evidence. To this we may add that in the Rothschild and the JCA phases there was serious deterioration, as described. The national enterprise was left to the *Second Aliya*, with the formation of the Bar Giora and Hashomer organizations.

2

The Second Aliya: *Ideology and Organization*

Judah fell in blood and fire –
In blood and fire Judah shall rise.
Ya'akov Cohen

THE TERM "*Second Aliya*" has chronological and sociological significance. Chronologically, it refers to the decade between 1904 and
1914, when this migration took place. The First World War period was
marked by events and problems essentially different from those of the
preceding years. In the period 1914–18 there was no immigration but the
reverse: the Jewish settlement (Yishuv) in Palestine suffered expulsions
and a reduction of population through the vicissitudes of war; the *Third
Aliya* commenced toward the end of 1918.

Statistically, the discussion centers on how many settlers entered the
country in the course of the *Second Aliya*, how many left, and how much
the Yishuv grew through natural increase.[1] In the absence of exact figures
it is estimated that the Jewish settlement grew by 55,000 persons in the
decade under review, to reach a total of 85,000.

Sociologically, the new arrivals in this period included traditionally
religious people, who built up the so-called "old" Yishuv, pious or
free-thinking folk with a national consciousness who mainly concentrated
in urban centers, immigrants from the Middle Eastern Jewish communities, a Yemeni immigration, and youths who came from eastern Europe
with nothing but a social and national awareness; some of them went to
work at the *moshavot* of the *First Aliya*. Ideologically, the *Second Aliya*
is associated with the last group, which although numerically small,[2] in
fact created the Palestine labor movement.

This last group overflowed with ideas about the society of the future
that was to be made in Palestine. A consequence of this ideological ferment
was a variety of social and economic experiments and the formation of
living frameworks based politically, economically and socially on new

ideologies. These gave rise to the unique features of the Palestine labor movement compared with other such movements around the world, such as the General Federation of Labor (Histadrut), the kibbutz, and the cooperative village (*moshav-'ovdim*: moshav), and they left their impress on the Jewish national movement, that is, Zionism, and on the Palestine Yishuv. Within this mass of national ideologies should be included the hope and desire to establish a Jewish defensive force as part of the process of national revival. As in the *First Aliya*, so in the *Second Aliya* the idea of creating a military defensive force arose in the agricultural settlements – in the *moshavot* where a sizable section of the active nationalist element was concentrated and where the young people of the *Second Aliya* worked. Moreover, it was the *moshavot* that stood on the front line of the confrontation with the problems of defense arising from the special circumstances of the country and from the new political processes taking shape since the first decade of the century.

The principle of "conquest of labor" (*kibbush ha-'avoda*) meant the replacement of Arabs by Jews in all work as well as the establishment of a Jewish working class as an integral part of the rebuilding of the nation in Palestine. The concept was elaborated in the early years of the *Second Aliya* by its young people, and in the first place it applied to conquest of labor in agriculture in the *moshavot* where they lived and worked. True, this approach derived from the situation in Palestine, where no real work was to be found in the towns and industry hardly existed, but it also contained an ideological component binding the idea of national revival to the idea of social revolution and the return to the land. These involved the wish to create a Jewish working class, firstly, by virtue of ideology and actual circumstances, in agriculture. Ideas on making the Jewish people productive and a return to working the land, it will be recalled, had formed as long ago as the first half of the eighteenth century, and they persisted as a silken thread throughout the Mendelssohnian enlightenment, the eastern European enlightenment and the Hibbat Zion movement, to be adopted by the Zionist movement and the labor movement during the *Second Aliya*.[3] This last added the element of self-realization and the creation of a working class.

Two other important forms of work in the *moshavot*, apart from labor in the fields, were in non-Jewish hands: the first was pasturing, the second guarding, which included guarding the moshava itself and its lands. While guarding meant defense of property and was not necessarily linked with safety to life, in the actual circumstances the two were connected, except, perhaps, in a few large *moshavot*.[4] The fact that guarding in the period under review was in the hands of outsiders[5] undoubtedly seriously damaged the image of the Yishuv in the eyes of the local population and weakened its own confidence and the belief in its viability.

Like "conquest of labor," "conquest of pasture" meant the transfer of pasturing to Jewish hands so that the new Jewish society might be self-sufficient in all areas of life and need not have recourse to outsiders as "hewers of wood and drawers of water." Similarly, "conquest of guarding," the notion of a Jewish defense force, assumed an important place in labor movement ideology from the start. The bearers of this idea were the Bar Giora association and later Hashomer. The roots of Hashomer arose from deep within the *Second Aliya*, but the life of this organization lasted far beyond that period and terminated well into the *Third Aliya*.

The Wellsprings of Bar Giora and Hashomer

The wellsprings on which the founders of Bar Giora and Hashomer drew were in part common to them and the people of the *First Aliya* and in part unique to them. The *First Aliya* and the *Second* were subject to the same influences: the national movements and the national struggles in Europe and the Balkans; the pre- and post-Herzlian awakening Jewish nationalism; the enticement of national romance. It was no accident that the people of the *Second Aliya* named their organization after Shim'on Bar Giora, a leader of the revolt against the Romans in AD 66–73. The encounter with the land of Palestine conjured up a fascination with the past and an intense sense of an immediate link with episodes and figures from the days of the First Temple and the Second. There were also the persons of Yisrael Belkind and Michael Halperin,[6] who imbued the people of the *Second Aliya* with the dreams of the *First*, which had not disappeared entirely and which also found expression in the complex and controversial figure of Avraham Shapira, head of the Petah Tikva guards, and also in the willingness and evident ability of at least some *moshavot* to protect their lives themselves, as distinct from their property, whose defense they entrusted to strangers.

But the founders of Bar Giora and Hashomer were influenced by separate factors also: the example of the Circassians who reached Palestine as recently as 1878 but were successfully maintaining two villages in the Galilee and several in the Golan. The *First Aliya* had not been aware of them because they lived far away in the Golan and the Galilee, remote even from the old *moshavot* in the Upper Galilee, while most of the *moshavot* in the Lower Galilee were established only in the period 1900–4.[7] The memoirs of the Bar Giora and Hashomer founders reflect the powerful impression made upon them by the Circassians who, despite their being few in number, new, detached from their homeland in the Caucasus now conquered by Russia, and settled in an alien and hostile environment, still showed great courage and won stature and respect.[8] Furthermore, the Jewish founders came from the ranks of the Poaley Zion movement, and the activist-revolutionary tradition of the international workers' movement generally and of the Russian movement in particular presumably played a part in fashioning their world outlook. There was a direct connection between the riots and the self-defense measures in Russia following the Kishinev pogrom (1903) and the founders, most of whom were involved in self-defense in the diaspora. Symbolically, it was a group from the self-defense unit of Poaley Zion, the "Heroes of Zion" (*Giborei tziyon*) from the town of Homel, who reached Palestine with their leader Yehezkel Hankin on 5 December 1903, after the riots in their city, that inaugurated the *Second Aliya*. Yisrael Shohat, Yizhak Ben Zvi, Yisrael Gil'adi, Mendel Portugali and others were connected with the organization of self-defense in the townships whence they came.[9] The self-defense movement in Russia grew up in the broader setting of general disintegration of faith in the Russian government, and not only as a direct result of the pogroms. For that reason, and because the Russian authorities were behind the pogroms, the popularity of terror and self-defense rose;[10] the ideology of Ber (Dov) Borochov, the founder of the Poaley Zion Social-Democratic movement, had a marked effect. A considerable number of the founders of Poaley Zion and the Bar Giora and Hashomer organizations, including Yisrael Shohat, actually arrived in Palestine before the establishment of Poaley Zion S-D in Poltava in 1906, but the latter's outlook became that of the movement in Palestine even before the immigration of Yizhak Ben Zvi; this is reflected in the "Ramla Programme" with its Marxist orientation, which was approved by the Poaley Zion conference on 5 January 1907.[11] Ben Zvi's arrival on 30 March 1907 reinforced Borochov's Marxist line, which is also in evidence behind the founding of the Bar Giora organization.[12]

In his essay "Our Platform," written in 1906, Borochov analyzed processes on the basis of Marxist historical materialism, and concluded that the production factors of a stronger society have a more absorptive capacity than those of a weaker society. Therefore, the Arabs would become assimilated, rapidly, but not without pain and friction, into the stronger Jewish society. That the Jews required the territory of Palestine he had no doubt, because as distinct from the Austro-Marxists Karl Renner, Victor Adler, and Otto Bauer, who severed the link between national autonomy and territory, Borochov held that every nation needed its own territory or it would be unable to develop its productive forces and would decay. Therefore, the Jews had to be in possession of territory, and this had to be Palestine. There the Jews would establish a strong society into which the Arabs would be assimilated, and there too they would win national autonomy as a result of a revolutionary political struggle, which would occur in three stages: (a) Jewish capitalism would develop the country, and would bring about social polarization and the strengthening of class consciousness; (b) a struggle would erupt between the worker and the capitalist that would lead to general unrest in Palestine, which would necessarily entail the involvement of the Turkish government on the side of the Jewish capitalist with the aim of suppressing the majority of the Jewish population; and (c) the Jews of Palestine, under the leadership of the workers, would arise against the oppressive regime of the Turks. The insurrection would be made into an international issue through the agency of the international proletariat, and would oblige the great powers to intervene. At the end of the process national autonomy for the Jews in Palestine would be attained. The Jewish worker would strive to make the autonomous regime democratic. Borochov confined himself to national autonomy, for like many other Marxist socialists he negated the dissolution of multinational states such as Turkey, and stood for their conversion into federative entities founded on the national autonomy of the oppressed peoples. This was the dominant ideology of the Poaley Zion party until the Young Turk revolution on 24 July 1908. From this viewpoint, an organization such as Bar Giora could be a potential military instrument of the Jewish proletariat in Palestine that would act against capitalism and against the Turks in the final struggle for Jewish and democratic national autonomy in Palestine, conducted by the Jewish proletariat.[13] In this light it is not surprising that not only Yizhak Ben Zvi but Borochov himself treated Yisrael Shohat's plans for the establishment of an underground armed organization in Palestine favorably and sympathetically, when Shohat told him of them at the Eighth Zionist Congress at The Hague in August 1907.[14] Only the Young Turk revolution in 1908 and the appearance of Arab nationalism, which had never previously been considered, changed the ideology of the Poaley Zion party.[15]

Naturally, the situation in Palestine, in which the Jews were almost the only group devoid of a military defense force, and therefore also devoid of prestige and status, in which the *moshavot* delegated the guarding of their property to outsiders, had a profound effect on the men of the *Second Aliya*.

The Founding of Bar Giora

Yisrael Shohat, the vital force in the establishment of the organization, arrived in Palestine aged 17, on 2 March 1904. The three and a half years intervening between that date and the founding of Bar Giora on 28 September 1907[16] were for Shohat and the other immigrants a time of encounter and impression with the conditions of Palestine, the formulation of thoughts and the formation of a group of people sharing common ideas. On his arrival he met Yehezkel Hankin in Petah Tikva, and later Alexander Zayd when working in a wine-cellar at Rishon Lezion. Shohat and Zayd developed a common language from the very start, and together they elaborated plans for "working the land and defending the country."[17] After finishing their work in the wine-cellar, Alexander Zayd went up to work in Jerusalem while Shohat got work at Shefaya as secretary and accountant of the Kishinev orphans' home set up by Yisrael Belkind. The two agreed that each would continue his efforts to win converts to their ideas until a group of about 18 people formed to become the core of the planned organization.[18] Thenceforward they operated, Shohat in particular, by the method of personal recruitment. In Jerusalem Zayd met Yehezkel Hankin, to whom he disclosed his secret dreams. The two of them easily found themselves talking the same language, for they came from a similar social and political background, were of similar mentality and had both fallen under the spell of Michael Halperin. Of this friendship Zayd wrote: "Michael Halperin lit this dream in my soul still in Vilna. Here in the land Yehezkel was the only man who understood me."[19] In Jerusalem Zayd recruited Moshe Goldstein-Givoni, Eliyahu Kamenetsky and Gad Avigdorov. But the main recruiting base was without doubt Shefaya, where Shohat was at work.[20] He picked out people whom he invited to Shefaya, where he tested their character. Only after the candidates for partnership in the "dream" proved equal to the criteria he set did he reveal his secret to them. In this way he enlisted Sa'adya Paz and Yehuda Zladin, who worked at Shefaya. Yisrael Gil'adi was also thus recruited, himself later bringing in his townsman Mendel Portugali.[21] In this manner men hailing from the Caucasus were let into the conspiracy – Zvi Beker and Yehezkel Nisanov, as well as Moshe Goldstein-Givoni after moving from Jerusalem to Samaria.[22] The standards set by Shohat were a good physique, courage, obstinacy, daring, willingness for self-sacrifice for the common good, and the desire to change the existing situation. So in Shefaya, at the end of 1904 and during 1905, the "intimate group" was formed that served as the basis for the foundation of Bar Giora. The company consisted of Yisrael Shohat, Alexander Zayd, Yehezkel Hankin, Yisrael Gil'adi, Mendel Portugali, Zvi Beker, Yehezkel Nisanov, Sa'adya Paz, Moshe Goldstein-Givoni-Yozover, Yehuda Zladin and Leibl Goldwag.[23] After the group took shape they tried to break into the work of guarding, and at first indeed succeeded in Shefaya, where Zayd and Gil'adi were taken on as temporary guards, working with Arabs. But in the end the effort failed, owing to the hostility of the Arabs, and Zayd was also severely beaten. But the first lessons were learned, both on the right way to guard and on the inadmissibility of mixed guarding.[24] With the transfer of the orphanage from Shefaya to Ben-Shemen in 1906

Shohat moved there too and the group dispersed, albeit with links still intact so that the dreaming and the planning did not stop.

In 1907 Yisrael Shohat and Yizhak Ben Zvi were elected as representatives of the Poaley Zion party to the Eighth Zionist Congress, held at The Hague on 14–21 August 1907. At about the same time the world conference of the Poaley Zion parties was held, during which the "world union" of Poaley Zion was founded.[25] Before journeying to the congress, Shohat assembled his comrades, Gil'adi, Portugali, Nisanov, Zayd, Beker, Hankin and Goldstein-Givoni, at an Arab coffee-house in Bustros Street in Jaffa. As far as is known, Shohat called the meeting for an exchange of views and to formulate guidelines for himself in his meetings with participants at the conference and the congress. According to the memoirs, at that meeting there was talk of the creation of a secret order ready to realize the goals of Zionism, including defense of the Yishuv. Some ideas were even voiced on the name of the nascent order, but the final decisions were postponed pending Shohat's return from the congress. Regarding the conference and the congress Shohat wrote that "the comrades charged me with acquiring the funds necessary to found our group and to finance its first steps." Shohat was to find allies among the leaders of both Poaley Zion and the Zionist movement.[26] In sum, Shohat's mission was to find financial as well as political and moral support for the planned organization. Clearly, this would have to be through personal contacts and by winning over individuals who could be let into the secret. Under no circumstances could the subject be raised for any kind of public debate or in any formal framework, even the most restricted. Any such discussion might embarrass the official bodies in their relations with Turkey, because at issue was an illegal organization. At the conference and the congress Shohat acted accordingly, and met Menahem Ussishkin, an outstanding leader of Russian Zionism, and Ber Borochov. But Shohat failed in his efforts. Nothing came of his meetings with Ussishkin and Borochov, apart from their sympathy to the idea. It was after this failure that Shohat related the plan, still at the congress, to Yizhak Ben Zvi, Borochov's colleague and friend, and a leader of the party. It seems that his failure instigated Shohat to bring in figures of high public and ideological standing, such as Ben Zvi.[27]

On their return, Shohat and Ben Zvi submitted their report to the Third Conference of the Poaley Zion party in Palestine, which opened on 28 September 1907 in Jaffa. It is likely that Shohat met his associates either at the opening of the conference itself or on its first day, between sessions. In his memoirs Shohat recalls that facing the group, "I gave them a brief account of my failure to obtain funds and we reached the decision that we had to begin operating on our own." Further on he writes that it was clear to them that "the idea of founding a secret order was timely."[28]

In his programmatic and apologetic article "The mission and the way" in the *Hashomer Volume*, Yisrael Shohat asserts that it was his report to his comrades that prompted them to decide to convene a meeting to found the organization following the party conference. He similarly states that already at this stage the tenets of the future body were established. Its goals were: "Liberation of the people and the homeland and the establishment of a Jewish state"; restoring the Yishuv to health; combating the halukka, that is, fund-raising among Jewish communities across the world to support the Jewish settlement in Palestine; striving for Jewish labor and guarding; socialist-Zionist education; unification of the working class; and the formation of a fighting defense force.[29] Some inaccuracies and anachronisms seem to be present in Shohat's account that need careful and critical examination. It is known that the founding conference of Bar Giora took place during the course of the conference, not after it. Similarly, it is very hard to accept that the basic principles detailed in Shohat's article were formulated in the short intervals between sessions during the first day of the party conference. Moreover, several of the principles he lists sound like later historical reflections.

The Bar Giora association was created on the night of 28 September 1907,[30] in Yizhak Ben Zvi's room in Batei Warsha (Warsaw Houses) in Jaffa where the group of founders gathered at the end of the first day of debates at the conference. The sources differ as to the number and identity of participants, although they agree that among the founders were Yizhak Ben Zvi, Yisrael Shohat, Alexander Zayd, Yisrael Gil'adi, Yehezkel Hankin, Zvi Beker and Yehezkel Nisanov.[31] In his memoirs Shohat adds to these Moshe Goldstein-Givoni-Yozover.[32] Ben Zvi expands the list to include Mendel Portugali and Berele Schweiger.[33]

Social and Cultural Background of the Founders

Socially, the founders came from the simple Jewish level. Some of them, such as Zayd, Hankin, Beker, Nisanov and Hazanovich, were discontented sons of poor people, and had themselves been apprentices or workers; most had no schooling at all, or very little. Nor was there much Jewish content in them, and very few could speak Hebrew. Mostly they spoke Yiddish or Russian; they were not ideologists and their nationalist or socialist fervor was basically sentimental rather than rational. They were youths who had come from the most impoverished social strata and they themselves were simple folk, not intellectual or well-read. It was no accident that such attributes among them came to be held in contempt. This social cross-section in general characterizes those who later joined Hashomer also. The description does not apply to the two leaders, Shohat and Ben Zvi. The former was from a prosperous family and was fairly well educated, while the latter had a wide education and evinced Jewish values and European culture in general. Shohat was physically weak and ailing, which was his justification for not actually practising the principles of the organization. He epitomized the charismatic leader who guided his adherents, but not by virtue of personal example at a time when personal example was almost vital. Ben Zvi's place was determined from the outset by his being the party ideologist and leader, most of his activity focusing on the party and public affairs. He served the illicit organization by acting as its bridge with the party, and he invested it with ideological and party legitimacy and the public and moral uplift that it required.

The principles of the organization were those that had crystallized in the long years prior to its founding. The slogan proposed by Ben Zvi had become accepted, this being a line from Ya'akov Cohen's poem *Habirionim* (The Mutineers):

Judah fell in blood and fire –
In blood and fire Judah shall rise.

From the very name "Bar Giora" it is possible to infer that the organization adopted the principle of forming a military defense force and seeking some kind of freedom for the people in their land. There was also talk of settlement and founding guards' colonies in the borderland, on the pattern of the Cossacks in Russia.[34] Regarding labor in agriculture, it was decided that every member had the duty of working one year at farming. Moreover, in addition to the idea of "conquest of labor" Bar Giora defined for itself two special goals of its own: "conquest of guarding" in the *moshavot* and "conquest of pasture."[35] The founders clearly perceived that the long-term goal was not "conquest of guarding" itself, but "conquest of guarding" was the means to forming a military defense force that could be used to achieve national aims.

In terms of organization Bar Giora was founded as a secret order and its members were conjured to fealty to the homeland, absolute discipline, devotion, willingness for self-sacrifice, and loyalty to the body. Potential new members were accepted only by unanimous approval. Yisrael Shohat was elected to head the clandestine organization and its members were committed to absolute obedience to him. From the start the organization was based on the avantgardism and elitism characteristic of the Russian political-revolutionary culture whence its founders came. The view was that a select, high-quality body, marked by the absolute discipline of its members, could move the masses and make gains that were out of reach of the unorganized and undisciplined masses. Such a body would be able to work through other groupings that it established and controlled. In the following years the separate framework of the "Labor Legion" was established as an auxiliary to the defense unit; likewise the Pasturers Association was formed, with the purpose of "conquest of pasture."[36]

The Eighth Zionist Congress at The Hague

From Shohat's description in his article "The mission and the way" of how events unfolded,[37] from the recollections of veterans of Bar Giora and Hashomer, and also from historiography,[38] it would appear that Bar Giora was created through internal evolutionary development and was quite uninfluenced by factors or processes outside the circle of founders. If this is so, it is strange that the process took so long, from the immigration of the self-defense group from Homel on 5 December 1903 to the founding of Bar Giora on 28 September 1907 – a span of almost four years. Even if we take the date of Yisrael Shohat's arrival in Palestine in March 1904 as the beginning, there is still a considerable gap of about three-and-a-half years. Furthermore, from the memoirs it is clear that already during the activity of the "intimate group" in Shefaya in 1905 the principles and future course had been formulated. It is not clear why it was necessary to delay implementation of the plans until after the Eighth Zionist Congress at The Hague.

Shohat stresses that the decision to establish the organization was not taken at the meeting he held with his group at Jaffa before he traveled to the congress, for on that occasion too they decided to wait until after his return. The linkage between the decision on the creation of the association and the journey to the congress is strange. It is not clear why such a decision was not taken earlier, nor why this connection was made between the decision and the Eighth Zionist Congress.

It is my belief that matters proceeded otherwise. Undoubtedly, it took time to assemble the founding group and to shape ideas, but both these were fairly well formed before the Eighth Congress. The decision to establish the organization was put off because it had no political and public backing in the Zionist movement or the Yishuv to catalyze the transition from theory to practice. Despite Shohat's personal failure and the words of disparagement he heard at the congress,[39] he most certainly became apprised there of the new trends being generated in Zionist policy opening up great vistas for actual advancement and development in Palestine. It was the Eighth Zionist Congress that resolved to concentrate no longer solely on political and diplomatic activity but to embark on practical work in Palestine. Following this change of policy, too, the Palestine office of the Zionist movement opened in January 1908 in Jaffa, directed by Arthur Ruppin. Shohat was without doubt aware of this change in Zionist spirit and policy. He doubtless knew too of decisions aimed at expanding horizons for national enterprise and initiative in Palestine. Therefore, influenced by the shift in the Zionist movement as expressed in its resolutions, Shohat concluded that the time was ripe to establish the organization that he and his comrades dreamed of. With this realization he returned to the country, heartened by the sympathy displayed by Borochov and Ussishkin and the support of Ben Zvi. Only then was the die finally cast on the founding of Bar Giora. Supporting evidence for this is present in the *History of the Hagana*, which states that after Shohat and Ben Zvi returned from the congress, where the "men of action" had prevailed over the "politicians," "the two decided that the time had come for deeds."[40] Shohat himself writes in "The mission and the way" that following his return from the congress and in the debates held in the group after he had delivered his report, it became clear to them that "that idea for establishing a secret order is timely."[41] Apparently, therefore, not only was internal organic development required, but also an external Zionist political change in order to generate the historical step of founding Bar Giora.

3

From Bar Giora to Hashomer

Guarding has ruined my health, there is much poison in guarding, and much, much has to change in the life of the guards. Spiritual satisfaction from guarding perhaps existed only at first, when everything was still new, but afterwards you see how empty the life of a guard is, and emptiness leads to lethargy and demoralization. There is nothing better than work, and however hard it may be the worker is fulfilled and always young in spirit.

Mendel Portugali

AFTER THE CREATION of Bar Giora an operational base for the group had to be found. According to Zayd, it was Yisrael Gil'adi, the man of action, who was the first to realize this and propose that they all concentrate at Mrah (Giv'at 'Ada), where they would take work in the fields, in grazing the livestock, and in guarding. Only after this proposal was rejected did the idea of Sejera come up.[1]

An Operational Base: From Sejera to Kefar Tabor

In contrast to Zayd, Moshe Goldstein-Givoni states that the proposal to obtain work and the task of guarding at Mrah was made by Shohat; then they tried to get work at Zikhron Ya'akov, and to make that place their base. Only after these plans fell through, so Goldstein-Givoni asserts, did the Sejera proposal emerge, which the group accepted and implemented. If this account, which derives from the recollections of Zayd and Goldstein-Givoni, is correct, it seems that the members of the organization stressed first and foremost the attainment of an operational base and even tried to acquire it in the area they had known in the Shefaya days; if so, the assertions in the histories on a preference for the Galilee do not hold. As opposed to Zayd and Goldstein-Givoni there is the version of Sa'adya Paz, who relates that at the end of the summer of 1906 he went from Shefaya to Sejera as the vanguard of the "intimate group" that was due to assemble there. This means that as early as 1906 the preference had been for Sejera as the operational base of the group members. Moreover, according to Paz, Shohat knew the Sejera farm very well, for in 1907 he had gone there from Ben Shemen and had stayed with Paz for several months, almost until he left Palestine for the Eighth Zionist Congress at The Hague. Shohat came to Sejera to recuperate from an illness, but also to check the possibility of concentrating the "intimate group" in the area.[2] On the basis of Paz's testimony it transpires that Shohat knew the place well when Manya Vilboshevich made her proposal.

Manya Vilboshevich was about 24 years old (born 1879) when she reached Palestine on 2 January 1904. The "Independent Jewish Workers' Party," of which she was a founder and leader and which was opposed to engagement in politics, preferring to concentrate on the economic and educational problems of the Jews, broke up in the summer of 1903. Manya then joined an SR (Social Revolutionary) terrorist group that sought to assassinate Pleve, the Russian Minister of the Interior. The plot failed, having been revealed by an *agent provocateur* and police collaborator within the SR party, Yevno Azef. Manya left Russia for Berlin, where she received an urgent call by her brother Nahum Vilboshevich to travel to Palestine on the false pretext that he was ill. When she went there Manya was not yet a Zionist, although from an early age she had had an emotional attachment to the country because her brother Isaac had been one of the Bilu in 1882 and his letters formed a link between it and her family. Another brother, Gedalya, was a Zionist, and had migrated to Palestine in 1892. Manya herself knew Hebrew from childhood. Only in Palestine itself did Manya catch the Zionist fever after being there several months, and also after she traveled the length and breadth of the country in a six-week tour together with her brother.[3] Yehoshua Hankin suggested that she visit the *moshavot* to study the problems of Jewish settlement. Manya was taken by the idea and began to study it assiduously. On her journeys she met workers of the *Second Aliya* in the *moshavot*, including the Shohat brothers Israel and Eliezer. Even before she left the country for Paris a plan began to form in her mind for the organization of groups of youth who would be trained for agriculture and defense, and a collective life. Manya dreamed of settlement on Baron Rothschild's lands in the Horan (to the east of the Golan), with which she had fallen in love. In 1905 she went to Paris where she met Baron Edmond de Rothschild and Max Nordau, but she failed in her efforts to win them over to her projects. In that city she read much on colonial methods of settlement and also on socialist-utopian thought. She was active in Russia in the winter and summer of 1906, after which she returned to Paris, whence she traveled to the United States to work there on behalf of self-defense in Russia and settlement in Palestine. In August 1907 she returned to Palestine without having made any real progress in her plans.[4] Through Yehoshua Hankin she won the approval of Eliahu Krause, director of the JCA farm at Sejera, to place the *falha* (field crop farming) in the hands of an organized group of workers who would operate on the basis of collective life. Manya hoped that the success of the planned group at Sejera would open the way to the longed-for settlement in the Horan.[5] The two workers' parties, Hapoel Hatzair and Poaley Zion, to which she applied for help, rejected the proposal, each for its own reasons. It was then that she met Yisrael Shohat, who accepted her suggestion. By her own account it was only at Sejera that she learned of the existence of Bar Giora.[6]

The Galilee in general and Sejera in particular had advantages that attracted the Bar Giora people. Apart from its historical memories the region had a topography favorable to clandestine activity and its *moshavot* cultivated field crops and pastured livestock, which suited Bar Giora's goals; the settlements were small, and as such could be useful for a small and active group. The farm at Sejera served for training agricultural workers.

The Bar Giora group arrived at Sejera on 2 October 1907. Shlomo Zemah, who was working there at the time, has left a very negative account of the arrival and militaristic, insolent manner of the young men.[7] This retrospective evidence of Zemah, who was a founder of Hapoel Hatzair, must be treated circumspectly owing to his unfavorable attitude to the Poaley Zion party, Bar Giora and Hashomer. According to his account the group that reached Sejera consisted of nine members.

Sa'adya Paz was a veteran at the place and experience in farming, and therefore Eliahu Krause put him in charge of the "collective," the cooperative organization set up there under the influence of Manya Vilboshevich-Shohat and to which the members of Bar Giora belonged. It seems that at first not all members of the "collective" belonged to Bar Giora. Among the collective Paz lists Ben Tsur, Gefen, Pik, Dov Ben Galil, David Yisraeli, and Yosef Shapira, who, as far as is known, were not members of Bar Giora. Thus, in the first phase of its existence the "collective" was not identical with Bar Giora, and the members of the latter were possibly a minority. Only gradually, with the departure, at times enforced, of the old workers from the collective did Bar Giora members replace them, until the two bodies were identical.[8]

The essence of the contract signed between Eliahu Krause and the collective was that the latter get work in the fields and in the dairy for one season according to the usual conditions of land tenancy. For the field crops the collective was given 2000 Ottoman dunams (an Ottoman dunam is smaller than a regular dunam), as well as work animals and tools. The collective ran itself with advice from Krause, and kept a common fund into which each member put his monthly wage of 40 francs.

The season ended successfully and with a profit, but the contract was not renewed when it terminated in the summer of 1908. At Krause's request Paz remained at the farm until the threshing in the granary was completed on 26 October 1908. Thus the period of the collective at Sejera was less than a year – from 2 October 1907 until 26 October 1908 at the latest.[9] At its fullest the collective numbered 18 people, including six unmarried girls. With the marriage of Manya Vilboshevich to Yisrael Shohat in May 1908 this figure dropped to five, these being the sisters Shifra, Esther and Sarah Shturman, and the sisters Kayle and Zipora Beker.[10]

The well-known story of the conquest of guarding at the Sejera farm has become a classic. From the moment of their arrival the Bar Giora people sought the right to guard the place, which the manager Eliahu Krause refused to grant them. Both before and after they won the guarding, the Bar Giora men engaged in physical exercises, weapons training, and target practice. On their free days they tramped across the country to get to know the region. They also learned Arabic and the customs of the Arabs.[11] Krause, despite his warmth toward the young people, was not inclined to hand over the guarding of the farm exclusively to Jews, for the same reasons behind the opposition of the moshava farmers to Jewish guarding: they did not consider it effective, they were afraid of endangering young Jewish lives, and above all they feared that the transition to Jewish guarding would further jeopardize the *moshavot* by kindling a desire for revenge in the non-Jewish guards. They were also afraid that the *gum* (the custom of blood vengeance common among the local population) might fall on the entire moshava should Jewish guarding be instituted. As for the Sejera farm, it is told that Krause's opposition was broken when he learned that the Circassian guard was not fulfilling his duties. The incident occurred one night when the Bar Giora men took a mule from the farm stable, and awoke Krause to show him just how good the Circassian's guarding was. Only then did Krause dismiss the Circassian, replacing him with Zvi Beker. The second gain was made when the farm manager agreed to attach three members of the group – Berel Schweiger, Meir Hazanovich and Yehuda Proskorovsky (Pross) – to the Circassian herdsmen-guards who pastured the farm's livestock.[12]

The story of the conquest of guarding at the Sejera farm, the first gain, became a legend which, the people of that generation, including those who did not belong to Bar Giora or Hashomer, embellished. In his memoirs David Ben-Gurion describes the event as "the capture of the first fortress,"[13] and elsewhere he uses the expression "after we captured the guarding at the farm and the moshava.[14] It was characteristic to use such bold words as "capture" and "fortress."

In reality, matters were more prosaic. The memoirs written decades later usually tend toward idealization, consciously or unconsciously. The tale of how Krause was persuaded to transfer guarding from the Circassian to Zvi Beker is typical. Sa'adya Paz, as stated, the Bar Giora man in charge of the collective at Sejera, in his own memoirs asserts that he was involved in the incident, and a cause of it. He tells that one night, when he happened to return late from the moshava to the farm, there was no one to open the gate for him because the Circassian guard was not at his post. Only after lengthy efforts did his comrades hear his banging at the gate, and went to let him in. Then, spontaneously, "we decided to take a mule from the stable to put it somewhere else." So that suspicion would not fall on him and the others, "I took the comrade Manya, who was the treasurer and book-keeper. We took one mule out of the farmyard through the wicket-gate, and handed it over to the guard at the dairy of the moshava, and then returned to the farm. We awoke the manager and told him everything."[15] In contrast to Paz, David Ben-Gurion wrote concerning the affair that the Bar Giora members tailed the guard and saw that he was not carrying out his duties. Although they reported this to Krause he paid no attention and was not inclined to take steps. Therefore, one night they decided to take Krause's "pure-bred Arabian mare" and hide it, etc. By now there is an element of planning and calculated action; and the mule, as if by magic, is now a mare – an Arabian thoroughbred no less. In her recollections Rahel Yanait-Ben Zvi too joins in with the motif of the Arabian mare.[16] Later historians also have pursued the tale of the fine Arabian horse, which stirs the romantic imagination more than a humdrum mule.

Moreover, it seems that the acceptance of Zvi Beker as a guard at the farm was not an innovation, because there had been a Jewish guard before him named Shalom Kurdi (or Hakurdi). During the Hannuka festival of 1907 there was a celebration at the farm at which this guard had too much to drink. He walked over to a window, and despite the late hour fired twice into the air. Krause was enraged and sent him away there and then, hiring a Circassian guard from Kafer Kama instead. Sa'adya Paz maintains that this greatly angered the workers at the farm.[17] Ben-Gurion also mentions the Jewish farm guard Shalom Hakurdi, but the reason for his dismissal, he states, was that "one night he was not on his watch, and put a Circassian guard there instead."[18] It is important to note this fact, which proves that Jewish guarding at the farm was not an absolute innovation. It also seems that Shalom Hakurdi too was not the first Jewish guard at the farm.[19] Moreover, it is questionable if Beker's guarding at the farm was exclusive to him or if there were others who guarded the farm, its live-stock, and its fields. In the latter case we are concerned with mixed guarding, like the mixed pasturing that took place later on, when Krause attached three members of the Bar Giora group to the Circassian herdsmen-guards. The latter, who were the regular guards of the farm and its property, opposed the addition of Jewish guards, and apart from firing warning shots they sued the JCA for 20,000 francs. The JCA was alarmed and a compromise was reached whereby the Circassians agreed to waive their claim in return for non-renewal of the contract with the Jewish guards. It seems that exclusive Jewish guarding at the farm was not achieved, and even the partial gain of Bar Giora was lost, at least temporarily, when in the summer of 1908 their contract to guard at the farm was not renewed.[20] It is difficult to accept Yisrael Shohat's account, that after the quarrel between Berel Schweiger and Hassan the Circassian during pasturing, Krause decided to fire the Circassian guards and to hand pasturing entirely over to Bar Giora. Thus, according to Shohat, the guarding of both the farm and the pasturing fell entirely into the hands of Jews.[21] Despite this querying the classic story, there is no doubt that the Bar Giora men won their initial gains at the Sejera farm, and in this respect there was great progress, but it is almost certain that this was only a partial achievement, namely, mixed guarding and that in a single season of one year only, from the winter to the late summer of 1908.

With the start of guarding by Bar Giora at the farm there arose the problem of financing and acquisition of weapons and horses, essential equipment for any guard. The group had no money to purchase these items. The necessity for financing from an outside source caused Shohat to turn to Ussishkin. In his letter Shohat requested that the matter be kept in strict confidence, and described the difficult circumstances of Jewish work and guarding in the *moshavot*. Next he clarified the nature of his organization, which was willing to contract both farmwork and guarding. To handle the guarding his group needed money to buy arms – in his words "instruments" – and horses. They also needed money as security, as they undertook responsibility for the property they guarded. All this necessitated the creation of a loan fund, which was where Ussishkin's help was required. The letter remained unanswered. At Sejera itself the problem was solved by Krause, who gave the group a loan of several hundred francs against the income of the collective. They used this money to buy arms.[22]

Still in 1908 Bar Giora made additional gains with the winning of guarding at the Sejera moshava. This was achieved after a farmer's horses had been stolen and suspicion fell on the Arab guard. Shohat relates that a Circassian guarded with the Arab, but it was the latter who was suspected.[23] According to the contract signed between the moshava and Shohat, not Bar Giora, which was a clandestine organization, it appears that the moshava got two guards from Bar Giora, Alexander Zayd and Mendel Portugali, instead of the two who were dismissed.[24] In July 1908 there began the episode of the defense of the moshava Mesha-Kefar Tabor against the Mughrabis of the village of Ma'ader. Following the success of this defense, principally by members of Bar Giora headed by Berel Schweiger, guarding of this moshava too was transferred to the group. The contract with Kefar Tabor was signed at the end of the summer of 1908, before the Jewish New Year festival.[25] Of the 16 clauses, clause 15 stands out. In it the moshava undertook to employ, in addition to the guards, 15 Jewish workers through the Hahoresh organization, the first non-party union of Jewish workers, which operated in the Galilee in the period 1906–10. The agreement applied the lesson learned at Sejera on the necessity for a strong backing in the moshava of Jewish workers, who would go to the aid of the guards in the hour of need.

The affair of the defense of Mesha-Kefar Tabor in the summer of 1908 is well known.[26] The moshava was guarded by Mughrabis from the neighboring village of Ma'ader, who quarreled with the farmers. One of them shot at a farmer, but the bullet ricocheted off a rock and fatally wounded the man who had fired it. This incident developed into a blood feud, in which the Mughrabis began to harass the moshava and threatened to attack it to take their revenge. Kefar Tabor appealed to the *moshavot* of the Galilee for help, and they responded, as was usual among the *moshavot* of the *First Aliya*. About 20 workers from the Sejera farm came to Kefar Tabor. Because of the tense situation a six-member temporary defense committee for the Lower Galilee was formed, and this body decided to organize routine defense for the moshava until the danger passed, with the help of reinforcements from the other *moshavot* and the farm. Berel Schweiger was placed in command of the few dozen defenders. The general mobilization, in which the role Bar Giora was outstanding, and the successful organization of the defense, prevented the Mughrabis from realizing their design. Following this episode the contract was concluded with Yisrael Shohat assigning the guarding of Kefar Tabor to his men, and four guards were stationed there.[27]

Summing up 1908, we may point to considerable gains made by Bar Giora. The collective did indeed disband in the summer of that year, and Manya Vilboshevich-Shohat's dream of settlement in the Horan faded, at least temporarily.[28] Likewise, the guarding at the farm was lost. But on the other hand, guarding the *moshavot* Sejera and Kefar Tabor was won. In the contract with the latter the principle of introducing Jewish labor as a necessary condition for the success of Jewish guarding was established. Horizons opened before the members of Bar Giora for further gains in conquest of guarding at the other *moshavot* in the Galilee. Bar Giora likewise came to exert a marked influence on the body of the Galilee workers through the Hahoresh union. Two of the five Hahoresh committee members, Yisrael Shohat and Yisrael Gil'adi, belonged to the organization. In light of these successes the group concluded that the time was ripe to found a "strong organization of guards" to be called Hashomer (The

Guard). Shohat states that this organization was to serve as "the first stage toward the establishment of a national security force." The gist of his account is internal organic development, followed, so it would seem, by the creation of Hashomer in Mesha-Kefar Tabor on 12 April 1909. In this respect the account is identical with that of the creation of Bar Giora in 1907.[29]

The Creation of Hashomer

The discounting of external influences and the wish to present all developments as the outcome of internal considerations alone, of organic processes within and of the philosophy of the founders themselves – this is the line that runs like a silken thread through the description of the creation of Bar Giora and Hashomer, as given principally by Yisrael Shohat. The other veterans of Hashomer, too, being men of action rather than ideologists or intellectuals, were ignorant of or were unwilling to admit the influence of outside factors on the founding and development of the two organizations.

Without doubt, the Young Turk revolution of 24 July 1908 and its successful overthrow of the despotic regime of Abdul Hamid II, the Ottoman sultan who had ruled for decades, resulted in two effects, ideological and practical. These, and not only internal developments, affected the transition from Bar Giora to Hashomer, that is, the transition to a legal organization able to gather the fruits of Bar Giora's success.

The Young Turk revolution came as a complete surprise to the Poaley Zion party, as it did to others. No one predicted it or took such an eventuality into account.[30] In an instant Abdul Hamid II's long-standing regime of absolute dictatorship ceased to exist, and Turkey became a constitutional monarchy to be governed by a parliamentary regime. Furthermore, as a result of the revolution, which promised much in liberalization and the grant of rights to Turkish-ruled peoples, there was a great awakening of Arab nationalism in the Ottoman empire, including Palestine.[31] These two new circumstances, the constitutional and political transformation in Turkey and the rise of Arab nationalism, necessitated a revision of the ideological and tactical stance of the Poaley Zion party. The party acted accordingly, and decided it was necessary to move from underground revolutionary activity to legal parliamentary activity in Turkey. This was the setting for the journey of David Ben-Gurion, Yitzhak Ben Zvi and Yisrael Shohat, the three party leaders, to study law in Istanbul as a preparation for legal political activity in the Turkish state. The revolution also reinforced the party's positive outlook on the continued existence of Turkey as a federative multinational state maintaining the cultural and national autonomy of its peoples. As late as 1917 at the twelfth party conference at Merhavia, a resolution was adopted supporting an integral and federative Turkey.[32]

Secondly, with the appearance of Arab nationalism the Borochovist prognosis of the assimilation of the Arabs among the Jews disintegrated. This collapse undermined the approach of striving for immediate national autonomy in Palestine. Similarly, a re-evaluation of Poaley Zion's position on the question of "Jewish labor" was called for. In the new circumstances of surging Arab nationalism the implications of a demand for immediate national autonomy in Palestine would be suicidal for the Jews. It is thus not surprising that already in October 1908 Yitzhak Ben Zvi declared that it was not worthwhile for the Jews to call for autonomy in the new conditions; this requirement should be postponed until they became the majority. In his view, national autonomy prior to this meant handing over the land to the Arabs. Poaley Zion became circumspect in its political predictions, and the resolutions of the sixth conference in 1910 stated that the goal was achievement of economic control in Palestine, the word "political" nowhere appearing. Henceforward the attitude to Arab labor on the *moshavot* changed, and in Poaley Zion, as in Hapoel Hatzair, hesitation was replaced by clear-cut adoption of the principle of Jewish labor. It was accepted that Arab labor on the *moshavot* would only exacerbate national tensions. With the recognition of the existence of Arab nationalism there also gradually arose the concept of a place for two nations in Palestine. According to this, the Jews would build up their national economy, based on national capital and Jewish labor, in the open spaces in the country beside the Arabs. A Jewish majority would be achieved in these areas without displacing the Arabs and without injuring their rights.[33] The change in the ideology and tactics of Poaley Zion certainly influenced the views of Bar Giora, whose members were activists and leaders of the party. It too changed from a clandestine revolutionary organization to a legal body seeking to realize its aims in more or less overt ways.

In addition to factors described, the situation on the ground dictated change. It has been mentioned that the revolution in Turkey opened the way for Arab nationalism, which in the circumstances of Palestine was largely directed against the Jews. The Arabic press in the country launched an anti-Zionist campaign, the most hostile paper being *El-Karmel*, edited by Najib Nasar and published in Haifa.[34] Arab enmity toward the Jews grew worse throughout the country, but principally in the Galilee, and the result was an increase in violent clashes and disputes over land. In his memoirs Ben-Gurion stresses the growing rift between Jews and Arabs in consequence of the revolution. The Arabs interpreted the word *hurriyya* (freedom) as lawlessness, "and the acts of plunder, vandalism, theft and bodily harm increased." The entire winter of 1908/9 resounded with gunpowder and there was a rash of skirmishes over land and trespassing between Sejera and Kafer Kanna and the Zbehs, a Bedouin tribe encamped at the foot of Mt. Tabor, and between Yavneel and the Arabs of Lubya.[35] The situation deteriorated to the point when, on 22 April 1909, the JCA management in the Galilee called an emergency council at Yavneel to consider the security situation in the area and the proper steps to deal with it. Three JCA representatives, three farmers' representatives and three workers' representatives participated. Following these consultations it was decided to recruit more Jewish workers to the Galilee, to reinforce the guarding at the *moshavot* through the addition of everyone capable of handling weapons, and also to raise a troop of Jewish soldiers with the permission of the Turks. To implement these decisions a committee of ten was appointed. But nothing came of all this, for after a short time the JCA resumed its policy of appeasement toward the government and the Arabs.[36]

    These, then, were the three factors that caused the transition from Bar Giora to Hashomer: (a) a fresh ideological and tactical stance was elaborated by the Poaley Zion party and the Bar Giora leadership regarding the Turkish state after the Young Turk revolution. (b) Arab nationalism generally, and in Palestine in particular appeared, leading to an exacerbation of national tensions between Jews and Arabs, and in consequence an increase in land disputes, clashes, and violent attack. The rise of Arab nationalism also necessitated a different ideological posture on the principle of national autonomy and Jewish labor. (c) The success of Bar Giora spurred the transition from a clandestine organization of limited ability to a legal organization with far more opportunities.

Ideology, Structure and Institutions

The Hashomer association, which was founded at Kefar Tabor on 12 April 1909, had an overt program,[37] defined as "to develop in our land an element of Jewish guards capable of this work."[38] Yet being the legal offspring of Bar Giora, the group was not meant to be a professional body of guards alone, but set itself, unwritten and secretly, the far-reaching goals of its parent. The aim of the overt program was "to mislead the Turkish government," while the unwritten, secret program sought "to impart to the Yishuv, on all its levels, the spirit of self-defense, the will and desire to create a defense force, which must in the course of time develop into a central element in the enterprise of national rebirth."[39]

    The creation of Hashomer did not mean the disbanding of Bar Giora, and at the founding assembly the latter was not mentioned, although a report was delivered to the meeting on the activities of the previous eighteen months. Not all members of Hashomer were members of Bar Giora, which continued as a secret and guiding body in the new organization. Bar Giora apparently ceased to exist only in 1911, but even then its members continued to direct and lead.[40] The structure described was the embodiment of the elitist concept, predicating a small, select and disciplined unit that moved larger bodies. Indeed, with the founding of Hashomer there were aspirations that it would become the large-scale framework controlled by Bar Giora, like the Labor Legion later, or other future frameworks. With the failure of these hopes there was no point in the continued separate existence of Bar Giora, and therefore it broke up. Hashomer took its place as an elitist-*avant-garde* organ.

Institutionally, Hashomer was directed by a general assembly of its members, which convened once a year. The meeting decided matters of principle by majority vote and discussed three main areas: guarding policy, that is, enlargement or reduction; breaking into new areas, such as conquest groups, the Labor Legion or the Haro'eh (The Herdsman) group; and it was empowered to decide on the admittance of new members by a two-thirds majority. The general assembly also elected the association's committee, which for many years consisted of three members.

Membership of the association was open to all, regardless of views and outlook or party membership. In this sense Hashomer was avowedly non-partisan, although most of its members were in the ranks of Poaley Zion. Some, however, belonged to Hapoel Hatzair, such as Shlomo Levkovich (Lavie), Haim Feinberg and Ya'akov Pat. The rules determined that each member merited one year of work after two years of guarding.[41]

The committee consisted of three members, of whom one was chosen by the others to represent the association outside. Until the First World War the committee members were usually Yisrael Shohat, Yisrael Gil'adi and Mendel Portugali, with Shohat playing the role of "foreign minister," in addition to his being the unacknowledged leader of the association. When Shohat left to study in Istanbul he was replaced by Shmuel Hefter. During the First World War the committee was enlarged to five, and its composition changed entirely.

Two funds operated in the association. One was for loans to members to help them purchase weapons and horses or other equipment needed for their guarding duties. The other fund, or foundation, was for guarantees to the *moshavot*. This was necessary, because when commissioned with the guarding of a given settlement, Hashomer undertook to pay compensation to the moshava if its members failed, through their own negligence, to prevent theft or destruction of property. This matter occupied a prominent place in all the contracts that were made.

As indicated, the admittance of new members was one of the thorniest problems that the association faced. Ideology required that quality be preferred to quantity, and therefore the most rigorous selection was applied in the acceptance of new members. This approach was reflected in a prolonged probationary period, supposedly a year but in reality two or more. The candidate was tested for a variety of qualities: courage, obduracy in pursuit of his goal, self-discipline and integrity. After passing all the "tests" the candidate had to be accepted by a two-thirds majority at the general assembly. In effect, it was extremely difficult to gain admittance into the association if any number of members opposed it. At times even a single negative vote, if cast by a man of standing in the association, could frustrate the candidate's entry into it. This was the background to several grim incidents, when men committed suicide because their probationary period was extended or they were rejected altogether. This intense selectivity, which led to testing periods lasting several years, created a bottleneck which prevented Hashomer from growing. A wide gap opened between the opportunities for missions that presented themselves and Hashomer's ability to accept them. The association bridged this gap by employing paid guards. In 1912–13, which were its peak years, Hashomer numbered only several dozen members but its salaried employees amounted to hundreds. The leaders and members of the association were not unaware of this unhealthy situation, but they preferred adherence to the principle of selectivity to bettering this poor state of affairs. Emphasis was laid on the help the association afforded its members when they were ill, imprisoned or out of work, the legal support it provided, as well as its method of equalizing wages in various cases.[42]

Operational Methods Take Shape: 1908–1913

Following its establishment, Hashomer began to develop successfully, and continued to do so almost uninterruptedly from 1908 (in the time of Bar Giora) to the beginning of 1913. As early as 1909 and the beginning of 1910 the organization took on the guarding at the *moshavot* Beit Gan and Yavneel.[43] The *moshavot* in Lower Galilee, except for Milhamiya (Menahamiya), came under its protection. In these *moshavot*, sparsely populated and enclosed by a wall, the operational methods of Hashomer took shape. In the main these remained the basis, even when modifications were introduced with the acquisition of guarding at the large *moshavot* in Samaria and Judea without a wall and with large tracts of land. In the Galilee the fundamental rules were laid down: there was to be no mixed guarding (meaning Jewish-Arab or Jewish-Circassian or any other combination); except for Milhamiya, Giv'at 'Ada (Mrah) and

Zikhron Ya'akov, where short-lived and unsuccessful attempts at such guarding were made, Hashomer was strict about exclusively Jewish guarding at the *moshavot* it took into its charge; the introduction and expansion of Jewish labor was required as a condition for taking on guarding. The number of guards that the organization could supply never satisfied the requirements of the *moshavot*, and therefore a rear echelon consisting of enthusiastic and supportive workers was essential; the effort was made to reduce the Arab presence in the *moshavot* and restrict their movement at night particularly. This strategy began in the Galilee, and later was applied and developed in Samaria and Judea; the response to attacks by Arabs was to be measured and considered, so as not to complicate matters or involve the association and the *moshavot* in criminal proceedings and blood feuds. These rules and others, including the personal conduct of the guard, had their beginnings in the Galilee and their continuation in the more southerly *moshavot*.[44]

In October 1910 Hashomer broke out of Lower Galilee southward to the northern Sharon, with the commission of guarding at Hadera. This was a different moshava from those in Lower Galilee in that it was unprotected on all sides, being without a defensive wall. In addition, it was surrounded by a large area of about 45,000 dunams, as compared with the approximately 5000 dunams of Kefar Tabor. These conditions necessitated a different disposition from that in the Galilee, in particular greater mobility of mounted guards responsible for the various sectors and a larger number of guards altogether. In parallel it was necessary to watch the large number of Arab workers at the moshava, who outnumbered the Jewish inhabitants. To achieve this, inspection and control of their movements had to be instituted.[45] On 6 November 1911 the association acquired the guarding of Rehovot, the large moshava in the south; and on 19 October 1912, that of Rishon Lezion and a few more small settlements. At the beginning of 1913 Hashomer was at its zenith. Its units extended from Lower Galilee through the Sharon and Judea, where it was responsible for guarding a sizable number of *moshavot*, including the largest and most important.[46] Apart from this, Hashomer won fame for its participation in the *kevutzat kibush* (a group of people that formed for a special task lasting a relatively short period of time) in 1909–10 at Um Juni, the future Degania Aleph, the mother settlement of the kibbutz movement, and in the pioneer group that went out to the lands of Merhavia on 24 January 1911, the first Jewish breakthrough into the Jezreel Valley. The drawback was that Hashomer could handle all these assignments only by employing candidate members, but chiefly many paid employees.

From the spring of 1913 the retreat of the association and its withdrawal to its source in Lower Galilee began. In March 1913 Hashomer was forced to give up Hadera,[47] and in October 1913 Rehovot (whither it returned only at the end of 1916). The reasons for abandoning the guarding were alike in most *moshavot*: Jewish guarding was, so it seemed, more expensive than Arab guarding. The farmers made no calculation of what they were saving in prevention of theft, only of what they were paying directly out of their pocket for the Jewish guarding. They were also apprehensive about rising tensions with the Arab environment, and inclined to blame Hashomer, which, they believed, treated the Arabs too severely; the farmers found it difficult to accept the almost absolute control that Hashomer imposed regarding movement of Arabs in the moshava and relations with the neighboring Arab villages and Bedouin tribes; the farmers also felt that very important areas of life were slipping from their hands to the benefit of the association, whose ambitions outreached the professional sphere of guarding. Quite naturally, it offended the farmers that some members of Hashomer did nothing to conceal their antagonism, arising from their socialist-Zionist world outlook, to those who gave them their bread.[48]

The Labor Legion

Parallel with the formation in 1909 of Hashomer, which was the legal offshoot of Bar Giora in the sphere of guarding, in the autumn of that year another branch was formed. This was the Labor Legion (*legion ha'avoda*), or for short Labor – Avoda – to remove the military connotation. It was the second general assembly of Hashomer, which convened in Haifa on 19 September 1909, that resolved to form the new body following the proposal by Shohat, who also composed its regulations, consisting of 14 items. The foremost of these were the aim of conquest of labor and assistance in the conquest of guarding; discipline as in an army; a collective way of life; absolute identity of membership of Hashomer and membership of Avoda, only the nature of the particular mission determining the placement of the member, which would thus be dynamic rather than static; semi-secret organization. Shohat's rules were similar to Ussishkin's plan published several years earlier calling on Jewish youth to volunteer for three years' work in Palestine, which implied the creation of a kind of neo-Bilu movement. The military character of Avoda found expression in the demand for rigid discipline, external ceremonial and a uniform: this was a broad red belt with a leather pouch full of bullets and a weapon at the side, and a Circassian *kolpak* (cap) on the head. Organization was in groups of five and ten, headed by commanders.

Avoda had two companies: one at the Sejera farm, the other at Hadera. The Sejera company broke up after a short while owing to the recalcitrance of the workers, but mainly owing to a strike that broke out there

in the summer of 1910 against Eliahu Krause. Because of the strike Krause
dismissed all the workers from the farm. At Hadera the Avoda company
also served as a bridge for the conquest of guarding at the moshava. At
its peak Avoda in its two companies numbered 30 to 40 people and it
lasted about a year. The break-up of the framework was due to the resistance of the workers to living as a clandestine body under harsh discipline,
in addition to which the general worker population was opposed to the
organization. It is quite certain that Hashomer's progress in the same
period drew manpower from Avoda to itself, which was bound to under-
mine Avoda in the absence of a solid kernel supplied by Hashomer. That
is, Avoda did not succeed in growing by enrollment of new members, but
on the contrary gradually lost its founding members, who were called
back to undertake missions with Hashomer.[49]

According to Yisrael Shohat, the special uniform was decided on so as
to satisfy the leaning toward romanticism among young men. He admits
that the political parties were against the organization that he created.
This applies in particular to Hapoel Hatzair, which saw it as yet another
arm of Poaley Zion and therefore forbade its members to join. Not even
Poaley Zion recognized Avoda, "because they regarded it as a contradiction to Marxism," but it did not forbid the organization. Shohat's claim
is that owing to the attitude of the parties and the few people in the organization, "the Bar Giora committee decided to temporarily disband the
Labor Legion and await a more auspicious moment." Shohat regarded the
labor battalion, named after Joseph Trumpeldor, and established in 1920
during the *Third Aliya*, as the continuation of the Labor Legion.[50] Despite
its brief existence, Shohat held that Avoda reaped successes. He considered these to be the participation of its members in the pioneer group at
Um Juni, working the field crops at the Sejera farm, and the conquest of
labor at Hadera. He maintained that "during the two years [Avoda]
succeeded in mobilizing more than one hundred workers."[51] Shohat's
summation may almost certainly be disputed, nor is his basis for "more
than one hundred workers" clear, and even if we assume that there was
a great turnover in Avoda, and he counts everyone who was connected
with it at any time during its existence – the figure is still dubious. He
seems to give the organization too long a life span. There is no supporting
evidence for his statement that Avoda existed from the autumn of 1909
to the end of 1911. It should be noted that there was no unanimity in
Hashomer over the creation of Avoda. One of the opponents was Yisrael
Gil'adi, who held that the new, additional, framework would damage the
conquest of guarding because it would draw from the few members of
Hashomer and would not supply it with new ones, as Shohat asserted.
There were grounds for Gil'adi's opposition, because Hashomer was
growing very slowly and numbered only 26 members in 1909. In fact,

Gil'adi was right, not Shohat. The contrast between Gil'adi and Shohat, not only on this matter, stemmed from their different temperament. The former, who was responsible for the operation and daily running of the organization, was pre-eminently rational, cautious and realistic. The latter, who was not involved in the practicalities of the association, either managerially or personally, and at times was absent, as during his studies in Istanbul, was extravagant by nature, forever dreaming of new conquests. In not a few cases the two clashed over their different positions, but at times they concurred with each other.

A fairly detailed report of the conflict between the expansive approach seeking to enlarge and make new conquests at any price, and the circumspect, restrained approach, is to be found in the memoirs of David Tsalevich. He describes the third general assembly of Hashomer at Hadera on 23 September 1911, when he was admitted as a member. Following the ceremony of acceptance of new members, a debate arose over a proposal to accept the guarding at Rehovot. Tsalevich relates that the supporters based their position on the claim that "our remaining in one place without expanding will be regarded as a retreat by us, because the idea of Hashomer is to create a political force in the land that will safeguard property and respect. How, then, will our strength grow if not by spreading across the land and thereby acquiring members for our association?

The opposing side argued that it was wrong for us at that moment to spread out to all parts of the country for the following reasons: (a) We would lose our reputation among the residents of places where guarding now exists because they would at once sense a decline in our strength. (b) Concerning acquisition of new members by expanding the guarding, this would not be achieved because we only admitted new members by the agreement of two-thirds of our number, who recommended them, knew them, and found them worthy of the task; this was not possible through guarding at Rehovot, for only three or four senior members would be stationed there and they would not have time to train and get to know candidates."[52]

Internal Problems

1 Blood feud (gum)
This was a serious issue, which for several years plagued the Hashomer people. The episode arose very tangibly and acutely with the murder on 13 February 1911, of Yehezkel Nisanov by Arabs of Sharona, when he was traveling by cart with Zvi Nadav from Merhavia to Yavneel. It was natural for the others to want to avenge the death of a much-loved and

admired comrade, a founder of Bar Giora and Hashomer. This was combined with the fundamental question as to whether Hashomer should adopt the usages of the surrounding Arab environment. There was also the fear that if it did not practise the *gum* (blood vengeance) the prestige of Hashomer would be lowered, as would the status of the Yishuv, which was slowly improving. Most members of Hashomer demanded blood vengeance, but the committee rejected it on the grounds that it would lead to difficulties for Hashomer and hence for the *moshavot* in which it operated. The main discussion in the drawn-out debate was at a secret meeting, apparently attended only by members of Bar Giora, held on the slopes of Mt. Carmel near Atlit in March 1911. While prior to Nisanov's death the majority had tended to reject the custom of *gum*, the balance in the association changed after it. The chief supporters of the adoption of the blood vengeance were the members of the "Caucasus group," but not exclusively. Finally, the committee's stance negating the *gum* was accepted, but the Arabs of Sharona were informed that Hashomer was in a state of *gum* with them. A decision was taken to find the killers and deal with them. According to Shohat three unnamed members were assigned the mission. In fact, the decision was not implemented, and the matter remained dormant for about two years; but at the end of 1913 it reappeared following a deterioration in the security situation in the Galilee.[53] Within a short time several people were murdered: Moshe Barsky (22 November 1913), Yosef Saltzman, a resident of Kinneret and former member of the Labor Legion (24 November 1913), and Ya'akov Feldman, a guard at Sejera (8 December 1913). The steady retreat of the association, the feeling of fatigue and failure, the non-implementation of resolutions on settlement and pasturing, the grave security situation in the Galilee, and finally these killings, which were the last straw – all led to the formation of an opposition to the committee, headed by Zvi Beker. The opposition demanded action, at least to execute the 1911 decisions. Furthermore, the opposition threatened to act alone if the committee did nothing. Only by immense effort, and with the help of Shohat who returned to Palestine from Istanbul, did the committee manage to gain control of the situation. This episode was one of a number of problems that then beset Hashomer and threatened it with anarchy. By hindsight it may be stated that the decisions of Hashomer against adopting the methods of the *gum* and of terror, and the preference for selective punishment, were fateful and became the guiding principles for the Hagana of the future.[54]

2 Agricultural settlement

The goal of agricultural settlement was a tenet of Bar Giora and Hashomer. Throughout the years of their activity efforts were made to find a suitable site for them to settle. Bar Giora imposed on its members the duty of working at farming for a year, and Hashomer gave each of its members the right to work in agriculture after two years' service at guarding. There was continuity here, as in other areas, from Bar Giora to Hashomer. According to Zvi Nadav, a decision was taken at the founding assembly of Hashomer at Kefar Tabor to continue efforts, through the JCA, to find a site for its members to settle. The actual place spoken of then was Bint al-Jabal, now the lands of Beit Keshet in Lower Galilee.[55] Sa'adia Paz records that the beginning of the dream was as early as the days of the "intimate group" at Shefaya in 1906, when the comrades yearned to establish villages on the model of the Volga and Don Cossacks.[56] Alexander Zayd too attests that in the days of the Sejera collective in 1908, and then at Kefar Tabor, his friends were much occupied with problems of settling the Horan, which they envisaged as a homeland for fighting men in the style of the Cossacks on the Sech.[57] We have here an obvious and persistent leaning, but in the conflict between the challenges of security and the desire for settlement the former predominated. At the same time, the wish to move from a life of guarding to a life based on farming became very firmly fixed with many of the founders. As their engagement in guarding lengthened over the years so did their desire to move from it to settlement. The chief proponents of this tendency were Mendel Portugali, Yisrael Gil'adi, Gad Avigdorov and Zvi Nadav, while the security tendency was led by Yisrael Shohat. The sharpest expressions of weariness with guarding as a way of life and longing for settlement are found in the letters of Mendel Portugali to his wife. In a letter of 1912, during the guarding at Rehovot, Portugali writes that he does not wish to leave the guarding lest the entire enterprise that he and his comrades have developed collapses, and this despite the fact that "I have discovered that guarding destroys the man and brings demoralization into his life." The solution, therefore, was "to create a settlement of guards, where each family man will have a plot of land and a farmstead."[58] In another letter Portugali remarks that he is sated with the kind of life he leads: "I need physical work, my body demands it and my spirit needs it. I will be happy on the day I go out to work." The next passage contains a cry of despair:

> Guarding has ruined my health, there is much poison in guarding, and much, much has to change in the life of the guards. Spiritual satisfaction from guarding perhaps existed only at first, when everything was still new, but afterwards you see how empty the life of a guard is, and emptiness leads to lethargy and demoralization. Most of the veteran guards are broken, dispirited, and listless. There is nothing better than work, and however hard it may be the worker is fulfilled and always young in spirit. The ideal of the guard is control, of the worker brotherhood. Guarding says: Take what is not yours, while work says: Only from the toil of your hands shall you live!

Were it not for the condition of our people in the land I would be the foremost opponent to the "Association of Guards." But the political situation forces us to take part in the guarding; therefore we must link guarding with work, so that we may be sound in body and in mind and so that others' property will not be fair game for us. These ideas have led me to think of a village for guards. Such a village would be on the example of the villages of the Cossacks, who made forays from them to fight their battles and returned to refresh their strength and to live lives of freedom.[59]

Mendel Portugali wished for a cooperative Hashomer moshava, whose members would live off farming, not guarding. He wanted intensive farming, which would provide work for women as well as men. On this cooperative village members would receive equal pay, and would enjoy its profits equally also.[60] Similar and no less clear-cut views are stated in the memoirs of Zvi Nadav, "the Fallah," who also complained about the guarding life, with which his comrades were exhausted because it gave them "the feeling of unproductive life and constant dissatisfaction." Those who dreamed of founding the kind of settlement described argued about the location. It was generally held that it should be far from town, in the mountains and close to hardy neighbors, so that it would be possible to rear a young and courageous generation. Alexander Zayd wanted the place be on the coast so that the young could learn seafaring. Shmuel Hefter emphasized the search for economic opportunities to foster the establishment of the envisaged settlement.[61] As distinct from the proponents of the settlement approach, Yisrael Shohat maintained that the future guards' village must be economically based on animal husbandry, so that the women could manage the farm while the men continued to work at guarding. For that reason he negated crop farming, preferring dairy farming and horse breeding.[62]

Presumably, while the Hashomer people were young and single, and the idea of guarding was exciting and clothed in romance, the goal of security predominated over the goal of settlement. To this should perhaps be added the successes that favored the association until 1913 and consumed the guards' energy, and seemed to justify the goal of security; but already inherent in this there was some erosion, with the result that this dominant tendency was weakened. As the guards grew older and established families, the romantic, exotic element that made guarding so attractive faded, at least for the senior men, and the obstinate demand began for realization of the old resolutions on settlement, which for years had received lip service alone. The failures of 1913 further intensified the demands and the pressures to create a guards' village, and so that year the Hashomer organs once more adopted resolutions on the vital nature of such a settlement. A special committee was even established, whose members went in search of a suitable site. They visited Benei Yehuda and Hittin-Arbel (near

Tiberias). The latter was particularly compelling owing to the historical memories that suffused it, as well as the marvellous view it commanded. The suggestion was dropped because of insufficient water, inability to accumulate enough land area for a viable settlement and the poor quality of the soil. Some members were also put off by the proximity to Tiberias.[63] As noted, the desires of Portugali, Nadav and Gil'adi were not shared by all to the same degree. The division between security supporters and settlement supporters hinged on where to concentrate the effort, which issues to emphasize, and what to determine as the center of gravity of their lives. One side did not negate the leanings of the other, but a difference in orientation did exist. Sharp expression of this, with bitter complaint, was made by Alexander Zayd when he wrote that many of his comrades had abandoned the idea of settlement, even though this was determined in the very essence of the association. "Yisrael Shohat himself has withdrawn from the notion of settlement at Tel Adashim and has gone to Turkey to study law."[64]

As we know, an attempt was made to establish a guards' village at Tel Adashim, whither the members of the association went as a pioneer group in October 1913. A further attempt, which persisted, was made by Yisrael Gil'adi's group in 1916 in Upper Galilee. Here a settlement was established, first called Bar Giora and later, following Gil'adi's death in 1918, Kefar Gil'adi.

3 Leadership

Yisrael Shohat was the acclaimed and sole leader of Bar Giora. In Hashomer, prior to the First World War, an elected three-member committee operated, usually consisting of Shohat, Yisrael Gil'adi and Mendel Portugali. When Shohat left to study in Istanbul he was replaced by Shmuel Hefter. Neither Bar Giora nor Hashomer was monolithic, and different shades could be discerned in them in respect of personality as well as policy.

Alexander Zayd and Yehezkel Hankin had personal friendship founded on deeply-felt common political sentiments stemming from the Poaley Zion party, and the influence of Michael Halperin. The two, it seems, had reservations about the nature and leadership of Yisrael Shohat. Zayd's words in his diary and in the *Second Aliya* volume create the impression of a critical attitude to the head of Bar Giora. It is possible that Zayd, more than the others, was disturbed by the absence of self-realization in Shohat, while for Hankin there was perhaps envy over the position of leadership that Shohat won and from which he himself was removed despite his past as a hero of the self-defense at Homel. In this context the marked social friction at Tel Adashim at the start of the war was evident, causing divisions in feelings, the build-up of many layers of resentment and finally the development of an ideological split which caused the Gil'adi group to move from Tel Adashim to Kefar Tabor and later to settle in Upper Galilee. In the sphere of ideology and policy mention has been made of the division between the security-oriented and the settlement-oriented members. Two disputes that brought the association to the brink of anarchy and even disintegration were those over the blood vengeance and the conquest of pasturing, which erupted with great force at the end of 1913 and the beginning of 1914. These were accompanied by the threat of the use of personal terror, which they knew well from the revolutionary movements in Russia, to achieve social and political goals in Palestine. Only the arrival of Yisrael Shohat at the beginning of 1914 from Istanbul and the adoption of the stick-and-carrot method – punishment of some of the opposition people together with the start of action toward conquest of pasture – prevented the demise of the association.[65]

4 The cultural aspect

The Bar Giora and Hashomer people were for the most part the product of the Jewish popular stratum, apprentices or workers, without general or Jewish education. Moreover, the historical image presents them as anti-intellectuals, demonstratively negating the various forms of cultural expression: being uneducated themselves, they were contemptuous of anyone showing a tendency to engage in philosophy, literature or culture generally. Once again, the image places them at the extreme pole, characterized by simplicity, anti-intellectualism and lack of culture.

There is no doubt that in part this portrayal is correct. But it should be remembered that in many respects it was not exclusive to the people of Bar Giora and Hashomer. To generalize, reaction to intellectualism in all forms, so characteristic of a section of the Jewish youth in the diaspora, marked sizable numbers of the people of the *Second Aliya*. The wish to break from the diaspora with its concepts, norms and way of life that seemed unacceptable to them, caused the elaboration of an antithesis fostering the values of productivity, simplicity, rupture from intellectual casuistry and excessive, effete intellectualism as a whole, and adherence to the tangible world – that is to life as it really was. This reaction, in its extreme and vulgar forms, negated engagement in culture and letters. It was as if the People of the Book were symbolically suing for divorce from the book as the token of the Jewish experience in exile. It was not by chance that for long years after the *Second Aliya* the Zionist labor movement in Palestine applied the terms "the Mount" (the Hebrew University of Jerusalem, situated on Mount Scopus) and "the Valley" (the working agricultural settlement in the Jezreel Valley) as opposites and antitheses. The Bar Giora and Hashomer people gave extreme expression to these currents in their day.

Furthermore, the lifestyle of the guards made for difficulties in engaging in cultural and intellectual matters. Exhaustion from guarding at night, the need to sleep during the day, illness, dealing with the mass of practical problems that the guard had to contend with in the few daylight hours at his disposal, the necessary preparations for setting out to guard – all these made an ordered daily routine impossible, physically denying any free time for matters of culture and mind that went beyond the daily round and the political and ideological requirements of their unique way.

For all that, the total image that has formed of Bar Giora and Hashomer regarding their repudiation of culture and the intellect is inexact. Although this area was not at the fore of their lives and experience, and therefore is not reflected in the sources and memoirs, there is evidence attesting to their attachment to the social component of life, and that they too were among its consumers. This is the spirit of the account by Atara Shturman, wife of Haim Shturman, one of the leaders of Hashomer and herself active in the association, in her memoirs:

The members of Hashomer were generally regarded as people who scorned cultural matters, hardened their heart against books and despised the Hebrew writer. At first glance this seems to be so, but only at first glance. True, the language they spoke was mostly Yiddish, with some Russian, but it should be remembered that at that time there were no evening classes. The members guarded at night, succumbed to the fever often, and lived in abnormal conditions. The lack of a sense of permanence and constantly being on the move are what produced in the Hashomer people the feeling that there was no possibility of studying and no chance of concentrating on reading. At times an expression denigrating books or slightly mocking the descriptions of the life of fictional heroes slipped out, for those were remote and different from the real life in which the guards were immersed in those days. There was no library where we were, and one had to content oneself with a book that Manya Shohat sometimes brought from town. This is what produced the impression that the guards denigrated books. There were members who boasted of their ignorance, but the truth is that they too at times settled down with a book in a corner of the granary. Finally there were those who had a profound inner feeling for all cultural things but they locked it away deep inside or obscured it with an expression of contrived scorn. It was as if they were deliberately suppressing within them any external show of culture, out of fear that this would disturb their simple ways. I recall Meir'ke Hazanovitch, who would laugh at anything "cultural," but really he had a soul that welcomed the experience of beauty and poetry. When he was in Rehovot he was among those that used to meet with Rahel Blovstein (the poetess Rahel) and, unobserved, learned to play the piano at her house. When he returned to Merhavia he brought many heart-rending melodies and songs with him.

They called the Hebrew writers *melamdim* (schoolteachers), but they drew deeply from their springs. Haim Shturman had a deep affinity for A. D. Gordon. He loved him to the core and Gordon returned his affection . . .

In Hashomer there was no lack of people with a healthy sense of culture, men of spiritual grandeur, but life in its vicissitudes and hardships created a form of world outlook that demanded simplicity of a man to the point of becoming stripped of everything and actively opposed to all external signs of accepted culture.[66]

Even assuming an attempt at apologetics here, there is other evidence altering the usual picture in the historiography on the cultural dimension of the Hashomer people. In her memoirs of the collective at Sejera in 1907–8, Kayle Gil'adi relates that in the evenings Eliahu Krause, the farm manager, "used to give us lessons on agriculture: on field crops and the life of the plant, animal husbandry and human nutrition. These classes left a powerful impression. He succeeded in planting in us love of the field and creating an attachment in us to trees and nature."[67]

Atara Shturman in her recollections of the period she spent at Tel Adas (Tel Adashim) wrote that "Rahel Katznelson stayed with us for some time too. She imparted something of her noble spirit to us, and in her lectures on literature she found us attentive listeners."[68]

The most striking evidence shedding light on the formal attitude of the Hashomer association is in a letter from Yisrael Gil'adi of December 1913 to Efraim Bloch-Blumenfeld, the director of *Kapai* (the Palestine Workers' Fund, PWF, the financing foundation of the World Union of Poaley Zion). It should be recalled that at the time of writing the letter, in the absence of Yisrael Shohat then studying in Istanbul, Gil'adi was the central figure in Hashomer. His letter thus reflects the position of the association on the subject under review:

[December 1913], Haifa

To the Member of the operational office of the Palestine Workers' Fund, comrade E. Blumenfeld, in Jaffa
Esteemed Comrade,
Recently we received a letter from Comrade A. S. Waldstein of Jaffa in which he requests us on behalf of the Lectures Committee to appoint a representative of the association who would participate in the meetings that organize the circuit lectures. The value of the circuit lectures is well known to us all, and it need hardly be said that for the Guards the lectures here will simply bring about a complete revolution in their lives for the better, and it is most desirable for us that the lectures do not cease their routine.
The financial situation of the Hashomer association is greatly strained and we have no means of expending monies on matters of the mind as long as our members are being held in prison or are ill; every month we spend hundreds of francs on them.
When we were in Jaffa you informed us of financial assistance for matters of the mind for workers and guards. We turn to you now to assist us with the fee that we must submit to the Lectures Committee as a society that

wishes speakers to fix special times to appear before the Guards in their places, because at night it is not possible for the Guards to participate in the gatherings when the speaker reads before all. If you do not give us a positive answer we will be obliged not to participate in the Lectures Committee. Please reply to us with all possible speed.Respectfully, on behalf of the Hashomer Committee,Yisrael Gil'adiWe do not receive Kefar Uria, reply to Karsani in our name.[69]

4

Hashomer and the Yishuv

Conference finds that Jewish guarding is one of the most important factors in the fortification of Jewish labor in the land.
Conference regards Hashomer as the beginnings of Jewish
self-defense whose importance has increased together with the
process of enlargement of the Jewish settlement.

Yisrael Shohat

O F THE TWO WORKERS' parties that existed in the country during the
Second Aliya, Poaley Zion and Hapoel Hatzair, the former had
generally sound relations with Bar Giora and Hashomer, at least until the
First World War. There were instances of the party criticizing actions of
Hashomer, such as the formation of the Labor Legion, but for the most
part there was support for the association, whose goals matched party
ideology.

The Attitude of the Workers' Parties

Members of Bar Giora and Hashomer – Yisrael Shohat, Rahel Yanait and
Yitzhak Ben Zvi – were in the first rank of the party leadership, and others,
such as Yisrael Gil'adi, Mendel Portugali and Shmuel Hefter, were among
its activists. Moreover, the recognized leader and ideologist of Poaley
Zion in the *Second Aliya*, Yitzhak Ben Zvi, was one of the heads of
Hashomer. In his personality a kind of personal link was forged between
the leaderships of the party and the association. So despite the independence and secrecy of Hashomer there was normally no marked friction
between the two bodies. But a certain element of opposition in the party
to the association cannot be ignored, although this was mostly beneath
the surface and was apparently fed in no small measure by the envy of
those who were not members of the secret society, with all its romance.
There were also those who propounded the necessity for party supervision of Hashomer. In the First World War, Ben Zvi and Shohat having

been deported, the dispute between the two organizations intensified, a further point of contention being the attitude to Turkey. In 1917, at the twelfth Poaley Zion party conference at Merhavia, the majoriy in the party continued to maintain the old ideology that stood for an integral and federative Turkey, while the minority, including Hashomer, abandoned this notion and adopted an anti-Turkish stance. The majority at Merhavia, with Efraim Bloch-Blumenfeld at their head, called for a line of non-identification with any side among the belligerents, while the minority, including Rahel Yanait, Dr A. Waldstein, Yisrael Gil'adi and Alexander Zayd, supported full identification with the Allies and the mobilization of an independent Jewish force abroad and in Palestine.

An interesting, if selective, description of the relationship between the majority with the orthodox ideology and the minority with the activist anti-Turkish orientation is found in the memoirs of Rahel Yanait-Ben Zvi. She relates that after the Hashomer assembly at Tel Adashim on 14 September 1917, she and several more active party members went to Merhavia to attend an urgent council of the party there. In the council Efraim (David) Bloch-Blumenfeld, the director of the PWF and a leader of the party and the World Union of Poaley Zion, expressed great fears in regard to the rumors over the espionage affair (meaning the exposure in October 1917 of the Jewish Nili espionage network, which had operated on behalf of the British). He thought that this might bring catastrophe upon the Yishuv. In his speech Bloch-Blumenfeld attacked the members of Poaley Zion and Hashomer, and was particularly ired by Rahel Yanait, a member of the party center, because "I [Yanait] did not consult with the party center on all matters concerning Hashomer." She states that she launched a counter-attack, asserting that everyone knew of the speaker's negative attitude to the activist spirit in Hashomer. If he had a sympathetic attitude, Yanait asserted, they would consult with him too. Enraged, Bloch-Blumenfeld interrupted Yanait's words, shouting that Hashomer activism did not conform to the line of Victor Adler. To this Yanait replied that she did not determine her positions according to Victor Adler: "What has he to do with our enterprise in Palestine? And today we must be ready to defend ourselves!" The moderate Yisrael Gil'adi tried to calm the storm by supporting Yanait's line in principle, but at the same time agreeing with Bloch-Blumenfeld's view on greater involvement by the party center in the activities of Hashomer.[1]

Another outburst against Hashomer occurred at the party council held on 9 September 1918, the eve of the Jewish New Year festival, at Mahanayim. Only representatives from the Galilee were present, because the south of the country was already in the hands of the British. At the meeting an extreme resolution was adopted, calling on all party members to leave Hashomer. The background to this was the incident of the "Nili money" and its ramifications. The "Nili money" was a sum collected abroad to support the Yishuv and sent illegally in 1917 by the Nili network from Egypt to Palestine. On 21 June 1917 it was handed over to Meir Dizengoff, a member of the Political Committee which then led the Yishuv. Dizengoff transferred the money to the treasurer, Bloch-Blumenfeld. The committee members, including Bloch-Blumenfeld, wanted to get rid of the gold coins, which might have incriminated them as spies if they were discovered. Therefore, Bloch-Blumenfeld was happy to remit the money to the Hashomer people, who used it for their own purposes, and also to help the many prisoners arrested by the Turks after the exposure of the Nili network in October 1917. The resolution was ineffective and was not implemented.[2]

The underlying source of the tensions and criticism was the opposition by many to Hashomer's secrecy, but above all to its independence of the party. Nevertheless, the basic position of the party should not be overlooked, as this was reflected in a resolution adopted as early as the ninth conference:

> Conference finds that Jewish guarding is one of the most important factors in the fortification of Jewish labor in the land. Conference regards Hashomer as the beginnings of Jewish self-defense whose importance has increased together with the process of enlargement of the Jewish settlement.[3]

The debate over the "Nili money" continued after the war and generated much heat and anger against the association. In an effort to remove all obstacles between the party and the association on this, the first party council to convene after the liberation, in Jaffa at the end of 1918, appointed a committee whose task was to clarify and conclude this dispute and thereby to restore the firm ties between the two bodies.

Relations between Hashomer and the Hapoel Hatzair party (a workers' party whose chief goal was to create a Jewish working class in Palestine, but which negated the Marxist-socialist outlook of its rival Poaley Zion party and adhered to a nationalist ideology), were incomparably worse. This was due primarily to the generally unpleasant atmosphere that prevailed between Hapoel Hatzair and Poaley Zion. For the former, Hashomer was an arm of Poaley Zion, not a non-party body as it claimed, and this largely determined the attitude of Hapoel Hatzair to the association. In addition, there were specific objections and different positions on the question of guarding and defense. Despite the pacifist sentiments of some members of Hapoel Hatzair, the party recognized the need for self-defense and guarding. Moreover, both A. D. Gordon and Yosef Aharonovich, among the guiding lights and leaders of the party, affirmed Hashomer as an organ for encouraging self-defense and Jewish guarding. The underlying difference was that they did not regard these as an ideal or an absolute value, or as the seed of an armed Jewish all-Palestine force. The ideal before their eyes was the creation of local defense and guarding organizations in each Jewish settlement, based on the awareness that every settler was obliged to defend property and life. In addition to their concept of local rather than countrywide defense, and their discomfort with the ideal of creating an armed Jewish all-Palestine force, the members of Hapoel Hatzair were against exclusive engagement in defense, which in their view detached the man from the chief thing, which was working the land. They also negated the extravagance and at times the insolence, arrogance and braggadocio of many Hashomer men. The romance of the association, expressed among other things in outward appearance, was not to their liking as proponents of a puritan, ascetic manner.

This attitude of reserve was met by a no less marked attitude of disdain, boasting and criticism of Hapoel Hatzair on the party of Hashomer, even though its ranks included several party members such as Haim Feinberg, Ya'akov Pat and Shlomo Levkovich (Lavie). This disagreeable relationship sometimes led to shameful acts. The worst of these, which was prevented from ending in disaster only at the last moment, was the Meir Rothberg incident. Rothberg was an exemplary and renowned worker in the time of the *Second Aliya*, who in the summer of 1910 was working at the Kinneret farm, where the Hashomer guards set a trap for him, which as stated almost ended tragically. One of the guards asked Rothberg to replace him on the pretext that he was not feeling well. Rothberg agreed, and during his watch that night some Hashomer men took his rifle from him by force. They then held him up to ridicule as one unable to protect his precious weapon – typical, they said, of the good-for-nothing members of Hapoel Hatzair, who let the Arabs steal their guns from them. Moshe Berman, the manager of Kinneret farm, who knew nothing of the plot, fired Rothberg, and he in his despair and humiliation at the wrong done him was close to suicide. At the last moment the Hashomer men admitted the evil of their act, returned the rifle, and revealed the truth.

It has been mentioned that the Hapoel Hatzair party was usually opposed to Hashomer and also advised its members not to join the association. Those who did were the exception in that they did not follow the party line. Nevertheless, at times Hapoel Hatzair defended Hashomer against accusers from outside the workers' camp. Shohat has set forth some of the arguments of this party against the association: it negated the Arab dress, Yiddish speech and sense of being "the chosen ones." In the setting of the poor relationship it is not surprising that the Hashomer men applied to the members of Degania, the first of the communal settlements whose members belonged to Hapoel Hatzair, the epithet "pure olive oil." Zvi Nadav, an adherent of settlement in the association, did not thereby renege on the principle that to create a farming village it was necessary to be devoted to it heart and soul, but "nor should the whole purpose of the creation of this village be forgotten." In addition to this nickname, there was no shortage of other terms of contempt, such as Poaley zairnik (a pun on Hapoel Hatzair, meaning "little worker"), "schoolteacher," "son of a householder," etc. These expressions reflect both attitudes and social and cultural differences. Many years later, describing the attitude of Hapoel Hatzair to Hashomer, Pinhas Shneorson attacked it bitterly claiming that the party journal "heaped abuse upon us"; the paper had also opposed the sacrifice of human life "for a bunch of grapes or a herd." In this approach by Hapoel Hatzair Shneorson found all that was distorted in the party's view of Hashomer, its goals and its deeds.[4]

This complex of bad relations with a large part of the working community, friction with their own party and criticism and resistance by the farmers resulted in Hashomer's being deprived of the consistent moral, social and political public support that it required.

Hashomer, Institutions of the Yishuv, and the Zionist Movement

Many of the leaders of the Zionist movement were ignorant of Hashomer's existence, or knew very little about it. Among those more aware of the facts attitudes varied from negation of the association, as in the case of Ahad Ha'am, by way of reserved favor, as with Yehiel Chlenov, to broad and material support as rendered by Shmariahu Levin and Menahem Ussishikin. The last-named maintained contacts with Yisrael and Manya Shohat and endorsed the association almost from the start. In 1910 Ussishkin attempted to found a Hashomer Fund in Russia for financial assistance to the group, but he failed. On the other hand, he succeeded in persuading the "Odessa Committee" of Hovevei Zion to come to the aid of the association. At the end of 1910 the Odessa Committee adopted a series of resolutions whose implications for Hashomer were very great: the Committee decided to guarantee the association financially when it contracted to guard on *moshavot*. Such a guarantee was a condition in every agreement, so that the Committee's decision in fact made the contract itself possible. Every agreement contained a clause whereby the association undertook to compensate the moshava for damage resulting from negligence on the part of the guards; this was the principal purpose of the guarantee. The Committee also allocated 7000 francs to Hashomer's "theft fund," which gave real backing to the guarantee. The

Committee underwrote loans to the association from financial bodies. The money was usually allocated to the purchase of essential equipment (horses, weapons) for the guards. The Committee also insured the members of the association. Through these steps the Odessa Committee became the central element in the provision of the monetary aid that made the work of Hashomer possible. Parallel to this, it also provided moral and public support, which was essential. On his travels outside Russia in 1912 Ussishkin also declared his support and esteem: "The idea of self-guarding is being realized; most of the Jewish *moshavot* have placed their guarding in the hands of the Jewish Hashomer association – bold and brave men, and wherever such guarding has been instituted, there the *moshavot* are safe and developing in peace. It is true that this association still lacks adequate forces, but the day is near when guarding will be Jewish everywhere."[5] Yehiel Chlenov too, despite his criticism, regarded Hashomer in a very positive light.

In 1908 Arthur Ruppin opened and headed the Palestine Office, the official representation of the Zionist movement in Palestine, which was in charge of all activities. Ruppin's backing for Hashomer derived largely from his overall support for the workers of the *Second Aliya*. Moreover, with the transfer of Yehoshua Hankin in 1910 from the JCA to the Palestine Office, Hashomer had an enthusiastic advocate and influential supporter within the very bastion of the Zionist movement in Palestine. Still, the heads of the establishment were apparently not happy with the independence of the association, and the reservations on the part of Ruppin and in particular Tehon, the second-in-command at the Office, surfaced during the First World War, especially after the deportation of Hankin from the country.

In the summer of 1913, during his studies in Istanbul, Yisrael Shohat traveled to the fourth world conference of the World Union of Poaley Zion, in Cracow. At its end he continued to the Eleventh Zionist Congress, held the same summer in Vienna. As early as 26 December 1912, Shohat sent a memorandum from Istanbul, on behalf of the Hashomer committee, to the large Zionist executive committee, in which he set out the plan for the creation of a countrywide organization for the defense of the Yishuv in Palestine. To realize the plan Shohat sought material assistance as well as public support. On his arrival at the congress he raised the subject of his memorandum, and the congress presidency appointed a special subcommittee to consider it. Shohat claimed that in its instructions the subcommittee was told that "if possible, [to] accede to our request." He attests that he himself appeared before the subcommittee, which he requested to recommend a grant of money and a short- and long-term loan as means toward creating the organization. The subcommittee agreed, but the executive committee rejected the recommendation. Shohat states that at the congress it was decided to set up a political body in Palestine in which the following elements would participate: a representative of the Palestine Office, a representative of Hovevei Zion and a representative of Hashomer. In respect of this Shohat states that "by this decision the status of Hashomer was officially recognized at the Eleventh Zionist Congress in Vienna. A connection was formed between it and the institutions of the Zionist movement. Hashomer became a unique organization in Palestine, responsible for the peace of the Yishuv in the land, a fact that doubled its responsibility and its devotion." The decision of the congress was brought before the members of Hashomer at their annual assembly at Karkur on 4 October 1913, and Yisrael Gil'adi was appointed their delegate to the planned body; but the idea was not realized and the decisions remained on paper. There is no doubt that the status of the association might have been different and perhaps the entire issue of guarding and security would have changed course if the Vienna decisions on the creation of the political body had been implemented. The winds blowing from Vienna, Shohat asserts, had no continuation. As stated, the support of Ruppin and Tehon during the war years fell away. These facts contributed to the decline in status of the organization that had begun as early as 1913 and continued during the war.[6]

Other Guarding Organizations in the Yishuv

The reservations and fears over Hashomer, its manpower problems, and local interests brought about the appearance of Jewish guarding outside this association. The idea of Jewish guarding was nourished and disseminated by Hashomer itself, but to a considerable extent it was also fostered by the the dangerous situation that arose in the country with the rise of Arab nationalism following the Young Turk revolution. Despite what has been set forth in the foregoing, the system of non-Jewish or mixed guarding had not disappeared from the *moshavot*. There were still a few villages, such as Mishmar Hayarden, Yesud Hama'ala, and Rosh Pina, which persisted in non-Jewish guarding, while others, principally Petah Tikva, went on with mixed guarding. A special case was Zikhron Ya'akov, where in the fall of 1913, at the time of the Tabernacles festival, the local youth organized the Gideonite association, which among others set itself the goal of establishing a guard for the moshava recruited entirely from local residents. Here and there individual Jewish guards worked independently of any organization, such as Aharon Ostrovsky who guarded at Kefar Saba.

It was encouraging that at *moshavot* left by Hashomer for one reason or another, such as Hadera, Rishon Lezion or Rehovot, the system of non-Jewish guarding was not restored and an effort was made to maintain Jewish or mixed guarding. At Rehovot, when Hashomer departed, guarding passed to the contractor Avraham Blumenfeld but the moshava made it a condition that he had to employ Jewish guards, not only Arabs. Despite this development, in itself favorable, there was still a great and fundamental difference in the attitude to guarding between the *moshavot* and Hashomer. While the former usually regarded the task as a professional matter only, Hashomer treated "the conquest of guarding" as a national value. As distinct from the *moshavot*, where there was some movement in the direction of Jewish guarding, in the towns there was generally no change. Only in Tel Aviv did Jewish guarding begin as early as 1910.[7]

Hanoter was formed in 1912 by Jewish guards acting outside Hashomer and in some cases rejected by the latter: the organization was shortlived, disbanding after about a year.

Hamagen was formed in the summer of 1915 by Yosef Lishanksy and others. Lishansky was the head of the association. It undertook the guarding at several farms and small *moshavot* in the south: Ruhama, Beer Tuvia, Gedera, and Ekron. Hamagen was active for about two years, until the summer of 1917, during which time it comprised about 20 members most of whom were from workers' groups, including some members of Poaley Zion. Even two members of Hashomer, David Tsalevich and Ben-Zion Mashevich, worked in it for a while. Hamagen maintained a strong link with the committee of the Judea Workers' Union, which also supplied it with guards. At the end of 1916, when Hashomer returned to guarding in the south, principally Rehovot, it demanded that the Judea Workers' Union committee cease in its support for the rival group, claiming sole rights of guarding. In this Hashomer based itself on earlier decisions by the union, which indeed recognized it as its sole representative in the sphere of guarding. The members of Hamagen appealed against this demand for monopoly by Hashomer, asserting they had operated and continued to operate only in places where Hashomer was not active, so that in principle and in practice they were not in competition. In their view there was room for the two organizations side by side and not in opposition. Moreover, to prove their good intentions they held up the regulations of their association, which forbade competition with Hashomer. The union committee, primarily Levi Shkolnik (Eshkol) and Avraham Hertzfeld, who were dealing with the matter, tended to accept Hamagen's claims. This aroused the anger of Hashomer, which began to regard this trend as a party plot hatched by Hapoel Hatzair and the "non-partisans" (*Second Aliya* workers who did not belong to either party) against it. Beyond the struggle over the monopoly in guarding that Hashomer sought in the workers' camp and beyond the struggle for work places, Hashomer on the one hand and in the Hamagen leader Yosef Lishansky on the other, both sought control of bases in the south, which were close to the front and thus facilitated the acquisition of arms. Lishanksy, who unknown to his comrades in Hamagen was involved in the Nili operation, wanted the guarding at these villages because this would allow him relative freedom of movement in zones close to the front. Because of his activity in Nili, Lishansky was forced to neglect the association he headed, and this caused its decline. When rumors of Lishansky's connection with Nili began to circulate, Hamagen broke up.[8]

In sum, during the decade 1904–14 tendencies toward strengthening self-defense of the Yishuv and freedom from dependence on non-Jewish elements in guarding property gained impetus. The expansion of the Yishuv and the manifestation of Arab nationalism enhanced these processes, but the major contribution to them was by Bar Giora and Hashomer.

5

The Organization and Ideology of Hashomer

> At the committee meeting a top secret decision was taken too,
> not to be disclosed for the time being even to our members; this
> was that Hashomer had to make preparations for the conquest
> of Jerusalem by the Jews.
>
> *Yisrael Shohat*

THE HASHOMER ORGANIZATION entered the First World War at a
serious disadvantage. The outbreak of the conflict found the association past its peak in strength and range of operations. The disposition,
readiness and functioning of the association during the four long and
arduous years of the war should be examined from the organizational and
practical aspect, as well as the ideological and political.

Organizational and Practical Aspects

In this aspect, the war years may be divided into several subperiods of
unequal length: (1) the first months of the war until the end of 1914; (2)
from the end of 1914 until August 1916; (3) from August 1916 until
September 1917; (4) from the end of September 1917 until the end of
Ottoman rule in Palestine.

1 Threshold of change (August 1914 until the end of the year)
In this phase the existing attitudes of the Yishuv, including the workers'
parties and Hashomer, toward the Ottoman empire persevered. The First
World War commenced with Germany's declaration of war against
Russia on 1 August 1914 and against France on 3 August. The following
day Germany invaded Belgium. This violation of Belgian neutrality
resulted, the same day, in a declaration of war by Britain against
Germany: the Great War was in progress.

The Ottoman empire did not enter the war at once, even though it had signed a secret alliance on 2 August with Germany. The latter applied heavy pressure on Turkey to join in the war, and succeeded when two German warships, the *Gaben* and the *Breslau*, showing Turkish colors, attacked Russian ports and ships in the Black Sea on 29 October. Following this provocation Turkey was forced to enter the conflagration, which it did the next day. Russia declared war on Turkey on 4 November, and Britain and France did so on 6 November.

The impact of the war was felt in the Palestine Yishuv even before Turkey's entry into the maelstrom. Turkey had on 9 September 1914 revoked the Capitulations, the grants of privileges to nationals of European states residing in the Ottoman empire, although the abolition was any way due to become effective on 1 October. This act stripped protection from tens of thousands of Jews, who had immigrated from Europe and retained their citizenship, and who suddenly found themselves classified as enemy aliens. Political and economic pressures tightened with the entry of Turkey into the war.

Enemy aliens were liable to deportation from Palestine. To forestall this action, which would have meant the loss of a large proportion of the Yishuv, and to prove their allegiance to the government, the leaders of the Yishuv initiated a campaign for the acquisition of Ottoman citizenship. To facilitate the process it was agreed, with the backing of the ambassadors of Germany, Austro-Hungary and the United States, that bestowal of citizenship would not involve a fee, which was usual. Similarly, a year's deferment of military service was granted.

The workers' parties and Hashomer supported Ottomanization, which meant surrendering previous citizenship in return for Ottoman citizenship, and they pressed for it. The effort resulted in 12,000–15,000 Jews being able to remain in the country. Ottomanization was also an important political demonstration by the Jews of their loyalty to the government.[1]

An episode meriting attention was the attempt to form a Jewish militia. This was not new, for as early as 1912 the idea had been raised by Yisrael Shohat during his days as a law student in Istanbul. Shohat's declared motive was to prove the loyalty of the Jewish Yishuv to the Ottoman empire on the eve of and during the Balkan War in 1912–13. Nothing came of the initiative.[2] With the outbreak of the war in August 1914 Hashomer and the Poaley Zion party revived the proposal to form a Jewish militia, this time in Palestine. The impression provided by the memoirs of those concerned is that two separate attempts, ideologically linked, were made to establish an armed Jewish force in the country. One was in Jerusalem, the other in the Galilee.

The Jerusalem effort to create a militia – the "Popular Defense" – was headed by Yitzhak Ben Zvi and David Ben-Gurion. They undertook it as an extension of Ottomanization following the abolition of the Capitulations. The two presented their proposal to Zaki Bey, the Jerusalem commander, with the stipulation that the unit formed would be deployed in the vicinity of the city. The initiators received encouragement by Zaki Bey, who also suggested the establishment of a joint Arab-Jewish militia, which would maintain order and, in the hour of need, defend the country. The Jerusalem Committee for Ottomanization undertook to further the activity of Ben Zvi and Ben-Gurion, and they gave the initiative their sanction on 17 December 1914. In accordance with the Committee's decisions a subcommittee for Popular Defense was formed under its auspices. A recruiting office was opened for volunteers on the Committee's premises. But in fact, in Jerusalem only about 40 Jews volunteered, including members of the editoral board and the printing shop of *Haahdut*, the organ of the Poaley Zion party. This handful was permitted to begin weapons training in the Russian Compound in Jerusalem. Shortly afterwards this was stopped by order of Jamal Pasha.[3]

In the Galilee, the Hashomer committee took the initiative for raising the militia. The proposal to the Turks was the formation of a mixed Jewish-Arab force, or, if this were unattainable, as they hoped, a wholly Jewish force, whose task it would be to defend the country. Only Ottoman citizens would be recruited into the planned militia. To implement the proposal Yisrael Shohat turned to Yehoshua Hankin and Meir Dizengoff for help. Hankin was taken by the idea and forwarded it to his friend the *mutasarrif* (governor) of the Acre *Sanjak* (region), who welcomed it. Following his agreement it was decided to set about the actual formation of the militia, which was to consist of two separate units, one Arab and one Jewish, each with its own commanders, who would be subject to the Turkish governor. The governor of Acre also accepted the condition that the units reinforce the police in maintaining order and not be sent abroad. According to Shohat's memoirs, hundreds of Jews all over the country volunteered for the militia and they chose their own commanders. Shohat relates that a dispute erupted over the commander of the Jewish unit "between myself and the Ahronson people at Zikhron Ya'akov," who demanded that Alexander Ahronson, head of the Gideonite Association which was hostile to Hashomer, be made commander of the Jewish unit. But Shohat was chosen. This effort too, however, was frustrated by Jamal Pasha.[4]

Regarding Hashomer, it might appear that a single motive underlay both the process of Ottomanization and the proposal to establish a Jewish militia: the desire to display fealty to Turkey. Undoubtedly, this factor was extremely important, arising from Poaley Zion and Hashomer ideology, which affirmed the continued existence and integrity of the Ottoman empire, and from the political need to prove to the government the allegiance of the Jewish Yishuv, which was generally suspected of lacking it. Such a step was essential, especially following the Turkish declaration of a *jihad*, or holy war, and the wave of Ottoman patriotism that swept the Arab population at the beginning of the war.

But it is also reasonable to suppose that there were other, nationalist, motives. Regarding Ottomanization, the obvious purpose was to keep as many Jews as possible in Palestine by preventing their deportation. Regarding the militias, the unstated purpose was to multiply cores of Jewish force and power, an attitude that well suited the overall orientation of Hashomer. Moreover, the militia idea contained the potential for armed frameworks parallel or alternative to Hashomer in times of trouble. Yisrael Shohat's words bear this out:

> It was clear to our committee, immediately with the outbreak of the war, that new forms had to be found to ensure the peace of the Yishuv and the actions of Hashomer itself. But it was equally clear that in those days of disturbances and decrees Hashomer had to be flexible: to be ready to evade every decree and at the same time not to concede the safety of the Yishuv.[5]

Rahel Yanait-Ben Zvi also states that Manya Shohat was highly enthusiastic about the idea of the militia, "seeing in it the opportunity to create kernels of Jewish strength in the spirit of Hashomer."[6]

Together with the caution required in treating recollections written decades after the events, they should be scrutinized, among other things, in light of the general tendency and basic aims of Hashomer. From this viewpoint the concept of the militia accorded well with the existing political needs of the Yishuv, Poaley Zion ideology, and the desire of Hashomer to create a series of strongholds that would promote the national interest. While there is no proof, it is reasonable to suppose that in the background were historical examples of peoples that grasped the chance of mustering military units to fight in wars, thereby accumulating greater political clout when it came to demanding the fulfillment of national goals. In the First World War itself various peoples – Poles, Czechs and others – learned this historical lesson in order to advance their cause.

2 The decline (the end of 1914 until August 1916)

The start of this period was marked by an abrupt change for the worse in the Ottoman government's treatment of the Jewish settlement in Palestine. Two consecutive stages may be discerned in this drastic turn of events.

The first stage began with the appointment of Baha el-Din to the post of *Kaymakam*, or district governor, of Jaffa. The new official, who enjoyed the services of Hassan Bey, the military governor of the *Kada* (district), and of Araf Bey, the chief of police, adopted, immediately on his arrival, an anti-Jewish and anti-Zionist stance in his area of jurisdiction. While the *Mutasarrif*s (regional governors) of Jerusalem and Acre continued with former policy toward the Yishuv, as early as October 1914 Baha el-Din embarked on the opposite course, as reflected in decrees and pressures which transformed the atmosphere, immediately and totally. The new official was a radical Turkish nationalist, who had previously served in Macedonia, where he had witnessed the strength of the local national movement. Through the intervention of the European powers, the national movement had caused the severance of Macedonia from the Ottoman empire. Baha el-Din was transferred to the ministry of the interior as head of the desk on non-Turkish nations. He arrived in Jaffa with preconceptions regarding the Yishuv, and what he saw there reinforced his view that the Jews constituted a hostile element, seeking to remove Palestine from the orb of the Ottoman empire. His wrath focused principally on the Zionists, the workers' parties and Hashomer: these he considered to spearhead the subversive tendency.

He began, in October 1914, by making threats. Very soon he moved from threats to deeds, issuing a series of harsh orders against the Jewish population in his jurisdiction: he tightened up the means of preventing Jewish immigration, forbade Jews to buy land from the local population, and ordered the removal of Hebrew signs. On 5 November 1914 house-to-house searches were conducted in Tel Aviv for hostile Zionist material. Baha el-Din prohibited the use of Jewish National Fund stamps and the Zionist flag, and Zionist institutions were declared illegal; the APC (Anglo-Palestine Company: the major Zionist bank) was closed; the illegal arms of the Jews, which meant almost all their weapons, were ordered to be surrendered; the holding of banknotes and cheques of enemy states was banned. Jewish guarding in Tel Aviv was abolished.[7]

The second stage in the worsening situation developed from December 1914, with the appointment of Jamal Pasha as commander of the Fourth Ottoman Corps, and as governor, to all intents and purposes, of Syria, including Palestine. Jamal Pasha had risen rapidly through the ranks of the Young Turks. In 1909 he had served as governor of the Adana *Sanjak*, and in 1911 he filled the same post in Baghdad. In 1912 he was made military governor of Istanbul. Later he was brought into the government as Minister of Public Works and then as Minister of the Fleet. From mid-1913 he became the third member of the ruling triumvirate of Young Turks consisting, besides himself, of Anwar Bey and Talaat Bey. This trio ruled the Ottoman empire until the end of the war. Jamal Pasha is described as a man of great energy and considerable administrative talents. But he acted on impulse and was therefore unpredictable. He habitually took decisions without consulting experts and advisers, or coordinating with his colleagues in the government. The latter succeeded in removing him from the capital by transferring him to Syria and giving him the command of the Fourth Corps. These posts, combined with his position as government minister and member of the ruling triumvirate, made him omnipotent in Syria and Palestine. He was essentially a Francophile, hence his reservations over and recoil from the Germans.

Jamal Pasha's hostility toward Zionism was the result of his radical Turkish nationalism and his xenophobia deriving from an Islamic-religious world outlook. These characteristics, together with the views he learned from Baha el-Din, whom he met in December 1914, consolidated his negative attitude to the Yishuv and to Zionism. Under the pressure of the Germans Baha el-Din was removed from his position in Jaffa, but Jamal Pasha appointed him his aide and political adviser. In his new role Baha el-Din influenced the formulation of Jamal Pasha's policy on the Yishuv.

In December 1914 and early January 1915, Jamal Pasha expanded Baha el-Din's policy to cover the entire country. His decrees included the disbanding of associations and unions, prohibition of the use of Hebrew in the mails, cancellation of the militia initiatives, and distribution among the Arabs of the weapons collected from the Jews. These edicts were appended to the earlier directives of Baha el-Din. In January 1915 a change occurred in Jamal Pasha's attitude when he declared his policies to be directed against the Zionists alone, not against the Jewish population as a whole. Thenceforward, with some ebbs and flows, this basic policy was maintained until the expulsion of the entire Jewish population from Jaffa–Tel Aviv in April 1917. Throughout the years under review Istanbul, which was subject to pressures of Germany and the United States, was the modifying element in Jamal Pasha's attitude to the Jews.[8]

As for Hashomer, its fortunes declined quickly. The promulgation of the law banning associations and unions placed the organization in a wholly new situation. Until then, Hashomer had operated officially and on a quasi-legal basis. The new order outlawed the association. From then on its members were obliged to conclude all guarding contracts with the *moshavot* in their own names personally. Activity went underground. The combination of the poor state of Hashomer on the eve of the war, the hostile policy of the government toward the Yishuv, and the laws that struck specifically at Hashomer created the dire circumstances in which the association found itself at the end of 1914.

Hashomer had to adapt to the new conditions, and so resolved on the following measures: the committee of the association would deal only with matters of principle; the committee members were individually given wide-ranging powers; the prohibition against carrying arms and the order to hand them in would be disregarded. It was also decided to continue acquiring weapons and stocking them in secret caches. On the subject of arms the association found itself under attack and charged with disobeying the institutions of the Yishuv and placing the Jewish settlement in jeopardy. Arthur Ruppin went so far as to accuse Yisrael Shohat of treason.[9] In the wake of all this Hashomer resolved to leave Judea entirely and to concentrate in Samaria, but more especially in the Galilee. A handful of individuals remained in Judea to gather information.[10]

On 6 December 1914 Manya Shohat was arrested and a warrant was issued for the arrest of Yisrael Shohat. On 4 January 1915 *Haahdut*, the organ of the Poaley Zion party, was closed down. Yisrael Shohat surrendered to the authorities in mid-January 1915. Yitzhak Ben Zvi and David Ben-Gurion were arrested on 9 February. Both were deported on 21–22 March, together with the Shohat couple, Yehoshua Hankin and several other members of the Yishuv establishment. Those who had been delegates to the Eleventh Zionist Congress in the summer of 1913 were particular targets. Apart from those who left voluntarily, within a short time a sizable section of the leadership of the party and of Hashomer was removed. Before the deportation a meeting was held on 5 March 1915 at the Amdursky Hotel in the Old City of Jerusalem, between the heads of the party and of Hashomer, where full coordination between the two bodies was decided on. To implement this Rahel Yanait was seconded to the Hashomer committee.[11]

In 1915–16 Hashomer concentrated in the Galilee. These were the years of deep recession in the association, continuing the trend of retreat that had been evident on the eve of the war. Naturally, the recession led to a narrowing of the vision. In the absence of alternative places to work or guard, many of the guards were forced to gather at Tel Adashim, the Hashomer settlement in the Jezreel Valley. In this small village, a social and economic pressure cooker, frictions, resentments, quarrels and short tempers were evident. Splits in opinions and trends widened. At the Hashomer assembly at Yavneel in Lower Galilee on 9 September 1915, a new committee was elected, but as a result of the troubled relations in the association its two central and authoritative figures, Yisrael Gil'adi and Mendel Portugali, were not on it. At this meeting it was also decided to conduct a "purge" at Tel Adashim, and the Gil'adi group were ordered to leave. The group moved to Kefar Tabor, where they barely scraped a living out of guarding. The new committee consisted of Shmuel Hefter, Zvi Nadav, Yosef Nahmani, Zeev Levinson and Rahel Yanait.

This committee was the largest since the establishment of Hashomer, but showed no initiative and did nothing. Each of its members was engaged in his/her own affairs. The committee also lacked authority and was in effect disunited. Individually and in groups the members of the association went their own ways, lacking any central uniting and directing force.[12] At that time, too, the attempt to break the barrier of pasturing collapsed, with the failure of the herdsmen, mostly members of Hashomer, at Beit Gan, Kinneret, and Mitzpe, all settlements in Lower Galilee.[13]

3 The awakening (August 1916–September 1917)

The revival of Hashomer began in summer 1916, several factors being responsible: with the failure of the Turks on the Suez front and the advance of the British in the Sinai desert, hopes for an early end to the war rose; the massacre of the Armenians instilled fear and served as a grim reminder to the Jewish Yishuv in Palestine that a similar fate might await it; the recruitment in Egypt to the Zion Mule Corps, which fought within the British Army at Gallipoli, and the efforts to form Jewish battalions in Britain, had repercussions in Palestine; and Zionist political activity was taking place across the world. These fresh circumstances and the encouraging war news sparked a renewed security effort in the Yishuv, to be ready for whatever was in store. Among the Hashomer people harnessed to this activity were Zvi Nadav, Rahel Yanait and Shmuel Hefter. Their enterprise resulted in contacts starting between Hashomer and the Jaffa Group in Jaffa-Tel Aviv. After several meetings, and owing to the reservations of the latter group about joining Hashomer, it was decided to recognize them as an autonomous defense group for the Jaffa-Tel Aviv district, without Hashomer operating there: "They did not want a closer contact." The awakening brought about the idea of the HTPY (Hebrew initials of a phrase meaning "continuous defense and direct action"), whose initiator was Nadav, "because it seemed to me that the matter of defense, or the idea of a force capable of fighting and taking part in conquering the country for the Jewish people, was so simple and obvious." The plan was approved at the eighth annual "activist" meeting of Hashomer, which convened at Tel Adashim on 29 August 1916.[14]

The improving mood and the warm sense of renewal were also nourished by the return to guarding in the south of the country, particularly in Rehovot. In December 1916 Hashomer, through the agency of Zvi Nadav, resumed the guarding at Rehovot following the failure of Blumenfeld's method of mixed guarding (Arabs, Bedouin and Jews) by contract. In fact, the guarding agreement between the moshava and Zvi Nadav was signed only on 11 March 1917. Nadav recruited the large manpower he required from the Judea Workers' Union. He received financial support from Kapai, the fund of the World Union of Poaley Zion parties, which acted on their behalf in Palestine.[15]

The return to the south was especially important for the association, for it permitted the renewal of arms acquisitions, which would now be on a considerable scale. It will be recalled that at the end of March 1917 the front was located on the Gaza–Beer Sheba line. Its proximity, the existence of arms depots close by and the large numbers of deserters from the Ottoman army presented many opportunities for obtaining weapons. Using the Ruhama farm in the south (now Kibbutz Ruhama) as its main forward base, Hashomer made acquisitions, in addition to guarding, its chief defense occupation in 1917.[16]

On returning to guard in Rehovot, Hashomer found itself in conflict with the Hamagen organization. The latter was formed in summer 1915 by Yosef Lishansky and others. With Lishansky's increasing involvement in the Nili (Hebrew acrostic for *netzah yisrael lo yeshaker* – "The everlasting of Israel will not lie," a spy ring working for the British), he neglected Hamagen, and the organization collapsed. Hashomer's monopoly was assured.[17]

Further encouragement for Hashomer derived from the settlement of the Gil'adi group at Hamara, in eastern Upper Galilee, in summer 1916. Yisrael Gil'adi drew to the Upper Galilee, parallel with his own people, a group of herdsmen who temporarily settled in the yard of Talha (the future Tel Hai), with the intention of establishing a cattlemen's settlement based on pasturing and agriculture combined. In 1916 the start of settlement by several workers began at Nijmat el-Subah, which was to become the kibbutz Ayelet Hashahar. Gil'adi strove for regional settlement of workers' groups in Upper Galilee, including a guards' settlement on the northern marches.[18]

The settlement of Gil'adi's people in the north, the special activity of the Haro'im (The Herdsmen) association, the restoration of guarding in the south, the feverish work of arms acquisition, the plan for the defense of the Yishuv put forward in summer 1916 and its reinforcement in 1917 as the front drew near – all these were excellent grounds for sense of uplift and revival, despite the Jaffa-Tel Aviv expulsion, and they were reflected at the ninth annual assembly of Hashomer, held at Tel Adashim on 14 September 1917. The Hashomer guards felt that they had escaped from confinement. Once more, new horizons for national deeds were opening before them.

During the Tel Adashim meeting, and all the more at the twelfth Poaley Zion conference at Merhavia immediately following it, news began to circulate that the Turks had got wind of the Jewish spy network, whose existence the conferees were aware of. Fears over the exposure of the Nili and the consequences that might be expected multiplied. The discovery of the Nili on 1 October 1917 brought about an end to hopes and the sudden collapse of Hashomer. With it, the activities described above halted immediately.[19]

4 The brink of dissolution (September 1917–April 1919)

The ninth Hashomer assembly, as noted, was already under the shadow of tension and fears of exposure of the Nili network, which, in fact, were vindicated. Acting cautiously, and in consideration of the future, the assembly resolved to freeze all activities of the association and to await the passing of the storm.

And indeed, the storm unleashed by the Turks on discovering the Nili was violent. The government's attitude to the Yishuv as a whole, and to the *moshavot* involved in particular, hardened. Especially hurt was Hashomer, which the Turks regarded as an insurgent military organization collaborating with their enemies. The hunt for Hashomer men began straightaway, and many of them were caught or gave themselves up. Most of them were concentrated in Nazareth, where they were interrogated and tortured, with many others. From Nazareth many were transferred to Damascus for trial. Many could not return to Palestine and wandered around Turkey. Some, among them the central figures in Hashomer, only returned to the country, via Russia, at the beginning of 1919.[20]

In addition to what has been described above, the conquest of the south of the country by the British in November–December 1917 led to the severance of the south from the north. Most Hashomer people who were not captured and deported were in the north. The few in the liberated zone in the south were obliged to operate on their own.

The explosion caused by the Nili affair – the manhunts, the arrests, the torture and the expulsions – caused the swift collapse and paralysis of Hashomer. The conquest of the south and its detachment from the north only served to exacerbate the process of dissolution.

Surprisingly, despite these desperate circumstances, disparate groups and individual Hashomer guards continued their activity. Those who found themselves in the south became the central workers in the volunteer movement of the Yishuv population, to *Hagedud ha'ivri* (the Jewish Battalion), which was established and was deployed in the framework of the British army. The Hashomer people in the south were also active, both before the volunteer movement and during their service in the Palestinian Battalion, in arms acquisition. In the north (that is, north of present-day Tel Aviv and Petah Tikva), where the Turks still ruled, the members of Hashomer who had not been arrested or deported devoted themselves to guarding and arranging the defense of the *moshavot*. To this end it was also decided, at the tenth annual assembly at Sharona on 27 July 1918, to organize groups of young people in the Galilee who would go out to work at guarding in the *moshavot*, and thus ease the burden on the farmers and the guards. Other decisions called for the arming of the *moshavot*, the enrollment of new members in the association, and to better manage the complex security situation.[21] This diverse activity attests to the great vital force of the association and its members. Immediately with the liberation of the north (in September 1918) the eleventh annual assembly of Hashomer convened on 17 October 1918 in Tiberias, where it was resolved to continue activities in several channels: continuation of guarding at the *moshavot* and enlistment in the army and police. This vitality found symbolic and demonstrative expression when the Hashomer guards, after their assembly in Tiberias, arrived *en masse* on horseback, ensigns aloft, at the conference of the Galilee Workers' Union then being held at Kinneret, the settlement on the shores of the lake.

Despite the energy and the will to continue to operate and influence, it must be admitted that the association had been dealt mortal blows. Our concern is with a small organization, whose members, together with their wives, numbered no more than a few score. The group lacked economic and financial reserves, and many of its people lived in poverty and want. In such straits Hashomer entered into the new era of British rule. At the end of 1918 and beginning of 1919 Hashomer found itself without its core of founders – some dead, some exiled. The group was without men of stature and without a central and authoritative leadership. Only from the spring 1919 did the rehabilitation process begin, itself short-lived, with the return to Palestine of the exiles and the Shohat couple.[22]

Ideological and Political Changes

Three stages are discernible in the development of Bar Giora and Hashomer: (1) the underground-revolutionary stage of 1907–9; (2) the legal stage from 1909 to the end of 1914 and beginning of 1915; (3) the ideological reversal from early 1915 until the British conquest of Palestine. In the first two stages there was a parallel and a mutual link between the security body and the mother party Poaley Zion. The third stage was more special to Hashomer, and the link existed only with a section of the party.

1 Underground-revolutionary stage (September 1907–April 1909)
Some of the founders of Bar Giora, like those of Poaley Zion, immigrated to Palestine before the Poaley Zion SD party was established in Poltava in 1906. The views of this party became the legacy of the Poaley Zion party in Palestine even before the immigration of Yitzhak Ben Zvi. The principle presented is reflected in the Ramla Programme, which was approved by the Poaley Zion conference on 5 January 1907. With Ben Zvi's arrival in the country on 30 March 1907 the Borochovist line in the party grew stronger. This ideology largely shaped the ideological and political concepts of Bar Giora also, from its establishment until the Young Turk revolution in July 1908.[23] Borochov, like many Marxist

socialists of his day, negated the dissolution of multinational states. The ideal was to convert them into federative frameworks based on national autonomy of the peoples.

It has already been explained that in the Borochovist outlook an important place was reserved for a self-defense organization such as Bar Giora, which could become the military spearhead of the Palestinian proletariat, destined to take the lead in the struggle in the country until democratic Jewish national autonomy was attained. A function of this ideology was, naturally, support for the integrity of the Ottoman empire. This pro-Turkish orientation predominated in the Poaley Zion party and in Bar Giora until the Young Turk revolution on 24 July 1908, and the revolution only served to reinforce this outlook.[24]

2 The legal stage (April 1909–late 1914, early 1915)
The Young Turk revolution introduced two new factors: the transformation of the Ottoman empire into a constitutional monarchy supposed to be governed by a parliamentary regime, and the appearance of Arab nationalism. These necessitated an ideological and tactical re-evaluation both in Poaley Zion and in Bar Giora.

As a result of these processes, Zionist ardor for the attainment of national autonomy cooled, but this did not alter the general basic political ideology of a pro-Turkish orientation and support for the integrity of the Ottoman empire. The change that occurred was merely tactical. The party shifted to overt and legitimate political activity directed toward merging into the new liberal political fabric.

The fundamental ideological and political outlook of Bar Giora, and from April 1909 of Hashomer, dovetailed with that of the mother party. On the tactical level, owing to the rise of Arab nationalism, which exacerbated national tensions, the pragmatic conclusion could only be to change from a revolutionary underground organization to an open organization, operating legally and better able to exploit the fresh liberal climate and the new political ground rules. Thus Hashomer was created, intended to serve as the mass legal arm of Bar Giora, itself designed to continue to act as a secret ruling elite.[25]

3 Ideological revolution (early 1915–British conquest)
The activity of the Hashomer people on behalf of Ottomanization and the militia has been described above. At first sight, loyalty to the Ottoman crown continued even after the turn for the worse in Turkish policy toward the Yishuv following the appointment of Jamal Pasha. In addition, the impression is that even the closing of the journal Haahdut, the arrests and the deportations from Palestine of the Shohats, Yitzhak Ben Zvi and David Ben-Gurion, did not shake the pro-Turkish orientation of

the party and Hashomer. Regarding Yitzhak Ben Zvi and David Ben-Gurion, historiography highlights the memorandum the two men presented to Jamal Pasha on 5 March 1915, which is replete with testimonials to their own loyalty and the loyalty of their party to the Ottoman empire. To counter charges of membership of a secret organization hostile to the empire, they asserted in the memorandum that "all our deeds, thoughts and hopes, just as they are aimed at the benefit of the Jews in Palestine, so are they aimed at the good of the Ottoman empire entirely."[26] Furthermore, historians claim that the two leaders continued in their allegiance to Turkey even after their expulsion from Palestine on 22 March 1915, at a time when they were imperiled by Jamal Pasha and his underlings.

The two men, reaching Egypt on 24 March 1915 *en route* for the United States, met Ze'ev Jabotinsky and Josef Trumpeldor, the leaders of the lobby calling for the establishment of Jewish battalions within the British army. In a conversation with these individuals, the two leaders of Poaley Zion voiced their opposition to the formation of the Jewish corps that was to be sent to Gallipoli and whose creation reflected a political orientation favoring the *Entente* powers. Evidence of this posture of Ben-Gurion and Ben Zvi is found in their memoirs. Ben-Gurion states it directly, writing that "we both expressed our opposition to this step,"[27] namely, the formation of the corps. Similar statements are found in Ben Zvi's memories.[28] According to the histories, the fealty of the two toward Turkey continued in the following years too. This posture was reflected, according to the history books, as late as 31 August 1916 in a memorandum handed by Ben Zvi and Ben-Gurion to Louis Brandeis (leader of the Zionist Organization of America), for him to pass on to the Turks. The memorandum was a petition by the two men that they be allowed to return to Palestine. In it they stressed once again their allegiance to the Ottoman empire and denied the charges leveled against them by Jamal Pasha. The petition to return to Palestine was made after the two men heard of the change for the better in Ottoman policy toward Zionism.[29]

According to this version of history, the shift in their political orientation occurred only in 1917.[30] Ultimately, accepted opinion holds that the views of Ben Zvi and Ben-Gurion characterized the Palestinian Poaley Zion party as a whole, and Hashomer, at least until September 1917, the time of the twelfth Poaley Zion conference at Merhavia.[31] Additional proof adduced for this view is the opposition by Ben Zvi and Ben-Gurion to the ideas of Pinhas Ruthenberg, on his arrival in the United States from Italy in mid-1915, on the need to set up a Jewish government and a Jewish legion that would fight beside the *Entente* powers for the conquest of Palestine.[32]

It is not possible, on the basis of the two memoranda described, to prove a pro-Ottoman orientation on the part of the two exiled leaders of Poaley Zion. They both wished to remain in Palestine, and therefore had to display their loyalty to the government in presenting their case to Jamal Pasha. The same is true for the memorandum to Brandeis. The moment they decided that their presence in Palestine was preferable to their activity in the United States and Canada it stood to reason that they would stress their loyalty in the memorandum to Brandeis, which was intended for the Turkish authorities, in protest against the wrong done them and in support of their right to return to Palestine.

Even if the memoranda cannot sustain the claim of allegiance to Turkey, there remains the issue of the orientation of the Poaley Zion party and Hashomer: first, ideologically, was there a fundamental ideological change in these bodies, as compared with the pre-war period? And second, practically, if there indeed was a fundamental ideological shift, did it remain on that level or was it put into practice? To contend with this issue, I shall deal briefly with the stance of the Poaley Zion party abroad during the war, but chiefly with the positions of the party in the United States, with the Poaley Zion party in Palestine and, of course, Hashomer.

As is known, the World Zionist Organization adopted a posture of neutrality in the world conflagration that broke out in 1914. The World Union of Poaley Zion followed the lead of the WZO.[33] Poaley Zion in the United States took a similar course too, influenced, moreover, by the pacifist and anti-war sentiments of the Socialist party of the United States. However, the Poaley Zion position in North America was not monolithic. As early as 1915 elements in the party accepted Pinhas Ruthenberg's ideas on the creation of a Jewish state and of Jewish battalions to fight on the side of the *Entente*. Among the leading proponents of this line were Nahman Sirkin and Haim Zhitlovsky. The longer the war went on the more this line could rest, beyond Jewish considerations, on the growing tendency of the American trade union movement, led by Samuel Gompers, to support Wilson and his policy of entering the war on the side of the *Entente*. From the Jewish point of view, the longer the war went on the stronger became nationalist feelings in the American Jewish community, including the Jewish workers' community, and these stimulated an enormous expansion of the Zionist movement in America. The political situation in the American and American-Jewish public generally and in the Poaley Zion party in particular was thus complex and heterogeneous, going beyond the official party line negating joining the war, affirming neutrality, and rejecting the idea of the Jewish battalions.[34]

The pro-Ottoman orientation with which the Palestinian Poaley Zion party began the war has already been mentioned. As a result of the economic and political hardships caused by the war, the political and cultural activity of the party withered and it entered into a deep depression. This was not the case with its financial arm, Kapai, which despite its limitations did much to succor its members. This difficult situation appeared clearly in the words of Efraim Bloch-Blumenfeld, the director of Kapai and a leader of Poaley Zion, at the party council on Rosh Hashana (the Jewish New Year) in August 1916, when he complained that "day-to-day problems weighed us down too much, and there was no creative perspective. The political functioning of the party ceased entirely." At the council, held on 29 June 1917, the same complaints were heard, including one that the central committee was inactive: "It is simply necesary to come to terms with the idea that at the moment there are no leading party forces in the country . . . "[35] It appears that the party stopped fulfilling its central role of a culturally consolidating body, guide and pointer in the sphere of political life, as it had been in the period before the war.

In these difficult circumstances of a void in ideological forces and in theoretical and practical politics, the party continued to tread the old path, unable to contend with the new situation brought about by the war. Only late in 1916, with the approach of the southern front,[36] did political activity revive. In December the party center adopted a draft resolution that "according to the latest information it is likely that the war is approaching its end." Another stated that "it is necessary to plan for the political situation, which is about to change."[37] The resolution was general, and it is difficult to infer from it what the preparations and the future political changes were to be. However, it does indicate the feeling that fresh political positions had to be established. The linkage of the resolutions to the comment on the coming end of the war, itself based on the approach of the British to the gateway to the country, leads to the conclusion that the coming political change involved a reorientation.

Hashomer retained a strong ideological, but not organizational, tie with the Poaley Zion party. The association belonged to the activist segment of the Yishuv, and its members constituted the activist wing of Poaley Zion. Hashomer activism was a consequence of the constant struggle by the association to create an independent Jewish force as an instrument for realizing national goals. Therefore, as already noted, the Hashomer people regarded the militia proposal also as "an opportunity to create kernels of Jewish strength in the spirit of Hashomer."[38] When the authorities ordered the Jewish settlement to hand over their arms Hashomer declined to do so, and acted to persuade other Yishuv elements to refuse also. Moreover, even in these hard times the association persevered in its policy of arms acquisition. In effect, its policies were anti-government. It is interesting that in the area of acquisitions Hashomer actually received financial support from Bloch-Blumenfeld, the director of Kapai, who was the foremost spokesman for the pro-Ottoman orientation.

Yisrael Shohat in his memoirs, presented chiefly in his programmatic article "The mission and the way" in the *Hashomer Volume*, states that Hashomer was forced underground in the wake of the decrees of Baha el-Din and Jamal Pasha in 1914. A *volte-face* took place in his attitude to the Ottoman empire, in parallel with his efforts at Ottomanization and the creation of the militia:

> At the committee meeting a top secret decision was taken too, not to be disclosed for the time being even to our members; this was that Hashomer had to make preparations for the conquest of Jerusalem by the Jews. It was decided that first of all we would make all the preparations, and at the right moment we would inform the members. It was certainly daring to dream of capturing Jerusalem with our meagre forces, but it was hard for Hashomer not to make plans in the circumstances that had been created by the world war. These circumstances caught us by surprise, before we were properly ready. But still, should they not be exploited for the benefit of the Yishuv?

Later, Shohat continues:

> Hashomer assumed that the Turks would lose and the British would conquer the entire land, including Jerusalem. The intention of the committee's decision was that we would deliver Jerusalem to the British, thereby signifying the special role filled by the Jews in the capture of the city. We believed that with the British advance the Turks would begin to retreat, and there would be confusion in the land; so that if Hashomer could then succeed in establishing a Jewish force, small though it may be, but organized and ready for action in the right place, it would be a simple matter to take control. To study the situation, I set out for Jerusalem with Yisrael Gil'adi. We reconnoitred the place, its topography, the lie of its fortifications, the locations of trenches and barracks. We drew detailed diagrams – Gil'adi was a perfectionist. But suddenly a great change occurred. Manya was arrested, and then I, and the preparations to take Jerusalem stopped.[39]

These words were written many years after the events and they should be treated with extreme caution; furthermore, at the time of writing the two other committee members, Yisrael Gil'adi and Mendel Portugali, were no longer alive, and Shohat's recollections are replete with anachronisms. Nevertheless, it would be rash to dismiss this passage and see it merely as the fruit of his imagination. Shohat's account is too detailed for it to be disregarded, particularly when it is juxtaposed to subsequent events.

At the beginning of March 1915, before the deportations of the Shohats, Yitzhak Ben Zvi and David Ben-Gurion, the Poaley Zion party workers and central figures of Hashomer met at the Amdursky Hotel in the Old City of Jerusalem. In various memoirs it is noted that the participants at the meeting were Ben Zvi, Ben-Gurion, the Shohats and Rahel Yanait.[40] In most memoirs the encounter is termed "historic," because at it the future path of the party and of Hashomer was forged. It was also decided to strengthen the links between the two bodies, and to this end Rahel Yanait was attached to the Hashomer committee.[41] For our purposes it is important to note that it was decided, among other things, that if Ben Zvi and Ben-Gurion were deported, they would travel to the United States, and act there for two goals:

> (a) The creation of a movement of pioneering and immigration to Palestine for work and guarding. (b) The idea of the Jewish battalion, which would fight in this war, when the right time came. True, the hour was not yet ripe, but we foresaw that it certainly would be during the war, sooner or later.

This version, by Ben Zvi, appears in two of his books: *Poaley Zion in the Second Aliya* and *Memoirs and Notes*.[42] In *The Jewish Battalions* Ben Zvi is even more explicit and outspoken: "We decided on a plan of action for the future: to strive by any means for the creation of Jewish battalions abroad to liberate Palestine."[43] Less incisive words, but in the same spirit, appear in the memoirs of Rahel Yanait-Ben Zvi.[44]

Important evidence is found in the the memoirs of David Ben-Gurion, who also refers to the decisions taken at the Amdursky Hotel: "We decided that first we would found the Hehalutz organization, and when the time was right we would set up battalions of volunteers for the Jewish legion that would come to Palestine."[45]

The most important document for our purposes is a letter from Ben-Gurion to his father dated 5 December 1919, written during his service in the 39th Battalion, a unit of the British army made up of Jewish volunteers from North America which operated in Palestine. While the other testimony presented here is memoirs written decades after the events themselves, this was written close to them; furthermore, it appears in an intimate letter from a son to his father. In it Ben-Gurion describes what befell him from the eve of his expulsion from the country to the time the letter was written. It includes the following passages:

> Several days before the departure we gathered in Jaffa. The police sent to keep an eye on us went off after we slipped them something, and we discussed the plan to organize in America Jewish battalions to fight for the Land of Israel, and with this aim I set off, after reaching Egypt, for America.
>
> When I arrived in America I saw that the time had not yet come. It is true that on reaching Egypt I found a Jewish battalion already being formed by Jabotinsky. But even then I realized that the timing was wrong. Britain was not yet ready to send an army to the Palestine front, and the participation of a Jewish battalion on a different front could only endanger the existence of the Jewish Yishuv in Palestine, without national gains or cover for the losses in pay . . .

The formation of the battalion was thus premature, so instead I set about founding Hehalutz . . . The purpose of Hehalutz was to emigrate at the first opportunity – regardless of the outcome of the world war – to Palestine for the sake of "work and guarding." But at gatherings of comrades I made it clear that the members of Hehalutz who might come soon would have to go to Palestine for another reason, more difficult and responsible – to liberate the land with sword in hand."[46]

It should be emphasized that the Hehalutz platform established in the United States by Ben Zvi and Ben-Gurion, and composed by them, contained the following in the clause on "Principles of Hehalutz":[47]

12. Hehalutz will establish a special division for the purpose of guarding in Palestine (Defense Group).

The clause on "Organization of Hehalutz" contains this:

13. The branches arrange for their members (a) lessons in Hebrew and knowledge of Palestine; (b) sports clubs and military training.

The memoirs and letters of the personalities themselves contain no evidence that the decisions taken at the "historic" meeting at the Amdursky Hotel, which imposed on Ben Zvi and Ben-Gurion the task of founding a Jewish force in America, meant the raising of battalions to fight on the side of the Ottoman empire, as a kind of direct continuation of the failed attempt to form the militia. By contrast, it may be stated with a high degree of certainty that two important decisions were taken at the Amdursky Hotel: (a) the need to create a Jewish force to act in the historic circumstances of the First World War; (b) on the basis of historical evidence, principally Ben-Gurion's letter of December 1919, this force was intended to fight on the side of the *Entente* countries against the Ottoman empire. It seems to me that this is the interpretation of Ben-Gurion's words to his father when reporting his clarifications to candidates for Hehalutz in America. They would be required to go to Palestine, he said, "to liberate the land with sword in hand." Such liberation could only be from the Turks.[48]

It follows, then, that Yisrael Shohat's testimony does not stand in isolation. What occurred at the "historic" meeting at the Amdursky Hotel in Jerusalem was the direct continuation of the revolutionary change in orientation that he relates. It seems that already at the end of 1914 and early 1915 a turn was made in the political ideology of Hashomer, and in at least some of the Poaley Zion people themselves. The essence of the change was the abandonment of the long-standing allegiance to the Ottoman empire and its integrity, and the beginnings of an orientation toward the *Entente* powers. It should be noted that the change was primarily ideological, while its practical application remained open, contingent upon appropriate political conditions.

On examination, the opposition of Ben Zvi and Ben-Gurion to the formation of the battalions after their expulsion from Palestine seems to have been purely on pragmatic grounds, with no ideological argument. Pragmatism likewise underlay their opposition to the battalion that was formed in Egypt. In his recollections of the conversation among himself, Ben Zvi and Josef Trumpeldor on the subject, Ben-Gurion wrote that he and Ben Zvi "both expressed opposition to this step. There were tens of thousands of Jews in the country, and this thing might cause the destruction of the Yishuv. Trumpeldor did not accept our view."

Ben Zvi wrote in a similar vein in his memoirs recalling the discussion among the two of them and Trumpeldor and Jabotinsky, in which the four men considered the issue of participating in the war against the Ottoman empire:

> The situation in the country was still not clear. There remained in it about 75,000 people, and their fate was in the hands of the government – for good or ill . . . At that time it seemed to us that [the time – Y.G.] had not yet come to raise battalions of Jews against Turkey. On the other hand, there was no guarantee that the Jewish battalion being formed in Egypt would be sent to the Palestine front.

Here an additional reason appears for their opposition to the creation of the battalion in Egypt. It was not only the danger that this brought to the Jewish population of Palestine: if a Jewish battalion was in fact being formed, then it should fight on the Palestine front, nowhere else.

This is exactly the tone of Ben-Gurion's letter of December 1919 to his father, cited above. He wrote that after his expulsion from Palestine, on arriving in Egypt he found Jabotinsky there, in the process of raising the Jewish battalion, "but even then I realized that the timing was wrong." Further in the letter Ben-Gurion notes that he was also troubled by the fact that Britain then was not yet planning to fight over Palestine and therefore the battalion was to be sent to a different front. This situation harbored perils, according to Ben-Gurion, and might "endanger the existence of the Jewish Yishuv in Palestine, without national gains or cover for the losses in pay."[49]

It becomes evident that the opposition of the two men to the initiative of Jabotinsky and Trumpeldor contained no trace of ideology. All the reasons they adduced for their objection to the battalion were practical and stemmed from a real political situation.

It is almost certain that the opposition of the two men, when in the United States, to the ideas of Pinhas Ruthenberg on the battalions also derived from practical considerations, as reflected in Ben-Gurion's memoirs. These state, concerning Ruthenberg's proposals, that "the two of us, Ben Zvi and I, were against any step that might lead to the destruction of the Jewish settlement in Palestine . . . " Ben Zvi elucidates their opposition from a different angle, writing that in the United States "we found that the groundwork for establishing battalions was not yet ready. Millions of Jews opposed the *Entente* allies (Britain, France and Russia), chiefly owing to the alliance with Tsarist Russia." [50]

It seems that already early in 1917, about six months before the Balfour Declaration, Ben Zvi and Ben-Gurion discarded even their practical reasons, and came out in open support for the *Entente* powers and the organization of Jewish battalions that would fight on their side against the Ottoman empire. Thereafter, the turn that had occurred in March 1915 became complete in practice as in ideology. The process received its ultimate affirmation in April 1917, with the entry of the United States into the war.

It was the set of political and military factors in the world and in Palestine that caused the two men to forsake their practical opposition to the idea of the battalions, and, as a consequence, to identify with the *Entente*. On the international level the Russian revolution of February 1917 and the rise of the liberal Kerensky government to power swept the ground from under the feet of those opposed to supporting the *Entente* owing to the alliance with Russia. Similarly, the entry of the United States into the conflagration on the side of the *Entente* was highly significant. Concerning developments in the Near East and Palestine, it should be recalled that at the end of 1916 the British crossed the Sinai Desert and were at the gates of the country. By the end of March 1917 they were poised at the approaches to the town of Gaza. These facts utterly transformed the political realities of the world and of the region. In addition, the hardening of Jamal Pasha's attitude to the Yishuv, expressed in the Jaffa-Tel Aviv expulsion, showed that there was nothing to be gained by extra caution. As stated, the process that began with Ben Zvi and Ben-Gurion in March 1915 at the Amdursky Hotel came full circle about two years later, in March–April 1917. [51]

In Palestine, the Yishuv was obliged to play a double role. On the one hand, it was essential to display loyalty, even if only superficial, to the government. On the other, with the prolongation of the war and its tribulations, and with the deterioration in the Ottoman government's stance on the Yishuv, hostility to that government expanded. There can be no doubt that the Ottoman orientation of the Yishuv was exhausted long before the British conquest.

Regarding Hashomer and a section of Poaley Zion, the turn in late 1914 and early 1915 has been mentioned. From the deportation of the

Shohat couple and others to the summer of 1916 Hashomer, like the party, was immersed in a struggle to survive, which brought it to the edge of collapse and drained it of all energy for any political thinking and activity. With the recovery, from summer 1916 on, political and security activity resumed, now bearing an anti-Turkish stamp. This was the background to the ties that developed then between Hashomer and the Jaffa Group, the new urgency in the quest for arms, the tendency of several members to support the Nili, and the overall program they attempted to formulate, together with the Jaffa Group, for the defense of the country as expressed in the "HTPY" plan.

The onset of the British campaign in late 1916 and early 1917 spurred Hashomer to intensify its practical plans for joining the *Entente* powers and fighting with them against the Ottoman empire. Zvi Nadav, one of the heads of Hashomer in the period under review and a leading activist, relates that with the approach of the front rumors spread about the existence of Jewish battalions commanded by Trumpeldor and Jabotinsky, deployed on the Palestine front. These were to be the first to invade the land and conquer it. These rumors gave heart to the Hashomer people, and impelled them to consolidate suitable plans:

> We thought that we could muster 300 men (at the Rehovot guarding alone about 70 men were organized) to crack the Turkish front and link up with the Jewish army. It was necessary to ascertain if the Jewish army existed and if it was on the front near Palestine. We followed matters carefully, and it transpired that they were not close by.[52]

It is important to note the willingness in principle, already in late 1916 and early 1917, before the Jaffa-Tel Aviv expulsion, for pre-planned military insurgency against the Turks. This means that in Palestine, too, the moment the actual political and military situation changed the Hashomer people were ready – not only ideologically but also practically – to rebel against the Ottomans and join up with the *Entente* powers.

Hashomer was essentially activist in national-security terms. The association was not firmly bound by ideological formulations but was of a more pragmatic bent. Therefore, already in late 1914 and early 1915 the ideological change had occurred whereby the pro-Ottoman orientation was deserted. The moment the opportunity arose for a change in the political and security situation in Palestine, Hashomer was ready for change in practical terms, with all its organizational and military implications.

Compared with Hashomer, the Poaley Zion party was not hewn of a single rock. Two orientations were active within it: pro-Ottoman and pro-British. These continued to exist in the party throughout the war years, until the conquest of the south of the country. This duality led to an open clash at the twelfth party conference at Merhavia in September 1917. There the adherents of the pro-Ottoman orthodoxy, all of them party members headed by Efraim Bloch-Blumenfeld, contended with the pro-British activist section, which included the members of Hashomer and some members of Poaley Zion. At the Merhavia conference a final and open battle was fought between the two currents, but it ended indecisively.[53] Toward the end of the conference everything collapsed with the exposure of the Nili network. Immediately afterwards came the conquest of the south by the British, which put an end to the quarrel.

6

The Status of Women in Hashomer

One Shabbat, while I was standing guard, Tzipora and Esther
Beker (Shturman) came out to me and said to me earnestly, "Go
on, go in and sleep. We'll guard for you." I was skeptical for a
moment, but without arguing too much I handed them the
whistle and the rifle and I went to my cosy bed feeling quite
alright. Several nights passed quietly under their guard, and
then they dared to make the same request to Meirke
Hazanovich. He accepted their offer and gave them his
weapon, but he stayed with them all night and sang his songs
to them.

Alexander Zayd

IT MIGHT BE EXPECTED that the participation and status of women in the
Bar Giora and Hashomer organizations would be based on the principle
of equality between the sexes, as part of the new normative world outlook
of the makers of the workers' movement in the *Second Aliya*. The reality
was quite different, however, and extremely unfavorable from the
women's point of view. The inequality was even greater for the women
workers of the *Second Aliya* who were associated with Hashomer. This
was because of the special problems of this body, which spearheaded the
labor movement in the "conquest of guarding" (*kibush hashmira*) and to
large extent in the "conquest of work" (*kibush ha'avoda*) also.

The *Second Aliya*

Most women who immigrated to Palestine with the *Second Aliya* and who
belonged to the labor current were young and single, and came from the
same socioeconomic and cultural background as their male comrades.
Most originated from Russia and were influenced by contemporary
circumstances in that country, such as the various shades of revolutionary
ferment, anti-Semitism, persecutions and pogroms. Most of the women
desired national revival, but at the same time the building of a new society,

one of whose aspects would be a changed status of the woman. Some way or other these attitudes characterized the entire community of women workers in Palestine, not only the younger ones who adopted the Marxist-socialist world view. Their ideology and the real conditions of their lives caused them to seek the concrete expression of their goals through work, primarily in agriculture, which was perceived as a symbol of the national and social renaissance. For these young women of the *Second Aliya*, working the land embodied the common link between the revival of the people in their land, the creation of a working society and the establishment of a workers' class. Precisely at this major junction the problems began, and the inequality[1] between men and women stood out. Sometimes it was evident even abroad, prior to emigration to Palestine. In her memoirs Haya (Drechler) Kroll relates that when she made the decision to emigrate to Palestine and set her mind on being an agricultural laborer there, she went to talk about it to the experienced Menahem Sheinkin, a leader of Russian Zionism and a founder of Tel Aviv. He laughed at her dreams. "He explained to me that agriculture in Palestine was not suitable for Jewish girls and advised me to learn dressmaking, and in that way prepare myself for an independent life in the country, and to buy a sewing machine too, and to take it with me there."[2] Sheinkin's advice was undoubtedly sound, arising from his knowledge of the land and his realistic approach to the actual circumstances in Palestine, but it is very likely that his attitude was also based on traditional values regarding the place of the woman in society.

The young woman worker who migrated to Palestine and attempted to achieve her goals encountered the same problems as the men. The land was a backwater, the climate was harsh and alien to them, the Turkish authorities treated them with hostility, the economy was undeveloped, there was no labor market and the Arab worker was preferred by the Jewish farmers; the latter were suspicious of the secular outlook of the newcomers, and their newfangled social ideas. But in addition to all these the young women workers had to contend with obstacles that were special to them.

These women of the *Second Aliya* demanded the right to an equal social status and equality of the right to work and rights at work. But in the setting of the actual situation and the traditional concepts prevailing in all social strata in the country, including the Jewish population, they encountered misunderstanding and difficulties. The status of the Jewish woman was inferior. For Jewish women of the traditional Sephardi community, working outside the confines of the household or ideas of equality with men were simply unthinkable. The farmers' wives and daughters did not usually undertake physical labor and agriculture, except, perhaps, in the *moshavot* of the Galilee. In all, the existing situation in the practical sphere was disheartening, and that in the normative sphere was more traditional, severe and extreme than in the diaspora society whence they came. Sara Malkin, among the earliest migrants of the *Second Aliya* and a founder of the women workers' movement, wrote: "The farmers found us strange. They could not and did not want to grasp the idea of a woman working not only out of necessity but also out of ideology; how much less could they comprehend how it was possible for a woman to occupy herself in work in the field and in the village."[3]. This is a generalization, but Sara Malkin clearly portrays the spirit of the Jewish settlement at that time.

Beyond the unfavorable circumstances of the women workers generally, the alienation and miscomprehension of their goals by the male Jewish workers hurt them particularly. This was so despite the identity between them in the remaining areas of national and social aims, and usually in day-to-day life and struggles. Suddenly the women found themselves alone, isolated not only from the general and Jewish society, but also within their own community, the workers' community. Sara Malkin writes scathingly of this: "In their eyes too we were ridiculous, and not only those of us who wished to tear down seemingly natural barriers and assume the hard work of agricultural labor, but also those of us engaged in work where the women could compete with the men. Even they were mocked."[4]

The men admitted women to the labor teams, known as "conquest groups" (*kvutzot kibush*) but this cooperation was limited. Usually the women were needed as kitchen workers and to manage living arrangements, and their equal right to work in general and to that labor in particular was not recognized. Sometimes there was not even equality in the area of expressing opinions and the right to vote. This was the case in the conquest groups at Um Juni, at Merhavia and in other mixed workers' teams.[5] This discrimination was made worse by the attitude of the philanthropic settlement institutions, and even of the Palestine Office, which in a considerable number of cases for years did not recognize women's labor as separate, entitled to its own wage.[6] Among the workers' teams that were recognized the collective at Sejera was exceptional, in that several women in it managed to get agricultural jobs for pay.[7] Here and there were some other exceptions, but these merely served to highlight the rule, which was the restriction of the woman worker to traditional service tasks and housework alone. As distinct from their male comrades, the young women of the *Second Aliya* did not realize their goals and did not bring about the general revolution in the status of the woman that they strove for.[8]

A lively debate on women's labor developed at the fifth assembly of Galilee workers' agricultural union, held on 12–14 March 1914 at the Poria farm. Yosef Baratz, a leader of Hapoel Hatzair and a founder of

Kibbutz Degania, who opened the debate on the labor situation, treated the issue of work by women, and stated that "Palestine is not yet able to solve the problem of women's labor. The role of the woman is not to become daily laborers, but to attend to the farmstead. Therefore, there is no place for women workers with the farmers, but in groups that will work autonomously." Eli'ezer Yaffe, the dominant figure in the Galilee workers' union, a founder of the workers' cooperative settlement movement (*moshav 'ovdim*) and a leader of the workers' movement, made no bones about revealing the whole truth about the attitude of male workers to females: "As everywhere in the world, the young men treat the girls as women. It seems to the boys that the woman should be secondary to the man."

As stated, the debate took place at the start of 1914, toward the end of a decade of the *Second Aliya*. The women workers had by then taken great strides since the beginning of the Aliya, in the area of awareness of their problems and in organizing themselves. They were on the eve of founding a countrywide women workers' movement. Not surprisingly then, the women who participated in the debate not only countered the assertions of the men, they also extensively set forth their own claims against the male workers. Sara Malkin complained that "the situation of the young women is far worse than that of the young men . . . Society and the young men do not understand the position of the young girl in the country . . . The girls have found no support on the part of the male workers . . . Most of them deride our work. We must be given a place to work not only in the kitchen but in the fields and a responsible role in all tasks." Yael Gordon, daughter of A. D. Gordon and a founder of the women workers' movement, also gave vent to the bitterness she felt. Her conclusion, even on the basis of that debate alone, was that the men were "not interested in the problem of the women," and hence the Galilee workers' union was not a general union serving the male and female workers equally. This held true as long as its primary or principal concern was the men, "and it ignored the problems of the women workers." Yael Gordon demanded that the young woman be treated as any person, and as any person possessing rights. She stated that "the lack of interest arises out of disregard for the woman as an individual . . . There is no internal (spiritual) respect . . . " Later she said, "It is not a matter of male workers and female workers separately; we must prove what Europe cannot." This meant breaking away from the norms of traditional European society and creating a new and egalitarian situation for the woman. The women's attack was taken up by Hanna Maisel, an agronomist, one of the educated women of the *Second Aliya*, who inaugurated agricultural training for women. She declared that the problems of women workers were not evident to most of the men taking part in the debate: "The young men, for psychological reason, cannot penetrate these questions." Later in her speech she demanded of her male comrades that "if you are capable of helping us a little, give us a place to work."[9] It is clear from the debate that toward the close of the *Second Aliya* the set of problems around the place of the woman worker in the creative society in Palestine – equality of her status and her equal right to work and equality in work – remained unchanged.

To cope with the harsh reality and to provide the young women with tools for their struggle, Hanna Maisel had in 1911 established a farming school for girls at the Kinneret farm, which existed until 1917. Women workers' teams were established also, and they fought collectively for their place in the male working society. They also developed new agricultural branches suited to women, such as vegetable plots. In parallel, a process of overall organization began, to help solve the problems described above on a countrywide scale, and also for the achievement of an equal social and economic status both within and outside the workers' camp.[10]

Services and Welfare

It has been mentioned that the fate of the women who were connected with the two associations was similar to that of the women workers of the *Second Aliya* in general, with the addition of an extra share of troubles partially owing to their being attached to the life and work of these organizations.[11]

The functions of the Hashomer women also were restricted to the traditional services and household duties: the kitchen and the laundry, repairing clothes, nursing the sick, cleaning, and later on caring for children. Kayle (Beker) Gil'adi explains why she was called to join the collective at Sejera in 1907: "And so an invitation came to me from Sejera – how marvellous it was for me! – to go there, to work in the kitchen at the collective that had been founded; the invitation was from Yisrael Shohat." Thirty-five people were fed from Kayle Beker's kitchen at Sejera, that is, most of the workers on the farm, and she single-handedly took care of them: she got in the food, prepared and cooked it, served it to the workers, and kept the kitchen and the dining-room clean.[12] Even after she married Yisrael Gil'adi and went with him to live at the Kinneret farm she continued in the same work: "I was a cook." Later in her travels with her husband she arrived in Zikhron Ya'akov, where they enjoyed the luxury of living in a room shared with three others and casual guests: "Here I used to cook the meal for the guards and here everyone slept on the floor."[13]

Atara Shturman, recounting her experiences at Merhavia, reinforces this picture of the concerns of the woman connected with Hashomer: "We had only one worry: how to make it easier for the men, what to do and how to behave so that the men would not feel any lack; how to spice the taste of the miserable food."[14] The serving and nursing functions of the women are still more evident in accounts of clashes with Arabs and tense security situations. The women were never involved in these and were not called on for consultations or decision making: "The women had no independent role in the skirmishes, but the succour they gave the men with great devotion and loyalty was very important." This support was expressed in repairing the clothes of those who had fought in the clashes with the Arabs, treating the wounded, supplying food and drink during the engagements and general nursing. Their most far-reaching operational activity was cleaning the weapons used by the guards.[15]

Evidence that the role of the Hashomer women too was limited to services and welfare is endless. A thorough description was given by Haya Kroll, who told of the days of her work at Hadera with the men of Hashomer: "The guarding at Hadera was very hard owing to constant strife with the Arabs and never-ending lawlessness. The girls took no part at all in the guarding. Our area of work – our mission – was limited to the kitchen and laundry alone."[16] With the perspective of years Haya Kroll permitted herself a measure of pique and irony.

The memoirs of the *Second Aliya* generation highlight cases where certain women managed to obtain not only men's work but also got into guarding and defense. Most stories are linked with the early glorious formative days of establishment of Bar Giora at Sejera in 1907–8. There are well-known accounts of the camaraderie of weapons training during the period at the farm, and of how some of the girls acquired pistols as personal weapons. The tale of Esther Shturman (Beker) and Tzippora Beker (Zayd) has been often told: In 1908 they subverted Yisrael Shohat's instructions and joined the group of Bar Giora members called urgently from Sejera by the Kefar Tabor farmers to help them defend the moshava against an imminent attack by the Mughrabis.[17] Alexander Zayd likewise tells of the effort made by the girls at Sejera to be included in guarding tasks:

One Shabbat, while I was standing guard, Tzipora and Esther Beker (Shturman) came out to me and said to me earnestly, "Go on, go in and sleep. We'll guard for you." I was skeptical for a moment, but without arguing too much I handed them the whistle and the rifle and I went to my cosy bed feeling quite alright. Several nights passed quietly under their guard, and then they dared to make the same request to Meirke Hazanovich. He accepted their offer and gave them his weapon, but he stayed with them all night and sang his songs to them.[18]

Here and there other brief inroads were made by the women in participating in the guarding and defense, as, for example, when Bar Giora's was commissioned to guard at Kefar Tabor prior to the establishment of Hashomer.[19]

All the tales recollected here, painted in such bold colors and with the *élan* of revolutionary transformation in values and in relations between the men and the women in the association – all were transient episodes of the early days of the organization, and they did not become the norm. The accounts of the brave deeds by the young women, the sagas from the time of "rage and fury," had no continuation. As the association became established, which occurred within a relatively short time, the Hashomer women became confined to providing services and welfare, the domain of women in all traditional societies. This indeed was continuity, on the real-life level and on the normative level, of the diaspora existence. The revolution in the natural order between the sexes, so yearned for by these young women, did not come about.

The problem of women's equality was especially serious in Bar Giora and Hashomer. These were elitist associations; their members lived highly tense lives of permanent vocation, which alone could carry them through and compensate for the harsh reality, replete with suffering and self-sacrifice. The men got their reward in the romantic aura and the sense of being the makers of a revolution, and in the social status that the organization won for itself. Out of all this very little remained for the women of Hashomer. Paradoxically, they "won" the lion's share of the hardships of daily life.

The Bar Giora and Hashomer women, with few exceptions, were not members with equal rights in the organization. From the slight, vague evidence some conclude that, despite the difficulties, a small group of young women – Manya Vilboshevich-Shohat, Esther (Shturman) Beker, Kayle (Beker) Gil'adi, Tzipora (Beker) Zayd, Rahel Yanait-Ben Zvi, Tova (Eliovich) Portugali, six women who were the wives or life-partners of the founders of the organization – had equal rights with the men in the two associations. Rahel Yanait-Ben Zvi records another list, with the names of the following as members of Hashomer: Manya Shohat, Rahel Yanait, Esther and Sara Shturman, Kayle Gil'adi, Haya Sara Hankin and Rivka Nisanov, seven women in all. Compared with the first list, Tova (Eliovich) Portugali is missing, and Haya Sara Hankin and Rivka Nisanov are added. Beyond this limited group of women, it is evident that other women were for many years deprived and without equal and full rights of membership in the organization.[20]

It is almost certain that among the women mentioned Tova (Eliovich) Portugali was not a member of the organization. A sign of this is found in Mendel Portugali's letter to her, in which he wrote: "I repeat that we should be equal, that is, in everything concerning our goals . . . And I also recall that you were hurt by the fact that I do not share everything with you. Do you think that I too did not sense the truth of your words? I did not feel good about this truth, but my mouth remained sealed because I did not know what to tell you." Rahel Yanait-Ben Zvi states plainly that Tova Portugali was not a member of Hashomer at least until September 1915, the time of the Yavneel assembly.[21]

Yisrael Shohat states that "Manya Shohat, Kayle Gil'adi, Esther Beker (Shturman) were members of Bar Giora from the start." His assertion must be treated carefully because it was written many years later and to a large extent was apologetic in nature. Kayle Gil'adi, in her memoirs concerning the Sejera days, corroborates Shohat:

> Shortly after I arrived they began to train me for the secret "order" that already existed. I was called to a meeting at which eleven members were present. The discussion was on the goal of the order and next steps that had to be taken . . . I was very happy at being attached to the group, but the responsibility imposed on me from that time on frightened me.

Esther Beker (Shturman), too, writes in her memoirs that she was present at the meetings of Bar Giora while they were still held in the famous cave at Sejera after her partner-husband prepared her and told her of the secret society. At the same time, her narrative does not elucidate unequivocally if she was accepted as a member with full, equal rights or as a passive observer at the meetings. Regarding Tzipora Beker (Zayd), her account is not clear; it states that Manya Vilboshevich Shohat at Sejera suggested that she join Hashomer [should be Bar Giora – Y.G.], but she refused. Only after some time did she change her mind, "and in a short time I became one of those whose entire might was devoted to this highly valuable and highly consequential service."

Ruth Kroll describes the life at Kibbutz Kefar Gil'adi after its restoration in the wake of the Tel Hai events in 1920; hence her account dates to the 1920s, the *Third Aliya* period. She complains bitterly that despite the equality between the men and the women in various tasks on the kibbutz, in matters of security the situation was different and discriminatory:

> We girls, products of the great Russian revolution, held different ideas about equality for women and the right of fighting for this equality. We sought equality with the men in the daily work of defense, and here we came up against one of the most painful features in the life of the country, especially at Kefar Gil'adi. Most of the women members of Hashomer were the wives or widows of guards. For objective reasons, arising from the special conditions of the country before the World War, it was impossible to involve the

women members of Hashomer in the practical affairs of Bar Giora, and only two of the women participated fully in running these affairs: Manya Shohat and Rahel Yanait (Ben Zvi).

Ruth Kroll is imprecise regarding Rahel Yanait-Ben Zvi, who was a member of Hashomer, not Bar Giora. The main weakness of her account is that she immigrated to Palestine only in 1922, after the disbanding of Hashomer, and therefore her testimony is indirect, not firsthand.

There is no evidence that Haya Sara Hankin and Rivka Nisanov were accepted in any way to the ranks of Bar Giora and Hashomer by 1915. This applies to Sara Shturman too; moreover, she later married Moshe Krigser (Ami'ad), who was a member of Hashomer but who ceased to be active in the organization after a few years. Regarding the names of women on the two lists, reasonable supporting evidence of some form of membership of Bar Giora and Hashomer seems to exist only for Kayle Gil'adi, Esther Beker and Tzipora Zayd.[22]

Only with two women is there no doubt that they were members of Hashomer with equal rights; these are Manya Vilboshevich-Shohat, who was accepted to Bar Giora as early as Sejera, and Rahel Yanait-Ben Zvi, who was accepted by Hashomer in 1909 at Kefar Tabor. Both achieved this owing to their special status. Manya Vilboshevich-Shohat enjoyed the aura of a fine revolutionary record in Russia and the privileges of being a founder of the collective at Sejera. Through her personality and the fact that she was several years older than most of them, Manya assumed the role of sympathetic listener and mother-confessor to the young people of the association. These passionate young men and women, far from the comfort and support of their families, poured out their sorrows before her and from her they sought solace. Manya was also the wife of the charismatic leader Yisrael Shohat, the partner in his dreams and his deeds. Rahel Yanait had a similar status, both as one of the first active women in Poaley Zion in Russia and in Palestine, and as the recognized life-partner of the leader and ideologist of the party and of Hashomer, Yitzhak Ben Zvi.

An interesting picture emerges. These two women were themselves not a part of the daily life of Hashomer (from mid-1909 the Shohats lived in Haifa and never returned to practical work with Hashomer), that is, they did not set about actually implementing its goals. Yet precisely they, and perhaps a few other individual women, enjoyed recognized status of full membership of the organization. Other woman, simple, without education or party position, did realize the goals of the association, with devotion and self-sacrifice, and they fulfilled its precepts; but they did not win similar full rights.

The heads of Hashomer had a way of explaining this paradox. Their main argument was that a women could not guard, and therefore could not be equal in rights to the man. In other words, the theory ran, the major criterion for membership was active duty as a guard, with all that that entailed, which the women could not undertake. It is interesting that this yardstick was not applied to Manya Vilboshevich-Shohat and Rahel Yanait-Ben Zvi. The service jobs that the women did, raising and caring for the family, and even farmwork, were not recognized as equal to the labor of the guard or as satisfying the major criterion on which the association was based. In this the leaders found justification for the discrimination that existed.

Most members of the association were unaware of the anomaly in which they lived, namely, that although the women shared the harsh life of the guard in every way, in most cases carrying a heavier burden, they were still denied the right to full membership of the organization to which they devoted all they had. Alexander Zayd was one of the few who fought consistently to eradicate the imbalance that was so unfair to the wives of members and the other young women who were attached to the association:

> The lives of our girls in the collective were hard. We wanted to transform our life root and branch, but we did not alter our conceptions of the role of the woman in society. For generations we had been trained to see the woman as housekeeper and mother only. The girls rebelled against this attitude, demanded changes in their way of life, and tried to pave new paths for themselves . . . It was not easy for our women comrades to win an honored place in our life. On the surface, we were all equal, members of a single collective, but we, the boys, were members of Hashomer and they, the girls, who suffered with us, bore the burden, nursed us, looked after us, worried about us, made our lives pleasant and bore us children – they remained outside the association, and were not officially deemed members.[23]

Rahel Yanait-Ben Zvi addressed the problem in her description of the seventh annual assembly of Hashomer at Yavneel, held on 9 September 1915. By her account this assembly, like all the others, was attended by all the women of Hashomer despite their not being members. "They 'assembled' outside the assembly, not being admitted to the conference hall. The Hashomer woman, if she was not a member, had no right to participate in the annual assembly."

At the Yavneel meeting there was a wide-ranging debate on the status of women in the association. Rahel Yanait wrote of the fiery advocacy by Alexander Zayd of equal rights for women: "He defended the stand of the few male members who said that a women comrade who became attached to a member of Hashomer, fully aware of what she might expect in family life, was by virtue of that alone a natural candidate for Hashomer." She stressed that Zayd felt the problem profoundly, and always sided with the women, as at the Yavneel assembly. There he declared that "not on sufferance but by right should they be accepted into Hashomer."[24]

There is no doubt that the disaffection over the imbalance between duties and rights, between the ideal and the actual, that existed in the lives of the Hashomer women was profound. An expression of it may be found in Haya Kroll's recollections of her work with the guards at Hadera:

> The situation of the woman in the unit of guards was hard. She had constantly to be prepared to lose her life partner, and her day was filled with the feeling that the child she bore would not see his father's face. But this was not all. The woman did not regard herself as equal in all things to her male comrades.
>
> It pained us to see that the man was regarded as one who was to be a future member of Hashomer, while the girls were regarded as workers, and that was all. For that reason we left the guards unit at the end of the year's work . . .
>
> In 1913 I went with comrades to found the Hashomer village at Tel Adashim. I was certain that from then on, at that place, the attitude to women would change . . . But there too the solution to the problem of the woman in Hashomer was not easy to achieve.[25]

All this bitterness burst out, not accidentally, at the seventh annual assembly of Hashomer at Yavneel on 9 September 1915, as noted. The assembly was held after the war had been in progress about a year. The general situation in the country was bad, and the condition of Hashomer was especially grave. Many of its members were without work and were obliged to retreat to the Galilee and crowd together, at Tel Adashim in particular. The political and economic distress was great. Many harbored a sense of failure, of loss of direction, and hopelessness. The vision diminished and no glimmer of light was to be seen on the horizon. This state of affairs was fertile ground for the reinforcement of opposed positions and internal quarrels, which no one could settle in the absence of the Shohat couple, who had been deported to Bursa in Anatolia. At the Yavneel meeting the conflict between the Gil'adi group and the Hefter–Shturman group was debated, culminating in a resolution forcing the former to leave Tel Adashim and move to Kefar Tabor. At Yavneel also a new committee was elected which, for the first time since the founding of Hashomer, did not include the two central figures apart from Yisrael Shohat, Gil'adi and Portugali.

The sense of urgency that hung over the Yavneel meeting caused those present to relent on their old positions and concepts, and this was expressed, among other things, in an official draft resolution by the committee "to expand the framework of the association and not to act with undue stringency in accepting new members."[26] It was most likely owing to this general flexibility that the debate on the status of women in the association came up. It is also possible that Rahel Yanait's appointment to the Hashomer committee about six months before the assembly, and her re-election to the wider committee at Yavneel, contributed to a fresh and favorable approach to this thorny problem. Indeed, following a bitter debate, in which several of the senior women of Hashomer spoke, there was a change in the position of the association, which adopted the following resolution:

A. As Hashomer has wider goals than guarding in the formal sense, such as general defense, the *moshav*, the *kvutzot* [*kvutza*: precursor to the kibbutz – Y.G.], etc., there is room in the Hashomer association for active female members, as there is for active male members, from among the wives of members and apart from them;
B. To bring the wives of guards closer to the Hashomer association, we allow room for passive membership;
C. Female members, like male members, are elected by the general assembly;
D. To admit to the association all the wives of members with the right to speak and without the right to vote until the general assembly finds them ready as active members;
E. The wives of guards may be present at our meetings without the right of expressing an opinion and of voting.[27]

In consequence of the resolution two groups formed of women with different status in the organization: (1) A group admitted to the association on the basis of full, equal rights – a status known as active membership. This rule apparently applied to women married to guards for a long period of time. (2) A group of wives of guards and other unmarried women who were granted a status known as passive membership, meaning equal rights, except for the most important, being the right to vote and hence be partners in determining the policy of the association, and likewise the right to elect the committee.

So the problem received a partial solution only. An entire group of young women continued to live in conditions of inequality and to feel unjustly deprived; not surprisingly, therefore, the ferment continued, and boiled over some years later in a document submitted by three women on the eve of the eleventh annual assembly of Hashomer at Tiberias, held on 17 October 1918:

To the members of Hashomer!
We, young women, who have been working together with you for several years and who are always with you in the most difficult situations, want there to be no chance of our having to continue henceforward with our work in the same way as hitherto. We want to present facts and instances: they are quite well known to you. We have reached the decision that work

is common and responsibility is common only when there are equal conditions in all things. We always must know in advance everything that is
happening with us and awaiting us. Only then will we be able to match our
work in the most desirable way to our goals and our aims. And if we have
been comrades in day-to-day work for years now, we shall be comrades in
all things. No assembly can take place without us, no secrets are withheld
from us, and if the men have insufficient confidence in us for this, they must
say so openly, then we shall know the situation as it is and we shall seek
other ways of carrying out the work that brings us closer to our goal, which
is also your goal.
Tel Adas, 25 September 1918
We await a reply.Atara, Dvorah, Yehudit
[Atara (Kroll) Shturman, Dvorah Drechler, Yehudit (Rozichansky)
Hurwitz][28]

Indeed, at this assembly all existing divisions between the men and
women in Hashomer were eliminated, and full equality was granted to all
women. But it was apparently difficult to forego habits of many years'
standing. In practice, discrimination against women continued for years
after Hashomer was disbanded in May 1920. Haya Kroll relates that even
in Kefar Gil'adi, after they returned and rehabilitated the settlement after
the events of Tel Hai,

girls were not involved in any communal activity. Our comrades could not
understand that we were not interested only in looking after the children
and service jobs. In those days the men were busy with guarding, defense,
obtaining arms in great secrecy and developing relations with the neighbors,
and they did not call on us to take part in their business. But we dreamed
of social and communal activity, of agriculture and building an economy.
The members of Hashomer, who were associated with members of Kefar
Gil'adi but were not members of the kibbutz, used to come to the place and
decide together on the fate of the kibbutz, and we, the women, were not
given the right to express our opinion in all this. Once a woman friend
alarmed me. She was all excited and her eyes were aflame. "Come on," she
said, "Let's go and break the windows of the schoolhouse, where the
Hashomerniks are meeting to decide our fate and haven't bothered to invite
us."[29]

It took several years more, and only after the development of kibbutz
life at Kefar Gil'adi, for the barriers to fall in practice also, and for women
to achieve the full equality they had been granted in 1918.

The Attitude toward the Arabs

It was permitted to use firearms and to shoot to injure "only as a last resort. Even in these cases we required the guard only to injure the attacker or kill the mare on which he was riding . . . It was deemed exemplary to emerge from a difficult situation honorably without having fired a single round."

Zvi Nadav

THIS CHAPTER EXAMINES the attitude of the associations to the Arabs up to the disbanding of Hashomer in 1920. A prime difficulty lies in the absence of documents defining the views of the organizations on the subject. Nevertheless, it is possible to reconstruct the positions of Bar Giora, and still more of its successor Hashomer. Because most of its members belonged to the Poaley Zion party it may be supposed that they took the party position in the political sphere, including its attitude to the Arab problem; there is also much information in the recollections of Hashomer people. These recollections are used here, but care must be taken given that they were written many years after the organization broke up. Many contain inaccuracies and a tendency toward apologetics, which sometimes distort the reality. But nevertheless, it is possible to gain much insight from the attitude of the associations to the Arab issue on the day-to-day level.

The Poaley Zion Party

Until 1908 the Poaley Zion party adopted the Borochovist view of the political developments that might be envisaged in Palestine. According to this doctrine, at a certain stage a Jewish rebellion against the Turkish rule in the country was likely to break out. The Palestinian Jewish workers' class would be the fighting *avant-garde* in this rebellion. In the end, owing to international intervention, Jewish national autonomy would be established in Palestine, which would remain within the heterogeneous and multinational Ottoman empire.[1] Ideologically, prior to the Young Turk revolution of 1908 the party did not regard the Arabs as competitors against the Jewish national movement for dominance in the future Palestinian autonomy. It was assumed that this Palestinian autonomy, which would be won through armed struggle against the Turks, would be Jewish in quality and controlled by the Jews. Moreover, the lack of discernment, and hence recognition, of the existence of Arab nationalism in Palestine caused Poaley Zion serious doubts about adopting the principle of "Jewish labor," which seemed to contradict the Marxist-socialist world view.

As stated, the turning point in the ideological stance of the Poaley Zion party on the question came in the wake of the Young Turk revolution of 1908.[2] This upheaval was followed by a rise of Arab nationalism throughout a region that encompassed the Arabs of Palestine. It could no longer be ignored. The awakening bore an all-Arab stamp, but as yet there was no separate Palestinian consciousness. Furthermore, it was clear that the Palestinian Arabs regarded themselves as the exclusive ruling element in the country. In view of this, the party began to retreat from the political goal it had set itself, namely, the attainment of autonomy for Palestine in the framework of the Ottoman empire. The ideologists of Poaley Zion in Palestine were well aware that in the given conditions of absolute Arab majority in the population and almost total Arab control of the physical assets of the land, the winning of such autonomy meant handing Palestine to the Arabs. The ideological and political change that came over Poaley Zion resulted also in a change in the party position on work relations and in the final adoption of the principle of Jewish labor.[3]

The broad ideological base, intended to solve the apparent contradiction between the universalist Marxist-socialist world view underlying the general brotherhood of the workers and the specific national needs of the Jews, was set out in a comprehensive programmatic article by Yitzhak Ben Zvi (Avner), entitled "National defense and proletarian outlook," published in the party organ *Haahdut* in two parts in January and February 1913,[4] and also in the debates and resolutions of the ninth party conference held in Jaffa at the end of April that year, as reported in *Haahdut*. The article and the resolutions determined unconditionally the absolute priority of the national interest over the universal Marxist-socialist ideal. Owing to the fundamental importance of the resolutions, they are quoted extensively:

> Conference has devoted great attention to the question of guarding and defense. For a long time now, many of our members, especially the guards, have faced the question of our socialist outlook and guarding. This question has been clarified in the pages of *Haahdut* and it also came up at the conference.

In the opinion of many members, guarding is only one of the forms of settlement labor. Therefore, it is impossible to take the question of guarding out of the overall context of Jewish labor. Socialism stands for international brotherhood and solidarity; we come forward in the name of national interests. Is there not a contradiction here? All the more so, in that our interests clash with the national interests of others! The matter requires elucidation.

International solidarity is for the time being only a vision for the future, the heart's desire of socialists. In conditions of the here and now, this ideal cannot be realized. The different peoples are subject to special conditions of life and work, each has its own needs, which sometimes contradict the interests of its fellow . . .

And still, the worker cannot be isolated from his community in the struggle for existence . . .

We have special needs, national needs, and if they are not satisfied we cannot exist. The question of our existence and our development is the seizure of fortified economic positions, the creation of a Jewish economic settlement, a place of work and life for the Jewish masses. This goal has brought us hither. Normally there is no contradiction to socialist theory here, stemming from the interests of the labor of the masses . . . We are not pushing our neighbors out of their own economy, but the contrary: the Jews have come to create a new economy, which must provide work for Jewish workers, because that is why we have come here – it is the neighbors who are pushing us out . . .

Now comes the question: Must the Jewish worker, ejected from the economy in all countries, give up his place in favor of others here also? Or perhaps the time has come for the Jewish worker to fortify a stronghold for himself in economic life. Socialist justice by no means requires the worker to forego his real-life interests; socialism was created for the worker, and the worker is not a means or material for it. From this aspect, guarding, like Jewish labor generally, is not opposed to socialism.

. . . Guarding in its present form does not protect private property, but our national assets as a whole, our respect and our worth in the eyes of our neighbors, and this is the sum total of its importance . . . [5]

The passages cited here show that after lengthy uncertainty the party responded unequivocally, and determined the primacy of the national interest. Morally, the party held that this tenet derived from the nature of socialism, and was not a contradiction to it. At last a theoretical foundation and ideological grounds were provided for the actual existential circumstances that prevailed in the country.

From the overall ideological and political viewpoint, there was no difference between the Bar Giora and Hashomer people and the mother party. Moreover, the act of creating Bar Giora was meant to provide the national movement with the armed element which it lacked and which was normally present in national liberation movements. In this sense Bar Giora and Hashomer considered themselves as the spearhead and the *avant-garde* of the Jewish national movement. The founders of Bar Giora and the creators of Hashomer were the first who consciously and intentionally formed, realized and developed the concept of the norm of armed strength as a part of the Zionist ethos. They therefore deemed themselves committed to stand in the first line in the contest with the Arabs. These views were inherent in the founding of Bar Giora in 1907 and were necessarily given overt expression in the creation of Hashomer in 1909 as a response to the rising wave of Arab nationalism in Palestine.

In Bar Giora and Hashomer it is possible to discern two parallel lines of thought and conduct regarding the Arabs, seemingly contradictory, but actually complementary. On the one hand, there was the position that regarded the Arabs as an enemy, with all the implications of this view point. The Hashomer people were certain that the Arabs would oppose the reawakening of the Jews in the country, a situation that necessitated meeting of force with force. They believed that the only chance of deterring the Arabs was through the enhancement of Jewish power and its effectiveness. In their view, only the development and expansion of Jewish power would create the opportunity for a balance of power and in consequence the possibility for mutual understanding and compromise. This basic position was adopted by their successors in the Hagana, and also became the heritage of the Jewish workers' movement in Palestine and of the Zionist movement, and its validity remains in force to the present day.

On the other hand, the Hashomer people believed in the need for coexistence of the two national elements side by side. A derivation of this belief was the awareness by Hashomer of the need to recognize the Arabs and their ways, developing neighborly relations based on mutual respect and consideration of the rights of either side. From this stemmed the tendency to adopt some of the manners of the Arabs.[6] Members of the association believed that through maximal application of these efforts it would be possible to prevent, or at least to temper, the clashes between the two sides and perhaps even to bring the two peoples closer together.

Furthermore, Hashomer regarded the norm of defensive armed force as only one of the essential components for realizing the Zionist dream, which among other things had to include the formation of a workers' class in Palestine, the development of the Jewish agricultural settlement, and also the establishment of a comprehensive Jewish economy. They treated the armed defensive force itself as a last resort, to be applied under control and very sparingly in everything concerning the development of relations between Jews and Arabs.[7]

Hashomer and the Arab Milieu

The relations of Bar Giora and Hashomer with the Arab milieu stemmed primarily from the overall nationalist outlook and the specific mission these organizations undertook, namely, to ensure security of life and property in the Yishuv. They regarded the conquest of guarding as the means to this end. Yisrael Shohat, in a paper written in Istanbul on the organization of general defense for the Yishuv and sent on 26 December 1912 to the larger Zionist executive committee, defined the goal of Hashomer as "to help in the defense of the Jewish Yishuv and to guard private and national property in Palestine against the foreign neighbors." Shohat believed that Jewish guarding attained other goals, and among them it awakened a feeling of national dignity in the youth of the *moshavot* and encouraged them to undertake self-defense. Hashomer, he felt, had strengthened the status of all the Yishuv in the eyes of the Arabs, who had stopped applying the epithet "dead sons," at least to the people of the new Yishuv.[8]

The primacy of the Jewish national interest was well expressed in a letter sent by Shohat to Shlomo Kaplansky, written in Stockholm on 15 October 1918, shortly after his arrival in the Swedish capital from Turkey. In his letter Shohat notes that in the given situation in Palestine the weakness of the Jews was obvious because they constituted only 10 percent of the Palestine population. Shohat was convinced that the strength and capacity of an enterprise were determined by practical facts on the ground, not formal documents, however important. He did not consider it possible to create in a short time a numerical balance between the Jews and the Arabs in Palestine, so his alternative was the creation of Jewish qualitative superiority to the Arabs, which would balance the forces. In parallel to refining the quality, Shohat believed that not for a moment should there be any relaxation in the effort to bring to the country masses of immigrants, who would enlarge the quantitative element of the Yishuv. But the needs of the moment were provisionally "to produce in Palestine a significant minority which in its productive and cultural level may compete, in the political sense, with the local majority which is less productive and uncultivated . . . "[9] The absolute priority given by the Hashomer leader to the Jewish national interest may also be inferred from his position in a later period, at the end of 1920. In a discussion in the executive committee of the general workers' federation (Histadrut) at that time on the need for Jewish initiative to establish Arab trade unions, Shohat stated that "from the humanitarian aspect it is clear that we must organize them, but from the national aspect, when we do organize them we will be setting them up against ourselves. They will obtain the best out of the organization and will use it for our ill. They will try to place more of their workers in it. This process is undeniable."[10] In a letter from Shohat to Nahum Hurwitz in the early 1950s he claimed that the goal of Bar Giora, from the start, had been to rise, when the time came, against the Turks. "We did not consider involving the Arabs in the revolt that we dreamed of raising when the moment came. On the contrary, it was clear that the Arabs were against us, therefore we wanted to learn their way of fighting so as to gain knowledge of the foe in his home . . . At meetings of Bar Giora the idea crystallized that the Arabs were against us and would fight with the Turks to destroy us, or at best to turn us into a minority in their state."[11]

In his memoirs of the First World War, Yosef Harit notes that as the the war went on, the expectations of casting off the Turkish yoke grew. But these expectations were accompanied by fears, because the clamor of national ferment was heard as it spread among the Arabs of the region. "And we, for all our desire to be free of the Turkish yoke, were by no means excited at the prospect of its being replaced by Arab rule, after which, or even before which, plunder and murder and attempted destruction of our enterprise would be rife."[12] Describing the unsuccessful effort to form a Jewish militia in the country in the months following the outbreak of the war, he stated that the initiative was heart-warming, and aroused the hope that the volunteers would be "among the first builders of the Jewish army."[13]

Zvi Nadav wrote in a similar vein when at the start of the war Hashomer invested the greater part of its energy in organizing the defense of the Galilee owing to fears that the moment the opportunity arose the Arabs would try to "attack us and kill us."[14]. Moshe Eliovich believed that the task of Hashomer was "to ensure the defense of Jewish life and property." To achieve this, the organization had to display strength so as to deter the Arabs. Among the means adopted, to prevent, or limit to the minimum the great expenses and at times casualties occurring from the clashes, was the promotion of neighborly relations with the Arabs and also gaining knowledge of them, so as to learn "their weak points, the disputes and quarrels among them, to be able to turn them to our advantage . . . The aim was to mingle with the Arab people around us, to become acquainted with the human and climatic environment as an organic part of it, as a people returning to its land by right and not on sufferance."[15] The policy of approximation to the Arabs, adopted by Hashomer as a part of the overall concept that such an approach was good in itself but also served the Jewish national interest, was also stressed by Pinhas Shneorson. He was critical of those in the Jewish Yishuv who accused Hashomer of assimilation because its members assumed some of the Arabs' habits, "but we felt that our policy had to be one of understanding and friendship, especially seeing that the strength of the Yishuv was so slight compared with the numerical strength of the Arabs . . . "[16]

It becomes evident that throughout the years the guideline was the supremacy of the national interest. This in itself caused Hashomer to regard the Arabs as an element hostile to the Zionist enterprise. For effective protection of Jewish interests, Hashomer adopted a policy of learning about the Arabs and their milieu. The approximation to the Arabs and development of friendship with them blunted Arab hostility. As long as disputes were avoided and the enmity and violence were held in check, so did conditions favoring the Zionist enterprise become enhanced.

Daily Relations with the Arabs

Hashomer's position derived from the respect the association bore for the Arabs on the personal level, from the recognition of their rights as an ethnic element that had lived in the land for generations, and from the consciousness that the Jews were fated to live side by side with the Arabs. These considerations led the founders of Bar Giora and Hashomer to a particular kind of conduct which developed as early as the Shefaya and Sejera days.

According to Yisrael Shohat, after the members of Bar Giora gathered at Sejera "to learn the language of our neighbors, we arranged lessons in spoken Arabic, for which we called in a special teacher who also taught us something of the Arab way of life."[17] In his article "The mission and the way" Shohat listed the principles on which the actions of the Bar Giora and Hashomer people were based. They included a special section on the nature of relations with the Arabs. The associations undertook "(e) to develop relations of friendship and respect with the Arab neighbors and to foster brotherhood among nations in the land."[18] Shohat dealt at length, retrospectively, with the issue of relations with the Arabs and formulated the position of the organizations he headed as follows:

> Hashomer paid particular attention to peaceful relations with the Arab surroundings . . . Hashomer tried in vain to instill a new character to links with the Arab environment. We knew that the Arabs were our neighbors and we would have to find a *modus vivendi* and to some extent match our life to theirs. The Hashomer members learnt Arabic, which helped them reach understanding with the Arab neighbors, and wished to learn from the Arabs whatever there was to be learnt and even to pay them for this. The guards tried not to limit themselves to visits to the effendis and the shaykhs, but preferred the *madafiya* [the guest house at the village – Y.G.] to meet the Arab fallah, the tenant farmer, the laborer. The guards learned Arab ways, the style of life of the Arab village. At every main place of guarding Hashomer set up a *madafiya*, a room to welcome guests, and every Arab passer-by, on horseback or on foot, rich or poor, worker or fallah, was welcomed warmly, as was customary in the Arab village. From his relations with the Arab environment the guard learned the way of thinking and the moral concepts of the Arab.[19]

Zvi Nadav augments Shohat's description, stating that the guiding principle of Hashomer was to foster in every way full friendly relations with the Arab neighbors, and likewise to maintain an attitude of respect toward their customs. All this was on condition that Jewish life and property, and Jewish national dignity, were not harmed.[20] As a function of this outlook a policy of a sort of "local integration" was adopted, such as the wearing of Arab dress, the practice of Arab customs, and the use of many expressions from spoken Arabic. To some of the workers of the *Second Aliya* this behavior by Hashomer members seemed like assimilation, and excessive extravagance, which contradicted the content and normatively puritanical life of segments of the Jewish Palestinian labor movement. One of the expressions of the integration is given by Zvi Nadav, who tells of Hashomer guards being invited to the wedding of Amin, son of the shaykh Mahmud of Shunam village (Sulam) near Merhavia in the Jezreel Valley, and their participation in a *maydan* (a warlike horseriding game), held on the occasion of the wedding, in which the Hashomer men were outstanding with their horses, their weapons and their prowess at riding.[21]

An important part in the development of good neighborly relations was the help the Hashomer people afforded the Arabs, such as medical assistance to people and animals, advice in agricultural matters, and sometimes intervention to attain a compromise between parties in conflict. Yitzhak Hoz, writing about his time at Merhavia, attests that the Arabs, after the first clashes to test the strength of the new settlers, came to terms with the Jewish settlement, and in consequence "the villagers began to visit us and also brought their children to our nurse for treatment . . . Our work methods in the field, which at first they disparaged, eventually found favor in their eyes, and the fallahs would come to consult us about seeds and their beasts that needed attention."[22] What Hoz has to say is not exceptional but was customary and widely accepted practice in most places where Hashomer was active.

The Test of Guarding

The greatest friction between Hashomer and the Arabs occurred when the former were conducting their duties during the "conquest" of Jewish land, as in the Kefar Tabor incident in 1908, or when they led "conquest" groups, as in the case of Merhavia in 1911; but chiefly the clashes were during the conquest of guarding and defense at the Jewish *moshavot*.[23]

It is important to note the rules whereby Bar Giora and Hashomer operated, such as insistence on Jewish labor, at least partially, at the *moshavot* where they guarded; checking and controlling the Arab workers at the *moshavot* during the day; prohibition of movement of Arabs in

Jewish settlements by night; and general supervision of the movement of Arabs by day and by night near to or through the *moshavot* for which the associations were responsible. All these created points of serious friction and tension between the guards and the Arabs and these led to violent acts by the latter, which at times ended in bloodshed. In addition, they caused serious disagreement, to the point of a split, with the moshava establishment, which viewed with disfavor the "extremism" of Hashomer in its treatment of the Arabs. There is no doubt that in all the areas mentioned, Hashomer was one of the most militant elements in the Jewish settlement.

At the same time, the method of guarding and the reaction to hostile Arab activity took into account the custom of the blood vengeance, the *gum*, which was common in the Palestinian population generally and among the Arabs in particular. The killing of a man automatically led to a blood feud, and to the danger of a chain reaction that might unleash calamity not only on Hashomer but also on the settlements it was guarding. Because of this mortal danger that hung over everyone, it was common that in the various quarrels and skirmishes among the Arabs themselves and among the Arabs and other ethnic elements, including the Jews, hundreds and even thousands of bullets were fired, but amazingly the number of casualties was very small. This was the result of intentional restraint employed by the combatants themselves through the fear of involvement in a blood feud. For that reason, too, an iron rule was determined in the training of a member of Hashomer, whereby he was required to develop the ability to absorb blows, and likewise to deliver only dry blows in clashes so as not to cause blood to flow; otherwise the complication of the blood vengeance would arise at once. According to Zvi Nadav, it was permitted to use firearms and to shoot to injure "only as a last resort. Even in these cases we required the guard only to injure the attacker or kill the mare on which he was riding . . . It was deemed exemplary to emerge from a difficult situation honorably without having fired a single round."[23] Mordechai Yigael, who considered Meirke Chazanovitch one of the bravest of the guards, complimented him in that he could "settle his business with the neighbors without using force."[24]

The skill of the guards was reflected in their ability to drive off any assailant without conceding private or public property, and at the same time without mortally wounding the robber or the thief; to have done so would have raised the danger of a blood feud. The Hashomer man was required to act in such a way as to elicit respect for himself and those he represented.[25] These rules of conduct crystallized as early as the Galilean period, before Hashomer broke out southward, to Samaria and Judea.[26]

To summarize, Bar Giora, and subsequently Hashomer, were a part of the Jewish Palestinian labor movement in general and of the Poaley Zion party in particular at the time of the *Second Aliya*. Like the mother party, these associations were based on an ideology expressed in the phrase "socialist Zionism." There seemed to be a parallelism and a match between the two components, but as in many liberation movements of a socialist shade, ideologically as well as practically, absolute priority was given to the nationalist element. In its very nature and the definition of its role, Hashomer, like Bar Giora before it, became the *avant-garde* of the Jewish labor movement in Palestine, of the Yishuv and of Zionism, in the defense of the Jewish national interest in the land. Its attitudes toward the Arabs bore the stamp of this character.

8

The Disbanding of Hashomer

Through this decision the status of Hashomer was officially recognized at the eleventh Zionist Congress in Vienna. A link was formed between it and the institutions of the Zionist movement. Hashomer became a unique organization in Palestine, charged with securing the peace of the Yishuv in the country, a fact that doubled its responsibility and its commitment.

Yisrael Shohat

THE CONQUEST OF PALESTINE by the British took place in three stages: by April 1917 the southern area had been captured and the front stopped at the Gaza–Beer Sheba line. Here the Turks, with the help of their German advisers, had established a strong defense which the British could not rupture, despite repeated assaults costing the lives of thousands of their troops.

The End of the War

After the British changed the command and redeployed, the second offensive opened, in October–November 1917; the south was liberated. On 16 November 1917 Jaffa and Tel Aviv were taken, and on 9 December Jerusalem fell to the British. The front was now located along the Yarkon river in the coastal valley and on the line between Jerusalem and Ramalla in the central highlands. This situation, in which the British controlled the south and Turks the center and north of the country, persisted until Allenby's second offensive, which opened on 17 September 1918 and resulted in the conquest of the entire country. Haifa was taken on 23 September, Damascus on 30 September, and the war ended on 11 November. From that date until mid-1920 Palestine was ruled by a British military government. In April 1920 decisions were taken at San Remo whereby the mandate for Palestine on both sides of the Jordan was entrusted to Britain, but the replacement of the military by a civil government came only several months later with the arrival of the first High Commissioner, Herbert Samuel.

At the end of the war the Jewish Yishuv in Palestine found itself in very straitened circumstances. In numbers, the population had fallen drastically from about 86,000 to about 55,000. This was the result of deportations, flight, emigration and the high mortality in the wake of the diseases brought by war. Moreover, the majority of the Jewish population belonged to the old Yishuv, most of the deportees and refugees being subtracted from the young and new population. Therefore, at the war's end the Yishuv in Palestine was of an old average age and growing older; it was mainly religious and non-productive. Only the *Third Aliya*, which commenced at the end of 1918, improved the negative balance, and saved the Zionist endeavor.

Hashomer endured the same suffering of the Yishuv, and more. Mention has been made of the harassment of its members following the exposure of the Nili affair. Large numbers were arrested, tortured, thrown into prison in Damascus and deported to Turkey. Many of the latter returned, after various adventures, only in 1919. That year, too, the Shohat couple returned after four years in exile. In all, the damage sustained in 1917–18 almost resulted in the total collapse of the association. In this tenuous state of negligible numbers, lack of power base, money and structure, and exhaustion of its members, Hashomer entered the new era of British rule.[1]

Nevertheless, scattered groups or individual members of the association continued to operate. This vitality, the will to prove that they had survived and that the war had not destroyed them, was symbolically and demonstratively expressed when in late 1918 the Hashomer men, after the close of their assembly in Tiberias, rode as a body, carrying their flag, to the conference of the Galilee workers' federation, then taking place at Kinneret.

A dire portent for Hashomer was that the appearance of this handful, the remnant of Hashomer, led by the moderate and much-loved Yisrael Gil'adi, rather than eliciting sympathy excited the anger of the conferees, who interpreted the parade as an excessive extravagance characteristic of the association.[2] After this conference, on 2 November 1918, Yisrael Gil'adi died. He had been a pillar of the association and beloved of it, the leading light after Yisrael Shohat. In late 1918 and early 1919 Hashomer found itself without central and authoritative figures.

Yisrael and Manya Shohat returned to Palestine, by way of Stockholm and London, several days after the Passover festival in 1919. On returning, Shohat began to work for the convocation of the remaining members of the association and its renaissance. After several months of preparation the Hashomer assembly gathered on 19 June 1919 at Tel

Adashim, where an attempt was made to renew the framework and breathe fresh life and vigor into it.[3]

Hashomer ordered part of its members to enlist in the police, which it saw as a means of defending the Yishuv. The association, in its elitist perception, wished to shape and direct the police force, which was then being established. This aim was frustrated by the national organization of policemen and by the "Delegates' Committee"; this body consisted of representatives of the Jewish communities in the Allied countries and leading Zionists, who went to Palestine in mid-1918 to assist the Yishuv and represent it before the British occupation forces. As an alternative Hashomer proposed creating within the framework and under the control of the Delegates' Committee a special section with their participation, which would be concerned with that issue of the police force; this proposal was not accepted either. Suddenly the association found itself hamstrung and restricted both by the paucity of its members, which severely limited its ability to act, and by Yishuv and Zionist institutions formed after the war. But the chief hindrance to Hashomer was the new party that was born then, on 26 February 1919, with the merger of Poaley Zion and non-party workers, the Ahdut Ha'avoda Union. Shohat and his colleagues found themselves without means and without any public backing, including that of the new party. In light of these circumstances a resolution was proposed, and adopted, at the wide council of Hashomer at Tel Adashim on 18 May 1920, to dissolve the association. At the Ahdut Ha'avoda conference held on 13–15 June 1920 at Kinneret, the Hashomer people handed over responsibility for defense to the party. Thus ended 13 years of existence of the association, starting as Bar Giora and continuing as Hashomer.[4]

Why was Hashomer Dissolved?

Essays written on the story of the painful passage from Hashomer to the Hagana are of the opinion that this was necessary and inevitable. The historiography generally agrees that Hashomer was essential during the Ottoman period, but the transition to mandatory times demanded a new ideological and organizational conception. Therefore, it was necessary to make way for the Hagana, which was constructed to meet the new conditions.

As presented, the heart of the debate between the Hashomer veterans, led by Shohat, and the proponents of the "new" conception, led by Eliahu Golomb and supported by the leaders of Ahdut Ha'avoda, centered, basically, on two issues: (a) the desired nature of the defense arm of the Yishuv, that is, if it should be a limited, select organization or a popular, mass organization; and (b) the sovereignty over the defense framework. The official *History of the Hagana* does indeed present other arguments against Hashomer, but there is no doubt that the Hashomer position on these two matters generated the main criticism against the organization and gave legitimation to the transition to the Hagana. This is attested by the assertion in *History of the Hagana* that "behind the debate over problems of organizational structure stood the fundamental question in all its gravity: Who determined and ruled on matters of defense, which was becoming more and more a political factor: the political leadership of the Yishuv or those active in defense themselves?" The official history cannot ignore the personal dimension in the dispute, being a bitter clash between the Hashomer veterans and Eliahu Golomb, but it dogmatically repeats its conclusion that "at root, however, the conflict was one of essence and principle." Later the authors of the work again argue that the organic form of Hashomer did not suit the new conditions, because "the center of gravity was passing gradually from guarding in the village to defense of the village and the town. The limited association of 'professional men' had to give way to the more popular and expansive patterns of defense, which drew their strength from the underlying recognition that defense was the duty and also the right of every Jew in the country."[5] And again, the authors state that the Yishuv, by means of its institutions, demanded the right to control and order the defense structure, "but the bearers of Hashomer were unable to 'change their spots' and wholeheartedly accept the logic and the necessity of the changing and renewing reality."[6] Similar views to those of *History of the Hagana* may be found in other studies.[7]

1 Rural and urban defense

In pre-mandatory times most security problems centered in the Jewish rural settlement, where Hashomer was active. Then, too, there was Jewish urban settlement, old and new, but this was not a focus of security problems. The situation was entirely different in the mandate period, for three reasons: (a) accelerated Jewish urban development; (b) accelerated Arab urbanization, especially in areas bordering on the Jewish settlement, and the enlargement and expansion of the Arab urban middle class, including the intelligentsia, which became the standard-bearer for Arab nationalism; (c) the intensification in Arab nationalism and the exacerbation of the struggle between the Jews and the Arabs. These processes were taking place when Hashomer no longer existed, and therefore it is quite strange to find a hypothetical argument raised against a body that had ceased to be, and was not constructed for some future set of circumstances. It is an *a priori* denial of any possibility of flexibility and evolutionary development. Moreover, in the 1921 disturbances, as in the 1929 disturbance, Hashomer veterans were to be found in the highest positions as organizers of urban defense. Therefore, the arbitrary assertion that they were incapable of adapting to contend with problems of urban defense appears untenable.

Furthermore, it was precisely the Hagana that proved helpless and, in the initial stages at least, incapable of managing urban defense in the events of both 1921 and 1929, and it was harshly criticized for this. A part of the ideological reason for the split in 1931 and the departure of Avraham Tehomi from the Hagana and the foundation of the "Parallel Organization" was criticism over the dearth of military acumen in the Hagana. Only after the 1929 disturbances, and in the 1930s particularly, were lessons learnt, and rapid development took place in the security organization. This means that there was an evolutionary process here of trial and error, and the 1920s were marked by the weakness of the Hagana, especially in urban defense. In light of this, the criticism of the authors of *History of the Hagana* against Hashomer does not reflect any objectivity, to say the least. It is possible that the Hashomer veterans, in view of their skills, would actually have been able to more quickly erect a defense structure suited to the expanding urbanization and the security problems that arose in towns during the mandate period.

2 Organization: limited and selective, or popular and general?

The ideology of the Bar Giora and Hashomer founders on this issue was affected by two factors: the actual conditions of Palestine and the Russian revolutionary tradition. The hostile Turkish rule necessitated clandestine organization in view of Bar Giora's broad national goals. By contrast, Hashomer appeared to the authorities as a professional association of guards only, and it could therefore operate overtly and legally. The wide national goals that it inherited from Bar Giora had of course to be played down. This objective state of affairs required partially or fully secret organization.

In addition, the creators of Bar Giora and Hashomer were schooled in underground activity, having been members of the self-defense in Russia, or of the revolutionary parties there. As such, they were influenced by and adopted the elitist, *avant-gardist* conception embedded in those currents of the Russian movement. According to this view, the well-organized, disciplined, idealist few, who were aware of their goals and were willing to sacrifice themselves for the ideal, were able to draw the masses along with them into action that would bring about the desired radical social changes. In this sense, it was held, the small, well-defined and selective body constituted the tempered steel and spearhead in the van of the camp, and expressed the true will of the people. Clearly, this outlook always contained the danger that the elite *avant-garde* would claim to know the "true" will of the people, and in its name would impose its mastery over the majority and subject them to its rule. The foremost historical examples appeared during the French Revolution and, in our period, the Bolshevik Revolution.[8] With their emigration to Palestine the youths took with them these patterns of the political culture, which, they averred, suited the Palestine circumstances. It should be stressed that the elitist outlook by no means negated broad frameworks, but rather the opposite. The condition was that these frameworks be managed by a professional, elite cadre of high consciousness, possessing the qualifications for realizing the goals of the people as a whole.

The Bar Giora organization was established along these lines, and it was not by chance that the association was not dissolved after the formation of Hashomer. Bar Giora was meant to be that restricted elitist body that would move and direct the various broad frameworks, some of which were of necessity legal. All the organizations were supposed to work toward the same nationalist and class goal, in some way or other. The consequence of this thinking was the creation of Hashomer, the Labor Legion, and later Haro'eh. Agricultural settlement was likewise planned: all were to be led by Bar Giora. In time, Hashomer took Bar Giora's place, and so the latter was dissolved too.

Bar Giora and Hashomer ideology did not negate but affirmed the organization of a broad popular framework of Yishuv defense. The selectivity related to the elitist leading body, not to the broad and essential popular framework. This was the spirit in which Yisrael Shohat wrote on 26 December 1912, in Istanbul, his program entitled "A proposal for the defense of the Yishuv," which he sent through Dr Viktor Jakobson to the Zionist executive committee and also to Menahem Ussishkin. Shohat proposed establishing a countrywide organization for the defense of the Yishuv, and to this end he requested the executive committee for financial help and political support. The program was based on the following ideological and organizational foundations: (a) The Jewish Yishuv had to attain the level of defensive capacity that would enable it to protect itself against the Arabs without assistance from the Turks; (b) for this purpose it was necessary to set up extensive defense frameworks that would encompass the farming and laboring population in the *moshavot*; and (c) the extensive framework would have to be managed by a skilled professional core – Hashomer.[9] Motivated by these ideas the Hashomer members, some years later, enlisted in the Palestinian battalion in 1917–18, and also in the police force, which was formed after the country was taken captive by the British.[10] This, too, is how Shohat's words are to be understood at the discussion held at the secretariat of the General Workers' Federation (Histadrut) executive committee on 25 June 1921: "There is need for a special group of men – only those willing to be at our disposal in all things – the type is rare, therefore."[11] The reference is to the leading core. Regarding the broad popular framework, Shohat and his colleagues were consistent throughout the years. Even at the broad council at Tel Adashim on 18 May 1920, which resolved to disband Hashomer, Shohat proposed a resolution, which was passed, on the formation of a countrywide defense organization.[12] He likewise presented proposals expressly concerning the creation of broad defense networks at the Migdal council of the Joseph Trumpeldor Labor Battalion, held on 18 June 1921.[13] It is very probable that for Shohat and his comrades it was important to activate the experienced Hashomer men in setting the tone in the broad framework and not to preserve the organizational framework of Hashomer in the new body.

The emergence of Eliahu Golomb as a public figure began on the eve of the First World War, but mainly occurred during its course. Already early in 1913 he initiated the establishment of the closed association of graduates of the Herzlia Gymnasia (high school), and the rules he proposed for it required among other things "the commitment to absolute devotion and firm discipline in work and secrecy outside."[14] Here, too, the Russian revolutionary political culture exerted its influence. Moshe Sharett (Shertok), his friend, attests that it was Golomb who inspired the young people of Herzlia with "the spirit of the Russian revolution."[15] It seems that Golomb and the founders of Bar Giora and Hashomer sprang from a common source. During the war Golomb worked with the Jaffa Group and was involved in arms acquisitions, and after the conquest of the south by the British he was prominent in the promotion of volunteering to the Palestinian battalion. Golomb joined Hashomer at the end of the war, and Shohat became acquainted with him only after his return to the country in April 1919. Unlike the Shohat couple, Golomb participated in the process of establishing Ahdut Ha'avoda, and was considered one of its young and promising lights, enjoying the sponsorship of Berl Katznelson.

Eliahu Golomb preached the establishment of a new and wide defense framework, and his speech at the council of the Labor Battalion at Migdal on 18 June 1921 reflected this orientation. "Now the assistance of the entire workers' community in the country is necessary for defense . . . The way of Hashomer 12 years ago was perhaps good, but now, when the problem of defense is widespread, it cannot be confined to a small group."[16] Note that these words were spoken no more than six months after the creation of the Histadrut and a year after the disbanding of Hashomer. The rivalry, the mutual anger, the enmity and the reciprocal suspicion were by then at their height, and Golomb was seeking to establish here a position in opposition to Shohat's in the council of a public body in which the remnant of his opponents found refuge. Golomb's purpose was to trap the bear in its lair. But his attack was pointless, because in fact it met no resistance. It has been shown above that Shohat and his colleagues did not negate but affirmed the broad defense framework, while Golomb by no means rejected the elite, *avant-garde* concept, as is clear from a letter he wrote to Berl Katznelson on 9 February 1922. In it Golomb argued that the way to a broad defensive framework "is perhaps really the way of a small group at first."[17] Only about two years after the dissolution of Hashomer did Golomb come round to the approach of its former leaders. He desired hegemony of the workers over the Hagana, but realized that this could not be achieved unless the workers' movement disposed of a devoted and organized kernel able to direct and lead the broad framework.[18] Golomb set these ideas out in a letter to his friend David Hacohen on 19 January 1922, thereby actually closing the ideological gap that seemed to exist between himself and the Hashomer veterans. The concepts were also expressed clearly in his aforementioned letter to Katznelson: "I agree entirely with Yisrael Shohat that the workers' community, apart from the Hashomer group, is unable to fulfill its role in the Hagana. The Hagana needs commitment and discipline, and these two are missing completely in our public." Later he proposed to Katznelson "the creation of a group of devoted and disciplined workers."[19] In his letter to David Hacohen, Golomb rounds out this line of thinking, remarking on the need to organize an elite group, which would set the course and provide leadership for the Hagana, "and within it, internal discipline and absolute obedience must reign."[20] In other words, after the dissolution of Hashomer it had to be created once again.

The wide gap between the two sides on the issue under study thus appears to have been superficial, one that with goodwill might have been bridged. The two sides favored a broad and popular defense framework, and at the same time they both affirmed and deemed important the existence of an elite body to direct and lead the broad framework.

3 Authority and sovereignty

This issue is more complex and difficult than the foregoing. As it is usually presented, the problem concerns two diametrically opposed positions. One derived from the elite, *avant-garde* approach, which did not accept, at least provisionally, the authority of the general community, but wished to lead it until the national goals were attained. The other was the democratic approach, which deemed the defense arm subject to the authority of the organized civilian institutions of the Yishuv. The first position is attributed to the Hashomer veterans, the second to Golomb and his adherents.[21]

There is no doubt that in the Ottoman period the Bar Giora and Hashomer people believed in the independence of their associations, in

the right of the members to shape their organization. The two bodies were
in fact run accordingly. From the start, and subsequently, their independent posture aroused anger, reserve and criticism on the part of luminaries
in the Zionist world such as Ahad Ha'am, Chlenov, Ruppin and Tehon,
as well as circles among the farmers and in the Hapoel Hatzair party. Even
the mother party, Poaley Zion, had doubts about the subject, and more
than once censure and reproof were voiced. The problem that arose in
1919 was not essentially new. The chief innovation was the new and
different political circumstances of the Yishuv.

In the timespan from the founding of Bar Giora to the First World War,
and during the war, the character of the Yishuv was diffuse, a situation
that benefited Bar Giora and Hashomer. There were no general and recognized representative Yishuv institutions. No body existed that could claim
to represent the entire Yishuv, and in its name demand the imposition of
authority over the guarding and defense association. There were some
exceptions to this only at certain times during the war. The Palestine
Office was the representative of the weak Zionist movement, working
within and influencing only a small minority of the Palestine population.
Beside it, stronger economic and philanthropic factors operated, such as
the ICA, the Alliance Israelite Universelle, and Ezra. The decentralized
political and institutional condition of bodies outside Palestine and the
absence of authoritative and binding institutional representation in the
Yishuv made the independent existence of Hashomer possible. Even in the
limited Zionist sphere, submission to the Palestine Office was by no means
taken for granted, insofar as the Office was not a decision-making body
in the economic sphere. Hashomer, which operated on its own financial
resources, and hardly relied on the Palestine Office for material support,
denied the latter any chance of demanding its own control and authority.

In the sphere of labor, Hashomer presented itself demonstratively as a
supra-party organization. Hence, non-party workers and some members
of the Hapoel Hatzair party could belong to the association or could be
active in the Labor Legion. The supra-party stance legitimized the independence of the guarding and defense organization. Moreover, regarding
the Poaley Zion party, from whose ranks most Hashomer members came,
for years the restraining and moderating influence of Yitzhak Ben Zvi was
at work. Throughout the years the Hashomer committee consisted of
party activists, and it could be argued that the party was involved and
influential with the defense body not as a matter of principle or institutionally, but in practice through its activists and its leaders.

For all that, in those years Hashomer was amenable to the cooperation
and involvement of other factors, of the Yishuv and of the nation as a
whole, in the area of defense. This was due to its sensitivity and awareness concerning the security needs of the Yishuv, which required broad

popularly-based defensive frameworks. The Hashomer position was stated in Shohat's memorandum to the Zionist executive committee of 26 December 1912, mentioned above. Shohat proposed establishing broad defense groups in every settlement; in every place the active defense would be controlled by a committee of Hashomer people. But the committee would also include a delegate from the moshava committee, acceptable, of course, to the other committee members. In principle, the right of the locally elected democratic body to be represented on the organ responsible for defense was recognized. Furthermore, Shohat, in describing his participation at the Eleventh Zionist Congress in 1913 in Vienna, asserts that as a result of his memorandum and his work at the congress this gathering decided to establish a "political institution" in Palestine, which would supervise the subject of defense. This institution was to be made up of three members, representing the Palestine Office, Hovevei Zion and Hashomer. If this account is correct, and there is no reason to doubt it, a highly qualitative change occurred here. Shohat is right when he writes:

> Through this decision the status of Hashomer was officially recognized at the eleventh Zionist Congress in Vienna. A link was formed between it and the institutions of the Zionist movement. Hashomer became a unique organization in Palestine, charged with securing the peace of the Yishuv in the country, a fact that doubled its responsibility and its commitment.[22]

This recognition was won at the cost of foregoing independence and accepting the authority and control of an all-national body. Shohat did not detail the nature and scope of the powers of this body, but it may be assumed that the "political institution" necessarily possessed meaningful powers. It is highly likely that the establishment of the institution alone, apart from the matter of the principle embodied in it, would create momentum toward expanding its function. Its composition is reminiscent of the civilian bodies that supervised the Hagana from the 1930s on. Shohat's initiative was taken with the approval of Hashomer, which received a report on the course of the congress and also elected Yisrael Gil'adi as its representative to the "political institution."

Here we have the most important ideological development since the Bar Giora days. The organization was formed in 1907 on a dual ideological foundation: national and class. In this, it was no different from the labor movement as a whole in the *Second Aliya*, which for the most part adopted the same ideology – later formulated as "Socialist Zionism." From the time of Hashomer onwards, the contacts and cooperation between the association and Yishuv and Zionist factions widened: the national elements among the farmers (Rehovot), Hovevei Zion, and the Palestine Office, culminating in Shohat's effort, approved by the association, won recognition at the Eleventh Congress. This trend led to willingness to accept authority at the national level. This process necessitated precisely the continuation of independence and a supra-party position on the labor level. The Hashomer people undoubtedly possessed socialist awareness and loyalty, and they were predominant among the workers in the defense body, but they held that this would be achieved not on the plane of principle and institution, where at once the overall national status of the association would be lost, but by the mass participation of workers in the defense organization. In this way the latter could influence and shape the defense framework. It is possible that the model envisaged was supervision and national authority in the general strategic area of policy making, while the day-to-day tactical sphere would be in the hands of the members. On the assumption that the workers would fill its ranks and be its activists, it may be assumed that its character would reflect the aims of the workers' class.

From this aspect, the resolutions of the first Hashomer assembly following the war, at Tel Adashim on 19–22 June 1919, were a serious aberration. They determined that Hashomer recognized Ahdut Ha'avoda as the body representing the workers' class in Palestine; Hashomer was part of that body. At the same time, clause A3 stated that in all matters of defense of the people and the country Hashomer would be autonomous on a neutral basis.[23] The resolution was an attempt to have the best of both worlds, without ideological consistency and organizational clarity. Ideologically, the moment Hashomer determined that it was part of Ahdut Ha'avoda it could not be independent because its entire essence concerned security and nothing else. Hence, the decision that in the defense of the people and the country it would be autonomous meant that in practice Hashomer was not a part of Ahdut Ha'avoda. Furthermore, the moment it determined that it was a part of the new political organism Hashomer yielded its independent national position. It should also be borne in mind that although Ahdut Ha'avoda claimed to be an all-class framework, it was in fact a political party in the usual sense, because Hapoel Hatzair remained independent. The resolution was absurd from the organizational standpoint also, because it was impossible to be both within and without simultaneously. Apparently this awkward resolution resulted from the pressures applied by Ahdut Ha'avoda, which Hashomer, in its weakened state, could not rebuff, although Shohat and his comrades left themselves a vague and narrow escape route. The continuation of this illogical line is found in the resolutions of the council dissolving Hashomer, which convened at Tel Adashim on 18 May 1920, where it was resolved again that the future Hagana would be a part of Ahdut Ha'avoda, but would be under the control of those who belonged to it. Similarly it was determined that at a second stage the Hagana would be obliged to serve as the basis for Yishuv-wide defense; in other words, in the first stage the Hagana would indeed be on a class basis, but in the second stage it would be national.[24] Surprisingly, a resolution in this spirit was adopted at the Ahdut Ha'avoda conference on 15 June 1920. Clause 3 of the conference resolutions stated that the Hagana must be under the authority of its members. The resolution, of course, allowed for a different interpretation by each side. Former Hashomer people considered it confirmation of their line, while Golomb, quite rightly, could not grasp how it was possible to be an integral part of Ahdut Ha'avoda yet at the same time be independent and outside its framework. Golomb demanded consistency and acceptance of absolute authority of Ahdut Ha'avoda over security matters. In fact, the Hashomer veterans were seeking a way to escape the Ahdut Ha'avoda bearhug via the back door. Despite their declaration that they were a part of Ahdut Ha'avoda they wished to create a relationship between themselves and the new political body similar to that between themselves and Poaley Zion in the *Second Aliya*. But in two major areas the difference between the circumstances of 1907–18 and of 1919–20 was marked: (a) the ideology of Ahdut Ha'avoda was different from that of Poaley Zion; (b) neither Bar Giora nor Hashomer were part of Poaley Zion, while Hashomer declared explicitly that it was part of Ahdut Ha'avoda. These facts created a new situation, which together with the changed Yishuv and national conditions forced Hashomer into its twisted and impossible position. It may be stated that deep within the Hashomer people knew intuitively that the ideological outline that had characterized them so far – non-party status, the quest for an all-nation position and national recognition – was correct; but the newly-created political and structural situation, the pressures brought to bear by Ahdut Ha'avoda, Hashomer's weakness and lack of an intellectual leadership that could contend ideologically with the new factors – all these gave rise to convolutions and to ambivalent and contradictory resolutions. To understand the events, it is important to scrutinize the new conditions of 1919 that underlay and influenced the course and conclusion of the episode under consideration.

At the end of the war Hashomer was in disarray. Its "golden age" had passed and it had been in retreat since 1913. The war harmed it seriously. In this conflict it had been forced underground, and its activity, as an organization, was slow and expiring, until it almost ceased altogether in the last year of the war. From this conflagration the association emerged exhausted. Moreover, some of the founding fathers, who were also its authoritative figures, such as Yisrael Gil'adi, Mendel Portugali, Yehezkel Hankin and Zvi Beker, had died. A large number of its activists had been deported, and they began to trickle back only in the first months of 1919. The Shohat couple returned in April 1919 after years of absence. Yitzhak

Ben Zvi was in exile in the United States, and on his return to Palestine at the end of 1918 with the American volunteer battalion he threw himself entirely into political work which led to the disbanding of Poaley Zion and the creation of Ahdut Ha'avoda.

Unlike the Ottoman period, when all-national and all-Yishuv institutions hardly existed, in 1918–20, the period of the British military government, the status of the Delegates' Committee as a central and permanent body in the Yishuv, representing it before the British authorities, became firmly based. Its position grew even stronger on its merger with the Palestine Office. At the same time, efforts were redoubled to establish a central Yishuv representation to act beside and together with the Delegates' Committee and with the World Zionist Organization. These were crowned with success with the elections to the Delegates' Assembly in 1920. Instead of the institutional decentralization that had characterized the years before the war, there was now a turn toward authoritative and institutional centralization in the Zionist movement and in the Yishuv. Naturally, the strongest body – the Delegates' Committee – wished to supervise what took place in the Yishuv. This was the background to the clash with Hashomer, as expressed in the police force episode. Hashomer realized the importance of the police, but held that its benefit to the Yishuv depended on the correct influence and the suitable leadership that its members could provide. Hashomer was not unaware of the new conditions, and offered the Delegates' Committee the supervision and authority over the police by means of a special section in which they would be included. The offer was rejected. The failure of their integration into the police force served as a portent. In reality, there was no reason to turn down the Hashomer proposal, which would leave control and authority in the hands of the Delegates' Committee, and at the same time would give the police an idealistic body of men, possessing a rich past and trustworthy and highly experienced in security. The Hashomer people failed in a considerable way owing to the notoriety that clung to them as a closed, domineering and sectarial group. This image outweighed the goodwill and the good intentions of the members of association. Rather than accept their help the Delegates' Committee rejected them. The path in respect of the Yishuv was closed to them.

No less significant was the change that occurred in respect of the labor movement. Ahdut Ha'avoda was formed in February 1919 through the merger of "non-party" workers and the majority of Poaley Zion. Hapoel Hatzair did not join the new body despite heavy pressure upon it to do so. Ahdut Ha'avoda did not consider itself a party but an economic and political body, uniting within itself the entire class of the workers. Its founders considered it a union (*hitahdut*), as its name reflected, of the entire class, and so saw no need for the existence of any workers' organization outside itself. The ideology was of a centralist body, which wholly embraced the entire class in all aspects of life. This was the cause of the particular bitterness toward Hapoel Hatzair which, by remaining independent, denied ideologically and practically the inclusive centralist ideology of Ahdut Ha'avoda, and proposed, as an alternative, the establishment of a federative framework. Only toward the end of 1919, when it was clear to the leaders of Ahdut Ha'avoda that they had failed in their efforts, did they modify their line to permit acceptance of Joseph Trumpeldor's proposals, leading to the creation of the General Workers' Federation (Histadrut) in December 1920 in Haifa.

From the foregoing account Ahdut Ha'avoda's attitude to Hashomer may be understood. From the party viewpoint, there was no longer room for an independent defensive body as at the time of the *Second Aliya*. The ideology of Ahdut Ha'avoda required the guarding body to be inherent in the class framework, while the centralist orientation sought to impose full control over all areas of life, including defense. Here lay the profound difference between Poaley Zion and Ahdut Ha'avoda in respect of Hashomer.

The leadership of Ahdut Ha'avoda was entirely different from that of Poaley Zion as well. In the latter, certain Hashomer activists had enjoyed important status. Their party loyalty, despite the frictions, was beyond doubt. They were considered the unofficial emissaries and representatives of the party in the guarding and defense organization. Moreover, the generally recognized leader of the party, Yitzhak Ben Zvi, was also one of the heads of Hashomer. On this foundation co-existence was possible, even if at times problematic, between the party and Hashomer. This was not the situation of Hashomer and Ahdut Ha'avoda. The Hashomer activists, headed by the Shohat couple, played hardly any part in the process leading to the formation of Ahdut Ha'avoda. Most of them were abroad and the remainder were distant from the arena of developments in Judea, being occupied in getting their living in the Galilee. The exceptions were Rahel Yanait and Yitzhak Ben Zvi. But the position of the latter was greatly attenuated in the new party. From the status of being recognized as leader of the Poaley Zion party, Yitzhak Ben Zvi was thrust aside by other figures. Henceforward he was never to belong to the first rank of the new party's leadership, nor that of the Mapai party later. The triumvirate that took over Ahdut Ha'avoda consisted of Berl Katznelson, David Ben-Gurion and Yitzhak Tabenkin. Of these, Katznelson was "non-party," having no sympathy for either Poaley Zion or Hashomer. Ben-Gurion had never won membership of Hashomer, and had no reason to show any warmth toward the organization that had ignored him so grossly. Tabenkin was indeed a member of Hashomer, but was accepted into the association in the days of its decline and dissolution at the end of the war, and he was not involved in it. It is quite certain that Tabenkin saw his chief power base as Ahdut Ha'avoda, and he desired its aggrandizement.

The explanation for the pressure exerted against Hashomer by Ahdut Ha'avoda, backed by Eliahu Golomb, is therefore clear. The goal was to eradicate the association, based as it was on a consolidated social group with a common past and a tradition that might threaten the orientation toward the homogeneity and centralism of Ahdut Ha'avoda. Hashomer was a potential kernel of an opposition to Ahdut Ha'avoda. It negated the existence of the Hapoel Hatzair party outside; how much the more was it opposed to an autonomous framework within.

In a discussion of the dissolution of Hashomer it must be understood that the drama was between the association and Ahdut Ha'avoda, which by late 1919 had become, even in the eyes of its leaders, a regular political party. Therefore, it is incorrect to claim that Hashomer refused to submit to *national*, or *Yishuv* or even *class* control over itself, as asserted by the authors of the *History of the Hagana*, or that the debate, in their words, concerned "who would make decisions and rulings . . . the political leadership of the Yishuv or the defense activists themselves?" The scene was enacted between Hashomer and the Ahdut Ha'avoda *party*. Any attempt to present the debate otherwise does not accord with historical fact. The debate, which continued after the disbanding of Hashomer and after the establishment of the Histadrut in December 1920, was by now of a different quality, and had to do with residues of ill-feeling, personal animosity, and the like. In the drama staged from mid-1919 to mid-1920 Eliahu Golomb played the leading role.

Furthermore, in the subject at issue Eliahu Golomb, who worked in the name and on behalf of a political party, is most remarkably depicted as the upholder of the democratic principle – the imposition of the discipline of the "whole," by way of its elected institutions, on the military arm – in contrast to the members of Hashomer, who allegedly opposed the democratic principle because they wished to maintain the all-national and non-party character of the security organization, without submitting to the authority of a single party.

Those favoring Golomb and his supporters usually take his subsequent positions as their grounds. It is true that several years later Golomb claimed that the Hagana had "to be linked and obedient to the whole, the Histadrut institution"[25] and that "it was to be under the leadership of an institution elected by the council of the Histadrut."[26] It is important to observe that these claims were made long after the dissolution of Hashomer, and also that at this stage Golomb places the emphasis on the authority of the Histadrut over the Hagana, not mentioning all-Yishuv authority; this was by no means accidental.

Eliahu Golomb underwent evolutionary development. Like Yitzhak Tabenkin, he joined Hashomer at the end of the First World War, and did not find his place in it. Unlike Tabenkin, whose primary concern was in politics, the young Golomb devoted himself to the problem of security, which he deemed his chief public occupation. There is no doubt that Golomb saw his power base and his future in the Ahdut Ha'avoda party, in which framework he sought to make his mark on the security sphere. Therefore, using the ideology and organizational structure of Ahdut Ha'avoda, and enjoying the personal support of Berl Katznelson, the young Golomb set his sights on the total elimination of Hashomer and its assimilation into the party, within which a new security system would be established. In this the Hashomer veterans would not be the decisive and dominating element. A historical blend occurred between party interests and the personal ambitions of Golomb, who did indeed succeed in destroying Hashomer and establishing the Hagana in the bosom of the Ahdut Ha'avoda party.

With the creation of the Histadrut, Ahdut Ha'avoda became the majority party in it. As such, it worked indefatigably to enlarge Histadrut authority at the expense of the parties. Security activity also, namely, the Hagana, was transferred by Ahdut Ha'avoda under the aegis and control of the Histadrut. In later years Golomb could speak of the control by the Histadrut of the Hagana, where formerly he had jealously demanded the rule of his party over security. Golomb's range of vision had expanded, but the objective decidedly suited his interests and those of his party, which was dominant in the Histadrut. The powerful party grip on this sensitive area never loosened, and through it neither did his. Something of Golomb's approach to the subject is revealed in a conversation he held with Zvi Nadav at the time of the debate. Nadav relates that at that time the Hashomer people made a proposal:

> On the question of the class composition of the Hagana we held that it had to be more general, of the entire Yishuv, but with the hegemony of the workers; at the same time we suggested local defense committees, elected, not appointed. I recall Eliahu's argument, when he asserted: If we want the discipline of a labor party – in this case Ahdut Ha'avoda – how is it possible for defense committees to be elected? The majority would elect its own people.[27]

Zvi Nadav's testimony is of course not beyond suspicion, but it is difficult to assume that he would have altered the content of the talk so tendentiously. It emerges, therefore, that at that point it was not the democratic principle that guided Golomb: his single goal was to impose the discipline of the party and to win its – his – control in this grave matter.

Ideological flexibility over the democratic principle was not foreign to

Golomb the politician, as attested by his conduct in the dispute between
Kefar Gil'adi and Tel Hai in 1925–7. As is known, most of the members
of Kibbutz Tel Hai decided, with the approval and support of the Labor
Battalion of which the kibbutz was a member, to unite with Kefar Gil'adi.
Only one-third of the members, 13 in all, were against the proposed
union, which was intended to improve the social and economic condition
of the two kibbutzim. Against this background a prolonged conflict broke
out, one side being the Labor Battalion, Kibbutz Kefar Gil'adi and most
members of Tel Hai, the other being the Histadrut, meaning the Ahdut
Ha'avoda party, which supported the minority in Kibbutz Tel Hai. It was
Golomb who vindicated or provided ideological reasoning for the decisions of the Histadrut executive committee supporting the minority.
Against the assertion that it was the democratic right of the majority at
Tel Hai to rule for union, Golomb wrote that this was a formalistic
perception of the democratic principle. It was to the advantage of the
minority that its members were among the founders of the kibbutz and
therefore held seniority over the majority. In addition, so Golomb
propounded, the majority was planning an isolationist act, working
against the larger majority, that is, the Histadrut.[28] Here we have an
example of the ideological flexibility of Golomb the politician. That an
evolutionary process did occur in Golomb in respect of the principle of
discipline is admitted even by the *History of the Hagana*. There it is stated
that the Hagana, in Golomb's opinion, was intended to be "in the first
place under the control of Ahdut Ha'avoda, then of the Histadrut and
finally of the entire Yishuv."[29] The authors of the book do not point out,
or explain – and not by accident – that this evolutionary process in
Golomb was not determinist but developed gradually, in step with the rise
of Ahdut Ha'avoda to dominance in the Histadrut and of Mapai to hegemony in the Yishuv and the Zionist movement.

In fact, it may be stated that Golomb's struggle, originating in a
combined party and personal interest, led through historical process to a
positive result, characteristic of democratic societies, in which the security arm is subject to the control of elected civilian institutions. As for
Hashomer, it is striking that the association had no difficulty at all in
submitting to national authority. Hashomer's problems were with the
Ahdut Ha'avoda party alone, whose ambition of wholly consuming and
ruling the defense organization it opposed. Hashomer wished to create an
organization with no obvious party label, so that it would be recognized
as a national body and fulfilling a national role. It sought to achieve labor
movement domination through the action of masses of workers in the
defense organization, which they could shape from within. The Hashomer
people were not guided by isolationism but the opposite. It is quite certain
that without the bitter taste left in 1919 they would have participated in

defense in the Histadrut framework and in the national development of the Hagana. In 1919 Hashomer in fact already accepted the principle of national authority, while Golomb was only then setting out on the path that would lead him to the same perception. History has dealt kindly with Eliahu Golomb but cruelly with the members of Hashomer, whose organization disintegrated in 1920. Its remnants, including its leaders, because they dared to rebel against their party, found no place in the various public and political bodies, and were cast aside from the stage of the future history of Jewish settlement in Palestine.

9

From Unity to Dissolution, 1920-1927

We are accused of sabotaging and preventing the establishment of the Hagana organization; of acting in a separatist manner: assuming that we did work in a separatist manner, did we hinder Eliahu and his friends in setting up the Hagana organization? Did we hinder Eliahu in continuing to acquire arms? After we stopped our arms acquistions because of Eliahu and his intrigues, what did he do? The year 1921 would tell . . .

Yisrael Shohat

I N THE GENERAL EUPHORIA that reigned in the Zionist movement and the Yishuv following the collapse of Turkish rule, the start of the British Mandate over Palestine and the appointment of a Jewish High Commissioner, Herbert Samuel, for many anxiety over security evaporated. Large sections of the Zionist movement and the Yishuv believed that henceforward concern for safety was a matter for the mandatory authorities, and the Jews were relieved of it.

The Mis-Step (12 June 1920–End of 1922)

Two clashes with Arabs did occur, in early 1920 and in April of that year. The first was an Arab attack against the Jewish settlement Tel Hai, located in the far north of eastern Upper Galilee, in which eight defenders fell, including their leader Joseph Trumpeldor. The modern town of Kiriat Shemona is named after them. The second clash was at the time of the Muslim Nabi Musa festival, which falls at about the Christian Easter. The festival originated in the Mamluk period and was characterized by the gathering of masses of excited Muslims in Jerusalem. However, these events were put down to special circumstances for which the British authorities were not deemed responsible, or they were blamed on officers of the British military government who had been in control from the start of the conquest at the end of 1917 until the inauguration of the British Mandate in mid-1920; they could not be attributed to the general attitude of Britain to the Zionist movement and the Jewish settlement in Palestine. Those holding such views did not alter them even after the disturbance of May 1921, in which there were assaults by Arabs against Jews, the worst being the murder of dozens of Jews in Jaffa, including the writers Zvi Shatz and Yosef Haim Brenner. These events occurred when Herbert Samuel was already High Commissioner. This indifference and complacency became more evident in the following years, because the May 1921 events were followed by a prolonged period of quiet that lasted until the disturbances of August 1929. These years were the most prolonged period of peace in the history of the Yishuv under the Mandate. This circumstance, together with the existence of many other kinds of hardship that the Yishuv had to overcome during the 1920s, changed the order of priority and caused a sharp fall in the interest evinced by Zionist and Yishuv elements in the question of security. There was disagreement over the nature of the security framework to defend the Zionist enterprise.

1 Attitude to the Security Issue

Zev Jabotinsky, who was then a member of the Zionist leadership, wanted the Jewish battalions of the First World War to continue to exist; these would provide defense for the Jewish settlement in Palestine. His proposal was that manpower as well as financing of the battalions should be from Jewish sources.[1] Jabotinsky emphasized the existence of an army that was overt, manned by Jewish troops but under British command. In his view the need for a Jewish army arose from the very nature of the Jewish-Arab conflict, which he saw as a clash of real interests and in which the Arabs, to safeguard their aims, would act against the Jews. Jabotinsky negated any alternative to an army, and therefore opposed illegal self-defense. He believed that two thousand Jewish soldiers were preferable to a ten thousand-strong underground.[2] He succeeded in imparting this concept, the importance of an army and its preferability to a clandestine defense organization, to the Zionist leadership. The latter, at its meeting on 1 April 1921, decided to call on Britain to renew the Jewish battalions, and it rejected Samuel's proposal to establish a "Defense Force of Palestine" composed of a Jewish and an Arab battalion. The Zionist Executive, which convened at Carlsbad in August 1921 on the eve of the Twelfth Zionist Congress, approved the position of the Zionist leadership by a vote of 23 to 9. Later, the Twelfth Congress adopted the decision of the Zionist Executive.[3]

This policy failed. The remnants of the battalions broke up after the disturbances of May 1921 and never re-formed. But despite the failure of his efforts, Jabotinsky adhered to his views throughout the 1920s and for most of 1930s, and also made the issue of a Jewish army, the idea of the Legion, a tenet of the Revisionist party, which he founded in 1925.[4]

The major and practically the only public body to persist in its concern for the subject of security of the Yishuv was the Ahdut Ha'avoda party. The party consistently supported Jabotinsky's efforts to sustain, and later to revive, the Jewish army battalions in Palestine. Resolutions in this spirit were adopted at the party's founding conference on February 1919 and at the second conference, held at Kinneret on 12–15 June 1920. In the report of the delegation of the World Union of Poaley Zion visiting Palestine in winter of 1919/20,[5] there was also a positive attitude to the idea of the battalions.[6] However, Ahdut Ha'avoda was also the chief proponent of clandestine self-defense, which it considered essential, parallel to a legal Jewish army, should this be achieved. This was the setting, already in the early 1920s, for a parting of the ways between the two elements active in the area of security – Zev Jabotinsky and the Ahdut Ha'avoda party. While the former consistently saw the chief thing as an overt army, and negated a Jewish underground, Ahdut Ha'avoda deemed this essential as a vital security instrument that would be entirely subject to the Jews; the envisioned overt army, whose chances of being created were slight, would be under British command.[7]

The Hagana organization should not be seen as arising from efforts made in late 1919 and early 1920 by the provisional committee of the Palestinian Jews or by the Delegates' Committee. Likewise, the body formed in February 1920 in Jerusalem headed by Jabotinsky, and including Pinhas Ruthenberg, Moshe Smilansky, Eliahu Golomb, Rahel Yanait and Dov Hoz,[8] was mainly active in organizing the defense of the Jews of Jerusalem in the Nabi Musa riots that erupted in the city on 4 April, but there was no continuation of this. The Hagana organization was, as stated, born in the Ahdut Ha'avoda party when, at the afore-mentioned Kinneret convention, it resolved to accept "the call made to it by the Hashomer association to undertake the arrangement of defense matters." The party charged Yisrael Shohat, Yosef Nahmani, Yissachar Sitkov, Eliahu Golomb and Dov Hoz with the implementation of the reso-lution. The latter were enjoined "in association with the Executive Committee of Ahdut Ha'avoda, to set about organizing a defense associ-ation."[9]

2 Ahdut Ha'avoda and the Histadrut

About six months after the above events the General Workers' Federation (Histadrut) was founded, in Haifa, in early December 1920, as an orga-nizing and guiding roof framework for the entire body of workers in Palestine. At the founding conference Ahdut Ha'avoda proposed trans-ferring the security issue to the Histadrut. The Hapoel Hatzair party opposed the idea with a series of reasons justifying its position: a special framework for security should not be created; it should be a local, not countrywide matter; security should not be inserted into the Histadrut constitution so as not to extend to it the existing differences in principle among the founders; security was not a matter for the Histadrut but for the National Committee (*hava'ad haleumi*), because the subject concerned the Yishuv as a whole.

In contrast to these arguments, Yisrael Shohat and Eliahu Golomb, the spokesmen for Ahdut Ha'avoda, stressed the great significance of transferring the question of security to the authority of the Histadrut, and of inserting it into the Histadrut constitution. Challenging his opponents, Golomb asked, "Is this the place to tell you that defense of the dignity and life of the Jews is the ideal of the immigrant to the land? Is it necessary to once again relate the valor of the Hebrew worker defending Tel Hai? The formation of the battalions? So closely linked is the life of the Jewish worker to defense that defense is bound to occupy a place in the Histadrut constitution." Shohat reinforced Golomb's words: "Throughout the entire existence of our work in the land we have been conscious that defense is an important part of our work and may not be separate."[10] In the end the majority approved the Ahdut Ha'avoda proposal, and so it became fact that from late in 1920 to the disturbances of August 1929 the Hagana, with its all-national goals, was under the aegis of the Histadrut. This actually recreated the situation in the time of the *Second Aliya*, when Hashomer fulfilled national security and defense functions but was politically linked to the Palestinian workers' movement in general and to the Poaley Zion party in particular. Despite the positive decision in principle adopted by the founding conference, several months passed, owing to the general air of complacency, until on 13 March 1921 the Histadrut council elected the first Defense Committee of the Histadrut. It consisted of Yisrael Shohat, Eliahu Golomb, Yosef Baratz, Levi Shkolnik (Eshkol) and Haim Shturman. Two candidate members were also attached: Zvi Nadav and Yitzhak Landoberg (Sadeh).[11]

In the period when security was the responsibility of Ahdut Ha'avoda, namely, June–December 1920, and also from December 1920 to the events of May 1921 and subsequently, when the issue was in the hands of the Histadrut, very little was done, nationally and locally, in organizing and preparing the Yishuv for emergencies. The May 1921 events threw this grave situation into sharp relief, highlighting the absence of a national defense framework as well as the glaring weaknesses of local defense. The events laid bare the bad state of the Yishuv, especially concerning weapons. The shortage was critical. Moreover, it transpired that some of the few arms possessed were not fit for use owing to the poor and makeshift conditions in which they were stored. Essentially the events revealed the extreme weakness of the young Hagana, which was devoid of all the vital components of a national defensive security organization: a national centralized organizational framework, a supreme command, trained officers and ranks, defined duties for officers and above all, disposition of necessary and acceptable quantities of arms.

It seems that not only were the Zionist and Yishuv institutions complacent and indifferent, failing to allocate necessary resources to defense: Ahdut Ha'avoda and the fledgling Histadrut did not pay much heed to the subject either. Some justification for this state of affairs may be found in the weakness of these two organizations. Ahdut Ha'avoda was a small and poor workers' party still lacking, in the early 1920s, influence in the Yishuv and the Zionist movement. The founding of the Histadrut indeed created an overall organizing framework for the workers in the country, but this community was still small and sparse, and the Histadrut was then taking its first faltering steps in organization, imposing discipline, and creating economic resources.

For all that, it cannot be overlooked that in both Ahdut Ha'avoda and the Histadrut security was the domain of only the very few. The leadership of these bodies was immersed in other concerns, and as in other organizations so in these was security pushed down low in the order of priorities.

The weaknesses described were so severe that even the riots of May 1921 did not cause a general and real change in attitude of the Zionist, Yishuv and even Histadrut institutions to security. Therefore, it is not surprising that those who did regard defense as their chief endeavor in the country and their historic course sought their own ways of giving actual expression to their wishes and plans in this field.

In the period under review, from June 1920 to the May 1921 events, and especially following those events, the real and imagined disputes, frictions and power struggles between Eliahu Golomb and the former Hashomer people developed and intensified. Mostly they were members of the the same party, Ahdut Ha'avoda, whose discipline, and later that of the Histadrut, all recognized. The main criticism of the former Hashomer people was on the practical level: the absence of real action by the Histadrut in advancing the security for which it was responsible. Golomb's group was identified with the party and Histadrut establishment, therefore criticism of the Histadrut to some extent encompassed Golomb and his supporters. There was serious and natural concern at Golomb's tendency to rely in security matters on his friends and acquaintances from the Herzlia Gymnasia (school) and on veterans of the Palestinian battalion, excluding former Hashomer men. Further discord arose over the direction in which the Hagana should be developed: toward qualities such as commitment, internal discipline, and consciousness, or toward externals such as appearance, parade-ground drills, etc. These positions are noted by Zvi Nadav, who criticized the organization of the Hagana in towns in the early 1920s, where secondary school pupils were indeed enlisted in the Hagana but all they did, according to Nadav, was drill, while the chief thing, weapons training, was neglected:

> I recall the arguments I had with Eliahu Golomb (we were friends from as far back as the Jaffa group) over the nature of the Hagana. We, the Hashomerniks, scorned and ridiculed the military character given to those exercises (such as standing to attention and saluting an instructor or commander). To us veteran workers those exercises were odd and alien, and valueless: we considered them tending toward militarism.
>
> Eliahu explained to me that in a mass organization it was impossible to introduce discipline without this ceremonial. We, who knew what discipline was to the death, and whose respect for an older member or a committee member came from within, without the paraphernalia, detested the parades, couldn't stomach them.
>
> Personal attitudes also arose from this. We did not care for the people that Eliahu and Dov Hoz (Dov was in the army then) brought into the Hagana organization. They included many from the intelligentsia, which we did not trust for their moral strength and seriousness. We demanded the attachment of our senior and younger members, who were experienced in the practical work and had also been tested in action. From this too the disputes arose between Yisrael Shohat and Eliahu.[12]

This account, with all the necessary caution, is reminiscent of the conceptual and sociological problems that arose in the Hagana on the eve of the War of Independence and the transition to the Israel Defense Forces (IDF), when friction arose between the Hagana school and the school of the British army veterans.

It is almost certain that the May 1921 events and the dispersal of the remnants of the battalions following their intervention in the events were the turning point for the former Hashomer men toward independent organization at the end of 1922. The events showed that the Hagana had no prepared infrastructure; they highlighted the lack of organization, the confusion, and above all the desperate shortage of arms; and the dispersal of the remnants of the battalions showed that no hopes should be pinned on the Mandatory government. All these generated despair and the realization that other lines of action had to be followed. This ultimately led to the separate organization of the former Hashomer people and their allies in the Joseph Trumpeldor Labor Battalion composed of immigrants of the *Third Aliya*.

During 1921 and most of 1922 there was no separate security activity by former Hashomer people. Hashomer members who joined the Labor Battalion were occupied in arms acquisitions in this framework, but Hagana activity throughout the 1920s was diffuse and decentralized. Any security initiatives by Hashomer people who were members of the Labor Battalion were, in 1920–2, unconcealed and known to the Hagana. This also applies to the work in arms acquisition of Gershon Fleisher, in 1921–2 in Vienna.[13] The *History of the Hagana*, which well represents the Golomb school, corroborates the above account for 1920–1, which is also applicable to 1922:

> Attention to the subject of defense in the Histadrut was dilatory. The Histadrut had a plethora of goals to attain from the time it was founded, and could not free itself from the question of defense. Similarly, the impression of the 1920 events [i.e., Tel Hai and the Nabi Musa disturbances in April 1920 – Y.G.] was dispelled and complacency reigned. To many it appeared that nothing would happen during the High Commissionership of Samuel. Work in defense dwindled throughout the land. In Jerusalem the defense association that had begun to operate forcefully following the Passover riots in 1920 broke up. In the Galilee too "they stopped being concerned about weapons (diary of the executive committee)." Many settlements refused to submit to the discipline of the Defense Committee elected at the Ahdut Ha'avoda conference, claiming that the resolution by the Histadrut had revoked its powers. A strange situation arose: Hashomer had been utterly eliminated and there was no body to fill its role (Y. Ben Zvi). The work of defense moved sluggishly. There was hardly any training; many arms depots, residues of the war, were neglected and much of what was in them was broken and rusty.[14]

This, together with the shock of the May 1921 events and the dispersal of the remnants of the battalions, gave rise to ideas about a separate organization of former Hashomer people. There is thus reason to doubt the slanted account in *History of the Hagana* claiming that the disbanding of Hashomer in May 1920 was not genuine but a trick, and at that very moment Shohat and his men were planning the re-establishment of Hashomer. Such a presentation at once casts the Hashomer people in a negative light, of hypocrisy, trickery, sectionalism and bad faith. This entirely tendentious rendering, discrediting the Hashomer veterans, is grounded in one short passage from the much later recollections of Yosef Harit – a passage, moreover, given to a variety of interpretations, not necessarily that adopted by *History of the Hagana*.[15] It is common sense that the dissolution was real, as was the wish subsequently to operate within the Hagana framework under the sponsorship of Ahdut Ha'avoda, and later under that of the Histadrut. Only the steady decline in security activity between 1920 and 1922, with the riots acting as a catalyst, caused the glimmer of thoughts on separate organization to appear, not even actual organization itself. Years later Yisrael Shohat claimed against his detractors:

We are accused of sabotaging and preventing the establishment of the Hagana organization; of acting in a separatist manner: assuming that we did work in a separatist manner, did we hinder Eliahu and his friends in setting up the Hagana organization? Did we hinder Eliahu in continuing to acquire arms? After we stopped our arms acquistions because of Eliahu and his intrigues, what did he do? The year 1921 would tell . . . [16]

3 The alternative: The Joseph Trumpeldor Labor Battalion

The political situation in Palestine with the exchange of rule held out many opportunities. Although the British government did not adhere to its early promises to help the Jews to establish their national home, there still remained a fairly wide range of possibilities for practical Zionist activity. The fate of the Zionist thrust, brought to a halt by the tribulations of the Great War, hung on a central question: Would Jews come to Palestine? The answer was the *Third Aliya*.

The *Third Aliya* period was critical for the three factors involved in shaping and determining the destiny of Palestine in the Mandatory era: The British, the Jews and the Arabs.

The *Third Aliya* came into being through the following circumstances. The old European empires had crumbled, and on their ruins new eastern European states arose. Concomitant with these upheavals was disappearance of the ancient concepts and ways of life of Jewish communities in Europe. Furthermore, the establishment of the new states in eastern Europe was associated with the rise of nationalism, which was directed against national minorities. Among the chief victims were the Jews; the long civil war in Russia and the war between Russia and the new Poland caused many casualties and cost the lives of hundreds of thousands of Jews.[17] Many felt that a new life had to be sought in different surroundings; the victory of nationalism in Europe effected the awakening of Jewish national consciousness. The revolutions in Russia fired the spirit and engendered faith in the possibility of building a new society, more just and equal. The Balfour declaration, the conquest of Palestine by the British and the fall of the Ottoman empire ignited nationalist fervor and messianic hopes. Many thought they heard the footsteps of the Messiah, and Herzl's vision appeared on the verge of realization. All these together gave birth to a wave of migration in the years 1919 to 1923: the *Third Aliya*.

The Joseph Trumpeldor Labor Battalion, formed near Tiberias Hot Springs on 25 August 1920, about six months after the death of Trumpeldor and a few months before the creation of the Histadrut, was the tangible outcome of this Aliya in general and of its pioneering current in particular. The original name was The Joseph Trumpeldor Defense and Labor Battalion, but the word "defense" was removed to avoid trouble. But the idea behind the word remained. The new body, conforming to

Trumpeldor's heritage, regarded itself as a pioneering organization fulfilling tasks in labor and defense equally.[18]

The small group of Hagana activists in Ahdut Ha'avoda welcomed the founding of the Battalion, which in a short time became a framework for hundreds of young people, among them those with much military experience from service in various armies. Not surprisingly, many saw the Battalion as the future bearer of the Hagana immediately on its foundation. Even after the creation of the Histadrut the few Hagana activists saw it as the main reservoir of human resources and the basis of the "chief army of the Hagana organization in the country," which would fulfill the tasks of a national military force.[19]

The Hashomer people were the first to establish close relations with the young people of the *Third Aliya*, and so broke the barriers of age and cultural–political differences. In Shohat's Tel Aviv apartment several meetings took place with Trumpeldor's disciples, and there the idea of establishing the Battalion on the model of the Labor Legion of the *Second Aliya* days was conceived.[20] Once founded, the Battalion was joined by a sizable group of Hashomer veterans including Zvi Nadav, Yosef Harit, Ya'akov Abramson, Arye Abramson, Moshe Levit, Zvi Nisanov, and others. Zvi Nadav and Moshe Levit were even elected to the first committee of the Battalion.[21] The warmth and welcome shown by the Hashomer veterans to the young people of the *Third Aliya* was reciprocated by the latter, who also identified with them ideologically and were attracted by the aura of glory and daring that enveloped many of the old guards and appealed to the romance of the *Third Aliya* people. It was natural that the Hashomer veterans would take charge of the security issue in the Battalion. They taught the young people about the conditions of the country and the local population, and trained novices in use of arms. The foremost problem was the great shortage of weapons, and as early as 1921 this spurred the Hashomer veterans, who were responsible for security, to renewed activity in arms acquisition.

Thus the people of the defunct Hashomer found an alternative to the party and the Histadrut in which to express their goals and their vitality in the area of security. Justly or not, in those frameworks they felt that their motivation to act struck no sympathetic chord, that the driving force inherent within them was paralyzed; they were misunderstood and redundant, elbowed aside by the Ahdut Ha'avoda party apparatus, which was practically indistinguishable from the Histadrut apparatus. But in the Battalion their experience, activity, contribution and primacy in security were warmly welcomed and appreciated by its youthful membership. So, starting from late 1920, but principally in 1921–2, the center of gravity in security activity by the Hashomer veterans shifted by slow degrees from the party and Histadrut to the Battalion. They set out on the path that would lead them to bind their fate indissolubly to that of the Labor Battalion.

In the development of the Labor Battalion, the council at Migdal on 18 June 1921 constitutes one of the chief landmarks. Here the platform was formulated and here the decision was taken to change from a provisional to a permanent body. It was also resolved that the goal of the Battalion was "to build the land by creating a general commune of Jewish workers in Palestine." It seems, then, that the aim was to impose the life desired by the Battalion on all the workers in the country; they and their institutions, including the Histadrut, were to be subject to Battalion ideology. This outlook carried the seeds of future conflict with the Histadrut, which regarded itself as an overall and binding framework for all the workers in Palestine, including the Battalion. Actualization of the Battalion's resolution adopted by the Migdal council would mean that in due course the communard way of life would envelop the entire workers' class, necessarily with the replacement of the Histadrut by the Battalion. Ostensibly the Battalion considered itself the *avant-garde* of the Histadrut, but the Migdal platform, which determined to "shore up the 'Histadrut' and direct it along the lines of the Battalion," reveals the Battalion's ambition to shape the Histadrut in its own image rather than to be subsumed by it; in other words, to become the substitute for the Histadrut.[22]

The set of circumstances in which the Labor Battalion was founded, several months before the Histadrut; the dynamic nature of the Battalion consisting of hundreds of young people and being the largest national coherent workers' body; the enunciation of the very ambitious Migdal platform – all projected the Battalion as a threat to the existence of the Histadrut and as a possible alternative. The potential of this menace was serious in light of the Battalion's strength at that time and the extreme weakness of the Histadrut.

The Histadrut was, after its establishment, merely a hollow framework, which had to be filled with content. Above all, the young institution needed to reinforce and consolidate its powers, and find the means of imposing its will on its membership, without which it would be impossible to overcome the traditions of independence, diffuseness and splits that had been rife in the small workers' community since the time of the *Second Aliya*. To the outside, too, it was vital for the Histadrut to appear exclusively as the body representing the entire workers' class. In 1921–2 all this was missing from the newly-formed workers' federation.

This was the setting for the forging of the unwritten alliance between the first nation-wide kibbutz, the broad organizational framework of the young people of the *Third Aliya*, and the members of Hashomer. The process was gradual, but the May 1921 disturbances and the dissolution of the last of the war battalions imparted movement to it. In mid-1921, and more markedly in 1922, the Hashomer veterans took the decisive, and mistaken, step which brought them several years later to a dramatic and tragic turning point with the break-up of the Battalion, and to their being pushed aside from the public stage.

The fateful tie between the former members of Hashomer and the Labor Battalion caused the abandonment of the historic path of Hashomer and a transposition between themselves and their rivals. For most of the years prior to the disbanding of Hashomer, its members had been guided principally by the overall national outlook. This was also the main reason for their opposition to the institutional subjection of the national issue of security to party authority, meaning the authority of Ahdut Ha'avoda, as Eliahu Golomb and his supporters wished in 1919-20. But following the establishment of the Histadrut in December 1920, the Hashomer members did not grasp the fundamental and qualitiative implications of the change that had occurred. For the first time in Palestine, an overall class framework had arisen, recognized, weak though it was, by all the workers' parties. This framework too was still partial, in that it was of a class, not a nation. Even so, with the creation of the Histadrut a genuine and all-embracing public matrix was formed, with ambitions toward centralism and the right to impose the discipline of the workers' class on all areas of life, including defense.

Adherence to the historic path obliged the Hashomer people to choose one of two alternatives: to continue to demand national authority over the Hagana and not to accept class authority, or, having undertaken to submit to the discipline of the Histadrut, to be consistent and accept its authority in practical matters of security as in others. It was their duty to impart real content to the Hagana framework, despite the difficulties, disputes and failings. The Hashomer people chose a third alternative: without refuting the authority of the Histadrut, they in fact abandoned the Hagana, leaving it prey to their competitors, and set up their own security framework in the Labor Battalion. This step was a *volte face* and a descent from the national or even class level to the level of partisan interest. In the best case the Battalion might, from an ideological viewpoint, become a possible substitute for the Histadrut, but it could never pretend to represent the national dimension. The linkage by the Hashomer people of their fate to that of the Battalion not only brought about their demise: henceforward Golomb and his adherents could speak on behalf of all and with the authority of all, first the class and then the nation, while the Hashomer veterans were forced into a particularist organization and were stigmatized with sectionalism, isolationism, and anti-democracy.[23]

The Intolerable Dualism (June 1920–End of 1923)

1 The founding of Hakibbutz

According to the *History of the Hagana* the foundations of Hakibbutz were laid "at the Tiberias assembly on 6 August 1921 when, for the first time, the readiness of a section of Hashomer members to form a separate defense organization was evinced. Many of the new immigrants of the *Third Aliya* were already involved. With the re-establishment of Kefar Gil'adi, which new members of the Battalion joined, and with its attachment to the Labor Battalion, a real basis for the organizing Hakibbutz was created."[24]

The name "Hakibbutz" was apparently the accepted one, and it is found in the letters of its members and in several documents.[25] But at various times other names appeared: "The Circle," "The Organized Circle," "The Secret Militia," "The Secret Circle," "The Secret Kibbutz," "Shohat's Company" or simply "Hashomer."[26]

Despite the importance of this secret security organization, which existed for several years, information on it is quite sparse. Its documents disappeared in uncertain circumstances in 1946 during the struggle against the British. The existence of such documents is known from Moshe Braslavsky, who studied them and even took some notes.[27] The leaders and activists of Hakibbutz, or those who happened at various times to deal with it, have preferred to recall this historical episode in a vague general way, or to overlook it entirely. This was so with Yisrael Shohat, Yosef Harit[28] and their comrades, and also other central figures. The most extreme case is David Ben-Gurion, who in his memoirs ignores the subject altogether.

Despite the paucity of documents, a few important papers are extant that shed light on the beginnings of the organization of Hakibbutz, its goals and ideology. From these, a question arises as to the date given by the histories for the founding of Hakibbutz, which, following *History of the Hagana*, is usually fixed as 6 August 1921.

The main document on which *History of the Hagana* bases this date is a form of minutes of an assembly held on that day at Tiberias. The date appears on the document, which also opens with a note of the number of participants – 45. At the end of the minutes there is a list of 56 names (one of them repeated), apparently covering a wider circle.[29] From the minutes this was obviously an open, not secret, meeting of former members of Hashomer who were active in defense and of certain members of the Battalion associated with them. In contrast to what is stated in *History of the Hagana*, the great majority of those gathered were from the former Hashomer and only a handful were *Third Aliya* people. The party and Histadrut institutions knew of the meeting, which they had not called, and naturally there was some senstitivity about it and its resolutions. On this Yisrael Shohat declared that "I informed them that we called together the active members to discuss and clarify our views, but this does not mean that this meeting will adopt any resolutions." In turn, the Ahdut Ha'avoda Executive Committee stated that "the organization of any group of members of Ahdut Ha'avoda on matters of defense in general, and in particular the group meeting tomorrow in the Galilee, must be with the participation and subject to the discipline of the Defense Committee of the Histadrut."

The participants at the meeting were well aware of the likely risk. There was the danger of a confrontation with the party and the Histadrut Defense Committee, and some of those present voiced ideas of separate action nevertheless. But the prevailing mood of the meeting was for continued activity within the Hagana, while striving for greater vigor in its work. Shohat adopted a clear position in this spirit, stating in his opening address that "the Hagana is of course for all the workers, and all the community takes part in it when there are incidents, etc., and no one thinks of taking over defense as a monopoly." Shohat was not unaware of existing frictions in the Hagana but hoped that David Ben-Gurion, who had just returned from his work abroad, would succeed in approximating the two sides and finding a unifying factor. Shohat repeated that "we must now plan on all fronts and at this time all are obliged to work jointly, shoulder to shoulder. The way of separatism will destroy the Hagana and no viable result can emerge from it." His speech did not retreat from the position of the Hashomer people on the organization of defense: "We say that defense is a general requirement of all the workers and all will stand ready to defend, but the drive to act can come only from a limited and organized group that will persevere in the work of defense not only in times of crises but also in times of quiet . . ." At the same time, he favored operating within the Hagana. Zvi Nadav and Haim Shturman held similar opinions.[30] Following the Tiberias assembly Yosef Nahmani wrote to the executive committee of the Histadrut, setting forth the position adopted by the meeting:

To the Executive Committee
Comrades.
I hereby submit to you, by the decision of the participants at the assembly (56 in number), their resolution regarding the question of defense taken on 6 August 1921 in Tiberias. "We, comrades from various places in Lower and Upper Galilee, gathered and spoke about the situation of disorganization and disorder prevailing in the defense of the places, and we see the chief cause of this as the lack of an association for defense to be at the disposal of the Defense Committee and which this latter can rely upon. Therefore, we demand that at once action be taken on creating a defense association that will itself determine its plans, its method and way of executing them.

Tiberias, August 1921.
On behalf of the participants at the meeting, Yosef Nahmani.[31]

The meeting, then, was open. The institutions knew of it, and its resolutions were reported to the Histadrut body responsible for the security issue. True, extreme statements were made at the meeting, but the general tone was of cooperation and encouragement of action from within. In light of this, it is not reasonable to suppose that the organization called Hakibbutz was founded at this meeting. Moreover, all the existing historical interpretations, which are critical of the Hashomer veterans and begin by assuming the existence from August 1921 of their underground within the Labor Battalion, are based on tenuous foundations.

Apart from the minutes of the Tiberias assembly there is another document, which almost certainly is the founding platform on which Hakibbutz was established. This paper is also minutes, but of another meeting, apparently attended only by Hashomer veterans. From these minutes, this was clearly a gathering with an express purpose and underlying ideology, intended to formulate goals and patterns of organization. Here, too, positions were stated against separate organization, but this time the predominant mood was different and the majority tended toward establishing a parallel and complementary framework to that of the Hagana. It is noteworthy that when steps toward forming Hakibbutz were being taken, the name was explicitly mentioned in the minutes. Furthermore, only Hashomer veterans were involved in this; invitations to the crucial founding meeting were not extended to other elements in the Labor Battalion, who were brought in only at a later stage. Hakibbutz was established in late 1922 or early 1923, as attested by the following evidence from the minutes: (a) Manya Shohat was among the participants: she had left the country on 27 or 28 June 1921 for North America as a member of the Histadrut mission to the workers of the United States and Canada. She most probably returned in July 1922, for on 24 July she reported on the mission to the Histadrut executive committee.[32] Hence, the meeting was bound to have been held after the date of her return from America. (b) The minutes mention Yosef Hecht, apparently as a leader of the Hagana. As far as is known, Hecht first joined the Defense Committee in November 1922, so that the meeting must have been held after that date. (c) The meeting considered such subjects as transfer of arms, storing arms at Kefar Gil'adi, the creation of an arms industry, and the establishment of a military school, all of which attest to a date later than that of the Tiberias assembly, namely, late 1922 or early 1923. (d) The minutes note that two former Hashomer members were on the Defense Committee: the provisional Defense Committee appointed at the beginning of November 1922 included Shmuel Hefter and Haim Shturman –

two former members of Hashomer. (e) If this meeting had taken place before the Tiberias assembly, there is no doubt that it would have been mentioned in one way or another there. The fact that at Tiberias there was no allusion whatever, not the merest hint, to such a meeting and that it resulted in the creation of a separate organization, shows that the meeting under discussion took place after the Tiberias assembly; from the participation of Manya Shohat and the status of Yosef Hecht it could only have convened at the end of 1922 or the beginning of 1923. From all the foregoing the founding of Hakibbutz, in consequence of this meeting, must be dated to late 1922 or early 1923, before the Ein Harod episode, and not 6 August 1921 as has been accepted until now.[33]

There is no mention of the location of the meeting deciding on the establishment of Hakibbutz. However, according to the testimony of Nahum Horowitz, Pinhas Shneorson and Yosef Harit, it was apparently at Kefar Gil'adi.[34] This is supported by the recollections of Moshe Levit, a Hashomer veteran. Levit was among the Hashomer people who joined the Labor Battalion early on, and, together with Zvi Nadav, was elected to the Battalion committee. After telling of his own and his comrades work in security in the Battalion, which included training young people of the *Third Aliya*, instruction in the use of firearms, which they took from the Kefar Gil'adi store, and night marches, Levit describes the place where Hakibbutz was apparently founded. Word of the planned meeting was passed from person to person in absolute secrecy, and the former Hashomer people gathered with the Shohat couple at Kefar Gil'adi:

About twenty of us literally squeezed into a cave at the foot of the southern slope of the kibbutz, by the spring. This cave had served as Hashomer's main arms store even after the official dissolution of the association. It was dark inside and the light of a few flickering lamps only added to the mystery of the event. The atmosphere was somewhat strange, gathering in secret and hiding it from our friends in the Battalion and the party, from our comrades in the Hagana and the Histadrut. In short, to form an underground. I, at least, had a feeling of uneasiness, as if a group of plotters was gathering there. But after some words spoken by Yisrael and Manya that sensation within me melted away. And why? Because then an accounting was made, and the finger of guilt was pointed at those who had forced us to break up Hashomer, but when the day of reckoning came, when the bloody events burst forth, they did not know how to stanch the flow.

Levit goes on to say that the gathering was so secret that many members of Kefar Gil'adi did not know about it. The discussions lasted an entire day, and the chief speaker was Manya Shohat, who largely set the tone. Her main argument did not include the revival of Hashomer at all, but the right means that the Yishuv must adopt in order to contend with the future security situation.[35] She harshly criticized the helplessness displayed by the Yishuv in the events of May 1921. As Levit recalled, she spoke with great emotion:

> "I do not understand – Where are we?!" Manya burst out angrily. "Jews are being slaughtered here as in the pogroms in Russia and no one reacts! If that is not enough, the English have taken Arab officers into the police, who cooperate with the rioters."

Later in her speech Manya Shohat demanded that her comrades sentence to death anyone who harmed Jews. Nor was she lenient with her partners from the Hashomer days: "If in the Yishuv, the Histadrut and the party they do not understand the gravity of the situation, the members of Hashomer must organize, secretly even, and take matters in their own hands." Manya Shohat's stirring words, Levit relates, were effective and swept away the hesitations of those present. After her speech, Yisrael Shohat read out the regulations and set out the course of action of the new body they had then established, which was then given the name "The Company."[36]

Levit's memoirs match the minutes of this meeting, not those of the Tiberias assembly. It seems, then, that Hakibbutz, the body with many names, was founded at Kefar Gil'adi. (The cave was most likely that near the rise called Giv'at Hashoket "Trough Hill". The rise was given that name because the Kefar Gil'adi flock was watered there, from the spring mentioned by Levit. Today the spring is run into a pipeline from the quarry, and the water is collected in tanks. The spring had three sources, and it still yields 20 cubic meters an hour. The cave was situated not far from Giv'at Hashoket, close by the path leading to Margaliot. It was spacious, with remains from the Crusader period in it. The cave was destroyed by heavy machinery, for no reason, in 1957–8.)

There is no doubt that what led to the Tiberias assembly, and eventually to the establishment of Hakibbutz, was the inactivity of the Hagana and the lack of trust, which constantly grew greater, in the British regime. The turning point may be seen as the May 1921 events, which were so traumatic, and also the dissolution of the remnants of the war battalions. Evidence that these were the main factors in the development of matters as portrayed may be found in Levit's testimony and in the recollections of the people themselves. The picture is of a drawn-out, evolutionary process, in which the Hashomer people became gripped by despair caused by the complacency and aimlessness of the Zionist and Yishuv bodies, and of the Hagana itself. These were the circumstances that impelled them to initiatives of their own. This is attested by Zvi Nadav, and it is generally the view even of History of the Hagana.[37]

In his diary Yosef Harit describes the grim effect of the May 1921 events. Following them, and after consultation with Manya Shohat, he decided to leave Kefar Gil'adi and head south to Tel Aviv to operate within the Hagana. Harit notes his distress at the negligence and indifference he found everywhere in Hagana activity. Harit, moreover, places the blame on Golomb's circle who, in his opinion, tried to remove his friends from acting in the Hagana because the rival group "wishes by all means to be in control, both for selfish reasons and for reasons of party status. This does not accord with our views." Everyone, including the workers, relied on the protection that the Mandatory authorities would provide for the Yishuv in times of trouble.

In light of this intolerable situation, he and his comrades decided to act on their own accord, and to concentrate on two subjects: arms acquisition and the formation of trained units in the Labor Battalion: "In every company a select group, unofficial but known to the members of the Battalion center, was organized." Harit himself was responsible for this activity.

To highlight the indifference to defense, not only among the general public and the workers but also among many in the Ahdut Ha'avoda leadership, Harit tells of a meeting between a delegation of members of the erstwhile Hashomer and David Remez, at which the delegation called for the mobilization of funds for arms acquisitions. Remez was entirely unmoved by the delegation's arguments and reasoning, and told them to drop the subject. As far as he was concerned, the time had come to stop playing with *bikselach* (Yiddish for rifles), because henceforth the British would attend to the safety of the Jewish Yishuv in Palestine.[38]

The central area of activity of Hakibbutz following its formation was in various frameworks of the Labor Battalion. But its vista transcended the Battalion and also extended to other geographical regions.

It is commonly held that Hakibbutz consisted of 60–70 people,[39] and included groups from various strata such as Hashomer veterans, young members of the former association, seven graduates of the Herzlia Gymnasia who had served in the Ottoman army and the Jewish Battalion, and young people of the *Third Aliya*.[40] A large part of these were concentrated in Kefar Gil'adi, which became the main base of Hakibbutz. The Hashomer veterans, headed by Yisrael and Manya Shohat, played a central role. Active with them were Pinhas Shneorson, Yosef Nahmani, Nahum Horowitz, Meir Spector, Zvi Nadav, Yosef Harit, Yerahmiel Lukacher (Luka) and others.

The Labor Battalion had its own defense committee, elected by the Battalion council. Not all members of the committee knew of the existence of Hakibbutz, whose participants had great influence over the committee. It should be stressed that the leaning of the Battalion toward wide autonomy included the security issue also, and this suited the interests of Hakibbutz.[41] Hakibbutz operated in such great secrecy that leading people in the Battalion did not know of its existence. Hanokh Rokhel, a leader of the Battalion, who appeared for the defense of the Hashomer veterans before the Clarification Commission of the Histadrut at the end of 1926, knew nothing of the existence of Hakibbutz.[42]

The organization had a managing committee, and also an elected council.[43] At times a general meeting of its members would convene.[44]

The ideology of Hakibbutz may be learned essentially from two documents. One is the minutes of its founding meeting in late 1922 or early 1923.[45] The other is a speech attributed to Meir Spector delivered in 1926.[46]

At the center of the founding meeting of Hakibbutz were Yisrael and Manya Shohat, who set forth its ideological grounds for and formulated its goals. In Yisrael Shohat's opening speech the *avant-gardist* note is already evident, with the faith in the ability of the few to forge the way and lead the masses to common goals: "In every people, in a historically difficult age some small group of people forms who are the living, vital material that appears boldly and vigorously, and they are able to draw the masses in their wake. We observe this manifestation in the Bolshevik revolution and in Ireland, etc." In the ensuing discussion no one disputed the need for the formation of the new body or the *avant-gardist* concept, but the question arose as to the nature of the relationship between the *avant-garde* and the national and class institutions – the classic question of the nature of the relations between the pioneer and the general camp. As Haim Shturman put it, "I really think that our Hakibbutz is best qualified to implement these tasks we define for ourselves. But we are also considering acting for the people or for the workers' class, and how shall we go about it without first making contact with the various institutions? Therefore, I propose making contact with the institutions involved in this work, because we shall not be able to accomplish all the activities on our own accord, and there are things that the institutions will not agree to. I raise this question and think it should be discussed." Others too raised the problem of the relationship with the Hagana in particular and the Histadrut in general.

Manya Shohat responded to all these doubts and hesitations in the classic fashion of every *avant-garde* since the days of the French Revolution. "If inwardly we are conscious that we are doing what is necessary and correct, then we have the moral right to do it without always considering the official institutions. We wish to fulfill tasks that make it impossible for us to be always under the control of the institutions. We of course must be careful not to err in respect of our morality. There should be no personal gain from this work, but we can only do what we find true and right."[47] In other words, here Manya Shohat fully applied Rousseau's doctrine whereby a social group representing the "general

will," which was the objective good, had the right, despite its being a
minority, to guide and lead the people. Rousseau held in addition that
freedom meant rational identification with the "general will," and that
whoever did not identify with it should have freedom forced upon him.
The meaning of this was that the element of coercion, in addition to the
element of belonging, was inherent in the *avant-gardist* approach. These
views expressed by Manya Shohat were not entirely alien and remote,
with certain qualifications, from Eliahu Golomb, Berl Katznelson and
David Ben-Gurion.[48] Not by chance, it was Manya Shohat who so clearly
and unequivocally presented the radical *avant-gardist* approach granting
the right of independence to the *avant-garde* group representing the
"general will." More than anyone else among the Hashomer veterans,
Manya Vilboshevitz-Shohat had been imbued with these views since the
early days of her activity as a revolutionary leader in Russia. Nevertheless,
she seems to have been left isolated in this extreme outlook. Her comrades
in Hakibbutz were pragmatic rather than ideological, and hence they also
took a different position throughout the years in their attitude to the
Hagana, which they wanted to encourage and stimulate; or they wished
to do what the Hagana failed to do, but not to replace it.

Great importance should be attached to the unequivocal position of
Yisrael Shohat, who replied to the above question that "in my opinion
this is not a question, because we are not a party; each of us can hold
whatever views he wishes and belong to any party he wishes. We do not
encompass all the liberation movements. We only grasp certain occasions
in that movement." Corroboration of this view of the founders of
Hakibbutz is found in Meir Spector's speech of 1926. True, regarding this
speech it may be argued that the Hakibbutz position crystallized much
later against the background of the splitting of the Labor Battalion, and
it was intended to save Hakibbutz from a similar fate by removing it from
the political cauldron; but such a claim cannot be made for the minutes
of the founding meeting held some four years earlier.

The conclusion arising from the foregoing is that from the start of its
existence Hakibbutz considered itself a body with no special political
goals of its own. Furthermore, it saw itself as a non-party group, which
in no way engaged in politics, and it centered entirely on one subject alone:
security. Therefore, its members might have included people belonging to
various parties. This clear picture, based on authentic documents,
dislodges the usual position in the historiography ascribing to Hakibbutz
political goals unconnected with defense and the liberation of the nation.

As stated, the concern of Hakibbutz was strictly security, but it still
had a political purpose, albeit a national one. In Yisrael Shohat's words,
"the last war showed us that justice and honesty have no value unless there
is a force behind it to protect it and insist on it. We wish to prepare in our

people that force capable of enduring and demanding their liberation as a nation . . . We desire to create an activist revolutionary force, which will protect the national and social assets of the people." Spector too, about four years later, identified with this view of Shohat's, and stated that the central motive that guided the people of Hakibbutz was "to fulfill an important and responsible task in the liberation of the nation." Although there were others who shared this goal, Hakibbutz was unique in that it was capable of translating a bare ideal into the language of action. In the speeches of others, especially Alexander Zayd and Manya Shohat, there is the assumption that the new body, despite its being non-party, will have a special link with the workers' class. Again, it is important to stress that the speakers emphasized the connection to the entire class, not just to a particular party or some political grouping.

As for ways and means of attaining the goals, the founding meeting took the following resolutions: infiltration of government ministries; planning a military school to prepare professional men "so that we shall have a number of members versed in the arts of war and strategy in the full sense of the term according to the latest method in Europe"; development of a military industry; and naturally, all to be accomplished in absolute secrecy. The principle of secrecy was repeated incessantly in the speeches of those assembled. One of the means determined for achieving the goals was terror, which Yisrael Shohat regarded as an additional educational method for the masses, indicating that not only was there mere talk but action as well. Another means was "taking by force."

Paragraph C of the founding charter concerns the acceptance of members. It was resolved that the committee would decide upon candidacy by majority vote, and actual acceptance of a new member required a two-thirds majority of the general meeting. Paragraph E deals with the discipline demanded of members of Hakibbutz, which must be absolute. For violations of discipline a member would face trial by his peers, and until the trial he would be subject to total prohibition from all activity. "For betrayal the penalty is expulsion from Hakibbutz until death." The term "Hakibbutz" as the title of the new body appears throughout the discussions of the founding assembly.[49]

From the second document, the speech by Meir Spector in early 1926, more may be learnt about the circumstances of the founding of Hakibbutz, the course it followed and its world view.

The speech opened with a review of the historic path of Hashomer, which in the *Second Aliya* era dedicated itself to "conquest and defense." After the hardships of the war "the horizons seemed to clear – the dream was on the way to realization; through certain causes the land was given to us and we were on the threshhold of the Jews' state." The *Third Aliya* began and the need was felt for the unification of the workers' class, "which would stress its stand on the creation of the Jewish state." When Ahdut Ha'avoda was founded the Hashomer members joined it and dissolved their own association. After that:

> A year passed – a wave of disappointment flooded the land. The dispersal of the battalions, the riots instigated through the government's incitement of the mob, the Galilee events [and] the decline in the political level in general manifestly showed that the issue of the national home served England only as a means of pursuing her goals in the Near East. In fact, England was turning Palestine into war booty, and it was to become one of the imperial colonies.

The speech went on to survey before the audience Britain's perfidy, expressed in the compromising policy of Herbert Samuel, the White Paper, and the pro-Arab posture of the makers of British policy in Palestine. Against this grave background Hakibbutz was founded: "A handful of people dared to declare to themselves that they wished to liberate the land, a group (*kibbutz*) that would consolidate around itself the revolutionary forces, and on the appointed day it would be they who would initiate and realize the liberation of the land."

Spector enumerated the means determined to reach the goal: infiltration into the government institutions and influencing them; training of men in various fields "which will facilitate the war of liberation for us"; an emphasis on propaganda and intensification of influence in the classes of the nation, particularly the workers, "the most fervent and revolutionary bloc . . . " These goals were not achieved even partially, and hence confusion and unease were felt in Hakibbutz.

In the speaker's opinion, the Jewish people in the given situation had to fulfill three tasks, without which it could not exist: territorial concentration in Palestine, transition to productive life with the creation of a laboring people, and achievement of self-rule:

> I envisage this complex work in this way. The first task is accomplished by the entire people by means of a single large organization. The second task is accomplished by the parties in various ways. The third task is undertaken by Hakibbutz. This is what necessitates the existence of this Hakibbutz.

If the people wished to win freedom they had to rebel against the overlord, namely, Britain. The revolt had to be of the entire people, otherwise it would not succeed. If Hakibbutz wished to play a part in this process it "cannot be narrow." The national struggle preceded the social-economic struggle, whose purpose was to shape the state that the liberated people would establish. At this point the speaker reached the formulation of his chief conclusion. This was that not only did the national struggle take precedence over the social-economic struggle, but the latter struggle must be left to the parties while Hakibbutz would devote itself solely to the former:

> We and all the ranks of the people must discuss, must involve everyone . . .
> All the people must be imbued with consciousness of the removal of the
> foreign rule over national life, life in their land. For us the structure of the
> Jewish state is decidely not important. For us first of all it is important that
> it exist . . . And I, facing the question if we should direct our steps toward
> constant preaching and calling on the people to liberate itself, or developing
> in our midst various social slogans, am for the first. Time will accomplish
> the second.

Spector repeated the same idea later in his speech: "With this I shall end this time. For us, it is completely unimportant what the composition of the future Jewish state will be. For us it is necessary that such a state will exist here in the land – and released from any foreign yoke. On two visions [or 'fronts' – the Hebrew word used is ambiguous – Y.G.] we cannot work."[50]

The circumstances of the speech are not clear, nor is there absolute certainty that the speaker was Meir Spector. In any event, as distinct from the previous document considered, the minutes of the founding meeting and the charter of Hakibbutz, this is the speech of one individual reflecting his own view; but it is highly likely that it was also the opinion of at least some of his comrades if not most of them. Therefore, the speech is of great value, contributing substantially to an understanding of Hakibbutz.

To summarize, the following picture of Hakibbutz emerges from the two main documents: (a) Hakibbutz was created as a result of prolonged inactivity by the Hagana which, in practice, was under the responsibility of the Histadrut, and as a result of disaffection with Britain. Obvious landmarks for the latter were the events of May 1921 and the dispersal of the remnants of the war battalions. The May 1921 events highlighted the nonexistence, to all intents and purposes, of the Hagana. A first overt, organized expression of dissatisfaction with the disappointing performance of the Hagana was the Tiberias assembly held on 6 August 1921, but Hakibbutz itself was founded about a year later at a secret meeting of members of the former Hashomer at Kefar Gil'adi. (b) The name accepted by the founders and subsequently was Hakibbutz. (c) Even after its establishment, for some years Hakibbutz cooperated with the Hagana because it did not consider itself an alternative but a stimulant, a goad, and a stopgap. (d) Hakibbutz was non-party and had no party-political ambitions. It saw its cause solely in the sphere of security activity. (e) In the setting of Weizmann's policy and that of all sections of the Zionist movement, which was for cooperation with Britain, the position of Hakibbutz was exceptional, regarding Britain as an enemy against which a war of liberation had to be planned. (f) Hakibbutz was non-party but had a link with the workers' class. (g) The express and unequivocal purpose of Hakibbutz was the creation of a Jewish state in Palestine. (h) To achieve the goals Hakibbutz affirmed terror and also "taking by force." (i) Regarding the means of achieving the goals, it exhibited far-reaching vision and planned the establishment of a military industry and of a military school. (j) Hakibbutz had a clandestine organizational structure, which was authoritarian but also democratic.

2 The period of dualism

Following the events of May 1921 some movement in security occurred, especially in arms acquisitions, in the winter of 1921-2. But in general, after the impact of the disturbances faded and matters were restored to normal, complacency set in again and with it the activity of the Hagana declined. A meeting of the Zionist leadership on 5 November 1922 in London discussed the security of the Yishuv and once more adopted Jabotinsky's policy, which strove for the creation of an official army. This had the effect of contributing to the overall tendency. Following the decision taken there was a notable fall in financial support for the Hagana by the Zionist leadership.

The Histadrut too was obliged, in the period under review, to devote itself to other vital matters and the issue of the Hagana was pushed aside. As a result of these circumstances the Hashomer veterans became more tightly-knit, and transferred most of their activity to the Labor Battalion, where they found fertile ground and wide receptivity for their initiative experience and contribution. At the end of 1922 Eliahu Golomb retired from direct involvement in Hagana affairs for a lengthy seven-year period, some of it abroad.[51]

After that the Hagana sank into decay. It was carried on the shoulders of one man – Yosef Hecht. In the 1920s the Hagana was a nationwide organization on paper only. It may in fact be described as a jumble of local defense organizations linked by loose ties of confederation and maintaining some kind of connection with the center in Tel Aviv. Every branch looked after itself. Arms acquisition too was conducted on a local basis. In retrospect Yohanan Ratner, a specialist on the Hagana, defined the situation in the 1920s as "a very primitive form of federation."[52] The History of the Hagana, which undoubtedly presents the official account of the Hagana, states in the same spirit that "the organization of the Hagana in the 1920s was a kind of weak confederation of tens of small cells and three large branches . . . which accepted the authority of the center out of goodwill if it seemed worth their while."[53]

In sum, there is no dispute in the existing histories, which all portray the condition of the Hagana in the 1920s in the same vein. All describe it as diffuse, extremely decentralized and low-key, operated by few people. Only against this background is it possible to comprehend the actions of the Hashomer veterans and the formation of Hakibbutz. Their separate activity, and even the establishment of Hakibbutz, were evidently not as outrageous as *History of the Hagana* would like its readers to think. The actions well suited the circumstances described. Only the riots in 1929 jolted everyone concerned into a rude awakening that changed the face of the Hagana entirely. Only this harsh, violent explosion had a traumatic effect that shook "the Zionist movement and the Jewish Yishuv, and opened their eyes to see that there would be no resurrection of the Jewish people in Palestine if it did not take steps in good time to establish its own defensive force that would serve it in times of trouble against its enemies plotting to cut it down."[54]

Hakibbutz arose out of this awareness, which all the others attained only after 1929. It was not founded to act against the Hagana, but to devote itself to security needs that had been left unattended. This was great boldness and extraordinary ambition on the part of a tiny handful who, owing to the difficulties, succeeded in actualizing only a fraction of their goals. The *History of the Hagana* too, despite its virulently critical attitude toward the Hashomer veterans in those years, is forced to confess that Hakibbutz did not arise in opposition to the Hagana and did not regard itself as an external, alternative body to the Hagana, but was formed and acted "without cutting ties in any way with the Hagana."[55] Elsewhere it is admitted that

> Hakibbutz did not see itself as a competitor with the Hagana, but as a complementary organization, especially in the field of acquiring and storing arms. The intention was "to do what it (the Hagana committee) was not doing. In fact, the members of Hakibbutz and the Labor Battalion worked together with members of the Hagana wherever they came into contact (for example, Jerusalem) and even maintained personal relations with many of its activists.[56]

From this it is possible to understand the dualism and at times over-lapping roles of Hakibbutz members, who simultaneously belonged to the Hagana. The Hakibbutz members were at peace with themselves and saw no contradiction in this duplication; they were merely filling those lacunae that should have been dealt with by the Hagana. Moreover, some duplication lay in the fact that members of Hakibbutz were for the most part also members of Ahdut Ha'avoda, and a number of them were among its activists and its representatives on various bodies. This situation was possible only because of their grasp of the area of security and their being a non-party body in the political sphere. Therefore, the label attached to them by their rivals and the accusation that they were not only a security body "but also a political underground organization with far-reaching goals," with all its implications, have no basis in fact. Despite the charges, and despite the efforts at delegitimizing the Hashomer veterans, their opponents were obliged to retract their words and admit in the same breath that they contributed the "dream of revolt against the imperialist regime and the liberation of the people in their land. The story of Hakibbutz is the story of the daring attempt by this handful of people to undertake responsibility for accomplishing this national historic mission." In spite of the unending process of discredit, the truth is beginning to emerge.[57]

The period of dualism in relations between the Hashomer people and the Hagana continued over the years, until the break-up of the Labor Battalion and the dissolution of Hakibbutz in late 1926, early 1927. However, in terms of the nature of the dualism, the years under review may be divided into several subperiods or stages. The first was the stage of ideological opposition to the Hagana apparatus, which rested on the Ahdut Ha'avoda and the Histadrut establishment. At this stage, which lasted until the formation of Hakibbutz, the Hashomer people sought full cooperation and there was no separate activity. The second stage opened with the formation of Hakibbutz at the end of 1922. This was the stage of separate organization, but there was still much continuity in practical cooperation. This phase continued to the end of 1923. The Ein Harod episode was followed by the final stage, in which even practical cooperation between Hakibbutz and the Hagana almost ceased, although some fragile channels of connection remained.

The stage of ideological opposition actually began even before the dissolution of Hashomer, when a debate developed between Yitzhak Tabenkin and Eliahu Golomb on the one hand and Hashomer on the other over the nature, organization and control of the kind of security suited to the new conditions after the British conquest. As is known, the debate passed to Ahdut Ha'avoda with the transfer of security to its charge, and following the establishment of the Histadrut and its acceptance of responsibility for the Hagana, the discussion continued there. The Hashomer people did not hide their views and their opposition to the concept of Golomb and his group. Their position was known and presented in several frameworks, insofar as so sensitive a subject permitted this. In the debate Golomb enjoyed the backing of the party and Histadrut establishment, and so had the advantage. The Hashomer veterans set themselves up as an ideological opposition to Golomb and his adherents.

Nevertheless, the Hashomer people wished to be fully active in all aspects of the work of the Hagana. It is notable that the years in question were marked by interminable quarrels and disputes between the rival camps, and particularly between their respective heads, Yisrael Shohat and Eliahu Golomb. The strife arose over the differences in ideological perception, but principally from the lack of "chemistry" between the two men and absence of mutual respect. In addition, the quest for prestige and the power struggles cannot be disregarded. These caused mutual suspicion, which magnified the friction. The mistrust was particularly strong on the part of Golomb, from two causes: his sense of inferiority and the residue of the past. In many respects Golomb's was a Pyrrhic victory, as he well knew. In the terrible state of impoverishment – economic and human – the Hashomer people had the upper hand relatively, because they disposed of several dozens of devoted activists, with experience, discipline and loyalty, who could be relied on in security operations. Moreover, it was precisely the Hashomer people who found a common language with the young blood of the *Third Aliya* in the Battalion, which all agreed was the main human reservoir for the Hagana. Golomb could not match any of this, and hence his deep frustration. In addition, he was ambivalent toward the Hashomer people. On the one hand he appreciated their endeavor, their ability and their idealism, but on the other hand he lacked basic trust and was highly suspicious. Golomb apparently acquired this attitude as early as the days of the Herzlia Gymnasia and the Jaffa group, with the vilification, hostility and reservations evinced by wide circles in the Yishuv toward Hashomer. As a result of the political and personal rivalry in the early 1920s, in Golomb the resentments predominated. From all this it is possible to understand the oscillation in Golomb's attitude to the people of Hashomer in 1920–2. The picture that emerges is a man pursued by fears, when in truth in those years there was no real proof or grounds for his suspicions and apprehensions concerning the Hashomer people. Golomb was able to impart his negative feelings about Hashomer to his political patron Berl Katznelson, and to many others among the former "non-party men" and his friends from the Gymnasia and the battalions; thus he was largely responsible for the emasculation of the image of Hashomer men and their removal from the public stage and from work in defense.

In the literature critical of Hashomer it is stated that the first real cause for mistrust and that which allegedly proved their separatist organization was the despatch of Gershon Fleisher to Vienna to obtain arms for the Hagana. The label of sectionalism and separatism was attached to them already at this early stage, "because the attitude of the Hashomer people was expressed in the sending of Fleisher without Golomb's knowledge."[58]

At first sight the impression may be gained that Golomb headed the Defense Committee, an active body that convened periodically, made decisions and supervised their ongoing implementation. In fact, matters were otherwise. The Committee hardly operated. Its members had just then been appointed by the Histadrut council and did not act in concert. Golomb was not the head of the "command" but a member of the Committee. His importance and status were no greater than those of his senior Shohat, who was revered for his deeds in the time of the *Second Aliya*. Furthermore, in the vague and decentralized circumstances of Hagana activity there was nothing remarkable in Shohat sending Fleisher to Vienna on his own responsibility.

Surprising as it may seem, Fleisher's mission was not secret at all, but undertaken with the knowledge and support of the secretary of the Histadrut Executive Committee at the time, David Zakai (Zhukhovitsky), who also furnished Fleisher with a letter of recommendation, as follows:

> To our comrades!
> 1 April 1921. We hereby request all our friends to help our comrade Fleisher in all matters for which he has traveled abroad – the acquisition of means and items required by us in the country.
> On behalf of the Executive Committee of the Histadrut in Palestine,
> The Secretary, D. Zhukhovitsky[59]

It is not clear when Fleisher left for Vienna. The letter of recommendation is dated 1 April 1921, but it is most likely that Fleisher left only after the outbreak of violence on 1 May, a vivid description of which is found in his memoirs:

> The young folk of Tel Aviv assembled near the Herzlia Gymnasia, and sought out the instructors and commanders; they looked for the many weapons that had been smuggled previously from the stores of the British Army, rifles, bullets and grenades, so as to rush to the aid of the 16,000 Jews of Jaffa.
> To their great dismay there was no one to turn to. No instructors, no arms and the commanders also were tardy. The rumor went about that the arms hidden in Tel Aviv had disappeared. Shifting sands had covered everything.
> Meanwhile Krinitzi and Aharon Sverdlov arrived and announced that one storehouse with 20 pistols, 8 rifles and 5 grenades had been found. They opened the storehouse, and lo and behold the arms had vanished.[60]

On his arrival in Vienna, Fleisher met Neta Goldberg (Harpaz), who then worked for the Palestine Office. He told Goldberg of the purpose of his visit and received a sum of money from him for expenses. He also went to the office of the World Union of Poaley Zion, which was active in Vienna, where he met Zalman Rubashov (Shazar), Berl Locker, Shlomo Kaplansky and others. Fleisher informed the group of his mission and from them too he received assistance for the arms acquisition. In the following months others cooperated with Fleisher, including Berl Katznelson, Rivka Shertok (Hoz), who was then staying in Vienna,[61] and

Dov Hoz. In November 1921 Yisrael Shohat joined the group and in 1922 so did Eliahu Golomb. In light of these facts, the claim that Fleisher's mission was kept secret and conducted behind Golomb's back, and the use made of Fleisher's mission to discredit the Hashomer people as plotters and troublemakers, disreputable, contentious and sectarian, are defamatory and remote from the truth.[62]

Another incident used to cast suspicion against the Hashomer people and to sow the seeds of bitterness against them was the so-called beehives affair. This originated with the need for large amounts of weapons in Palestine, so the arms acquisition group in Vienna looked for cheap ways of transporting the necessary consignments to the country. Eventually it was decided in Vienna at the end of 1921 to send the arms in small wooden beehives fitted with a double wall. To save money it was planned to sell the hives in Palestine after they had served their purpose. The hives containing the hidden arms were sent to Palestine to the address of a carpentry cooperative in Haifa managed by Yitzhak Rosenberg, a member of Hashomer, to be forwarded to Yehuda Wolfson, also a former Hashomer man and a member of the Labor Battalion at Ein Harod. By misfortune, on 17 December 1921 one of the hives broke open at Haifa port when it was dropped by an Arab porter, and the arms were discovered. The authorities confiscated 300 pistols and 17,000 rounds of ammunition; this was a serious blow. The police arrested Yitzhak Rosenberg, who was later acquitted for lack of evidence.[63] After the event Eliahu Golomb spread rumors that the shipment had been intended for the Hashomer people and not for the Hagana. On the basis of this claim/assumption Golomb considered the affair an act of treachery against the Hagana and yet another demonstration of the disloyalty and separatism characteristic of the Hashomer people.

Shortly after the arms were discovered, in January 1922, Golomb arrived in Vienna. After a brief clarification conducted there he realized he had been utterly wrong. He was forced to withdraw his accusations and admit to the innocence and devotion of the Hashomer men in Vienna who were engaged in acquiring and shipping the arms, but the damage had already been done. The constantly repeated charges of splitting and disloyalty, the suspicions that had been spread, the vilification – all generated deep resentment in the offended parties. Therefore, the withdrawal of one specific accusation was insufficient to rectify relations, which continued to deteriorate.[64]

Throughout the entire period of frictions and quarrels attempts were made to continue with joint work. One such effort, among many, was in January 1922, when the two rivals found themselves involved in arms acquisition in Vienna. Shohat and Golomb held several awkward and unpleasant conversations, in which they leveled mutual charges against each other, but for all that they agreed to continue the common work. According to Golomb, the reasons for the renewed internal peace was his realization that the time was not right for strife "at home," for

> our task now is to fortify the land and organize the work so that the workers and those really responsible for this task – the working community – will not be removed from directing it. In the country there is a clearly recognized tendency to remove us from directing the work. Therefore, we decided to place the entire management of the effort in the hands of a committee that would be elected in the country, and it would appoint the workers in Palestine and abroad who would be answerable to it. After this agreement (on Y's part) we began to work in cooperation.[65]

In terms of historical fact it is agreed that the work of arms acquisition in Vienna began with the arrival of Gershon Fleisher there, apparently in May 1921. By January 1922 a highly successful operation was under way. The backbone of the group was the Hashomer people: Fleisher, Moshe Levit, Shmuel Hefter, Moshe Zhaludin and Yisrael Shohat. Eliahu Golomb joined them only in January 1922 when the acquisitions had been proceeding intensively and successfully for about six months; so it is strange that *History of the Hagana* sees fit to praise the great contribution to the arms acquisitions, of which there is no proof at all, by Golomb: "With the arrival of Eliahu Golomb in Vienna the work was reorganized." On 16 July 1922, as a result of carelessness on the part of Golomb, the network was discovered by the Vienna police. Golomb himself was arrested and others were obliged to wind up their business in the city, depart and seek alternative, less favorable bases for the work of acquisition.[66]

Another incident that aroused fierce anger, intensified mutual mistrust and added to the bitter resentment, was the "millstone business" at the beginning of July 1922. In March 1922 Shmuel Hefter opened a new route for smuggling arms into Palestine, overland from Beirut port to Kefar Gil'adi. After making the necessary arrangements Hefter informed the group in Vienna, who despatched 15 machine-guns and ammunition concealed in a cement mixer and steamroller. The consignment arrived at Beirut port at the end of March. It was registered there as tax-exempt agricultural implements, and therefore did not require inspection. Hefter and Nahum Horowitz of Kefar Gil'adi hired Arab carters with mules, which were harnessed to the cement mixer, and by devious routes they arrived at the village of Dir Mamas, not far from Metulla. Members of Kefar Gil'adi went there with transport animals to replace the Arab carters. The journey to Metulla took two days. At Metulla the cement mixer broke down, and so the Kefar Gil'adi people had to remove the hidden weapons at night and transport them to their kibbutz. The steamroller was brought by a different route later by lorry. The contraband weapons were sold to Hagana branches throughout the country. From then on the Beirut–Kefar Gil'adi route became the highway for smuggling arms into Palestine. The members of Kefar Gil'adi invested great effort, many workdays and not a few sleepless nights in operating the new route. All this was done with great devotion and unstinting loyalty arising from the sense that they were engaged in sacred work. It is important to stress yet again that the arms smuggled in were sold to all the Hagana branches across the country that had the money to purchase them.

At the beginning of July 1922 Yehoshu'a Ztolovsky, a supporter of Eliahu Golomb, was sent by the latter to Beirut to handle a regular consignment of arms that had arrived from Vienna. But this time Golomb gave express instructions to Ztolovsky to break with the usual system, namely, to involve the Kefar Gil'adi people in the transport of the arms but to bypass the kibbutz and take the consignment, which was hidden in two millstones, directly south. Ztolovsky did as Golomb ordered and on reaching Beirut took the items from the port, hired an Arab carter, loaded the two millstones onto the cart, and set off for the south. Ztolovsky's aim was to reach Rosh Pina, where he was supposed to hand over the shipment to Haim Shturman, who was then the Hagana quartermaster. Not far from the Arab village of Waziya (to the west of the northern shore of Lake Hulah on the Metulla–Rosh Pina road), the cart struck a rock and overturned, and one of its wheels was shattered. Having no other alternative, and anxious about the weapons, Ztolovsky turned to the Kefar Gil'adi members for help, telling them about the hidden arms. They persuaded him to rest at their kibbutz until dawn, and not to worry about the arms until then. The following day, when Ztolovsky returned to the place, he found to his surprise that one of the two millstones was missing. After informing the Kefar Gil'adi people about this a search was made for the stone but to no avail. Ztolovsky had no choice but to go to Kinneret, where he found Haim Shturman to whom he related what had happened. Shturman sensed that the Kefar Gil'adi people were behind the loss. After clarifications, which reached as far as David Ben-Gurion, who had then taken office as a member of the secretariat of the Histadrut Executive Committee, and with the intervention of Manya Shohat, Yosef Hecht and Haim Shturman, the contents of the millstone were sent to the Hagana stores.

The *History of the Hagana* presents the episode in full detail, concluding with the following charge against the members of Kefar Gil'adi:

There was a clear hint here that the strings of the arms smuggling into the country were in the hands of the Kefar Gil'adi members, and they refused to release their hold. The complex of mistrust and fears on the part of Eliahu and his men grew even worse. Eliahu Golomb and his comrades reached the conclusion "that it was necessary to put an end to their tricks, for if we do not have the strength for this we had better give up all this business."[67]

The conclusion reached is not only surprising in itself, but remarkable for its one-sidedness. Reading the story it is impossible to ignore several obvious questions, one of them being, who empowered Golomb to instruct Ztolovsky to bypass Kefar Gil'adi? It should be stressed yet again that Golomb was not the commander of the Hagana. The Hagana had an appointed directing body, the Defense Committee, in which Golomb was a peer, but not the first among his peers. In terms of age, seniority, prestige and experience, Yisrael Shohat was superior to Golomb. The latter operated, in those months, with Shohat and with the entire group in Vienna, and on Golomb's own testimony he at that time settled the differences between himself and Shohat, and joint work was agreed upon. Moreover, in the minutes of a meeting they held on arms acquisitions in Vienna in Janury 1922, it was expressly stated that "no decision is taken except in the presence of members of the directorate in Vienna. Copies of all letters written are kept."[68] In light of these facts it seems that Golomb skirted the decisions and the understanding between himself and Shohat, and in secret, of his own accord, without the knowledge of any of the leaders of the group in Vienna, he instructed his trustee how to act regarding arms sent to Beirut. By any objective standards this was an unacceptable deed, and therefore the account rendered in the official history of the Hagana is contrary to fact. Instead of making charges against Golomb it makes them against the Hashomer people and the members of Kefar Gil'adi.

Furthermore, the stigma attached to the members of Kefar Gil'adi is manifestly unjust, and the description given, particularly its conclusion, is wrong and a grave perversion of truth and logic. The truth is otherwise: essentially, the members of a small settlement, beset with hardship and grinding toil in the far north, devoted days and nights to the central need of national defense, namely, arms smuggling for the Hagana. These dedicated people learned by accident that someone was questioning their loyalty for no reason, and secretly, without their knowledge and against all accepted practice until then, was attempting to bypass them in moving weapons south. The depth of their dismay, humiliation and anger is clearly understandable, and so, therefore, is their reaction. Here too the history books have turned matters upside down, and instead of blaming and criticizing Golomb they accuse Kefar Gil'adi. Not only this, but to add to and exacerbate the discredit of the Hashomer people, *History of the Hagana* uses this episode as a pretext for applying to the Hashomer people in general and the Kefar Gil'adi members in particular epithets such as subversive, divisive, sectarian, disloyal, and the like. This is in fact the conclusion that emerges explicitly and implicitly from the book's account of the affair. Again the facts have been utterly corrupted. From the summary of the incident it is clearly implied that in the disputes at the time in the Hagana not only was the allegedly separatist and self-seeking group of Hashomer people active, but opposing them stood "Eliahu and his people," and later "Eliahu Golomb and his comrades." The presentation makes it appear that two groups were struggling for control and power. In any event, it was impossible to accuse the members of Hakibbutz or "The Circle" of the deed, as the historiography does, because it was done by the members of Kefar Gil'adi alone. This was determined as early as 1926 by the Histadrut committee known as the Clarification Commission on the Tel Hai issue appointed by David Ben-Gurion.[69]

Thus, none of the instances intended to prove the existence of a separate framework of Hashomer people already at the end of 1921 and during 1922 is grounded in reality. In one of the three incidents supposedly attesting to the disloyalty, sectionalism and separatism of the Hashomer people, Eliahu Golomb himself withdrew his accusations; in another, the Fleisher affair, History of the Hagana is wrong and misleading; and in the "millstone business" the innocence and justness of the Hashomer and Kefar Gil'adi people as against the absolute guilt of Eliahu Golomb are easily proved. Therefore, all the claims set out in the historiography approving the "proper" conduct of Golomb by virtue of the assumption that an underground of Hashomer and its allies in the Battalion existed already in 1921–2 are without foundation. Golomb's behavior in those years may be put down only to the residue of his hostility toward Hashomer, his excessive suspicion and his sense of inferiority arising from helplessness and power struggles.

As stated, occasionally there were attempts at peacemaking between the combatants. After the temporary peace achieved in January 1922 between Shohat and Golomb in Vienna, a further effort was made in August 1922 when Ben-Gurion, Katznelson, Yisrael Shohat, Golomb and Dov Hoz met in Carlsbad and discussed the Hagana in the hope of bringing about renewed cooperation between the two. At a meeting held in Shohat's absence, Golomb adopted an extreme and ultimative position, demanding a decision between himself and Shohat. Katznelson and Ben-Gurion calmed the atmosphere at that time, and called for the continuation of joint activity, with the promise that on their return to Palestine they would convene for a comprehensive clarification of the issue.[70]

In October 1922 Golomb returned to Palestine and renewed the struggle with the aim of removing the Hashomer people from activity in the Hagana. At Tabenkin's suggestion the two sides stated their positions, first before the Executive Committee of Ahdut Ha'avoda. Eventually the debate moved to the Executive Committee of the Histadrut, which was not versed in the issue because not all the details were presented to it. Neither the party nor the Histadrut succeeded in settling the matter by compromise and understanding, and they did not attempt to rule between the two sides. As a way out, a new Defense Committee was elected in November 1922, consisting of Golomb, Shaul Meirov, Yosef Hecht, David Yaffe, Shmuel Hefter and Haim Shturman, which was intended to operate until the convening of the second Histadrut conference in February 1923. In the new body only Shaul Meirov (Avigur) and Yosef Hecht were in fact active. Nor was the new committee able to win domestic peace between the sides. When Golomb sailed for Europe in January 1923 on a mission, and when the Hashomer people shifted the focus of activity to the Labor Battalion at the end of 1922, the conflict between the two rival groups within the Hagana suddenly disappeared. The *History of the Hagana* admits that

> with the departure of the Hashomer people and their adherents in the Labor Battalion the young Hagana organization was struck a severe blow. Among the seceders were the finest activists of the Hagana, men with rich experience, who considered this work the purpose of their life, men with vision and broad perception; there was no one to replace them. The Hagana organization, whose wings were clipped, was forced into a corner and continued its existence in isolation and without support from the Yishuv institutions and in ceaseless conflict with the general indifference of the Yishuv.

It is not clear how these words of praise accord with the almost systematic effort by the authors of the official history of the Hagana to discredit and delegitimize the Hashomer people. The anomaly may be explained only by the ambivalence present even in that book over the Hashomer people, as it was present in the leader of the victorious camp in the Hagana, Eliahu Golomb, whose version the volume seeks to perpetuate. Moreover, at the end of 1922 the Hashomer people quitted the Hagana and left the arena free for their rivals, who now could realize their desires and elevate the organization to the high road. In fact, the opposite occurred.

The people of "vision and broad perception" withdrew, but there was no one to fill the gap they left. Golomb, who in fact got what he wanted, set off for Europe in 1923 (for six months), leaving behind a Hagana adrift in a sea of problems.[71] This is the time of passage from the first stage, of ideological opposition but full cooperation in the Hagana, to the second stage, of dualism, after the establishment of Hakibbutz, which was marked by separate organizational frameworks and continuation of partial cooperation.

3 Activities of Hakibbutz: separate frameworks

The Hakibbutz organization, as explained earlier in this chapter, was apparently formed at the end of 1922. This assumption, based on documents, well matches the foregoing account, namely, that the end of 1922 marked a turning point for the Hashomer people, who in fact concentrated their efforts in the Labor Battalion. But they did not leave the Hagana, nor did they consider leaving in the future. They saw nothing extraordinary in their being members of Hakibbutz and of the Hagana at once. However, *History of the Hagana* is right in stating that "in August–September 1922 two defense organizations in fact existed in the country, although formally the Labor Battalion had not severed its links with the Hagana organization of the Histadrut."[72] The clearest expression of this new stage was the actions carried out by Hakibbutz.

The assassination of Tawfiq Bey. Tawfiq Bey was an officer in the Jaffa police. He was regarded by many as directly responsible for the massacre at the immigrants' house in Jaffa in the disturbances of May 1921. In summer 1922 Tawfiq resigned from the police, and the rumor spread that he was the leader of a terrorist band that attacked Jews. The leadership of Hakibbutz, under pressure of Manya Shohat, resolved to assassinate him both for his part in the May 1921 events and as a warning for the future. Shortly before the day appointed for the act it was brought to the knowledge of Yosef Hecht, who was a kind of chairman of the Hagana Defense Committee, for his approval and also to prepare appropriate measures should the killing spark off riots. The Hakibbutz people obtained the impression that Hecht approved of the action that was to be taken.

The mission was given to Yerahmiel Lukacher (Luka), one of the Herzlia Gymnasia graduates in Hakibbutz. For support he took his friend from the Gymnasia and the Turkish army, Binyamin Bichman, and on 17 January 1923 the two set an ambush, in Manshiya-Jaffa, for Tawfiq Bey. The assassination was carried out as planned. It was the only political killing performed by Hakibbutz. After the action the Hakibbutz people resumed their other occupations.[73]

The great X ("the carriage business"). To realize visions, desires and plans, large financial resources were required which, of course, were not to be had. In the absence of real support from national and Histadrut bodies it was obvious that if Hakibbutz wished to break the stranglehold of lack of resources it had to find alternative financing. Bold plans were floated and the slightest shred of real or imagined information that could help them in their distress was eagerly grasped. Such was the attempt, which ended in disappointment, to raise chests of gold that the Turks, it was said, had dropped into the River Jordan in their flight.[74] Eventually the hopes were fulfilled through the great X.

The term X was the abbreviation for the word *expropriatsia* – expropriation. Its origins were in the revolutionary movement in Russia, in which various circles who found themselves in financial straits, which hampered their activities, "expropriated" money from capitalist institutions or personalities on the principle that the end justified the means. It is not surprising that ideas of this kind were rife among the Hashomer veterans and the Hakibbutz people. The minutes of the founding meeting of Hakibbutz refer explicitly to the concept of "taking by force."

The great X action, or "the carriage business" as was its code-name at the time, was carried out in November 1923 by members of Hakibbutz disguised as British policemen. So dressed, they arrested, in eastern Upper Galilee, Jewish smugglers who brought gold rings from Lebanon, which was under French Mandate, to Palestine. The action was performed with the aid of Avraham Haikind, a veteran of the American-Jewish battalion who had settled in the country. A sum of 15,000 gold sovereigns was stolen. The police found a lead to the perpetrators of the theft, but with the help of Jewish police officers the traces were erased.

The sum that was taken was extremely large in terms of those days, and it allowed Hakibbutz to achieve some of its goals in the following years, until its dissolution.[75]

The central arms store at Kefar Gil'adi. Following "the carriage business" Hakibbutz possessed the means for obtaining large quantities of arms. Once acquired, these had to be stored in suitable conditions, and for this purpose the central arms store was dug at Kefar Gil'adi. The quarrying was done in conditions of extreme secrecy, at night and only by a very small group of people. These were Zvi Kroll, Matityahu Stein, Mordechai Teitelman and Yehiel Brinman. The work took an entire year. This was the store whose contents were placed at the disposal of the Yishuv in the 1929 disturbances. The arms accumulated at Kefar Gil'adi through ceaseless toil over many years by those stigmatized with sectarianism, isolationism and other such calumnies were a contribution of tremendous importance in the stormy days of 1929.[76]

"Valley Industry". In 1924 the Hakibbutz members attempted to lay the foundations of a military industry by establishing an arms factory. A cooperative was formed in Afula with the name Valley Industry, with the intention of manufacturing arms and ammunition under the camouflage of agricultural machinery repairs. The head of the enterprise was David Fish, a Hashomer veteran and member of Hakibbutz. The professional man was Naftali Shneorson of the Labor Battalion, who had some experience, having worked in an arms and ammunitions factory in Russia. The

plant was set up on a five-dunam plot obtained from Yehoshu'a Hankin near the railway station. It operated for two years and was then closed owing to the losses it made. It seems that the settlements in the northern valleys and the Galilee preferred to send their agricultural machines for repair to the German experts working in Tiberias and Haifa, rather than Afula. Unable to survive economically, and with no subsidizing factor, the factory closed during the days of the great crisis in 1926.

In parallel Hakibbutz attempted to establish a chemicals factory as a future subsidiary of the arms industry. This effort was with the help of Dr Yeivin, who hailed from the same town in Russia as Yisrael Shohat. Shohat helped him to emigrate to Palestine and establish the factory. Attached to Dr Yeivin was Yisrael Simkin, a member of Hakibbutz from the Gymnasia, who was given the task of learning the subject.[77]

The military school at Tel Yosef. In May 1924 Yisrael Shohat, Pinhas Shneorson and Yerahmiel Lukacher traveled to Europe for several purposes, among them arms acquisition; this was now conducted in Germany, and the arms were transported over the well-worn route – Beirut port and thence to Kefar Gil'adi. Another purpose was the enrollment of Lukacher at a military academy in Germany to study military science there and then bring his newly acquired knowledge to Palestine. Through Dr Yeivin's help Shohat made contact with a German general of the First World War, one of the commanders of the successful partisan war waged by the Germans in their colonies in Africa. (This was General Paul von Lettow-Vorbeck, who won fame as a brilliant tactician in the war against the British in South Africa which ended only in 1918. On his return to Germany he joined the General Staff and became renowned as a nationalist officer. He took part in the famous putsch of Kapp in 1920, and for that reason was obliged to resign. In 1924 he had no official standing.)

Lukacher failed to be accepted at the German military academy, and it was settled that the General, and other military men, would give him private tuition. In some of the classes he was joined by Yehoshu'a Isaac (Eshel), who was then studying at the art school in Berlin. The level of studies was high. Lukacher also learned what was required to establish an officers' school. Both Shohat and Lukacher were greatly influenced by the concept then dominant in the German army – namely the limitation by the Versailles peace treaties of the army, to 100,000 men. Because of this restriction the Germans built up a core army of officers and sergeants which, in the hour of need, could in a very short time become the backbone of a far larger army. Lukacher had the task of bringing this method to Palestine and creating the kernel of a Jewish army in secret.[78]

Meanwhile, even before Lukacher completed his studies in Berlin, the first military school for instructors and commanders was set up at Tel

Yosef in July–September 1924. Dr Zev von Weisel and Dr Otto Hahn, who had served as officers in the Austrian army, were invited to direct the first course. This was attended by several dozens of young men from the Batallion, who for that purpose were released from work. The level was that of sergeants. A great obstacle was that the two chief instructors delivered their lectures on theory in German, which most of the participants did not know. Nor were the lecturers knowledgeable in the conditions of Palestine, and they made no effort to adapt the teaching they imparted to their students to the local circumstances. Practical training, namely field exercises, was more effective. The course was a one-time event, and had no continuation. Nevertheless, most of the participants were chosen to study at the military school that opened about 18 months later at the same place.[79]

This was in winter 1926, after Lukacher completed his studies in Berlin and returned to Palestine. The administrator of the Tel Yosef military school was Yosef Harit and its chief instructors were Yerahmiel Lukacher, Yehoshu'a Isaac (Eshel) and Binyamin Bichman. The students spent half the day at farmwork and half the day studying military theory. As camouflage the course was entitled "Course for Trainers in Physical Exercise." Each course lasted three months; three courses were held, at which over 50 people studied. The students had at their disposal a library of military literature in German and Russian, brought from Germany by Lukacher and Isaac. The curriculum was based on a combination of theory and practical training. There were also field exercises, in which dozens of members of the Battalion participated, in addition to the students. The worsening disintegration in the Battalion that year, and the growing conflict between the "right" and the "left," put an end, among others, to this enterprise too.[80]

Development of aviation. Yisrael Shohat and Zvi Nadav were among the first in the country to realize, as early as the 1920s, the importance of the development of aviation. This was then taking its first steps in the country, in the civilian and military spheres, and Shohat and Nadav were among those who were highly impressed by the new field of activity. Nadav spent the latter half of the 1920s and the early 1930s in France, where he studied aeronautical engineering. On returning to Palestine he became a pioneer, together with Shohat, in civil aviation in the Yishuv.

Already in the May 1921 disturbances aircraft had proved their worth as military equipment; in addition their performance on the western front in the First World War was well known. In the disturbances British aircraft played an extremely important role in saving Petah Tikva and Hadera from the Arabs. In addition, flying and the opportunities inherent in its development fascinated people of a qualitative *avant-gardist* world outlook.

From Shohat's own account, he showed initiative in this subject as early as 1921, when he requested Harry Sacher, an English Jewish lawyer prominent in the Zionist movement, to obtain a licence for him to form a private aviation company in Palestine. The Mandatory authorities rejected the application despite Sacher's efforts. According to Shohat, he still did not concede, and even when occupied with other matters he studied aviation and collected literature on it.

The development of flying in Palestine required skilled and trained people. Shohat concluded that to achieve this, reliable men had to be trained at flying schools abroad. In early 1924 Shohat left for Paris with the aim of furthering this goal. The snag was that the flight schools in France were military, under the control of the war ministry. Most of the students were French citizens or from countries under French protection. Foreign students were admitted only after a complicated selective procedure. In Paris Shohat found ways of reaching Leon Blum, a Jew and leader of the Socialist bloc in the parliament (a leader of international socialism and Prime Minister of France in the mid-1930s). He also made contact with de Monage, the Minister of Culture. Shohat succeeded in establishing a public committee for the development of aviation in Palestine, whose members, apart from the two men noted, were Edmond Fleg, Narcis Louan (renowned Franco-Jewish public figures), and others. But ultimately these efforts failed, and the entire enterprise came to naught.[81]

To summarize, the relationship between, on the one side, the Hashomer people and their allies in the Labor Battalion and, on the other, Golomb's people in the Hagana and his supporters in Ahdut Ha'avoda and the Histadrut, was complex and ambivalent. Even in the first stage, up to the end of 1922, when the Hashomer people did not yet have a separate organization and were no more than an ideological opposition, relations were nevertheless on the verge of explosion and intolerable. Ambivalence in relations was characteristic of both sides. From the second stage, the end of 1922 onwards, after the founding of Hakibbutz, relations declined into a dualism, which in the long run proved untenable for three reasons: those of practice, structure and principle.

The practical reason. Experience showed that the human composition of the two rival groups in the Hagana, and particularly the personalities of their two leaders, Shohat and Golomb, left no possibility for cooperation. Consequently, the organization, meaning the Hagana, came off worse from the unending tensions and rivalries, which, without ignoring the ideological element, essentially stemmed from intense mutual suspicion and mistrust, absence of "chemistry" and antipathy between the two leading figures. Hence, the two groups neutralized each other in a great many cases, undoubtedly wasting much energy on competition and power struggles. The only way out of this complicated situation could be a decision in favor of one side or the other. Such a decision was never made over the years, so the festering situation deteriorated. In the second stage, when the Hashomer people withdrew from activity in the Hagana and left the field to their rivals, Golomb for some reason preferred to abandon his work in the organization. Those of his adherents who remained could not contend with the objective and subjective difficulties that the Hagana faced.

   The structural reason, or the "constitutional" reason. With the decision in December 1920 at the founding conference of the Histadrut that the Hagana was to be subject to itself, a decision enthusiastically supported by the Hashomer people, it was clear that the Histadrut would insist, one way or another, in imposing its authority on the sensitive issue of defense. As long as the Histadrut was weak and decentralized, or quasi-feudal in structure (loosely encompassing the Solel Boneh, Hamashbir Hamerkazi and Tnuva cooperatives, the parties, the workers' cooperative villages [*moshavim*], the kibbutzim, etc.), there was room in it for such a body as Hakibbutz, which considered itself an organic part of the Histadrut but in fact at times operated of its own accord. As the Executive Committee of the Histadrut grew stronger from late 1921 under the leadership of David Ben-Gurion, it strove for centralism, and the life expectancy of such organizations as the Labor Battalion and Hakibbutz, as elements in the Histadrut, would predictably grow shorter. Here the fate of Hakibbutz was tightly bound to that of the Battalion, which served as its nursery, its supportive and protective framework. From the structural–constitutional aspect, these two bodies were one, and to a great extent shared a common dilemma. The collapse of the Battalion destroyed the structural and practical basis of Hakibbutz, which therefore fell with it.

   The reason of principle. Hakibbutz was faced with the classic problem of the nature of the link between the pioneer marching in the van of the camp and the camp itself. The question was how far a small group, regarding itself as an elite *avant-garde*, could act independently, free of the authority of the overall social and political framework of which it considered itself a part. In Hakibbutz the radical position of Manya Shohat and several of her adherents stood out, but even she, and certainly her comrades in the organization, did not deny in principle the authority of the Histadrut – rather the reverse. In this sense, the condition of Hakibbutz was more difficult than that of the Labor Battalion, which in ideology and potential deemed itself a substitute for the Histadrut, or a "Histadrut" in due course. By contrast, Hakibbutz regarded itself, despite its goal of national liberation and the establishment of a Jewish state, as firmly attached to the workers' class and as a part of the Histadrut and obviously of the Hagana. Therefore, ideologically an impossible dualism arose here, which could not persist long and had to be resolved. But the resolution, when it came, was in tragic circumstances, through a development quite unconnected with Hakibbutz; this was the collapse of the Labor Battalion.

The Rift and the End (1923–1927)

In the elections to the founding conference of the Histadrut in 1920, four national lists competed for the votes of 4433 voters: Ahdut Ha'avoda, Hapoel Hatzair, the New Immigrants' list (including members of Hehalutz, Hashomer Hatzair and Tze'irei Zion), and the Jewish Socialist Workers' Party (JSWP) – a communist list.[82] Ahdut Ha'avoda won 1864 votes, Hapoel Hatzair 1324, the New Immigrants' list 842, and the communists 303. Of the 87 delegates to the founding conference, 38 were from Ahdut Ha'avoda, 27 from Hapoel Hatzair, 16 from the New Immigrants' list and 6 from the JSWP.[83]

Although these elections did not give Ahdut Ha'avoda a majority in the Histadrut, it was still the largest and therefore the dominant party. However, its lack of an absolute majority required that it be flexible and willing to compromise to win the necessary support of the other political groupings, and also to coexist within an organization that still had to build itself up.

In the elections to the second Histadrut conference, held on 20–27 February 1923, there were 6549 voters, who had to elect 127 delegates; to these were added the secretariat of the Histadrut Executive Committee, making a total of 130 delegates to the conference. There were by now 12 lists in contention, indicating the politicization and splitting taking place in the workers' community in the short time since the founding conference. The Labor Battalion appeared on a separate list, to the displeasure of Ahdut Ha'avoda. In the elections that party won an absolute majority in the Histadrut, with 69 delegates out of 130. The second largest party, Hapoel Hatzair, trailed far behind with 36. The other lists received the remnants of the votes, the Labor Battalion gaining 6 delegates, the Hashomer Hatzair list only 4.

Without doubt, these elections enhanced the self-confidence of Ahdut Ha'avoda in readiness for its coming struggles against the Labor Battalion and Hakibbutz. Its much-desired majority in the Histadrut gave it political power and economic and organizational means for the future.[84]

Two events stand out as clear and tragic landmarks in the complex relations between the Labor Battalion and the Histadrut: the episodes of Ein Harod and Kefar Gil'adi-Tel Hai.

The Ein Harod episode (1923). Until late 1922–early 1923, that is, until the appearance of the Battalion as a separate list in the elections to the second Histadrut conference and the start of the Ein Harod episode at the beginning of 1923, the Battalion concentrated essentially on internal problems and social and cultural issues concerning the most desirable structure of the Battalion and of the Jewish society being built in Palestine. True, Battalion ideology contained the seeds of possible future clashes between itself and Ahdut Ha'avoda and the Histadrut, but so far these remained latent. Any disputes there had been until then had no direct link to party-political matters. Nor did the Battalion have official ties with any party, and each member could belong to whatever party he chose. The parties themselves, including Ahdut Ha'avoda, had no active relationship with the Battalion. Ahdut Ha'avoda actually viewed the Battalion in a positive light.

The turning point and the rapid deterioration in relations between Ahdut Ha'avoda and the Battalion began when the latter appeared as a separate list in the elections to the second Histadrut conference and with the Ein Harod episode. From that time a left-leaning tendency began in the Battalion, and this burst into the open in a debate on the relationship between the Battalion and the party and the Histadrut. The sense of crisis that became manifest in the Battalion deepened with the onset of the *Fourth Aliya* in 1924. The success of this Aliya in the first two years sharpened the awareness of the contradiction between the social-economic dream of the Battalion and the actual state of affairs in the Yishuv in the period 1924–6.[85]

The dispute that erupted at the start of 1923 between the Battalion and Ahdut Ha'avoda and the Histadrut over Kibbutz Ein Harod is among the most famous in the history of the labor movement in Palestine generally and of the kibbutz movement in particular. At stake was the chief ideal of the Battalion, which envisaged an all-nation commune – a national kibbutz, with a single common fund for all echelons of the Battalion and an egalitarian life for all its sections; this was opposed to the conception of the *Second Aliya* people, led by Shlomo Lefkovich (Lavie) and Yitzhak Tabenkin, which posited economic and organizational autonomy for the settlements. It was, in other words, the principle of centralism as opposed to the principle of decentralism. In parallel, there was the problem of Histadrut responsibility and authority in building the workers' economy, the method of settlement and the building of each individual village. Ahdut Ha'avoda and the Histadrut aligned themselves with the Ein Harod members who were veterans of the *Second Aliya*. This was deemed interference in what was an internal dispute within the national kibbutz movement. As the dispute supposedly centered on the imposition of Histadrut discipline on a kibbutz movement, with no party-political content, all members of the Battalion consolidated in this struggle against

Ahdut Ha'avoda and the Histadrut, regardless of political outlook.

Within a short time the lines of the struggle and of the contesting camps were drawn: the party and Histadrut establishment side by side with the veterans of the *Second Aliya*, versus the vast majority of the Battalion, people of the *Third Aliya*. As stated, this clash involved a wide range of elements: *Second Aliya* veterans against the young people of the *Third Aliya*,[86] different views on the nature of the national commune, and on reciprocal relations between the Histadrut and the first national kibbutz.[87] The development and outcome of the episode are well known. After the dispute began, the Agricultural Center (*Hamerkaz hahaklai* – the representative institution of all the farmers organized in the Histadrut) entered the fray on behalf of the Histadrut and accepted the following tenets as guidelines in the running of the Tel Yosef and Ein Harod kibbutzim: (a) the permanency of members in the places, and their supreme responsibility was to the Histadrut; (b) the individual kibbutz had financial and administrative autonomy; (c) the acceptance and expulsion of members was by members of the settlement and with the agreement of the Agricultural Center; (d) the budgets of the settlements required the approval of the Agricultural Center; (e) the leadership of the settlements was chosen by people in them, but required the approval of the Agricultural Center; and (f) the determination of a settlement location as well as its master plan required approval by the Agricultural Center. These decisions removed supervision of the kibbutzim in general and Ein Harod and Tel Yosef in particular from the hands of the Battalion. On 17 March 1923 the Battalion submitted its appeal against the decisions of the Agricultural Center to the sixth council of the Histadrut, but the appeal was rejected. On 4 April 1923 the Battalion center officially requested the Executive Committee of the Histadrut to partition the two kibbutzim. The Battalion demanded Tel Yosef for itself. On 3 June 1923 the joint kibbutz Tel Yosef and Ein Harod was partitioned. Tel Yosef remained in the hands of the Battalion. By decision of the Histadrut Executive Committee and Agricultural Center, the kibbutz was divided equally between the two settlements, without consideration of the number of members of each settlement.

The Ein Harod episode resulted in the final shaping of the ambivalent relationship between the Histadrut and the Labor Battalion in the direction of increasing hostility and separation. From then on the Battalion felt itself beseiged and persecuted by the Ahdut Ha'avoda and Histadrut establishment. These sentiments were shared by all in the Battalion, including Ahdut Ha'avoda members in it; "Members of the Battalion who vehemently opposed the left shared the feeling that the Histadrut, and especially its dominant party, Ahdut Ha'avoda, were hostile to the Battalion and sought to ruin it . . . "[88] The last act in the tragic drama of the relationship between the Battalion and the Histadrut occurred several years later, with the episode of the Kefar Gil'adi and Tel Hai settlements. *The Kefar Gila'di and Tel Hai episode (1925–7).* The facts of this episode were as follows: At the dual Battalion council held at Tel Yosef on 1–8 September 1925 it was decided to unite the Battalion settlements in Upper Galilee, namely, the kibbutzim Kefar Gil'adi and Tel Hai and the quarrying unit. A total of 150 people were involved. The considerations were economic, and the union, it was hoped, would bring about the creation of an economically sound agricultural–industrial bloc.[89] The economic and social condition of Tel Hai was particularly difficult. The decision of the Battalion council was put to the vote separately at the settlements and by the quarrymen. The results were that the quarrymen and Kefar Gil'adi accepted the decision without stipulation (there was a small minority opposed to it at Kefar Gil'adi), while at Tel Hai a majority of 22 people were in favor and 15, or 12, were against (some sources give figures of 28 for and 12 against).[90]

In a memorandum of February 1926 Alexander Zayd, who was in the minority at Tel Hai, explained his opposition on the grounds of disagreement with the Battalion over education and farm management. An additional reason was that he opposed "the ambition of Kefar Gil'adi for dictatorship in Upper Galilee . . . "[91] It should be noted that the Zayd family had been obliged to leave Kefar Gil'adi and move to Tel Hai shortly before the dispute owing to a serious disagreement with the members of Kefar Gil'adi.[92]

Following the decision by the Battalion council, its Executive Committee began to elaborate the plan for the union. At the beginning of October 1925 an executive committee was created for the united bloc. The minority opposition to the union requested the Agricultural Center to intervene on their behalf and prevent it. The Agricultural Center responded favorably and called on the Battalion to delay the union until it had studied the issue.

After clarifications the Agricultural Center announced that it overturned the decision on the union, although it accepted the economic wisdom of the idea. The settlements were not satisfied with the decision, and the subject was brought before the Histadrut council, which met on 1 July 1926, and for this purpose was declared secret and closed. The council decided that Tel Hai was to be detached from the Battalion and transferred to the supervision of the Agricultural Center. The council thus affirmed the earlier decision by the Histadrut Executive Committee. Next, the Executive Committee announced the appointment of a Clarification Commission on the issue of Tel Hai. In fact, however, the real purpose of this commission was to consider and rule in respect of Hakibbutz.

The Battalion center decided to submit, and accepted the dictate of the

Histadrut council. By contrast, the majority in the two settlements rejected the decision. On 25 July 1926 the members of Kefar Gil'adi went out to plough Tel Hai land, which resulted in a violent clash with members of the minority at Tel Hai. When the majority in the two settlements dismissed repeated demands by the Histadrut Executive Committee to accept its authority and to obey its decisions, the latter declared their administrative expulsion from the Histadrut.[93]

Finally, the Histadrut placed sanctions on the two rebellious settlements, and denied them the support of its economic institutions as well as the services of the sick fund. The incident threw the entire public into turmoil and did not quieten down. The Executive Committee decisions, which had been stringently applied by David Ben-Gurion, were the target of harsh criticism by the minority parties in the Histadrut. In particular, Hapoel Hatzair came out in opposition both to the radical means adopted against the settlements and to the administrative expulsion of hundreds of the most senior comrades in the country, and this without a trial by their peers. By a decision of 1927 the sanctions so severely applied by Ben-Gurion were lifted and the settlements returned to the Histadrut fold, but by then the Battalion had been disbanded. The episode was the final nail in the coffin of the relationship between the Battalion and the Histadrut.

The Kefar Gil'adi–Tel Hai episode would not have taken place at all, nor would it have had any logical foundation, had not interests entirely unconnected with the welfare of the settlements been forced into it. The Histadrut, under the leadership of Ben-Gurion, exploited the affair to test the strength of the Battalion and Hakibbutz with the aim of suppressing them.[94] Even Golomb admitted that the entire social and economic issue, that is, Histadrut protection of the minority of veterans at Tel Hai, was a ploy, and the propaganda squeezed out of the affair by Ahdut Ha'avoda and the Histadrut for the benefit of the public at large was hypocritical and intended to vindicate themselves. "If the Histadrut institutions had discussed the matter of Tel Hai only for regular economic and social reasons, even then it would have been very complex and difficult . . . But all these economic and social claims are cast aside because of the special situation of the Upper Galilee settlements . . . " Later Golomb presents, in disguised form, the real political factors hidden behind the dispute.[95]

All the quarrels and the turmoil described occurred in the last dying stages of the Battalion. The years 1925–6 were marked by the hard struggles between the left and the right in the Battalion. The final split occurred at the Battalion council on 16–17 December 1926. About 300 Battalion members went to the right and about 200 to the left. The absolute majority both in Kefar Gil'adi and at Tel Hai went to the right. This fact, the attachment of the majority to the right in both settlements, was known to Ben-Gurion, who acted with great force in leading the attack that has been described. The obvious inference is that all claims that the cruel struggle against the two settlements was to save them from the claws of the left are groundless. It transpires that the entire harsh and relentless battle waged by the Ahdut Ha'avoda and Histadrut apparatus, with the help of all the political means and propaganda at its disposal, was based on false premises, as the directors of the battle well knew. This was a cynical and self-seeking use of all the enormous means at the disposal of the establishment against a handful of people who dwelt in the far north, and it had one aim: to eliminate the Hakibbutz organization.

The last days of Hakibbutz. The Hakibbutz people were an inseparable part of the Battalion. The various developments and struggles in the Battalion affected them also. However, it seems that most Hashomer members were not among the elements that caused the leftward shift in the Battalion. Contrary to the existing histories, which identify the left in the Battalion with Hakibbutz, the available facts show that the opposite was the case. The division of the people themselves after the split in the Battalion is incontrovertible evidence of this. In the stormy days of the struggle in the Battalion, Hakibbutz had a vital interest in retaining its non-party and non-factional character and in concentrating exclusively on security matters. Most Hashomer people fought for this approach by Hakibbutz, although some members of the organization, mainly the young people of the *Third Aliya*, were drawn into the political whirlwind. The charge of a coherent plot made by the enemies of Hashomer and the absolute identity they allege between the left and Hakibbutz are unsubstantiated and run counter to the truth. The party and Histadrut establishment used this weapon to discredit the Hashomer veterans in their struggle against Hakibbutz.[96]

Some maintain that Golomb began to suspect not only separate organization by the Hashomer people but the actual existence of Hakibbutz already in late 1921–early 1922.[97] Therefore, when the Carlsbad meeting took place in August 1922 among himself, Hoz, Ben-Gurion and Katznelson, Golomb even then demanded that this separate organization be terminated. On his return to Palestine in October 1922, Golomb began preparing data and collecting material for this fight, which he wished to conduct by means of a Histadrut trial. Nothing came of his efforts, but he was assured of the creation of a Histadrut commission to investigate the matter. To further this, before his departure abroad in January 1923 Golomb left with Dov Hoz an envelope containing material that he believed would prove the existence of a separate organization of Hashomer people.[98] Golomb returned to Palestine in July 1924. Instead of the Histadrut commission of inquiry and the Histadrut trial that he wanted, a clarification was held by the Histadrut of the case of the millstone related above. The matter was quietly settled after the people of

Kefar Gil'adi returned the arms. In summer 1923, after the Ein Harod conflict, the links of the former Hashomer members and Hakibbutz with the Hagana were severed almost completely when Shmuel Hefter and Haim Shturman, both Hashomer veterans and members of Hakibbutz, were not re-elected to the Defense Committee. Still, even in 1924 attempts were made to hold talks. Ben-Gurion noted in his diary that Yitzhak Ben Zvi and himself arranged a meeting with the former Hashomer figures Yisrael and Manya Shohat and Shmuel Hefter on 6 April 1924. The meeting was not held, for reasons that are not clear. It seems that the mediators in these efforts were the Ben Zvi couple, who over the years had maintained sound contacts with their old comrades from Hashomer.[99] As described, the decline in relations continued in these years.

In winter 1925 the Ahdut Ha'avoda Executive Committee appointed a committee of three to investigate the Hakibbutz issue. The three were Zalman Rubashov (Shazar), Golda Meyerson (Meir) and Zev Feinstein (Shefer), and the committee was known as the "trial committee." This was not the Histadrut commission that Golomb had demanded at the end of 1922, but it was a commission of inquiry on a respectable level. The two sides appeared and set forth their positions before the committee. In addition, the committee was presented with secret material for perusal only by the members of the party's Executive Committee; it also heard about 20 witnesses.

On 19 March 1925 the committee drew up its findings. According to Ben-Gurion's diary, he received them the following day. In the main they were these: (a) The disbanding of Hashomer in 1920 had not been contingent on any commitments by Ahdut Ha'avoda whatever. Since the disbanding of Hashomer the Hagana issue had passed to the party, and later to the Histadrut. These steps were binding on all. (b) The existing disputes on the nature of the Hagana did not release anyone from the duty of obedience to it. The charge of Yisrael Shohat, that Golomb's attitude hindered the smooth functioning of the Hagana, had not been proved. (c) No one was to blame for the collapse of the arms acquisition operation in Vienna in the summer of 1922. (d) Shohat's charge that Golomb had behaved improperly in Vienna was not supported by others, therefore Golomb had not exceeded his authority. (e) Golomb's accusation in the beehive affair was not proved; on the other hand, nor was Shohat's charge that Golomb was responsible for this failure. (f) The accusation regarding the millstone was proved to be correct. (g) It was clear to the committee that a secret circle existed.

The findings of the committee were raised for discussion at a session of the Ahdut Ha'avoda Executive Committee on 15 April 1925 and in his diary Ben-Gurion summed up the meeting: "We decided to demand that the Circle cease its separate activity. Transfer of all means and equipment.

The findings would be submitted to the Exec. Comm. of the Histadrut." The members of Hakibbutz, or "the Circle," as it was termed by the committee, rejected the conclusions totally, and called the commission the "family committee" instead of the "trial committee" – a pun in Hebrew, meaning that its considerations were not objective. The Battalion gave its backing to this stance.[100]

Ben-Gurion's interest in the security issue grew greater in 1925. This might have been the result of fears of a violent Arab reaction to the peak of the *Fourth Aliya*, which occurred in that year. This was perhaps the reason for several meetings held with the commander of the Hagana, Yosef Hecht, to clarify the state of the organization and how prepared it was for disturbances should they break out. At a meeting with Hecht on 3 November 1925 (possibly in connection with the anniversary of the Balfour Declaration – Y.G.) Ben-Gurion received a report on the scope and composition of Hagana membership in the three large cities. Hecht informed him that in Jaffa (apparently including Tel Aviv – Y.G.) there were 350 members in the Hagana, of whom 90 percent were workers and the remainder students. The local defense committee was headed by Fachter, Shoshani, David Yaffe, Gefen and Bader. In Haifa there were 250 Hagana members, as there were in Jerusalem. Two days after this meeting Ben-Gurion received a report from Hecht on the quantities of arms possessed by the Hagana. According to Ben-Gurion's diary the Hagana at that time had 26 "big" and 100 "medium." In addition the community at large possessed 1500 "medium" (the reference is apparently to rifles ["medium"] and machine-guns ["big"] – Y.G.).[101] Ben-Gurion held further meetings on the situation in the Galilee with both Menahem Elkind and Yisrael Shohat on 18 November 1925, and with Hecht after the latter returned from a special tour of the Galilee. At his meeting with Hecht on 23 November Hecht gave Ben-Gurion a reassuring report of the situation in the north.[102]

The stick-and-carrot method in respect of the Hakibbutz people continued. On the one hand, there was the flaunting of the decisions taken by the Ahdut Ha'avoda Executive Committee in light of the trial committee's findings and the threat of action through the Histadrut, to which the findings had been submitted; on the other hand, there were attempts at negotiation. Ben-Gurion wrote in his diary on 30 November 1925 that being in Jerusalem, "in the evening I met Shmuel [Hefter – Y.G.]. Rahel said that the 'Circle' wished to come to terms. Matters were set before Manya, Harut [should be Harit – Y.G.] and Elkind, they admitted their lack of internal talent."[103] Efforts at discussions continued at the beginning of 1926. On 13 February Ben-Gurion noted in his diary: "Shmuel and H [possibly Shmuel Hefter and Yosef Harit – Y.G.] this morning gave me the opinion of their friends. They agree to cease special action, to place their inventory at the disposal of Ahdut Ha'avoda, except for the inventory that belongs to the Battalion, which will remain the property of the Battalion. They will propose well known people of whom one will be selected, and are willing to sign a protocol."[104]

The efforts at discussions on the part of the Hakibbutz leadership should come as no surprise: (a) As recalled, only on account of their inability to act within the Hagana did the Hashomer people concentrate in the Battalion, and eventually form Hakibbutz. (b) They considered their task in Hakibbutz to be to stop the gaps opened through the inaction of the Hagana and complementary to the work of the latter. (c) By the end of 1925 the Battalion was rent by splits and dissent, and was in fact paralyzed. Only hostility to the Ahdut Ha'avoda establishment and the Histadrut was still capable of uniting the fragmented elements within it. (d) In light of the grim reality the Battalion seemed to have reached the end of its course. As a result of all these it was logical that the Hakibbutz people attempt to be reintegrated into the Hagana.

Ben-Gurion presented information on the feelers put out for discussions by the Hakibbutz members at an Ahdut Ha'avoda Executive Committee meeting on 28 February 1926, and he recorded in his diary: "At eleven meeting of AH Exec. Comm. on matter of negotiations with Shmulik, decided to postpone the matter until my return from abroad."[105]

On 4 March 1926 Ben-Gurion journeyed abroad and returned to Palestine on 10 June, after which he began a meticulous examination of the balance of power among the rival factions in the Battalion in readiness for the expected final rift. From his trusted informants Ben-Gurion received exact data, which he recorded with his usual thoroughness in his diary. On 14 June he wrote there that according to information he had obtained from Moshe Shapira the situation at Tel Yosef was the following: 74 members belonged to the right, the same number to the left and 40 belonged to the center: "(the center of Hashomer people and their supporters). The left is dismayed and angered with Hashomer. Through Shneorson Poaley Zion went to the center . . . " It seems to have been entirely clear to Ben-Gurion that at Tel Yosef at least the Hashomer people and their friends were not to be identified with the left but with the right. It is true that at a certain stage the "center" tried to produce a compromise between the two sides, but ultimately it went over to the right. Moreover, Pinhas Shneorson just then abandoned Ahdut Ha'avoda and joined Poaley Zion (Left), thereby causing his comrades to join the center and thus weaken the left in the Battalion.

Furthermore, on 17 June 1926 Ben-Gurion recorded in his diary information that Moshe Shapira published in an article in *Davar* on the division of forces at two other Battalion settlements, Tel Hai and Kefar Gil'adi. Ben-Gurion noted that at Tel Hai all 28 members belonged to the right and at Kefar Gil'adi 25 members belonged to the center, and 25 belonging to Poaley Zion (Left) went with the center.[106] From these notes there is no doubt that Ben-Gurion knew that the Hashomer people and their allies, including the members of Poaley Zion (Left) influenced by Pinhas Shneorson, were not to be identified with the left in the Battalion. Obviously, therefore, all attempts made at that time to identify the Hashomer people with the left in the Battalion were nothing but cynical demagoguery, and in fact this was an utterly baseless charge.[107]

The battle for Tel Hai, which led to the appointment of the Histadrut Clarification Commission with the real purpose of dealing with Hakibbutz, was the last in the war waged by the party and Histadrut establishment against the Battalion and Hakibbutz. The Clarification Commission was appointed by the Histadrut Executive Committee on 8 August 1926, and after certain changes it consisted of the following: Yosef Aharonovitch, Meir Ya'ari, Hugo Bergman, Yitzhak Ben Zvi and Studenich of the Battalion.[108] It was charged with studying the questions examined by the "trial committee" of Ahdut Ha'avoda. Its first session was on 31 August 1926, but its actual work commenced only in October. It held six formal sessions and submitted its findings to the Histadrut Executive Committee in January 1927. Its major purpose had been to obtain a public admission of the existence of Hakibbutz, a fact that was already known to Ben-Gurion and to at least some members of the Commission itself. The public admission was meant to serve as a weapon in the battle of destruction and the elimination of Hakibbutz, the final overthrow of the band of Hashomer veterans, who possessed so threatening a potential for opposition. Ben-Gurion had no need for information, for this he had. He needed a public admission, in the wake of which he could deal the *coup de grâce*.

The Commission encountered difficulties. Its work did not progress and it entered a dead end. Surprisingly, despite all the cards in the hands of Ben-Gurion's and Golomb's group, no one would testify and confess to the existence of Hakibbutz. Only two days before the Commission was due to conclude was there a change, when Meir Koslovsky, a veteran of Hashomer and Hakibbutz, testified to the existence of the latter and gave an account of its activities. The goods were supplied and Ben-Gurion had what he wanted.

On 27 January 1927 the Commission submitted its findings to the Histadrut Executive Committee, in which it determined that there existed an independent "Circle" in the Battalion consisting of former members of Hashomer and members of the Battalion and acting separately. Yisrael Shohat stated his objections to the Commission's findings, but declared he accepted them, including the disbanding of Hakibbutz.[109] In fact, Hakibbutz had been inactive since 1925, and with the dispersal of the

Battalion on 17 December 1926, Hakibbutz too had reached its term.

The Central Committee of the "right" Battalion, which most members of Hakibbutz joined, dismantled the separate "defense center" that had existed in the Labor Battalion before its dissolution. The Committee agreed to transfer supervision of the security issue in the "right" Battalion, including its arms stores, to the Histadrut Defense Committee. This in fact was done, except for the central arms store at Kefar Gil'adi. This store remained in the hands of the former Hashomer people, and they agreed to show its contents only to the Hagana commander Yosef Hecht. He put this knowledge to use later, in the 1929 disturbances.[110]

10

The Hapoel Association, 1930–1935

Constitutional means and influencing public opinion – these are no longer sufficient in our war against Betar . . . You have nothing more ridiculous and wrong than to combat by constitutional means a force that is wholly anti-constitutional. In our war with Betar it is impossible to make do with methods of moralizing, and it is necessary to set our own organized force against it.

David Ben-Gurion

A T FIRST SIGHT there were many areas of proximity between the two chief workers' parties in Palestine in the 1920s, Hapoel Hatzair and Ahdut Ha'avoda, and the Revisionist party, formed in 1925. Nevertheless, the ideological, social and political differences were far more significant and fundamental. These differences, among other things, shaped the circumstances of the Yishuv and the Zionist movement in the second half of the 1920s and the last half of the 1930s. They were characterized by a titanic struggle, at times violent, between Revisionism and the Palestinian labor movement for hegemony over the Yishuv and Zionism.

Struggle between the Palestinian Labor Movement and Revisionism for Hegemony over Zionism (1925–1933)

1 The ideological-political clash
Hapoel Hatzair, which was established in 1905, drew on various sources of influence,[1] which created in it a range of opinions.[2] It placed its entire weight on the theme of realization (*hagshama*). For long years it regarded the "conquest of labor" as its special mission, and also the fight to revive Hebrew language and culture in Palestine. Hapoel Hatzair negated the Marxist-Borochovist world outlook as unsuited to Palestinian conditions.

In terms of its national coloration on the one hand, and its rejection of the idealist-Marxist world outlook on the other, it was, on the surface, in some way similar to the Revisionist party, when the latter appeared on the Zionist stage.

In fact, Hapoel Hatzair became a hard and uncompromising opponent of Revisionism from the moment of its appearance. The rejection of the new party took place on the background of sharp and deep differences in the social-economic and political arenas. In the former, there were substantive disputes over the way of building the land, and consequently over the respective preference for social elements. Hapoel Hatzair saw the focus of the national revival as the return of the Jewish people to its soil, that is, working the land and social experiments, and emphasized the value of physical labor – primarily agriculture – and therefore also the role of the Jewish worker as a national normative concept. Revisionism, by contrast, stressed the town and the middle class. In the political arena Hapoel Hatzair stood for Weizmann and opposed Jabotinsky from the moment the latter left the Zionist leadership in January 1923.

At the beginning of 1925 Yitzhak Lufban attacked Jabotinsky, writing: "The politics of Jabotinsky and a third or half of those flocking after him . . . is nothing other than a political parody devoid of any real and rational grasp, and it has no roots in the Palestinian conditions or in the National Zionism of the Jewish people." In this Lufban expressed the view of his party.[3] After the establishment of the Revisionist party it was criticized by several leading personalities from the party, such as Shlomo Shiller,[4] Yitzhak Wilkansky (El'ezri-Vulcani), who spurned Jabotinsky as a statesman and also accused him of anti-democracy. He saw him as a nineteenth-century romantic, possessed by the ghost of Garibaldi.[5] The critics were joined by Eli'ezer Kaplan and Yosef Sprinzak.[6] It emerges that for Hapoel Hatzair, Revisionism was almost entirely negative, and therefore the party attacked it from its first appearance at the Zionist congresses, beginning with the Fourteenth Congress in 1925. In a letter to his wife written at that congress, Yosef Sprinzak describes Jabotinsky's speech, stating that "from the point of view of rhetoric Jabotinsky's speech was technically perfect, but from the point of view of content it was a political and moral scandal, and its premises an indication of weakness in Zionist thought."[7] It should be stressed that the enmity was not one-way but mutual.[8]

Relations with Ahdut Ha'avoda were far more complicated. Most surprisingly, despite the latter's Palestinian socialist world view, the points of proximity between the two parties during the twenties were numerous[9] and concerned certain issues of great importance: (a) Both parties affirmed the imparting of greater and more respected weight to the Palestine Yishuv in the deliberations of the Zionist movement. For them, the Yishuv, meaning the population who had migrated to Palestine and was reaching Zionist ideology, had the right to greater political clout than its numerical and economic strength might merit. The two parties negated the custom that had become rooted in the Zionist leadership of usually ignoring the views of the Yishuv as expressed through its elected institutions. (b) The two parties evinced great sensitivity toward the safety of the Yishuv and the creation of a Jewish security force to defend the Zionist enterprise. This attachment to defense issues, or defense activism, characterized the two parties and their successors throughout the Mandatory period. (c) Also common was the concept of Zionist activism, that is, the constant striving for large *aliya* (immigration to Palestine) and the speedy building of the land. (d) The two bodies were united in censuring the Mandatory administration, including that of Herbert Samuel's High commissionership, and the separation of Transjordan from the area of the Jewish National Home. (e) Both organizations argued against the policy of the Zionist leaderships under Weizmann and were opposed to Weizmann and his policies. Until 1927 the two parties were together in their opposition to the "expanded" Jewish Agency – Weizmann's great desire in the 1920s. It may generally be stated that in most matters on which Ahdut Ha'avoda differed from Weizmann it was close to Jabotinsky and Revisionism.[10]

Despite all the foregoing, the areas of dispute were more numerous and substantial, and these gave rise to the rift between the two parties that steadily widened in the second half of the 1920s prior to the 1929 disturbances: (a) Precisely in the field of defense a serious conflict arose, in 1921–3, between Ahdut Ha'avoda and Jabotinsky. As stated in an earlier chapter, the latter was a great proponent of the overt army and negated the underground, while Ahdut Ha'avoda, which supported his goals, believed in the necessity for the existence of a clandestine Jewish security organization. (b) As for the mode of building Palestine, Jabotinsky developed his concepts under the title "the settlement regime" – a central tier in Revisionist ideology. For Jabotinsky, the entire Jewish enterprise in Palestine before the Mandatory period had been merely experimental, while mass Jewish settlement could be implemented only as a government project based on the resources of the Mandatory government. The Jews were incapable of realizing the aims of Zionism on their own. It was possible to absorb mass immigration principally in the town. Therefore, urbanization, in all its aspects, including social, had to receive absolute priority in Zionist policy. As against these views Ahdut Ha'avoda identified with Hapoel Hatzair on the way of building the land, the place of agriculture, the value of labor and the status merited by the laborer on the land and the worker in the town. (c) While Jabotinsky negated national capital as the central lever in building the land but relied on the middle class and private enterprise, Ahdut Ha'avoda, like the other workers' parties, believed in national capital as the chief, necessary, means of building the land and as the major instrument in the socioeconomic revolution in the nation, which did not depart from the principal of territorial concentration. (d) Jabotinsky and his party rejected the Palestinian version too of the socialist world view, and so stood for monism and combated the theory of the existence of classes in the nation and the right to class war. Jabotinsky saw this as a peril to national unity, without which national goals would not be achieved. As for Ahdut Ha'avoda, only the parallel struggle for socioeconomic and national goals could ensure the success of Zionism.

In the socioeconomic sphere the views of Jabotinsky and his party contained all the elements rejected by the workers' parties: aggrandizement of individualism and its preferability to the various kinds of cooperative experiments; absolute negation of socialism and the class war, and the affirmation of capitalism; the view of the bourgeousie as the class of the future; denial of the superior status of the farm laborer and city worker. All these views made Jabotinsky and his party undisputed enemies of the workers' parties.

Ultimately, in choosing between Weizmann and Jabotinsky, Ahdut Ha'avoda, like the labor movement as a whole, preferred Weizmann's course to Jabotinsky's. Ahdut Ha'avoda moved into the Weizmann camp at the Fifteenth Zionist Congress in 1927, joining the supporters of the "expanded" Jewish Agency. Henceforward, the location of this party in the Weizmann camp made it Revisionism's enemy not only in the socioeconomic sphere but also in the political. In fact, already on the eve of the 1929 disturbances the chasm between the two parties was opening. From 1927 the entire labor movement "foresees" almost unanimously enmity toward and total negation of Revisionism and its leader Zeev Jabotinsky. The latter came to the conclusion that a condition for the defeat of Weizmann and his own victory in Zionism was the destruction of the labor movement. As a consequence of these contrary positions, the hostility between the streams became absolute.[11]

2 Struggle over Weizmann's succession (1929–1931)

In 1926 Jabotinsky could still make a round of visits to the kibbutzim of the Jezreel Valley and be welcomed there with kindness and even in friendship.[12] In Haifa, too, thousands came to hear him speak and he was not interrupted.[13] Two years later, however, on his return to Palestine in October 1928, the division between him and his party and the Palestinian labor movement was total.[14]

The 1929 disturbances erupted into this tense state of affairs. They caused a series of political moves that brought relations between the

Zionist movement and Britain in 1929-31 to their lowest level ever. This in turn caused the outbreak of harsh conflicts within the Zionist movement, where a struggle over its course and its leadership burst out. There was polarization in inter-party relations, increasing militancy that flared up into violence, and the final crystallization of positions among the parties in conflict over the succession to Weizmann. In the end, two alternatives took shape in the Yishuv and in Zionism between which no compromise was possible: the Weizmann camp centered on the Palestinian labor movement on the one hand and the Revisionist movement with its allies on the other. This serious political situation had implications for all other areas of life in the relations between the fighting camps and brought them to the verge of civil war. The crisis of the drama, in this period, was the Seventeenth Zionist Congress of 1931.

After the publication of the Passfied White Paper in October 1930 Weizmann officially tendered to the Zionist Executive his resignation from the presidency of the Zionist movement. This step caused an escalation in the struggle within Zionism.

Weizmann himself, who had sensed the storm gathering against him throughout the Zionist world since the 1929 disturbances, announced on various occasions that he did not intend to continue as president of the Zionist movement after the Seventeenth Congress.[15] However, there is certain evidence that his own feelings on the matter were divided. At any rate, the impression he created among his supporters was that within his heart he wished to continue his presidency. It is most likely that Weizmann did not wish to resign because, in the given circumstances, this would be interpreted, as indeed it was interpreted, as a personal defeat of himself and his policies and a dishonorable departure. And above all, it would leave the presidency open to his chief rival for many years, Zeev Jabotinsky.[16] If Weizmann had really been firm in his decision to quit the presidency he would have convinced his supporters of it and the whole conflict around his personality at the Seventeenth Congress would have been avoided.

At the end of 1930 and in the first half of 1931 the Central Committee of Mapai (the largest labor party in Palestine, created in 1930 through the merger of Hapoel Hatzair and Ahdut Ha'avoda) formulated the party position on the subject of Weizmann's presidency. While opinions on this were divided, there was complete unanimity in rejecting the possibility of allowing a coalition with the Revisionist party to be created or of joining such a coalition.[17]

A summary of the future strategy of Mapai in particular and of the "workers' faction" in general at the Seventeenth Congress was adopted at the meeting of the Mapai Center on 1 June 1931. The Center decided on its maximalist goal and a minimal target. The maximum plan strove to establish at the congress a leadership without the Revisionists, with the "workers' faction" as its focus, and to keep Weizmann in office. The minimum plan was based on forsaking, if necessary, support for Weizmann's presidency in order to achieve the chief and fundamental aim of Mapai and the "workers' faction" – the creation of a coalition without the Revisionists and with the workers at its Center. In the Mapai platform for the Seventeenth Congress, section B contains a very significant paragraph: "to keep away from any coalition that includes circles of a Hitlerist outlook or that reject the popular-political program of Zionism."[18]

In a letter from David Ben-Gurion to his wife Paula dated 20 July 1931, after the closing of the Seventeenth Congress, he notes the three chief goals of the "workers' faction" at the congress: retention of Weizmann, as president; convincing the congress to adopt the policy of the "workers' faction" and not of the Revisionists; election of a Zionist leadership without the Revisionists and with the workers at its Center. It seems that two of these three goals were connected with ridding the Zionist movement of Revisionist influence. The workers indeed succeeded in these two goals but they failed regarding the continuation of Weizmann's presidency.[19]

Chaim Arlozoroff also, in a letter to his wife Sima dated 16 July 1931, wrote that the policy of the "workers' faction" at the congress, when it became clear that Weizmann would not be elected, was to form an anti-Revisionist coalition. The faction also wished to win decisive influence over the Zionist leadership so that it would continue Weizmann's policy and at the same time combat Revisionism.[20]

There is no doubt that the chief battle of the Palestinian labor movement and its allies abroad in 1929–31, and especially at the Seventeenth Congress, was against the Revisionist party. Moreover, this struggle contained a certain innovation and signs of the revolution, beginning in the early 1930s, in the Zionist movement. While in the 1920s the movement had been dominated by the authoritative figure of Weizmann and most of the conflicts were around him, at the 1931 congress a new circumstance arose, inter-party strife for hegemony over the Zionist movement. This was the first instance of the party war that was to characterize Zionist life in the future.

The Palestinian labor movement saw Revisionism as its great foe. For it, Revisionism was the embodiment of Jewish fascism. Although Weizmann had been forced to resign from the presidency of the Zionist movement, the workers' parties won a great victory. Not only did they succeed in blocking Jabotinsky, keeping the longed-for presidency from him, they also routed the Revisionist party, coming to opposition while they themselves became an important central element, as early as 1931, in the new Zionist executive headed by Nahum Sokolov.[21]

This crushing defeat of Jabotinsky and Revisionism at the Seventeenth Congress at the hands of the Palestinian labor movement led by Mapai brought the enmity between the two parties to its peak. The two sides were characterized by bitter mutual hatred. In Jabotinsky and his party this was especially profound owing to the enormous frustration they suffered at the close of the congress. The great prize of conquest of the Zionist movement, which had appeared easily within their grasp, was snatched from them at the last moment. The abyss yawned ever wider. Offshoots of the hatred, which arose in the political sphere, ramified, and spread their poison to cause ferment in other areas of life involving the two parties, labor relations in particular.

3 Labor relations and violence

As stated, Jabotinsky and his party held socioeconomic views completely different from those of the Palestinian labor movement.[22] These did not remain abstract ideology but were converted into real political positions in the area of economics and labor relations in Palestine. The social and political element carrying these views to implementation was the workers of Hatzohar (tsiyonim revizionistim – Revisionist Zionists) and Betar (the youth movement of the Revisionist party) in Palestine, and these brought about a head-on collision with the Histadrut in a very sensitive area, that of labor relations.

From the start, the Revisionist party in Palestine included several groups. Its social and economic policy and its attitude to the Histadrut were influenced in the second half of the 1920s principally by members of the former Amlanim group and by the Menora group.[23] The former pressed for a separate organization, while the latter wished to act as a faction within the framework of the Histadrut. At the end of 1926 Jabotinsky still supported the Menora position, and on this basis a Revisionist faction appeared at the third Histadrut conference in July 1927.[24]

About six months later the approach changed and a separate organization was begun. On 10–11 February 1928 a national convention of Revisionist workers was held at Nahalat Yehuda and as a result the Revisionist Labor Block (gush ha'avoda harevizionisti) arose, which still remained in the framework of the Histadrut. At this convention three men appeared, former socialists who had left the workers' parties and joined the Revisionist party. They were the poet Uri Zvi Greenberg, Dr Yeivin and Abba Ahimeir. Henceforward these three exerted great influence in shaping the Revisionist image in Palestine.

At the convention not only was the organization of Revisionist workers formed, but its socioeconomic outlook took shape also, as did its view of the desired organizational structure of the Histadrut and the way to settle labor relations in the country. The ideology formulated was diametrically opposed to that of the labor movement in that it required (a) the Histadrut to consist of trade unions only; (b) complete separation of the cooperative and economic institutions from the Histadrut; (c) neutral and not Histadrut labor exchanges; and (d) the establishment of an organ for compulsory national arbitration to settle labor disputes and prevent strikes and lock-outs.[25] From then on the gap between the two currents widened in this area also. Two of the requirements in the program essentially caused the subsequent radicalization in relations and the slide into violence: the demand for a neutral labor exchange and the demand for compulsory national arbitration.

The first serious labor dispute in which the Betar people were involved erupted in April 1930 at Kefar Saba. At the beginning of the month 17 Betarists arrived at the moshava (now a city), at the invitation of the local Agricultural Committee of the Betar command. The invitation had not been made through the Histadrut labor exchange, which sought to impose order and to organize the Jewish workers' labor market. On 9 April David Ben-Gurion arrived at the moshava in his capacity as quasi-secretary of the Histadrut, and spoke with the Betarists. He explained that the Histadrut recognized the equal right to work but this must be arranged through the Histadrut labor exchange. The Betarists referred Ben-Gurion to the Betar command, who responded that they were not willing to accept work through the Histadrut exchange. When the Betarists set out to work in the citrus groves a serious and a violent fight broke out between them and the workers organized through the Histadrut exchange. The dispute was settled only on 29 April.

The Kefar Saba dispute was significant in that it was the first such confrontation to occur in a clearly political setting: the rejection by the Revisionists of the Histadrut labor exchange and their demand for a neutral labor exchange. The Histadrut was willing to compromise over a "joint" labor exchange, namely, one managed by workers and employers which through negotiation would solve labor problems. The Histadrut had set up such exchanges with the Industrialists' Association and with the *moshavot* Magdiel and Ra'anana. But it dismissed out of hand the Revisionists' demand for a "neutral" labor exchange, meaning one run by neutral officials, arguing that the labor exchange had to be managed directly by the workers and the employers.

The fight by Hatzohar against the Histadrut labor exchange stemmed not only from the ideological angle, but mainly from the political. The aim was to weaken the Histadrut, the bulwark of the Palestinian labor movement, by nullifying its control of the labor market. This goal could be achieved, so Hatzohar believed, by means of a neutral labor exchange.

The Kefar Saba dispute markedly affected the deterioration in relations between the two sides. The conflict served to induce the Revisionist workers to abandon the Histadrut and continue their separate organization.[26]

At a convention at the moshava Nahalat Yehuda on 31 May 1930 it was resolved to establish the Organization of Hatzohar and Betar Workers in Palestine, outside the Histadrut framework. Some years later this body served as the basis for the creation of the National Workers' Federation. Now a special organizational framework was added, which together with the Revisionist party and Betar stood behind the labor disputes. The year 1931 passed without major disputes in labor relations, but in 1932 tension rose once more in this area. That year Jabotinsky published his barbed anti-Histadrut articles "Red Swastikas"[27] and "Yes, Break."[28] The ferocious battle against the Histadrut was entered by the Palestinian newspaper *Hazit ha'am* (The People's Front) which, from the end of 1932, was the journal of the Organization of Hatzohar and Betar Workers in Palestine. The fierce anti-Histadrut line was formulated by the threesome of Uri Zvi Greenberg, H. Yeivin and A. Ahimeir.[29] Serious labor disputes, in a political setting, broke out that year in the construction branch in Tel Aviv.[30] The foremost of these, in 1932, was at the Frumin factory in Jerusalem, which was focally settled only in February 1933 and apparently gave impetus to the establishment of the National Workers' Federation that year. Another dispute, which led to bloodshed, occurred in Petah Tikva on 23 February 1933.

A study of the basic causes of the various labor disputes, from Kefar Saba on, shows that the conflict was political. The Revisionist movement was battling the pro-Weizmann camp. The chief support of the latter was the Palestinian labor movement. The Histadrut was the main organizational framework on which the labor movement rested. Therefore, the Revisionist party in all its aspects was at war with the Histadrut. To this underlying cause, naturally, was added Revisionist ideology in the socio-economic and labor spheres. The Revisionist demand for a professional workers' federation (consisting of trade unions only), compulsory national arbitration and a neutral labor exchange could by no means be countenanced by the labor movement.

The disputes, therefore, were rooted essentially in Zionist politics. The struggle spread thence to the socioeconomic and labor spheres. At the end of the 1920s and early 1930s these spheres nourished each other. This reciprocity was particularly evident in Palestine, where labor relations were the most sensitive area owing to their vital nature. Therefore, the clash in this area was of the greatest force and extended to violence and bloodshed. The man who led this struggle, and stood in the front line in the war against Revisionism, was the leader of the Histadrut, David Ben-Gurion.

182

The Hagana: From Histadrut Control to National Control

1 The 1929 disturbances and split in the Hagana

It has been mentioned that on 23 August 1929 disturbances broke out in Jerusalem, and spread thence to all parts of the country. Their peak was the massacre of the Jews of Hebron on the Sabbath of Saturday, 24 August and of the Jews of Safed on Thursday, 29 August.

The disturbances highlighted the flaws in the Hagana. Although without the Hagana the situation might have been worse, the disturbances still revealed the many weaknesses and faults of the Hagana, which did not fulfill its expectations.

The Hagana showing in the disturbances sparked severe internal self-criticism by its commanders. This was especially voiced by Avraham Tehomi, the Hagana commander in Jerusalem, after the disturbances. His censure referred to the professional aspect and railed against the low level of training, the desperate shortage of arms, and the lack of order, organization and planning. Whatever planning there had been was out of date. There was no intelligence section and lack of professionalism generally. Tehomi and others declared the need for a speedy and comprehensive transformation in organization, conception and battle array of the Hagana on a professional semi-military basis, instead of the slovenly militia that existed. In the public sphere, Tehomi called for the transfer of the Hagana from Histadrut control to national control.[31] Into this maelstrom of wound-licking and self-criticism and external criticism there erupted, at the start of 1931, the clash between the Hagana and Avraham Tehomi, which led to the splitting of the former and the creation of the "Parallel Organization," or Organization B, or Etzel (*Irgun Tzvai Leumi* – National Military Organization) Stage A.

The details of the dispute between Tehomi and the Hagana commander have been covered in various essays,[32] and this is not the place for a discussion of the episode. Nevertheless, it is difficult to avoid the feeling that the split in the Hagana in Jerusalem in 1931, with all its consequences for the future, would not have occurred if the quarrel had broken out at a more peaceful time. There is no clear-cut proof of Tehomi's wish to transfer personally to the Revisionist party, or of a prepared plan on his part to move sections of the Hagana into some kind of link with that party. Moreover, his behavior in the years following the split does not support the version presented by his opponents, who accuse him of a predisposition toward Revisionism. As stated, if the Tehomi affair had occurred in a calmer atmosphere, not in the tense, explosive, suspicious and hostile spirit prevailing between Revisionism and the Palestinian labor movement in 1930–1, the quarrel might have ended differently and without a split.[33] *History of the Hagana* admits that "the influence of Avraham Tehomi on the command staff in the city was very great. In his discussions with them he spoke of the need to turn the Hagana into an organization of more military character . . . These views were wide-spread in Hagana circles even before the 1929 disturbances . . . " But those were days of struggle against Revisionism, and therefore "the Histadrut people viewed with disfavor the Jerusalem Hagana commander, who had shown excessive independence and who held personal ties of friendship with the Revisionists (Eliahu Ben Horin). His views on the conduct of the Hagana tended to be regarded as Revisionist and the attitude toward him was charged with mistrust."

As stated, apart from friendship in his youth with Eliahu Ben Horin, the accusations against Tehomi on his being a hidden Revisionist and on his desire to transfer the Hagana to the Revisionist camp have not been clearly proved.

2 Transition from Histadrut control to national control

It has been noted that in the 1920s control of the Hagana lay with the Histadrut. The heads of the Hagana were appointed by the latter and they recognized its authority. It is important to stress that the Histadrut conceived of the Hagana as a national instrument and the goals of the organization were national also, but in practice, in terms of decisive influence and control, the Hagana was subject to the Histadrut. The situation in the 1920s was as follows: "The central committee of the Hagana was appointed by the organs of the Histadrut and was also subordinate to them in practice. The connection of the Hagana central committee to the general institutions of the Yishuv, the Zionist leadership and the National Committee was not one of clear-cut subordination . . . " The man who in the eyes of many in the 1920s was the embodiment of the Hagana was Yosef Hecht.[34]

The disturbances displayed the great importance of the Hagana and therefore also placed it at the center of renewed public interest. The institutions of the Yishuv and the Zionist movement roused themselves from the complacency that had settled on them in the long years of quiet, and also from the naïve belief in the desire and ability of the Mandatory government to defend the Yishuv. The functioning of the Hagana in the disturbances and the rise in its importance made necessary its reorganization as a defense implement.[35] The first step was taken by the Histadrut, which wanted, immediately after the disturbances, to reconstitute the Hagana center, and it was this that led to the dispute with Yosef Hecht.

The Hecht affair. In 1923 Yosef Hecht had been appointed by the Histadrut to the Hagana central committee. During the years prior to 1929 he accepted Histadrut authority and periodically submitted a report to David Ben-Gurion, the leader of the Histadrut.[36] Hecht was opposed to the wish of the Histadrut at the end of 1929 to reconstitute the Hagana center on the pattern of the early 1920s. The available evidence on the dispute is one-sided. *History of the Hagana* presents it as follows:

> Yosef Hecht saw himself as the sole person in the Yishuv with the right and the ability to stand at the head of the organization. He reacted with bitterness and skepticism to the revived interest shown by the Yishuv after the disturbances, and regarded the establishment of the Hagana center as a blow to his own authority. At most he was willing to accept a fictitious "center," in which leading public figures would participate who could not devote themselves to this work owing to their other commitments; when his proposal was rejected he announced that he did not want a Histadrut center and he did not need the Histadrut.[37]

From this account it appears that Hecht's opposition to the reconstitution and renewal of the Hagana center was due to the following causes: fears of curtailment of his personal powers; and rejection of Histadrut authority over the Hagana.

On Hecht's opposition to the proposed changes there is also the evidence of David Ben-Gurion, as noted in his diary for 13 September 1929, that is, very soon after the disturbances:

> This evening Manya came to me. She had met Asaf [Yosef – Y.G.] and spoken to him about his refusal of the center. He told her that he agreed to a national center, but did not want any center of the Histadrut. He is against the Histadrut people and does not need it. The youth is with him and K-sh [Kisch – Y.G.] has complete confidence in him. He is willing to work with Yisrael, he is willing to work with M.S. [Moshe Smilansky – Y.G.]. He told her that I wanted to see him but he got out of it, and will get out of it in the future too . . . He is certain and believes that "the youth" will be with him. I told her what he had said to me a week ago – the opposite of what he told her on certain points. I said that I was willing to be patient with him, and explain his error, but we will settle this thing with or without him.[38]

It is important to note that the Histadrut tendency at this stage was to tighten its grip and its control of the Hagana, and the transfer of the latter to national authority was not considered. This position is clearly evident from what Ben-Gurion had to say to Hecht, as recorded in the former's diary:

> This evening Asaf [Yosef – Y.G.] came to me and I said to him: Until two weeks ago I had complete trust in you. Even now I believe in your devotion to your work, but I have no confidence in your loyalty to the Histadrut. We know that you operate in the name of the Histadrut, but apparently you now rely on other forces.

Ben-Gurion goes on:

We cannot allow his continuation in the work without the control of the Histadrut. We are not covered by a defense federation. All the operatives in the Hagana worked on behalf of the Histadrut and fulfilled its mission. In this profession, as in other professions, the Histadrut did not have the means necessary to carry out its tasks. The work must now be placed on an entirely different footing, and the Histadrut connection is even more necessary than before.[39]

After harsh exchanges between the Histadrut executive committee and Hecht a new Hagana center was appointed, composed of David Ben-Gurion, Eliahu Golomb, Yosef Aharonovich, Shaul Meirov and Yosef Hecht. Shortly afterwards Aharonovich resigned, on the grounds that the center was a fiction and in fact Hecht was continuing to act alone and on his own account. Hecht replaced him with Meir Rothberg.[40] This center did not enjoy good fortune, because differences soon arose between Golomb and Hecht. *History of the Hagana* describes the clash as follows:

The objective content of Yosef Hecht's "rebellion" (regardless of his personal intentions) was not connected with the problem of replacing Histadrut control by general Yishuv control, but with the question of real public authority over the Hagana or the retention of actual control of its affairs in the hands of its commanders exclusively. The Histadrut, which had founded the Hagana as a national organization in the early 1920s and had appointed its leadership in those years, had always and consistently stood for handing control of it over to general national organizations, and the struggle of its leaders with the tendencies represented by Hecht was not about their control of the organization but about the organized public's control over the Hagana arm.

In light of the evidence in Ben-Gurion's diary there is room for doubt concerning this unequivocal statement by the author of *History of the Hagana*. Ben-Gurion's reservations about Hecht arose explicitly because "I have no confidence in your loyalty to the Histadrut. We know that you operate in the name of the Histadrut, but apparently you now rely on other forces." The rest of the entry in the diary is in the same spirit.

It is most likely that following the 1929 disturbances Yosef Hecht reached the conclusion that it was time to eliminate the anomaly whereby the national defense body was in practice under the supervision of the Histadrut. Therefore Hecht demanded, possibly out of personal interests also, the transfer of the Hagana to national control. In opposition to him, Ben-Gurion, Eliahu Golomb and their supporters wished to retain, at least in late fall of 1929 and early 1930, Histadrut authority over the Hagana.

In the ensuing conflict the forces were not balanced and tended to Hecht's disadvantage. At first the officers in the field were on his side. One of his foremost supporters was Rosa Cohen, a Hagana leader in Haifa. *History of the Hagana* admits that this group of Hagana commanders sustained "a theory whereby the Hagana should be 'of the Yishuv' and not 'of the Histadrut.' These actions aroused the opposition and even the ire of the members of the Executive Committee [of the Histadrut], who regarded Hecht as a sort of emissary of the movement who was betraying his masters' trust, while Hecht now saw himself as the leader of the Hagana, which stood above any organization and party."

The truth, then, has emerged. *History of the Hagana* itself explains what stimulated the rage of the Executive Committee. In the Histadrut the desire to retain and even to strengthen the grip on the Hagana continued.[41]

With the changes in the summer of 1930 in respect of authority over the Hagana the fate of Yosef Hecht was sealed. After various transitions he was finally removed from activity in the Hagana in the summer of 1931;[42] he had lost the trust of the Histadrut.

The parity national command (NC). In the ferment aroused in the Yishuv following the disturbances, a considerable role was played by groups of citizens castigating Histadrut control of the Hagana. Some even spoke of the formation of a "civil defense" in parallel to the Histadrut force.

After the disturbances the Va'ad Haleumi (National Committee of the Yishuv) appointed a defense commission composed of Pinhas Ruthenberg (chairman), Eliahu Golomb, Yisrael Rokah, Rahel Yanait, Sh. Gordon, Berl Repetor, Dr Weinshal, Moshe Smilansky and Avraham Shapira. In summer 1930 this commission began to consider the question of authority over the Hagana, and resolved to transfer it to a parity national command, consisting, in equal numbers, of representatives of the Histadrut and of the public at large. The defense commission also determined the five members of the first provisional parity command. These were Eliahu Golomb and Dov Hoz of the Histadrut and Sa'adia Shoshani and Zvi Butkovsky (of Hadera) from the general public. Gershon Agronsky (Agron) was appointed on behalf of the Zionist leadership.[43]

With the creation of the parity command, authority over the Hagana, at least formally, was transferred to a national body resting on the support of the Va'ad Haleumi and the Zionist movement. In practice, the provisional command did not succeed in gaining control of the functioning of the organization and as a result the citizens' groups continued to rail against their being passed over and to claim that Histadrut control of the Hagana in fact turned it into a kind of workers' *Schutzbund*. The demand to establish a civil defense organization did not diminish. Finally, in the citizens' groups those supporting the creation of a single national defense organization gained the upper hand.

After drawn out negotiations, in 1931 a permanent parity national committee (NC) was formed. Its members were Eliahu Golomb, Dov Hoz and Meir Rothberg for the Histadrut and Dov Gefen, Yissachar Sitkov and Sa'adia Shoshani for the general public. This command received the approval of the Va'ad Haleumi and the Jewish Agency. From then to the establishment of the state of Israel the principle of parity in the Hagana command was maintained. The command formed in 1931 operated on the original pattern until July 1938, when the Jewish Agency leadership decided to appoint a neutral figure as the seventh member of the command who also served as its chairman.[44]

The Histadrut, then, was in late 1929 and early 1930 still seeking to strengthen its hold on the Hagana, and to this end it attempted to rehabilitate the Hagana center purely with Histadrut people; but in the summer of 1930, by virtue of pressures exerted by the public and Yishuv and Zionist institutions, it was forced to transfer authority over the Hagana to a national body, namely, the parity national command. This development created a difficult and complicated situation for the Histadrut, precisely at a time of polarization in the factors jostling for position in the Yishuv. Just when militantism and enmity between Revisionism and the Palestine labor movement was in the ascendant the Histadrut became vulnerable to its opponents following the loss of control over the Hagana. In light of this new circumstance, and in light of the inferences made from similar situations in Europe, the idea arose of the creation of a new security instrument, a kind of Palestinian *Schutzbund* exclusive to the workers. The man who came up with this notion and tried to realize it with the help of members of the erstwhile Hashomer was the leader of the Histadrut, David Ben-Gurion.

Special Concepts, Special Tools: David Ben-Gurion in 1928–1931

1 Struggle for creation of The League for Labor Palestine

In basic outlook, Ben-Gurion and the members of the Ahdut Ha'avoda leadership were generally of a single mind. Nevertheless, more than his comrades in the leadership, Ben-Gurion was given to fierce outbursts and sudden, dramatic *volte-faces* in the political and ideological sphere. Nor did he adhere to organizational frameworks, which he saw only as means for achieving the overall aims and ultimate goals in which he believed. Furthermore, his impulsive and energetic nature, and his tendency toward centralism, characterized and shaped his political course. More than once these qualities led Ben-Gurion to unique views and the attempt to create unique organizational and political tools. A leading example is the episode of the rise and fall of The League for Labor Palestine.

Even in the first half of the 1920s Ben-Gurion occasionally expressed dissatisfaction with the Zionist Organization. This criticism was fairly widespread in his party particularly until 1927, the year in which Ahdut Ha'avoda moved from opposition to support of Weizmann, when it adopted the idea of the "expanded Jewish Agency."[45] Ben-Gurion was unique in the extremity of his criticism, which at times reached the point of negating the right of the Zionist Organization to exist and viewing it as a factor inhibiting the realization of Zionism.[46] Because of this stance he maneuvered himself, at the beginning of 1927, into a minority in his own stronghold, the Histadrut Executive Committee, and even in his own party leadership, when his demand for the resignation of the workers' representative from the Zionist leadership failed, rejected not only by the Hapoel Hatzair party, to which the demand was addressed, but also by his own party.[47]

Despite his isolation among his comrades for his extreme disfavor of the Zionist Organization he did not yield. Indeed, from the beginning of 1928 Ben-Gurion strove relentlessly to establish an instrument which he saw as a future alternative to the Zionist Organization, namely, The League for Labor Palestine.

During 1927 two events occurred that helped Ben-Gurion to obtain the assistance of the Histadrut in his efforts to establish the League. First, an outcome of the 1927 Zionist Congress was that for the first time since 1921 Hapoel Hatzair was not included in the Zionist leadership under Weizmann. This betrayal by Weizmann, as it was perceived by many, created a favorable background in Hapoel Hatzair for the absorption of new ideas. Second, with the shift by Ahdut Ha'avoda to support for the "expanded Jewish Agency" there seemed to be some logic in Ben-Gurion's efforts to organize potential allies of the workers' movement throughout the world, who would be represented on the "expanded Agency" in which they would support the interests of the Palestine workers' movement.

Despite these events Ben-Gurion won only limited support from his comrades in the Histadrut and the party for the establishment of the League. Even this was given only after Ben-Gurion made it clear that his aim was not to create a body in competition with the Zionist Organization or the Jewish Agency, but to forge a worldwide instrument that the Palestine labor movement could rely on to protect its interests. Only after Ben-Gurion assured the doubters and skeptics as to his real aim did he win, in February 1928, the support of the Histadrut Executive Committee to convene a world congress for labor Palestine. The reservations and suspicions about Ben-Gurion's true goals for the League did not disappear even then, so the work of forming the League actually fell solely on Ben-Gurion's shoulders. His colleagues in the leadership, including Berl Katznelson and Yitzhak Tabenkin, came to his aid only in the last stage before the congress, and then only after he applied heavy pressure on them.

In the end, the mountain brought forth a mouse. The desired congress did, in fact, convene in Berlin on 27 September–1 October 1930, and its result was the creation of The League for Labor Palestine, but the new framework was anemic and the complete opposite of the high hopes that Ben-Gurion had placed in it and elaborated around it. In the following years the League served as a roof organization in the diaspora in the struggle against Revisionism and in election campaigns.

It is reasonable to suppose that when Ben-Gurion calmed his comrades by explaining that he had no intention of establishing a parallel or alternative world body to the Zionist Organization his inner feelings did not accord with his words. In his heart he never abandoned the view that the time of the inefficient and fractionary Zionist Organization had passed. An inkling of these sentiments and of his despair at the Zionist Organization was revealed to his comrades in the Mapai center when in a debate on 29 May 1931 he proposed not joining the Zionist leadership that would be formed at the Seventeenth Zionist Congress but to leave the running of the Zionist Organization to the Revisionists who, in any case, would lead it to perdition.[48] Before his friends he argued that, instead, a new body should be created, under the workers' hegemony, that would work more industriously and efficiently for the realization of Zionism. It may be supposed that at this stage he still saw the League, for which he had fought for almost three years, as the alternative to the existing Zionist Organization. His abandonment of the League was actually associated with the revolutionary events that took place in the Zionist Organization following the Seventeenth Congress in 1931, as a result of which there appeared, for the first time, a real possibility of the conquest of the leadership of the Zionist movement by the Palestine labor movement.[49]

2 Tendency to convert Hapoel into a Palestinian Schutzbund

In parallel to his efforts to establish the League, Ben-Gurion had begun working on the Hapoel association with the aim of turning it into a reservoir for the Hagana. From the end of 1930 he took upon himself an even more ambitious goal, namely, to organize Hapoel so that it would become or give rise to a semi-military framework like the defense organizations of the workers' movements in eastern and central Europe, of which the most famous was the *Schutzbund* of the Austrian workers.

The sources recounting the birth and establishment of the Hapoel association are identical, except for the date and place where the first association called "Hapoel" was founded. It is generally considered that the beginnings of sporting activities by groups of workers throughout Palestine were in 1923–4. In Tel Aviv and Beer Sheba the workers formed football teams. The Petah Tikva workers' council created a sports association called Masada. In 1923 the 1 May celebrations at Ein Harod were marked by a soccer match arranged by Avraham Shlonsky. Sports were organized by the members of Hashomer Hatza'ir from Russia who later established Kibbutz Afikim. All these were spontaneous acts by the youth, some of whom had been sportsmen in the past and some of whom found sports an outlet for excess energy.

It is generally held that the first sports association called "Hapoel" was founded on 24 April 1924 in Haifa by a group of former members of Maccabi, ex-members of the workers' sports movement in Austria, ASKO, and some of the workers in the groups then concentrated in Haifa.[50] Another view states that Hapoel had already appeared in 1923. The first association of this name was established in Tel Aviv before October 1923, and so preceded that in Haifa.[51]

Efforts toward a more comprehensive organization were made at the end of 1924, and then in 1925, by workers' groups in the northern valleys and Haifa. These met at a founding convention on 1 August 1925 in Afula, at which an overall body was set up, as well as a secretariat, which decided to locate its offices in Haifa.

On 15 May 1926 the founding council met in Petah Tikva and resolved to create the national association of Hapoel.[52] The third conference of the Histadrut, which opened on 5 July 1927, affirmed Hapoel's membership of the workers' sports association of the Socialist International, SASI, whose offices were in Lucerne.[53]

It seems that the development of Hapoel in its first years was not spectacular. Evidence of this is found in a report presented by Yosef Hecht on 20 January 1928 to Ben-Gurion in which he depicted Hapoel as a total failure as a sports association. Hecht believed that Hapoel should be merged with Maccabi to create a new single national athletics organization, in which it was likely that the workers would be the majority. To reinforce his proposal Hecht pointed to the danger of the increasing penetration and growing strength of the members of the (communist) "Fraction"[54] in Hapoel. For emphasis Hecht gave the example of the Hapoel branch in Tel Aviv, of which 22 members belonged to the "Fraction." At the conclusion of his report Hecht called on Ben-Gurion to place a leading figure at the head of Hapoel.[55]

Ben-Gurion's interest in Hapoel at the beginning of 1928 appears to have arisen from two causes. First, he believed that Hapoel could not be a sports association only, but must serve as a human reservoir for the Hagana. Therefore Hapoel must engage in quasi-military activities. Secondly, in the period in question Ben-Gurion was fiercely fighting the "Fraction," which had grown extremely powerful in consequence of the painful economic crisis that the Yishuv was suffering and was therefore gaining strength in the Histadrut branches, including Hapoel. Ben-

Gurion's fears undoubtedly increased when at a meeting with the Hapoel center on 26 January 1928, despite encouraging data presented on the organization, which, its representatives stated, had about 2000 active members in 19 branches, they nevertheless warned of the marked infiltration by members of the "Fraction" into Hapoel branches, especially in Tel Aviv and Haifa. At the meeting Ben-Gurion complained to those gathered that "there is no perception of Hapoel regarding its role and importance as a preparation and a corridor to the Hagana. Lack of connection with the Histadrut deprives Hapoel of its class and national value, and harms Hapoel and the Histadrut." Ben-Gurion required that the center apply a strict social and political test to any candidate for membership and that admission to Hapoel be only with the approval of the center.[56]

In light of the great importance that Ben-Gurion began to attribute to Hapoel for these reasons, he conceived of transferring its offices from Haifa to Tel Aviv so that they would be under closer supervision. By economic lures and exploitation of the severe financial straits of the organization, Ben-Gurion achieved his aim. The financial difficulties of Hapoel were so great that the center elected in the spring of 1927 had been unable to convene since then because the traversing expenses of its members could not be met. The secretariat staff in Haifa were so short of funds that the connection between them and the branches was by mail only. It is not surprising, therefore, that when Ben-Gurion offered direct and indirect financial support and strengthening of links with Histadrut institutions such as the Sick Fund, Kapai (the Histadrut financial organ), etc., as an incentive to move to Tel Aviv, his proposal was accepted; the move was made in the first months of 1928. In his diary Ben-Gurion relates how he managed this step at a meeting of the Hapoel center on 3 February 1928: "I suggested that the center move to T.A. and the Exec. Comm [of the Histadrut] would have two representatives on the secretariat. I required a re-examination of membership – so that the Fractionists could not get in – and clear direction for Hapoel activities." The decision on the move to Tel Aviv was made at a meeting of the center with Ben-Gurion on 4 February 1928.[57] Henceforward Ben-Gurion could keep an eye on the organization that he had begun to appreciate as a highly valuable political-security instrument.

From all the foregoing it is evident that Ben-Gurion's interest in the subject of Hapoel in 1928, as well as the transfer of its offices to Tel Aviv, arose from the two reasons described above. At that time he was concentrating assiduously on his war against the penetration and strengthening of the communists in the Histadrut branches. In this struggle Ben-Gurion ascribed great importance to Hapoel, which he saw as a "corridor to the Hagana" and not merely as a framework for developing the physical culture of the workers. From 1928 Ben-Gurion continued to follow Hapoel, albeit loosely. His interest and the importance he saw in the organization grew after the 1929 disturbances because of the Hagana's failure.[58] His attention and interest in Hapoel took on special significance and a fundamental change occurred in them in mid-1930 in view of the moves then under way to transfer the Hagana from Histadrut to national authority. Moreover, owing to the intensification that began that year in the Histadrut's struggle against Revisionism in the political and the labor sphere, Ben-Gurion embarked on steps whose purpose was to turn Hapoel, or part of it, not only into a "corridor to the Hagana" but into a semi-military defense organization of the Palestine labor movement, a kind of *Schutzbund*, parallel to the national Hagana.

In mid-1930, then, Ben-Gurion created an alternative to the existing Zionist Organization by establishing the League for Labor Palestine. Toward the end of that year he strove for the establishment of a defense organization exclusive to the Histadrut that would parallel the national defense organization. His outlook was colored by events in Europe, where a widespread and violent struggle was proceeding between social-liberal forces and the nationalist-fascist right in all their varieties, and by the militant conflict that burst out between the Palestinian labor movement and the Revisionists, after the 1929 disturbances, in the Yishuv and in the Zionist movement. Because of the transfer of the Hagana to national authority, and against the background of the events described, Ben-Gurion, the Histadrut leader, believed that the labor movement was becoming exposed and vulnerable. Therefore he concluded that there was an immediate need to create an alternative to the Hagana, which would protect the Histadrut and all its affiliates. Ben-Gurion found models for such an organization in the countries of eastern and central Europe.

As stated, Ben-Gurion's plan to turn Hapoel, or part of it, into a defense organization exclusive to the Histadrut rested on the history and contemporary events of Europe. Historically, it was a common phenomenon that the sports organizations of subject nations before 1914, such as the Slavic *Sokol*, provided the basis for the military-defensive organization of those nations in their struggle for national liberation before and during the First World War. After the war several workers' movements in eastern and central Europe set up their own quasi-military organizations. In 1924, in Germany, the *Reichsbanner Schwarz-Rot-Gold* association was created, which was common to socialists, other democratic bodies and even certain groups in the political center. In 1931 the "Iron Front" was established on the basis of this organization, it too a quasi-military defense association. With the Nazi takeover of power in 1933 the two organizations were, of course, dispersed and banned. In Austria, in 1923, the most famous workers' quasi-military organization was created, the

Republikanischer Schutzbund (Republican Defense Society), which was attached to the Austrian workers' sports organization ASKO. It was headed by Dr Julius Deutsch, who was also a leader of the sports association of the Socialist International (SASI). It should be recalled that the *Schutzbund* was at the head of the rebellion of the Vienna workers in 1932 and was defeated, despite a heroic struggle, by forces of the right-wing government. The sports movement of the workers of Latvia was also a quasi-military defense organization, the SSS, which fought, weapons in hand, against the forces of the right that finally took control of the state and destroyed its democratic regime.[59] It is no surprise, therefore, that in the reality of the Yishuv and the Zionist movement Ben-Gurion drew inferences from these organizations and set about establishing a similar body on the basis of Hapoel and within its framework. To realize this goal he used the former members of Hashomer, whose leader, Yisrael Shohat, he attached to the Hapoel secretariat in March 1930.[60]

3 Integration of Hashomer people in Hapoel (1930–1934)
Yisrael Shohat joined the secretariat of the Hapoel center at Ben-Gurion's initiative on 10 March 1930. He was followed by the incorporation into the center and the secretariat of his wife Manya Shohat, she having received the approval of her kibbutz, Kefar Gil'adi, for this, and also by a group of former Hashomer people: Yosef Harit, Eli'ezer Kroll and Haim Tzipori. Their attachment to these activities, at the highest level, was also through Ben-Gurion's backing. The entry of the group of Hashomer people to the Hapoel institutions was not due to their sporting past or their interest in physical culture. The group, headed by Yisrael and Manya Shohat, came to Hapoel at the beginning of 1930 to realize the concept of Ben-Gurion, who for years had held that Hapoel had to be converted from an organization concerned solely with physical culture to a semimilitary framework, or in Ben-Gurion's definition, "a corridor to the Hagana."

It is possible that before the 1929 disturbances Ben-Gurion regarded Yosef Hecht as most suited to this task, but after the serious rift that opened between him and Hecht following the disturbances nothing could come of this. By contrast, following the disturbances the former Hashomer people were rehabilitated and legitimized once more. In these circumstances Ben-Gurion could charge Yisrael Shohat and his people with the mission. That this move could be made only through the will, initiative and support of Ben-Gurion is attested by various evidence, including that of Yisrael Shohat, who in his memoirs relates that "he suggested that I pick up the dry bones of Hapoel and create a living and vital association." Elsewhere he says that "then Ben-Gurion invited me to work in Hapoel."[61]

By Yisrael Shohat's account, when he and his friends joined Hapoel they found a small organization, marking time and in a state of decline. In the four years of his own and his group's activity Hapoel, in his opinion, experienced a quantitative and qualitative revolution, credit for which Shohat ascribed to himself and his group. When he came to Hapoel "it numbered 400 and was in a very sorry state. I went to Hapoel, I brought in my people, in a short time we increased from 400 to 4000. We appeared in Vienna at the Olympics . . . "[62] Elsewhere he repeats his account in greater detail: "We worked in Hapoel for about three years. We invested hard work and energy, we held a trainers' course whose curriculum suited the conditions of the country *and the requirements of the Hagana.* Hapoel thrived, and was bold enough to appear at the Workers' Olympic Games held in Vienna in 1931. In a few years Hapoel grew from 400 members to 4000. The impressive parade in the streets of Tel Aviv in 1932 demonstrated the strength of Hapoel . . . "[63]

Shohat's self-praise requires criticism and should be treated with great caution. The almost magical numerical leap that Shohat adduces, from 400 to 4000 members between 1930 and 1934, in itself seems highly suspect. Quite different testimony, apparently more accurate, is found in Ben-Gurion's diary. The entry for 1 October 1929, written following a meeting with the members of Hapoel and a report from them, records that the organization had 2590 members distributed in 24 branches.[64]

There is no doubt that in the years in question the association developed, but this should be attributed in the first place to the revolutionary enlargement of the Yishuv during those years, especially the period 1932–5, when the Jewish settlement in Palestine doubled, significantly expanding demographically and economically. All this was the outcome of the *Fifth Aliya,* which flowed into the country during the "golden age" of the High Commissionership of Sir Arthur Wauchope. The great *Fifth Aliya* from eastern and central Europe also carried many young people into the sports organizations, including Hapoel. Nevertheless, the contribution of the Hashomer group to Hapoel's remarkable leap forward in that period should not be underrated: the attachment to Hapoel of such illustrious people as the Shohat couple and their comrades raised the status and esteem of the organization within and without; the Hashomer people imparted to it a greater measure of national awareness and Histadrut and class awareness, seeing no contradiction between the two; regular patterns of organization took shape; military-type discipline was introduced; Hapoel first entered the international arena at the Vienna Workers' Olympics of 1931, an appearance largely made possible through the efforts of the Shohat couple; Hapoel was emerging from obscurity and winning international recognition. Sizable financial support flowed into the association, raised by Manya Shohat from sources in Britain and the

United States; a process of integration of Hapoel members into the Hagana began too; it was around the kernel of the Hashomer group that the Hasadran society was established;[65] relations with the Histadrut progressed and improved, and joint meetings were held with the Histadrut Executive Committee to iron out problems that arose; and the Histadrut enlarged its monetary contribution to Hapoel activities, Kapai (the Histadrut bank) doubling its allocation to the organization in 1930. A second impressive convention of Hapoel was held in Tel Aviv on 10-12 October 1931; during the Vienna Workers' Olympics Yisrael Shohat was behind the decision to establish in Tel Aviv a world bureau of socialist-Zionist sports organizations of Jewish workers; in Haifa the first course for gymnasts was held from 20 March to 20 May 1931 with the financial aid of Manya Shohat and under the direction of Yosef Harit. In Petah Tikva, in December 1931, the first Hapoel conference was held, at which Yisrael and Manya Shohat, Yosef Harit and Eli'ezer Kroll were elected to the new center.[66]

It is very difficult to distinguish between the input of the objective process and the special contribution by the former Hashomer people to the development of Hapoel in those few years when they were active in it. But it is quite certain that on the eve of the sixth council of the association held on 3-4 January 1930 in Tel Aviv, Hapoel was in the throes of a serious crisis. And only subsequently did it attain the notable achievements listed in part above.[67] The role of the Hashomer veterans is to be found in the frame of these achievements.

The Conflict Years (1931-1934)

1 Debate over the nature and purpose of Hapoel

The establishment of Hapoel in the 1920s reflected a widespread trend in the European labor movements to form workers' sports organizations on the grounds that workers had special needs and interests. The Sports Association of the Socialist International (SASI) arose on the basis of the national workers' sports associations, and workers' Olympic Games were held. In the period under review there were two such Olympics in which Hapoel participated, one in Vienna, the second workers' Olympics, in 1931, and the second in Prague in 1934.

Hapoel was formed out of the same interests operating in Europe, with the addition of local conditions in Palestine. A few years after its founding, but mainly in 1930, Hapoel became caught up in an ideological debate on its nature and its purpose. The discussion centered chiefly on if its goals were limited to sport exclusively or if it should also be an instrument for achieving security and political objectives.

Already at the start of 1928 Ben-Gurion complained that Hapoel had no conception of its role and importance, and that the flimsy connection between Hapoel and the Histadrut caused a decode in the awareness by the former of its working-class nature and in its value to that class.[68] Ben-Gurion's war against the penetration of members of the (communist) "Fraction" into Hapoel showed his concern for the political shading of the organization. Ben-Gurion was undoubtedly convinced that Hapoel had security and political goals, and hence may not esconce itself in the area of physical culture alone. His position is well reflected in that he defended the organization against its critics' charges of indiscipline in its ranks, detachment from the Histadrut as shown among other things by the non-membership of the Histadrut of many Hapoel members, etc., yet at the same time he called for the introduction into Hapoel of Histadrut norms and the preservation of the correct political coloration. Ben-Gurion insisted that only members of the Histadrut were "fit to join the organization. Hapoel has to fulfill Histadrut functions" – *inter alia* workers' picketing and strikes.[69]

Ben-Gurion's views on the nature and goals of Hapoel were clearly expressed in his greetings address, in October 1932, before the third national convention of the association. In his speech Ben-Gurion stated that "membership of Hapoel requires the member set an example to the workers' community, an example at work, in the organization, in relationships with comrades, in creativity, in pioneering, in awareness and *in war . . . For us sports, with all its biological and social importance, is not an aim in itself, it is nothing but a means.* It has the right to exist and to the association devoted to it within our midst if its desires and its efforts are directed to creating in our public the excellent core, the bastion of our workers' society." Later in his speech Ben-Gurion called on Hapoel to become an instrument for the absorption of immigrants also.[70]

These views were shared by many. They were upheld by political elements to the left of Ahdut Ha'avoda and later Mapai. In the latter were many, especially from 1930 on, with the intensification of the struggle against Revisionism, who regarded the subject of sport, on which Hapoel was founded, as only one of its purposes. One of the most fiery, outstanding and extreme among those holding this position was Abba Hushi (subsequently mayor of Haifa for many years). He was a leader of Hapoel, and expressed his opinions on the matter in a speech at a general meeting of Hapoel members in Haifa in January 1933:

If we wish to see a difference between ourselves and other sports organizations, we shall see a great difference. If for all the "neutral" associations sport is an aim, for us sport is a means to free the class and the people. We wish to educate an organized and consolidated force that will fight for realization of national and class ideals . . . Hapoel should be the one showing the way and bringing about socialist realization . . . Members of Hapoel should be active in the Histadrut, be the first among the fighters for the workers' class.[71]

In the ideological debate that developed, principally in the first half of the 1930s, on the nature and purpose of Hapoel, three schools of thought crystallized, which waxed or waned according to circumstances and the political climate prevailing in particular years. The first school held Hapoel to be purely a sports organization, and nothing more. True, it was a sports organization of workers in the framework and under the sponsorship of the Histadrut, but it was not concerned with politics, concentrating solely, or essentially, on developing physical culture among the workers.

In the years closely following the founding of Hapoel this seems to have been the dominant view. Even in the turbulent thirties there were not a few in Mapai and in Hapoel who held it, the foremost among the major political figures being David Remez.[72] Most supporters of this school were people concerned purely with sports in Hapoel. This is evident from words spoken by Abba Hushi at a meeting of Mapai members active in Hapoel on 24–25 May 1935 in Tel Aviv. Hushi referred to the three main schools of thought. Regarding the first, which he called the third, he noted critically that it "exists in most members of Hapoel. They confuse the skin for the content and see the authorization of Hapoel in the sporting field exclusively."[73]

The diametrically opposed second school, the most extreme, was represented by the organizations on the left in the Histadrut, especially a sizable group of young leaders, from the *Third Aliya*, in Mapai. The foremost spokesman among them was Abba Hushi. Among the veterans of the *Second Aliya* this school was supported by the former Hashomer people, it being the cause of their joining Hapoel. For many years the unquestioned head of this extreme, militant school was the leader of the Histadrut, David Ben-Gurion. At the aforementioned meeting of Mapai activists in Hapoel, Abba Hushi pronounced his and his adherents' credo on the matter:

In my opinion, Hapoel is not an organization for bodily culture alone. Something essential differentiates us from other sporting associations, and this is what justifies our separate existence. For us, sports are only a means to an end, which is the creation of a conquering, pioneering camp, the avant-garde of the Histadrut and the entire movement. Hapoel must be a force for realization, a shield and fighter for the Histadrut.[74]

In the following years too Abba Hushi remained faithful to his views. But he did not reach extreme political conclusions, as did the Hashomer people, these conclusions being only partially accepted.[75] The third school was intermediary, seeking to grasp the stick at both ends. Those of this outlook admitted that the chief pillar and nature of Hapoel was the development of physical culture among the workers, yet they held that the association had additional goals in the political and security sphere. These were expressed by Dov Hoz:

> Although Hapoel is at root an organization for physical culture and realization of order and discipline, and it constitutes a social organizational framework for youth, Hapoel additionally has special tasks as we clearly see at *special times*. We know that in times of emergency for the Histadrut, when it is subject to difficult conditions and needs special recruitment of qualified forces, it looks to Hapoel.

Hoz indeed recognized that Hapoel was primarily a sports organization, but in practice, in the stormy years when this debate was raging, there was no real difference, at least until 1934–5, between Hoz and Hushi. This was not the case regarding the views of these two and of David Remez and the pure sportsmen.[76]

The dispute over the nature and purpose of Hapoel was not unique to the Palestinian labor movement. As a rule it was to be found in workers' sports organizations in Europe, in a situation of similar problems of serious, violent political clashes. It was natural that the hard-fought struggle of the Palestinian labor movement, led by the Histadrut, against the Revisionist right in the Yishuv and the Zionist movement, would engender an ideological debate, of practical implications, as described. As in Europe, so in Palestine the aggravation of this struggle and its escalation into violence resulted in the workers' sports organization – Hapoel – being made a superstructure within which a semi-military body was established exclusive to the Palestinian labor movement, like the Austrian *Schutzbund*. As noted, this move, from late 1930 on, was initiated, directed and led, ideologically and practically, by David Ben-Gurion.

2 Debate on violence in Mapai

At the beginning of this chapter it was noted that the disputes between the Revisionists and the labor movement were rooted primarily in politics, that is, the struggle for supremacy in the Zionist movement. They spread thence to work relations. In Palestine these constituted the most sensitive area, owing to the real economic interests they entailed. Therefore, the clash in this area had the greatest force, and spilt over into violence. The murder of Haim Arlozoroff in the summer of 1933 added a dramatic dimension to the conflict. Relations between the two movements were replete with hatred and violent outbursts. In Palestine and the diaspora, particularly eastern Europe, there was a sense of civil war.

Violence, as fruit of political enmity, had actually first occurred at the end of the 1920s. In 1928 Betar members set upon a May Day parade organized by the communists.[77] On 5 October 1928 an assault was again made by the Betar people against a meeting being conducted in Yiddish, organized by the "Left" Poaley Zion in Tel Aviv in honor of Ya'akov Zerubavel.[78]

These were isolated outbursts, which did not yet create an atmosphere of violence, although they contributed to the negative image of the Betar people and the Revisionists among the workers. Violence as a regular occurrence began in 1930. Until the second half of 1933 the workers were usually, apart from the "seventh day of Passover," those attacked and on the defensive, but at the end of 1933 and in 1934 the initiative passed to them. Against this background a serious debate ensued on the position the party and the Histadrut should adopt toward violence.

The debate, which took place mainly at the beginning of 1934, started when on the last day of the Passover festival, 17 April 1933, workers attacked and dispersed a parade of Betar members in Tel Aviv. The event was dubbed the "seventh day of Passover" affair. In protest against the deed, Berl Katznelson tendered his resignation from the Mapai center on 20 April 1933. Yosef Aharonovitz published an article condemning violence by workers, which was published in Davar under the title "Ye shall not walk in their laws" (a play on a biblical phrase). In his article Aharonovich argued that the premeditated and preventive use of force against the opponents of the labor movement would boomerang and in the end destroy both the labor movement and the Zionist enterprise.[79] The protests of Katznelson and Aharonovich did nothing, and six weeks after the "seventh day of Passover," on the festival of Weeks, another organized attack by workers was made, in Haifa, against a parade through the city streets by Betar members wearing brown uniforms and led by Abba Ahimeir.[80]

The issue of the planned and preventive use of force by the workers stimulated in Mapai enormous passions and acrimonious quarrels. Although the discussion had begun in 1933, after the Katznelson's resignation, the marathon debate, which led to practical conclusions, was held at the party center only at the beginning of 1934. These discussions, on how to wage war against Revisionism, opened at the Mapai center on 31 January 1934 and continued at sessions of the center on 5 February and 14 February, and were summed up on 21 February 1934. The intensive debates evinced the existence of two currents regarding the question of how to fight Revisionism and the use of force: the moderate current and the militant-extremist.

The moderate current did not promote pacifism but supported only token measures against Revisionist violence. Its partisans wished to shift the center of gravity of the war to the plane of education and ideology. In their view, the planned and preventive use of force was morally destructive, and ultimately would harm the workers themselves by undermining their moral foundations. For them the planned and preventive use of force would only expand the civil war and could wipe out the Zionist endeavor. This camp included Yitzhak Lufban, Moshe Beilinson, Yosef Baratz, Shmuel Dayan, Avraham Haft, David Remez and Berl Katznelson.[81]

The militants were led by Ben-Gurion, who drew a parallel between the situation in Palestine and the Jewish-Zionist street in the diaspora and the world struggle of the socialist-liberal forces against national-fascism then in progress. In contrast to the moderates Ben-Gurion put forward an entirely different vision: "Constitutional means and influencing public opinion- these are no longer sufficient in our war against Betar . . . You have nothing more ridiculous and wrong than to combat by constitutional means a force that is wholly anti-constitutional. In our war with Betar it is impossible to make do with methods of moralizing, and it is necessary to set our own organized force against it."[82] In Ben-Gurion's view the reaction of the masses, which usually were passive, was not to be relied on. Therefore his intractable position was that it was necessary to meet force with force, but this must be organized. "It is necessary for there to be an authorized Histadrut organ that will strike in the hour of need deliberately." Elsewhere Ben-Gurion continued to argue, in the same spirit, that "the war against Revisionist violence must be waged by special organs under severe military discipline."[83] Ben-Gurion admitted that the use of force was dangerous and at times destructive, and this was precisely the reason why it must not be delivered into the hands of the masses. The alternative, therefore, was to create a small organized and disciplined force.

Ben-Gurion was supported by Zalman (Ziama) Aharonovich (Aranne), who reasoned that because of the lack of response by the workers to Betarist violence a psychosis of fear and submission had been created in the public. Referring to the similar situation in Germany, Aharonovich maintained that there the workers failed because the German SD (Social-Democrats) had not trained them to contend with such a state of affairs. The militant current also included A. Rabinovich, H. Shorer, Y. Duvdevani, Y. Bankover and also Abba Hushi, who defined his position unequivocally: "I'll say it openly – I'm for blows, and I don't call this violence. Everyone agrees that if anyone hits me I have to hit back. And if there is a movement whose central idea is to strike us to the very core, must we wait until it is strong enought to destroy us and we have no power to resist it?" Hushi demanded that the Revisionists be prevented from reaching a position of strength from which they could threaten to destroy the workers' movement. He also justified the onslaught in Haifa on the festival of Weeks (*Shavu'ot*) in 1933. In his view it was actually the use of organized workers' force that had prevented bloodshed. His conclusion was that the organization of force was more necessary for deterrence than for application.[84] Also in the militant camp were Berl Repetor, Yitzhak Ben Aharon, Yona Kesse, Eliahu Dobkin and Avraham Katznelson. Yitzhak Tabenkin complained, at the meeting of the center on 31 January 1934, that the center was already holding its fourth discussion on the subject: the first had been on account of the strike at Petah Tikva in February 1933, the second following the "seventh day of Passover," the third was after the assassination of Arlozoroff, and the fourth was the present one. In fact Tabenkin supported Ben-Gurion's position and approved of the use of organized force. This camp also included Shaul Meirov (Avigur), Bat-Sheva Haikin, Dov Hoz and George Landauer.[85]

Toward the vote and taking of practical decisions three positions took shape: (a) approval of the use of force only for defensive purposes; (b) approval of the use of force in an organized and controlled manner; and (c) approval of the use of force actively, by initiative and unconditionally. The first was supported by such persons mentioned as Lufban, Beilinson, Remez, Katznelson, etc.; the second by Ben-Gurion, Tabenkin, Ben Zvi, Aharonovich (Aranne), Meirov (Avigur), etc.; the third by Ben Aharon, Duvdevani, Hushi, Bankover, Repetor, Shorer, etc. Those in the last group claimed that Revisionism was a fascist movement and the war against it had to be waged uncompromisingly. Moreover, in their view there was no chance of reaching any understanding or peace with this movement. Influenced by the events in Austria and Germany they warned that the fate of the workers of Palestine must not be like that of the workers in those countries. The fascist-Revisionist enemy understood only force, and therefore it was incumbent to use force, planned and preventive, against him until his elimination.

Finally, victory went to the holders of the middle position led by Ben-Gurion, who affirmed the use of disciplined and organized force subject to the control of suitable institutions. The Mapai center, at its meeting on 24 February 1934, took a vote and approved the establishment of a security organization charged with the task of contending with and repelling Revisionist violence.[86]

The decisions of the Mapai center were extremely important, because they provided the support of the dominant party in the Histadrut to the harnessing of the latter, with its resources and machinery, to the establishment of the "organization." In fact, Ben-Gurion had pre-empted the move. The decisions taken gave formal democratic authorization not to a future organization, but to an organization that in fact actually existed, the Hasadran Association.

3 Establishment of the Hasadran ("Attendants") Association

The first Hasadran company was apparently founded in Haifa by Abba Hushi in 1927, as a section of Hapoel.[87] Other branches followed Haifa's lead.[88] The function of Hasadran was to work at various ushering jobs for pay. Hasadran had no political or security significance and the nature of its work was simply economic, with the addition of very few elements of sport.

In 1928 Ben-Gurion's interest in Hapoel had had nothing to do with Hasadran. As mentioned, his concern with Hapoel arose from his wish to turn it into a "corridor to the Hagana" and also a weapon in the war against communism.[89] Again at the beginning of 1930 Ben-Gurion resolved to implement his views on Hapoel and therefore he brought Yisrael Shohat and his people into the association in order to put his ideas into practice and actually convert Hapoel into a "corridor to the Hagana," while retaining its legal front and activity. At a joint meeting of members of the Histadrut Executive Committee and of the Hapoel Center on 10 March 1930 Ben-Gurion declared that "Hapoel should not be involved in matters of security. Hapoel is a legal association . . . The association must remain an overt organization." For Ben-Gurion this was indeed possible because Hapoel was meant only as a training ground for the Hagana, not as a replacement.[90] It should be recalled that at this stage Ben-Gurion was still investing effort to ensure the authority of the Histadrut over the Hagana.

The Hasadran companies in Hapoel experienced serious problems over their essence and their direction. These stemmed from the failures they suffered in the chief area of activity, which was supposed to be economic, that is, to make profits from various forms of ushering. There were also difficulties owing to the slight occupation of Hasadran with sport, despite its being part of a body whose entire purpose was concern with physical culture. The result was frustration, confusion and demoralization, which spread throughout the Hasadran companies. This situation is well reflected in the discussions of Hasadran in Tel Aviv in 1931. From these it clearly arises that the framework was not attractive and therefore it had very few members. Only 17 people were present at the Hasadran general meeting in Tel Aviv on 21 July 1931. The Tel Aviv company attempted to engage in drilling exercises and jujitsu, but the feeling of the members was of economic failure, lack of direction and bewilderment, with the resultant chaos and demoralization. At the general meeting of the company on 18 December 1931 hard questions were raised, the outcome of the state of affairs: "What is the role of the section? Is the section not for sports?" The participants also complained that the little sporting activity that had been introduced and the drilling exercises were devoid of meaning or point. It may be supposed that the situation in the other companies throughout the country was no different. So from the documents available it seems that in 1930 and 1931 there was still no change in the old character of Hasadran, which also became perhaps the most problematic element in Hapoel, in the absence of a viable basis and clear purpose.

The change in perception of Hasadran began to appear in the spring of 1932. Only then, for the first time, did a new concept make itself heard on the nature of Hasadran. It is true that in theory the economic functions were not entirely abandoned, but they were pushed aside and made merely marginal. The essence of Hasadran was by now becoming defused in completely different terms. The revolutionary change is clearly reflected in the discussions of the selfsame Tel Aviv company that only a few months earlier had been in a mood of aimlessness, frustration and despair. At the general meeting of this company on 20 May 1932 a quite different spirit was in the air, in which very different words were spoken from those heard there in December 1931. The general call at the meeting was that Hasadran prepare itself for a range of activities different from those it had engaged in formerly, with the aim of becoming an organization similar to "the *Austrian Schutzbund*" (my emphasis – Y.G.). "The Histadrut has two enemies that hate it: the Fraction on the one hand and the Revisionists on the other. With fist [ ] against [ ] fists the company must be first of all and Hapoel in general" (original writing in document unclear).

This was the first time that the demand was made to turn Hapoel as a whole and the Hasadran company in particular into a semi-military force of clear political and class shading and with a well-defused aim – defense of the Histadrut. It was the first time that the comparison was made between Hasadran and the Austrian *Schutzbund*. At a meeting of the Tel Aviv company leadership on 26 June 1932 the subject of training members in arms and marksmanship was already discussed. At the meeting of the company on 5 August 1932 one of its activists declared that "the Hasadran company is called on for activities vital to the worker without being ashamed that this takes on the form of a gendarmerie. But this is the way by which we shall succeed."[91]

Only in the spring and summer of 1932, then, was the awareness sufficiently mature and the ideology formulated, among the rank-and-file as well as the leadership, for the necessary change of direction in the nature, purpose, organization and operation of Hasadran. Such awareness and the ideology, however, still did not lead to real steps toward organizational and institutional expression of the conceptual revolution.

It seems that it was Ben-Gurion who elaborated the first program intended to provide an organizational basis for the ideological change that had taken place regarding Hasadran. The program for the creation of Mishmar Hapoel (or Hamishmar – The Hapoel Guard) is undated, but it is most likely that Ben-Gurion wrote it in 1932. In it he listed the tasks that were to be imposed on the members of Hamishmar. The Hamishmar member had to be "a fighter of the labor war, protector of the Yishuv, nurturer of physical culture and the spirit of the workers' class, constant in the realization of socialist Zionism." According to the program the Mishmar Hapoel command would be appointed by the Histadrut Executive Committee so that the Histadrut would have full control. Ben-Gurion determined that those worthy of acceptance by Hamishmar must be imbued with socialist-Zionist consciousness. The volunteers–recruits would be aged 18 to 25, apart from exceptional cases. Applicants would be accepted through the local branches, but acceptance would require confirmation by the command. The volunteers would serve in the planned body for two years. Ben-Gurion even decided that the uniform of Hamishmar was to be identical to that of Hapoel, with the addition of a special badge.[92]

Ben-Gurion's outlook, from which the reform of Hasadran grew, is also attested by the content of his speech at the third national convention of Hapoel at the end of October 1932 in Tel Aviv. There Ben-Gurion made clear that for him sports were a means, and the essential thing was to turn Hapoel into the fortress of the workers' society so that it would be the "shield of labor." He continued in the same spirit:

> Those who assumed the name "Hapoel" [the worker] knew first and fore-most that there was no greater sin and calamity and danger than for the workers' community to be weak. We have been commanded by history, by our mighty mission, to be strong and to repel any instigation and provoca-tion against the labor movement. Hapoel is called on to serve as a model of loyalty and *to consolidate a reliant force for our movement.* [My emphasis – Y.G.][93]

More concrete organizational moves were made by Ben-Gurion at the end of 1932 and beginning of 1933, when tensions in the conflict with the Revisionists rose throughout the country following the outbreak of the strike at the Frumin factory in Jerusalem and after Jabotinsky published a series of articles fiercely attacking the Histadrut. The workers' commu-nity interpreted the articles as a call to destroy the Histadrut. They saw this expressed by the actions of Jabotinsky's followers, the strike-breakers in the field.

Late in December 1932 Ben-Gurion assembled a small group of people who were involved in security matters and were also active in the struggle against Revisionism. Among those gathered were Yisrael Shohat, Dov Hoz, Shaul Meirov (Avigur), Eliahu Golomb, Zalman (Ziama) Aharonovich (Aranne) and Abba Hushi. The outcome of the meeting was that Abba Hushi presented a proposed program for the reorganization of

Hasadran and its conversion into a semi-military defense force. The proposal stated that:

> 1. The Histadrut requires today and will especially require in the future an organized, consolidated force, possessing consciousness and exemplary discipline, which will be forever at its disposal in order to protect the organized workers' class and its gains.
> 3. The Hapoel association is the framework in which this force will be formed.
> 6. The groups-kernels will everywhere constitute the Hasadran company and to this purpose there will be appropriate reorganization of the Hasadran company.
> 9. The groups [i.e., Hasadran companies – Y.G.] will place themselves immediately on their formation at the disposal of the leadership to fulfill practical daily tasks and in accordance with the goal stated in paragraph 1.[94]

Other clauses of the program determined that the Hapoel center would select the candidates for companies in every local branch, but final approval of acceptance would lie with the Histadrut Executive Committee. Similarly, Hushi proposed that the Hapoel center would appoint the top leadership of Hasadran, but with final approval by the secretariat of the Histadrut Executive Committee, namely, of Ben-Gurion.

The program also proposed preparing members of the renewed Hasadran for their tasks through intensive educational, cultural and ideological activity. Professionally, they would be trained in wrestling, jujitsu, long-distance throwing of objects, marksmanship, cycling and horseriding.

Abba Hushi's program, together with Ben-Gurion's own – Mishmar Hapoel – formed the basis for the reorganization of Hasadran in July–September 1933, after the triumphant election campaign, brilliantly conducted by Ben-Gurion, for the Eighteenth Zionist Congress in 1933. This sweeping victory and the course and results of the congress greatly strengthened the status of the labor movement *vis-à-vis* Revisionism and brought enormous prestige to the architect of the victory, David Ben-Gurion. Evidence that the reorganization of Hasadran did not commence prior to Ben-Gurion's departure for eastern Europe to lead the election campaign for the congress may be found in a letter from Ben-Gurion to Yisrael Shohat, sent from the vessel in which he sailed to Europe:

> To Yisrael Shohat. Esperia 3.4.1933. I was hesitant about beginning with the organization of Hasadran, knowing that I was due to travel, and I was not sure that the matter would continue, and in my opinion a thing like that should not be started and left in the middle. I had the feeling that in the first stage my active participation would be needed. If I had not been obliged to travel I would have devoted myself to this matter as my chief task, and this

is what I shall do immediately on my return to the country after the congress. Meet Eliahu and Dov and ascertain if it is possible to find already now a suitable comrade who will devote himself here even now to this subject. If not, it is necessary for the time being to swell the ranks of Hapoel in town and village. The aim should be that there is not a single member of the Histadrut under thirty who is not a member of Hapoel.[95]

In his letter Ben-Gurion gave approval and authorization to Yisrael Shohat to begin the first cautious steps toward reforming Hasadran, although, as noted, its major reconstruction took place some months later after the triumphal return of Ben-Gurion to Palestine.

In July, but mainly in August and September 1933, the process of recruitment of selected people to Hasadran began. The aim was that simultaneously with the change in purpose of the organization its human material, deemed unsuited to the new tasks, be totally replaced. To this end all the new volunteers- recruits were obliged to complete a detailed questionnaire, which underwent meticulous checking by the national command set up by the Hapoel center and approved by the Histadrut Executive Committee to establish the Hasadran Association.

The reorganization also led to a partial change of the official name of the old-new association. Instead of the usual name Hasadran Company, or simply Hasadran, appeared the new title *Igud Hasadran* – Hasadran Association.[96] In practice the new name did not take hold with the public, who continued to call the entirely new creature by the old name.

From the volunteers' answers to the questionnaires it is evident how they perceived the new nature of Hasadran. The question "What are the causes and reasons" for the candidate's application to the association elicited replies of a purely ideological and political shading, such as "to create a consolidated, organized and trained unit possessing discipline that can serve as the *avant-garde* for Hapoel and the workers' community in their daily war for the working Jewish Palestine; the last year in the world and the country has made special organizations necessary;[97] considering the world situation with fascism on the rise, and especially that among us, the Jewish people, there is already the start of a fascist movement (the Revisionists), there is need for a workers' movement in Palestine to form like the *Schutzbund* in Austria and other countries companies whose task will be to guard the Histadrut from any dark forces wishing to break it; on the other hand to protect the lives of the Jews in the country against savage attacks that may break out always."[98] Some of the responses of volunteers to the major question of why they volunteered are laconic, but all, in different variations, were similar in content and reflected keen awareness of the real danger overhanging the labor movement, the insignificance of the events in Europe on the Jewish street, etc. A sizable proportion of the answers were lengthy, detailed and effusive, such as "To protect our status *in organized Jewish labor*. To fight to the finish the fascist peril which is the Betarist movement that is assaulting us, and I think, 'Whoever comes to kill you, kill him first' [a Hebrew saying]. To protect the workers' movement and its institutions from this danger. To organize the majority of the workers and to fill them with socialist activization so that we can meet force with force." As stated, the influence of events in Austria and Germany was clearly marked in the volunteers, who applied them to the state of affairs in Palestine.[99] Similar replies were made by volunteers not only in Tel Aviv but also in Rehovot, Hadera and elsewhere.[100]

The process of qualitative and structural reorganization of Hasadran in the summer of 1933 is highlighted in the report submitted by the Tel Aviv Hapoel branch to the general meeting of the branch on its activity from July 1932 to December 1933, entitled "The Hasadran Companies":

> In view of the situation in Hapoel and the Histadrut, the Hasadran Company was charged with special tasks, which weighed greatly on the members of the Company, and the branch saw it as its particular duty to devote additional attention to this Company. The need of the hour was to make the Company the active element most loyal and dedicated to the concerns of Hapoel and the Histadrut of all times. We were called on to conduct a first-class recruitment of dozens of members to fulfill special tasks daily, and *in light of this need the committee decided to alter the organizational structure of the Company, in accordance with the instructions of the Hapoel center. A re-registration of Company members was announced; each person who registered was the subject of an individual discussion; some who registered were not approved. The existing leadership was disbanded and in its place a leadership approved by the center was appointed.*

A similar account appears in a letter sent by the secretariat of the Hapoel branch in Haifa to the secretariat of the Hapoel center in July 1933. The letter states: "I hereby submit to you a report of activity in our branch regarding the renewed *Hasadran organization* . . . I have drawn up a list of members from the branch, which amounts to more than 90 members. I am also to receive a list from Abba Hushi . . . "

It is perfectly clear that following the change in essence and purpose of Hasadran its human material was entirely replaced also. In organization, the elected leaderships of the companies were dismissed and in their stead commands were appointed by the Hapoel center with the approval of the Histadrut Executive Committee. The intention was to form a company of the Hasadran Association in every important Hapoel branch. In the large branches such as Tel Aviv and Haifa more than one company was planned. A commander and his deputy headed each company, which was divided into groups under group leaders. Intensive educational and ideological activity was undertaken among the Hasadran Association membership. Henceforward the Hasadran Association was conceived as the fighting *avant-garde* of the Palestinian labor movement.[101]

Beyond the Hasadran Association, Hapoel was concerned for educational and ideological activity among all its members, in the spirit of the view that Hapoel in its entirety must enroll in the defense of the labor movement. This was done through explanatory material orally and in writing, as in the following document:

> In light of the situation in the country, with the expansion of the fascist onslaught, the propaganda of plunder, and the attacks against the organized Jewish labor movement – the Histadrut, the clashes against the Jewish worker's organization and his gains, the incitement and provocation in the fascist and liberal press in Palestine and abroad . . . we deem it necessary to approach you with the following words: . . . It is incumbent upon us to consolidate the Hapoel camp from within . . . to stand ready, as a united and strong *avant-garde* to repel any attack against the Histadrut . . . Hapoel is that which is obliged to and must be the loyal *defense army* of the Histadrut, which will be able to rely on it and be confident in it in its war and in its work every day."[102]

Ben-Gurion's interest was not confined to the establishment of the Hasadran Association in Palestine, which he charged with the task of contending, also by initiated and preventive actions, with the threat from the right and Revisionism. He strove equally to create a similar instrument for the same purpose in the diaspora. The aim was to set up branches of Hapoel in the working communities there, and especially in Hehalutz. Within the Hapoel branches it was planned to create companies of the Hasadran Association, which would act to drive Revisionist violence off the streets. In his letter to his colleagues in Palestine, sent from Warsaw on 9 July 1933, the eve of the Eighteenth Zionist Congress, Ben-Gurion among other things suggests sending emissaries from the country with the purpose of realizing the goal described, "and against the forces of the underworld now gathering in the hooligan *brit hehayal* (Soldier's League) of Jabotinsky to form an all powerful physical force, pioneering and cultural, to protect the honor and strength of the movement in the diaspora." Ben-Gurion believed that if they worked for several years in the diaspora in the spirit of his proposals they would succeed in creating a large movement there: There is ample strength, there are huge camps, there are human resources – lacking is leadership, *military commandership*, direction, rule!"[103]

The above-described stages of development in the creation of the Hasadran Association–the Palestinian *Schutzbund* – are based on available documentation. In the Regulations of the old Hasadran Company of the Hapoel branch in Tel Aviv, dated 21 July 1931, it is stated:

Name: Hapoel Tel Aviv, Hasadran Company.
Purpose: to introduce order, discipline and precision into the workers' community.
Means: a. Participation in keeping order at various activities . . .
       b. Study of drilling and physical training.
       c. Self-study of order and discipline and introduction of these
          ideas into the ranks of the community.

Membership of the old Hasadran companies was open to any Hapoel branch member aged 18 years and over who was found suitable for attendance duties by the company administration. This body consisted of four members: one representative of the Hapoel branch committee and three elected by the general meeting of the company and consumed by the branch committee. The administration handled all internal company matters while external activity required the approval of the branch committee. The administration distributed the functions of the company, which were essentially three: head of the attendants, company secretary and financial manager.[104] The Regulations are in great detail and cover three printed pages. It is most likely that these regulations were a feature of all the old Hasadran companies.

About 18 months later, in the resolutions of the Hapoel center of 2–3 December 1932, paragraph 2, clause (b) contains the key decision:

> b. To engage in planned reorganization in all the Hasadran companies; every member entering Hasadran requests special approval by the special committee to be created by the central secretariat.[105]

This decision expands and somewhat alters the picture presented above. It seems that Hapoel center decided on the reorganization in Hasadran already at the beginning of December 1932, and therefore Abba Hushi's proposal, which was put forward later, was the result not only of the talks initiated by Ben-Gurion at the end of December 1932, but had already taken shape following earlier discussions in the Hapoel center and the resolution taken by this body at the beginning of December 1932.

From Circular no. 1 of the chief command of the Hasadran Association dated 27 August 1933 and its two appendices, several facts may be learnt: Reorganizational activity in Hasadran had already begun, the new name "Hasadran Association" appeared at the head of the circular, the Hasadran Association had a national chief command; the circular portrays the new organizational elements characteristic of the Hasadran Association. Appendix A gives details of the organizational structure and the following picture emerges: there was a chief, national, command, which is described as having been approved by the Hapoel center and the Histradrut Executive Committee. The local company was headed by a command composed of 3–5 people, including the company commander and local Hapoel branch coordinator. These two were appointed by the Hapoel branch committees but required approval by the chief command of the Hasadran Association. According to the plan, the company command was supposed to operate in close connection with the local Hapoel branch committee, but it received its instructions from the chief command of the Hasadran Association. The basic cell of the company consisted of 8 people, including the cell commander, who was appointed by the company commander and approved by the local company command. Two cells constituted a group of 17 people, headed by a group commander. The appointment of the group commander proceeded like that of the cell commander. Two groups constituted a company of 34 people or more, headed by the company commander. The instructions of the chief command of the Hasadran Association to the company commander were issued in the form of quasi-military orders, bearing a serial number also. The instructions of the company commanders to those under them were similarly given. Appendix B contains details of the form of training of the company. The new subjects that the companies engaged in are typical. In addition to the wider occupation with sports, there were now in addition first aid, marksmanship, jujitsu, wrestling, topography, map-reading, compass skills, day and night orientation in the field, all types of communications and, of course, educational and ideolgical activity.[106] The range of subjects covered by the companies of the Hasadran Association was radically different from those that had occupied the old Hasadran. These were undoubtedly the subjects of a semi-military defense organization, if not something more.

The Hasadran Association was an autonomous national organization. It was, indeed, connected to the Hapoel framework on the national and local level, but nothing more. Its principal authority was the Histadrut Executive Committee.

Something of the history of the Hasadran Association, or the renewed Hasadran, may also be learned from the report on it submitted by the Hapoel secretariat to the second national conference of the Association, held in Haifa on 20–23 March 1936. The report states:

> With the enlargement of the workers' movement in Palestine . . . with the sharpening of contradictions within the Yishuv in economic and political areas, the intensification of aggressive attempts by "zealous Zionism," awareness increasingly crystallized on the need for *the establishment of an organization that would be charged with the task of protecting the gains of the movement in the face of their attackers* . . .
>   The Hapoel center expressed the willingness of the Association to undertake, in cooperation with the institutions of the Histadrut, the creation of this organization within the Association.[107]

The report notes that the Histadrut Executive Committee and the

Hapoel center began constructing the organization at the beginning of 1934. It was determined that supreme and direct authority over the body would lie with the Executive Committee. On this basis, "the Hapoel center formed a national commission which was appointed by the Histadrut Executive Committee after consultations with the Hapoel center. This commission was set the task of organizing and training the organization, the "Hasadran Association." The report notes with satisfaction that although matters were conducted hastily the organization achieved the purpose for which it had been created, to halt and repel the violence of the Revisionists. In circumstances of attacks by the right, the body imparted to the workers self-confidence, which they had previously lacked.[108]

According to the documents presented in this chapter, the author or authors of the report were inaccurate in the timetable they gave of the establishment of the Hasadran Association, although it is possible that the final "polish" was applied at the start of 1934. It may also be that official report to the conference, concerning the timetable, was written to conform with the resolutions of the Mapai center. As noted, the center only voted at its session on 24 February 1934 to establish the Association. Most members of the party center apparently did not know that what they called by the casual name the "Association" already existed, and was called the Hasadran Association."[109]

The "Organization" or "Hasadran Association" or the renewed "Hasadran" had as its appointed commander at the time in question Yosef Rokhel (Avidar), who writes in his recollections:

> I was requested to organize this body and to stand at its head. The essence of the role of Hasadran . . . was to ensure the safety of the workers' movement and the Histadrut with its institution, its meetings and its conferences . . . According to the tradition of the workers' movement this body, entitled "Hasadran," was given additional practical tasks, such as organizing the struggle for Jewish labor on the moshavot, "dealing" with informers on illegal immigrants, help in bringing the illegal immigrants in off the ships, etc. I devoted myself to this task until the beginning of 1935, when I was asked to give it up. I was told to find a suitable commander to replace me. Not without effort I persuaded Moshe Zalitsky (Carmel) to accept the command of Hasadran.

It is important to note that Yosef Avidar's description is very general and concentrates primarily on the national tasks of Hasadran, which were secondary in terms of the aims of the organization. Regarding the area of occupation and the chief goal, Avidar confines himself to a very broad statement that conceals more than it reveals.[110]

It was the Hasadran Association, or the "Organization," headed by Yosef Avidar that led the premeditated attack against the Betarists in

Haifa on 17 October 1934 on the occasion of the address by the Revisionist leader W. von Weisel. The Mapai center discussed the clash on 21 October 1934 at a very stormy session. From the minutes, and particularly the words of Yosef Avidar, something more may be learned of the history of the Hasadran Association in 1934. It transpires that the Organization indeed had a supervisory body, but from a certain stage the latter existed on paper only, and in practice ceased to operate in July 1934, and close to this date it actually disintegrated. Hence, in mid-1934 a situation arose that Avidar described as dangerous, and he even warned his superiors – the Histadrut Executive Committee – of it. In his speech at the meeting of the center Avidar stressed the danger that lay in the existence of a semi-military organization with a commander but without a supervisory Histadrut organ. The example that he and at least some of his listeners most probably had in mind was the condition of the Hagana under the command of Yosef Hecht until 1929. In light of this, Avidar demanded one of two alternatives from the Mapai center: either to renew the supervisory body of the Hasadran Organization or to disband it. Avidar himself threatened to resign if the supervisory body was not created at once.[111]

From the foregoing account, by mid-1932 a new mood was already prevalent in Hapoel generally and in Hasadran in particular toward the change in the latter as described, turning it into a central and eastern European-type defense organization for the labor movement, like the Austrian *Schutzbund*; its task would be to protect the labor movement, upon which the political, economic and social pressure brought to bear by the right and the Revisionists had been felt increasingly since the 1929 disturbances and the labor dispute at Kefar Saba in April 1930. This mood and the fresh outlook undoubtedly sprang from a leading and activist group in Mapai and the Histadrut, headed by David Ben-Gurion. In December 1932 the Hapoel center already decided on thorough reform, in organization and manpower, of the old Hasadran in light of the new goals placed before it. At the end of 1932 or at the beginning of 1933 Ben-Gurion and Abba Hushi each composed documents that served as the ideological and structural foundation for the Hasadran Association. The first organizational steps toward the creation of this body were taken in June and July 1933, when the election campaign to the Eighteenth Zionist Congress was still in full swing. The work of establishment was taken up with added vigor in August and September, 1933, at which time the questionnaires completed by the new volunteers to the new body were distributed and collected. This was after Ben-Gurion's great victory in the election campaign for the congress and the triumph of the Palestine labor movement, headed by Mapai, at the congress itself. In fact the Hasadran Association already existed at the end of 1933, although the finishing touches were perhaps applied at the beginning of 1934. In the middle of that year the supervisory body of Hasadran Association broke up, for various reasons. This collapse was perhaps one of the first signs of the change that began to appear in the political and personal conditions that led to the foundation of the Hasadran Association. The change in these conditions in the second half of 1934 and early 1935 ultimately caused the value and prestige of the Hasadran Association to decline, and in 1936 it was replaced by another body, the Hapoel Companies.[112]

Swan-Song (1934–1935)

1 From "Class to Nation" – Ben-Gurion's change in attitude to the Zionist Organization and the struggle against Revisionism

Ben-Gurion's basically negative attitude to the Zionist Organization, which he displayed in the 1920s, did not alter in 1930 and the first half of 1931.[113] But in the aftermath of the Seventeenth Zionist Congress in Basel in July 1931 a qualitative change occurred in Ben-Gurion's outlook. The successes of the workers at the congress led him to the realization that an alternative organization was unnecessary because the workers were capable of taking over and transforming the Zionist movement from within. At the Seventeenth Congress the workers had indeed made impressive gains. Not only did they prove able to repulse the onslaught of Revisionism and its allies and to keep it in opposition, they themselves entered the Zionist leadership, where they became a major element. Moreover, the election of the weak Nahum Sokolov to the presidency of the movement instead of the strong and authoritative Weizmann enhanced the workers' capacity to direct and shape the Zionist movement. These new circumstances led to the change in Ben-Gurion's outlook, with the result that he abandoned the issue of the "League" to dedicate himself to instilling his party with the consciousness of the need to conquer the Zionist movement and to convert the labor movement into an *avant-garde* that represented and led the people. To this orientation he applied the slogan "From Class to Nation."

Ben-Gurion was consistent in his view of the "old" Zionist Organization, which he voiced on various occasions, including the Mapai Council at Kefar Yehezkel in July 1932, where he spoke of "the crisis in Zionism and the workers' movement." "What then is the meaning of the crisis in Zionism, expressed in the paralysis of activity by the Zionist Organization, its disintegration and helplessness?" he asked. "The crisis in Zionism did not follow the 1929 disturbances but preceded them by several years." For Ben-Gurion, the negative manifestations began in the Zionist Organization as early as the time of the *Fourth Aliya*, even, before the eruption of the economic crisis of 1926. Since then there had been a deterioration in the Zionist Organization, and the "expanded Jewish Agency" had gone the same way after its creation in 1929. The causes for this momentous crisis stemmed, Ben-Gurion believed, from the draining of General Zionism, which for years had led the Zionist movement, of its national content. In light of this it was essential that there be "a change of guard in the Zionist Organization. For the sake of maintaining the necessary accord between the Zionist enterprise in the land and the Zionist movement in the world, the workers' movement is called on to become the decisive force in the Zionist Organization, to constitute the overwhelming majority."[114] At the second Mapai conference on 3 November 1932, Ben-Gurion again stated that "the time has come for our movement to cease being a wing of Zionism, but to undertake the entire burden and all the responsibilities of the Zionist Organization fully and completely . . . It is incumbent on our movement now to identify absolutely with the Zionist Organization, to be a majority at congresses and in the Zionist Organization and to stand at its head."[115]

The irony of history is that after the defeat sustained by their major foes, the Revisionists, the hour came for the workers to win the coveted prize that they had denied their opponents, the conquest of the Zionist movement.

Suffused with a powerful feeling that it was possible to realize the ideas he preached, Ben-Gurion left for eastern Europe to lead the election campaign for the Eighteenth Zionist Congress in the summer of 1933. The mighty victory by the labor movement in these elections must undoubtedly be ascribed in large part to the successful election campaign conducted by Ben-Gurion in eastern Europe. The labor movement won a crushing victory, and the workers' faction at the congress accounted for 44 percent of all the delegates. In comparison with the Seventeenth Congress, the workers' strength had grown by 15 percent. The 1931 victory was consolidated and expanded. Henceforward the labor movement was to be the dominant and shaping force of the Zionist Organization.[116] Ben-Gurion's dream was achieved and made real. From that time on the labor movement, Mapai at its head, was responsible for the fate of Zionism and the fate of the nation. The new accountability broadened horizons and affected the formulation of positions.

Concurrent with these major changes in the status of the labor movement, there was also a binding and fateful change in the personal political career of Ben-Gurion. After the assassination of Arlozoroff, Ben-Gurion accepted the demand of his party and assumed the direction of the Zionist movement in place of the murdered man. After over ten years of work and leadership of the Histadrut, Ben-Gurion transferred the continuation of his public life to the national arena. Henceforward the sphere of Ben-

Gurion's activity was the nation. For a year, from 1933 to mid-1934, he attempted to continue operating on the two levels, but at the end of that time he made his decision and finally left the Histadrut. From then on he concentrated entirely on Zionism in the broadest sense.

Ben-Gurion's new position caused a re-ordering of his priorities with regard to the problems of Zionism then at issue. Matters seen through the eyes of the Histadrut secretary and leader of the labor movement seeking a position of power had now to be seen through the eyes of a senior leader in the national movement. Moreover, with the hegemony of Mapai in the Zionist movement and institutions firmly in place, the party's apprehensions faded and its self-confidence mounted. The change in status of the labor movement in general and of Mapai in particular and the alteration in Ben-Gurion's personal standing led, as noted, to changes in his views. The most outstanding and significant of these concerned the struggle against Revisionism.

As described above, in 1930–4 it was Ben-Gurion who was in the van of the struggle against Revisionism. Among the leaders of Ahdut Ha'avoda and Mapai, the people of the *Second Aliya*, Ben-Gurion was the most extreme and militant in his attitude to Revisionism. Because of his position and high status in his movement and in the Histadrut he united around himself the militant and radical "Young Turks" of the *Third Aliya*. It was Ben-Gurion who conceived the idea, and for years instigated, supported and urged the creation of a semi-military defense organization on the lines of the Austrian *Schutzbund* to replace or parallel the national Hagana as an exclusive instrument of the Histadrut. Without Ben-Gurion's support and leadership the creation of the Hasadran Association in 1933 is unimaginable. It was Ben-Gurion who succeeded in winning a majority in his party for the establishment of the Organization at the beginning of 1934. In the eyes of many Ben-Gurion appeared as the angry prophet and warring commander, leading the labor movement in the extreme and uncompromising struggle against the right and Revisionism. At the fourth session of the Mapai Council held in March 1934 in Tel Aviv he declared: "I do not believe that there is any hope or way of repentance for the Revisionist movement after the dizzying example to them of the victory of Hitler and Dollfuss. There is no remedy, only total extirpation from the Zionist movement."[117] Ben-Gurion's extreme stance on Revisionism was also evident during the year, when he uttered such characteristic statements as: "We must direct our activity toward expelling the Revisionists from the Zionist Organization"; or "If they do not leave now the next congress is liable to turn into a battlefield"; or "they will never change their skin, for such is their nature."[118]

In view of Ben-Gurion's position, all were thunderstruck by the acute and sudden *volte-face* he made at the end of August 1934. Ben-Gurion transformed his approach completely, and began to call for colloquy with Revisionism. His argument was that it was impossible for the existing situation in Zionism to continue and it was impossible to remove the Revisionist movement from the Zionist Organization because of the objections of the other parties. His conclusion was that in the given circumstances, when the labor movement was responsible for the fate and future of the national movement and the nation, there was no alternative, and it was obligatory to communicate with Revisionism in practical areas of violence and labor relations; the struggle against it would continue only in the ideological sphere. The change in Ben-Gurion was startling, because as late as 14 August 1934, at a discussion of the Mapai center, he still adopted an extreme position and was, in principle and in practice, for the expulsion of the Revisonists from the Zionist movement. Then, suddenly, a mere week later, at a discussion of the center on 21 August, he presented his new and astonishing views.[119] This dramatic change brought him to the signature on 27 October 1934 of the famous agreements with Jabotinsky in London. The rejection of the labor agreement in a referendum held among the Histadrut members early in 1935, as well as the insistence on the duty of discipline by Revisionist party members to the Zionist Organization, led finally to the departure of the movement from the Zionist Organization and the creation of the New Zionist Organization.[120] There can be no doubt that the political processes described, and also the change in Ben-Gurion's personal position with all that ensued, determined the status and the future of the Hasadran Association and its disbanding in 1936, for the following reasons:

(1) After the Eighteenth Zionist Congress the labor movement, headed by Mapai, became dominant and responsible for the future of the Zionist movement. Hegemony and national accountability expanded horizons and shifted focus and emphases. These changes in both consciousness and in practice developed in an evolutionary process.

(2) As a result of the processes mentioned, and also for practical reasons, the persistent influence of the labor movement on the Hagana did not vanish. The Hagana was indeed subject to the national parity committee, but in practice the Histadrut representatives on the committee were the determining and predominant factor. Fears of loss of influence, in a certain sense control, of the Hagana, proved groundless.

(3) In 1934 Ben-Gurion finally detached himself from activity in the Histadrut and concentrated entirely on his work in the Zionist movement. Ben-Gurion's departure from the Histadrut created a situation in which the Hasadran Association lost its creator, its ideologist and its chief patron. Ben-Gurion the member of the Zionist leadership was not the same as Ben-Gurion the all-powerful leader of the Histadrut.

(4) The change in Ben-Gurion's attitude to the struggle against

Revisionism at the end of August 1934, with all that this involved, the relaxation of stresses that had arisen in the Yishuv and in the Zionist movement despite the failure of the labor agreement and the Revisionists' leaving of the Zionist Organization – all these caused an alteration of climate in the Yishuv and in Zionism in relation to violence. The militant inter-party tension eased. From 1936, with the outbreak of the Arab rebellion, the situation changed entirely. These developments, which had begun in 1933, when the Hasadran Association was only in the process of creation, found more marked expression in the second half of 1934, grew in force in 1935, and became decisive in 1936. The lessening of internal strains and the replacement of the centers of interest to the national sphere did not work to the benefit of the Hasadran Association.

(5) As a result of all the above processes, the former Hashomer people lost not only the ideological foundation that had been the reason for their activity in Hapoel and the Hasadran Association, but also their patron and sponsor. From 1934 they became utterly exposed to their old and new enemies, who excelled them in political talents and party power. For them the countdown had begun.[121]

2 Why did Hashomer people resign from Hapoel institutions?

The understanding reached between Yisrael Shohat and his people and Ben-Gurion at the beginning of 1930 was based on the common desire to convert Hapoel into an organization that would be a "corridor to the Hagana," in which occupation with sports would be a very important but not exclusive element. In the *Hashomer Volume* Yisrael Shohat describes the understanding that was reached. "We spoke of a special mission, kept secret from the government, which was to train comrades for defense activities. Ben-Gurion assured me of his support and help whenever I might turn to him. This association was to be under the direct control of the secretariat of the Histadrut Executive Committee."[122]

In his memoirs Yisrael Shohat mixed later events with earlier, that is, the episode of the Hasadran Association with the subject of Hapoel. At the beginning of 1930 Ben-Gurion was striving for the more modest goal of providing education and semi-military training to the members of Hapoel in accordance with the concept he had expressed in 1928, that Hapoel should be a "corridor to the Hagana" on the model of the sports organizations in eastern Europe. Such an idea undoubtedly held great attractions for the Hashomer people. Ben-Gurion's proposal did not, in fact, invite them to enter the chamber itself, that is, the Hagana, but only the "corridor" leading to it, yet for people whose being and whose entire lives were dedicated to defense the proposal and its legitimization by the public and the movement were an enticement impossible to withstand. Not surprisingly, therefore, they agreed to harness themselves to work in

Hapoel. The host and the guests knew clearly that they would have to operate cautiously because suspicion and opposition toward the Hashomer people were still considerable.[123]

The return to public activity of this kind was possible only on the basis of repentance by the Hashomer people for the past and commitment to accept Histadrut authority. Even Eliahu Golomb was convinced, at the initial stage at least, that their contrition was sincere.[124] A few years later Golomb reversed his view. The intention to accept Histadrut authority unconditionally was expressed by Manya Shohat to Ben-Gurion soon after the disturbances.[125] She repeated this position in the wider forum of the Histadrut Executive Committee at a meeting on 10 February 1930, when she requested the support from the Histadrut for her journey, on behalf of public matters, to the United States. In her speech at the session Manya sought to remove any suspicion from the minds of those present as to her political motives, or any doubts about her loyalty to the Histadrut. "After all the attempts at separatist activity I have made in Palestine I have discovered that *ich hob sich genug shoyn oyfgebrihet* [Yiddish – 'I have been burnt enough']. And I know that this causes only damage and I shall no more do such things."[126] Manya Shohat repeated her stand in the following years also.[127] This was absolute remorse and unconditional repentance on her part. It is almost certain that her comrades shared this posture.

From other scattered recollections of Yisrael Shohat too, and from the memoirs of Yosef Harit,[128] the same picture emerges: The attachment of the Shohat couple and the Hashomer people and others to Hapoel was strictly on the basis of Ben-Gurion's outlook that Hapoel had to be turned into a preparatory framework for the Hagana. Only at the end of 1930, but chiefly in 1931–2, after Ben-Gurion again formulated his views on the need to establish a Palestinian *Schutzbund* within Hapoel, did the Hashomer people join the small circle of his adherents who strove to realize the idea.

The departure of the former Hashomer people from Hapoel resulted from two principal causes: (a) the general debate on the essence and purpose of Hapoel, but particularly the place, and purpose and organization of the Hasadran Association; (b) the status of the Hashomer group in Hapoel.

(a) *The general debate on the place, purpose and organization of the Hasadran Association.* The members of Hashomer belonged to the extremist-militant wing of Hapoel, which considered sport an instrument and a means of achieving overall and class defense goals. In their perception the organization was a fighting *avant-garde* and a shield over the Palestinian labor movement. The Hasadran Association was intended to spearhead this trend, to be the *avant-garde* of the *avant-garde*, so to speak, the Palestinian *Schutzbund*, the yeast in the dough of Hapoel. This orientation of Ben-Gurion was the progenitor of the effort to turn the Hasadran Association into an autonomous national framework under direct Histadrut command and control, acting in coordination with the secretariat of the Hapoel center but not subject to the latter's supervision and authority despite being a part of it.[129] The establishment of such a semi-military force as the renewed Hasadran created problems over the relations between itself and the Hagana. Above all, in the air hung the question if the Histadrut defense organization would be supplementary to the Hagana or would operate in parallel to it and compete with it. These problems were expressed in the discussions on the organizational structure of the Hasadran Association. Two conflicting views arose in these debates. The first demanded that the Hasadran Association be subject to the local Hapoel branch and that its status be like that of all the other sections; the second held that the Hasadran Association should be an autonomous national organization under the direct authority of the Histadrut, and merely coordinate actions with the Hapoel center. Additionally there were those, including the Hashomer people, who argued that the Hasadran Association units should join the Hagana and operate within it as integral units and not on an individual basis. This debate proceeded in various forms from 1932 to 1935. As the tension of the struggle against Revisionism subsided the self-confidence of the labor movement rose, the fruit of its hegemony in the Zionist movement; as the mood grew calmer regarding the continuation of Histadrut influence over the Hagana after Ben-Gurion left to work in the Zionist movement, the second position, the maximalist, weakened, while the first, the minimalist, grew stronger.[130]

In figures, in 1934 the renewed Hasadran numbered 307 members organized in 12 companies.[131] In 1935 the companies encompassed a total of 678 people.[132]

(b) The status of the Hashomer group in Hapoel. Despite the rehabilitation and legitimization accorded to the Hashomer people after the 1929 disturbances, past resentments toward them did not disappear. They were moderated and pushed aside, but the embers of enmity and suspicion still glowed and could burst into flame at any moment.

A distinction should be made between the attitude toward Manya Shohat as an individual and the general attitude toward the Hashomer group. Manya too joined the Hapoel institutions in 1930, where she concentrated principally in mobilizing public and financial support abroad, which was essential for the development of the organization. Here she enjoyed considerable success.[133] For all that, with her, more than others in the group, a sense of mistrust surrounded her activities and her understanding of her political goals. Perhaps more than others, Ben-

Gurion had extreme reservations regarding Manya Shohat's political tendencies and acumen, to understate the case. He voiced his opinion to her and others on various occasions, without mincing words (see note 127 to this chapter). The ambivalence toward her – appreciation of her ability to mobilize resources and setting at naught her political activity and understanding – led more than once to crises in her work in Hapoel. In a letter to Ben-Gurion dated 5 November 1932, Manya complained about this attitude and the mistrust shown toward her. The letter reflects the distress she felt. As an act of protest she resigned, and for a while returned to Kefar Gil'adi. In her letter she charged Ben-Gurion that owing to his negative view of her "there is only one way out, to remain at Kefar Gil'adi, and the work to go on without me until you change your judgment."[134] Shortly afterwards she resumed her work at the Hapoel center even though Ben-Gurion remained adamant in his opinion of her, believing that she had no understanding of political affairs and therefore should refrain from engaging in them.

As noted, the Hashomer people belonged to the militant, maximalist wing of Hapoel. Echoes of the flaring of tempers between the two currents – the moderate and the extreme – in Hapoel could be heard in Manya Shohat's letter of 5 June 1933 to the Hapoel center. At that time she used the pressures on her by Kibbutz Kefar Gil'adi to return there as a pretext for ending her work in Hapoel, while settling accounts with the opponents of the maximalist camp to which she belonged. As the excuse for her resignation, which she announced on 15 June 1933, she gave her feeling that she was no longer contributing to or influencing developments in Hapoel. "I have reached the absolute conclusion that without creating active nucleus within the Hapoel branches there is no great value in all my endeavors." Since in her opinion she was being prevented from establishing the activist groups, she ceased believing in the future of Hapoel.[135] On this occasion too Manya displayed hastiness and and rash conclusions, for less than two months later practical and organizational steps toward the creation of the Hasadran Association began to be taken.

Findings of another kind from which deductions may be made about the deteriorating condition of the Hashomer group are present in the letters of Manya Shohat to her son Gid'on (Geda) written in June 1934. In one dated 20 June 1934 she wrote that "affairs in Hapoel are bad. We are looking for a way of leaving this mess with honor. There is no peace between us and the Histadrut Executive Committee, nor does it seem that there ever will be." The word "we" in the letter should be noted. It is also important to observe the emphasis Manya placed on the nature of the relations with the Histadrut Executive Committee, which were poor, meaning that a rift had opened on the political level. It transpires that the election of David Remez to replace Ben-Gurion as Secretary-General of the Histadrut caused a strengthening in the Executive Committee of the moderate elements with reservations concerning the Hashomer group. Remez himself was undoubtedly among them.[136]

In another letter to her son dated 27 June 1934, Manya repeated that "things here, in Hapoel, are rotten. Tomorrow there is a meeting of the full Hapoel center to change the way matters are going radically, or we Hashomerniks will abandon the leadership of Hapoel *en bloc*."

From the letter it seems that some of the friction arose for political reasons, namely, struggles within the party among groups with differing political loyalties and postures. But another part of the friction was due, in her opinion, to the ancient hostility and suspicion toward the Hashomer people. Elsewhere in the letter Manya wrote that "Yisrael works hard, is angry mostly because of the disorder and internal demoralization in Hapoel, which he can't do anything about."[137]

In a letter from Manya Shohat to Dov Hoz of 21 June 1934, matters are set forth and exposed even more. The writer complains of what she believes was the intentional postponement of the meeting of the Hapoel center, because:

> You know that we, the few Hashomerniks who have stood at the head of Hapoel for the last four years, do not agree with the way things are going as you are now directing them. You want to gain time and to present us with a *fait accompli*. What you are doing now is a crime against Hapoel and spiteful to us. You know that we will not become an opposition to you in these difficult times, when the whole atmosphere is filled with hatred and poison against the Histadrut. You know that we shall be silent, but we do not wish to be responsible for your deeds, and it seems that we will have to go, because you want to push us aside automatically. You, Dov, are among those . . . you are guilty of *deliberately* neglecting the affairs of Hapoel for 20 months, you were afraid of giving us an opportunity to influence, at that time none of "your" people could be found for this work, and you thought it better to leave matters in a state of stagnation rather, God forbid, than allow us to affect the reorganization of Hapoel.

Manya goes on to complain that in 1930, when she was on a mission in the United States, she received no help from home, because "Manya Shohat is a Hashomernik, and you have to be careful of them altogether."[138]

Manya Shohat's grave charges must be treated with caution. She was well known for her cutting and direct tongue, albeit not always accurate. The accusations hurled against Dov Hoz and his allies are at first sight not clear either. The militant activist wing actually won its victory in 1934, with the establishment of the "Organization," or Hasadran Association, as a national autonomous body headed by special commander, Yosef Rokhel (Avidar), and under the direct authority of the Histadrut

Executive Committee. Hence, almost all the goals of the maximalists were achieved. Therefore, the extreme displeasure expressed in Manya Shohat's letters to her son Gid'on and especially in her accusatory letter to Dov Hoz is all the more strange.

In this letter there are no details of the causes of the dispute, but it may be supposed that at the height of victory of the activist trend an undercutting of its gains was started by political elements in Hapoel, the party, the Histadrut and the Hagana. This undermining stemmed in part from fears harbored by Eliahu Golomb and his supporters of the potential danger to the Hagana from the Hasadran Association if the latter developed and became entrenched as a semi-military autonomous national body, exclusive to the Histadrut and headed by its own commander or command. At the same time, in Golomb and his adherents the old enmity and suspicions of the hidden goals, secrecy and separatism of the Hashomer people surfaced once again. It is possible that the reason for the exclusion of the Hashomer people from any form of command over the companies of the renewed Hasadran, and the placement at the head of the Association, or the "Organization," of Yosef Avidar, a Golomb loyalist, lies here. Reinforcement for this assumption may be found in the words of Eliahu Golomb himself, spoken before the Hadera Hapoel branch on 20 November 1935, when he tried to explain the need for a change in the organizational status of the renewed Hasadran:

> We wanted to educate special companies. If this had taken place in that way, we would have had to find a way of correcting and determining the relations between the two bodies [i.e., Hapoel and Hasadran – Y.G.]. The fact is, instead of strengthening activity Hasadran does the opposite. Hasadran has not succeeded in establishing itself in the country. There is no authority, and this makes for *separatism and anarchy*. A situation cannot be allowed in which there are in a branch different bodies, some of them self-governing. Until this state of affairs changes Hasadran will remain a section in the branch and under the directorship of the branch. It may carry out special tasks, but without songs of autonomy. There is no national Hasadran, there is no national directorship. All of Hasadran is fully obedient to and under the authority of the branch leadership.[139]

So the wings were clipped of the "monster," which to Golomb's dismay had been constantly developing. A body that might have complicated matters in the area of the defense organs of the Yishuv, and whose very existence might have legitimized the separation of Avraham Tehomi's "parallel organization," or Organization B, was significantly reduced. Golomb was apprehensive of what he called "anarchy." Above all, the secret was out. Golomb conjured up the frightful and menacing word "separatism." In the dense political atmosphere of the Yishuv and the party artificial or genuine suspicions were let loose of a revised edition of

Hakibbutz. The immediate target of these suspicions was the Hashomer people, and then apparently their removal from the Hasadran Association.

The fears of Golomb and his supporters cannot be lightly dismissed. The crystallization of the renewed Hasadran as a semi-military autonomous national organization with its own command created the potential foundation, according to Ben-Gurion's original plan, for a defense organization of the Histadrut in Palestine, namely, a *Schutzbund*. As long as a powerful Revisionist threat existed, and the labor movement was struggling for its place in the Zionist Organization, vital considerations surpassed other considerations. With the attainment of hegemony by the labor movement in the national movement, to which the Hagana was subordinate, and with the attenuation of Revisionism, self-confidence and the sense of national responsibility mounted. The latter required the strengthening of the status of the Hagana and the elimination of any possibility of legitimization for the separate existence of Avraham Tehomi's organization.

For all that, there was no basis for the suspicions of Golomb and his people regarding the separatist tendencies of the Hashomer group. They had learned the lessons of history, and moreover the gloomy past of the 1920s had left them scarred. Hence the injustice and unfairness of being sidelined in Hapoel generally and in the Hasadran Association particularly was all the more painful to them.

The swan-song of the Hashomer people was sung when they resigned from the Hapoel organs in mid-1934. The hasty resignation was actually on account of their recent past. They left of their own free will, so as not to constitute a focus for opposition or to be tempted to join an opposition and so give some basis to the indictments of their old and new enemies. By leaving they wished to sweep the ground from under their enemies' feet over the old claims of separatism and rejection of authority. This they did, but politically through resigning they played into their rivals' hands. Above all, in leaving Hapoel they sentenced themselves to final disappearance from the public stage as a group.

The Hapoel council at Kiriat Haim on 21–22 June 1935 considered the subject briefly and in a minor key. The council accepted the resignation and elected a new center for Hapoel. It is important to stress that the Hashomer people were not alone in their resignation.[140] The Kiriat Haim council also elected a commission charged with presenting concrete proposals to the second conference of Hapoel on the future of the Hasadran Association. Yisrael Shohat and Abba Hushi were included on the commission. It is noteworthy that Abba Hushi, who was one of the most radical leaders of the maximalist current in Mapai, the Histadrut and Hapoel, continued in his political career and did not follow the path of the Hashomer people. In his memoirs Yisrael Shohat states that "Abba Hushi betrayed us."[141]

As stated, the final departure of the Hashomer people from Hapoel in 1935 was also the swan-song for their public activity as a group. Henceforward most of them were entirely removed from the public stage and only few of them succeeded in maintaining a hold at its edge.

3 Epilogue: the Hapoel Companies (1936)

In 1934, concurrent with the resignation of the Hashomer people and those of similar mind from the Hapoel center, the national directorate or supervisory body of the Hasadran Association also broke up. On the eve of the Hapoel council at Kiriat Haim on 21–22 June 1935 activity by the Hasadran Association in fact ceased. Various companies continued to exist and operate at different levels, but the process was of withdrawal toward the former economic activity. The renewed Hasadran descended from the heights it had attained.

The Kiriat Haim council elected a new center for Hapoel, and the latter at its first meeting in Tel Aviv on 27 June 1935 elected a new secretariat consisting of Yisrael Carmi, Yosef Rokhel (Avidar), Zeev Sherf, Efraim Perlstein, Dov Hoz and Mordechai Zhilist. The secretariat was given the task of preparing the second Hapoel conference.[142]

In readiness for this event the Hapoel center and the Histadrut Executive Committee formulated the new Regulations of Hasadran. The document was presented for approval to the second conference, which was held in Haifa on 20–23 March 1936. It read:

(1) Attached to the Hapoel center there will be established a national commission, composed by the Histadrut Executive Committee after consultation with the Hapoel center, which will guide the Hasadran companies.
(2) The Hasadran companies are a section of the Hapoel branches and subject to their discipline, except for matters made known by the national commission to the branch. In other matters they will be like any other section.
(3) The local company leaderships are appointed by the national commission in consultation with the branch committees.
(4) Immediately after the conference a clarification will be made in every place regarding the individual composition of the companies and the necessary arrangements will be made for the continuation of their work.
(5) Prior to this clarification the companies are not to accept new members and companies are not to be formed in places where they have not been formed so far.
(6) With the division of the sections into groups – in connection with general sporting activity – the groups will be able to join Hasadran.[143]

The second conference approved the new Regulations.[144] On the surface they looked like delicate cosmetic surgery, and it was entirely in the organizational area. In fact, Hasadran lost its spirit and its quality, that of being a Palestinian *Schutzbund*, although it did not resume its old shell. The new–old creature born at the second conference soon evolved into what became known as the Hapoel Companies. The conversion and integration of Hasadran into the Hapoel Companies were gradual, lasting about a year. The first national commander of the Companies was Azaria Kiriati.[145] The new name – Hapoel Companies – entered the consciousness of its members and obliterated the old name.

Even after their resignation, in a certain sense the Hashomer people could rejoice in a partial ideological victory: (a) the concept that Hapoel was not only a sports association but also a means for other goals gained ascendancy; (b) the Hapoel Companies that formed and operated after 1936 inherited marked features of the Hasadran Association in the area of defense of the labor movement and also as auxiliary elements to the Hagana; and (c) Several elements of the Hasadran Association survived in the organizational sphere also.

Conclusions

There is ample strength, there are huge camps, there are human
resources – lacking is leadership, *military commandership*,
direction, rule!

David Ben-Gurion

BAR GIORA AND HASHOMER were among the outstanding creations of
the *Second Aliya*, of which they were a part. Their all-embracing
national vision was one of the basic characteristics of the Palestinian labor
movement from the start of its activity. In the few years of their existence
(1907–20), despite the small number of their members, they displayed
fertility of thought and contributed to the Yishuv. Rightly, therefore, they
have been placed in first rank of the renewed history of the Jewish people
in its land. They were the first to successfully establish a countrywide
organization that combined guarding with a broad national defensive
concept; the first to recognize the importance of the dimension of force
and also to create and integrate it as an essential component in the process
of national revival. For them the element of force for physical defense was
not the only component, but it was highly significant and vital for the
building of the Yishuv and the realization of Zionism; they contributed
much to the raising of independent awareness in the Yishuv of the need
to protect property and life and of the connection between the two. Even
the *moshavot* that dismissed Hashomer did not, at least in part, restore
non-Jewish guarding entirely. Bar Giora and Hashomer elevated the
standing of the Yishuv in the eyes of the non-Jewish population; the role
of Hashomer in the creation of a Palestinian police at the time of the military government was not insignificant; the idea of the kibbutz is linked to
the "collective" of Sejera. Even those who assert that Kibbutz Degania
was different from the collective are bound to admit that the conquest
group at Um Juni in 1909 was formed on the basis of the Sejera precedent. Only with the success of the latter did the Degania continuation
come about; Hashomer contributed enormously to the enterprise of the
various kinds of conquest groups; the Haro'eh group and the idea of

conquest of pasture sprang out of Bar Giora and Hashomer, even though its ideological fathers were Yisrael Belkind and Michal Halperin. Members of Hashomer were among the volunteers to the Palestinian Battalion; they worked for the establishment of settlements in the eastern Upper Galilee, thereby helping to draw the map of the country. All these were momentous contributions, which became an organic part of the history of Zionism and the Palestine Yishuv.

Contrary to the concept imprinted in the historiography, Hashomer was not a closed and separatist sect with narrow goals. The clandestine structural framework with its high self-discipline was essential in the setting of a hostile Turkish rule. The Russian revolutionary tradition and the necessity for deepest secrecy owing to the regime shaped the patterns of Hashomer's activity. It should be stressed that although Bar Giora and Hashomer grew out of the socialist Zionist current in the *Second Aliya*, although they were associated with the norms of the labor movement and although they regarded themselves as an inseparable part of the Palestinian labor movement, their ideology and the goals embraced the entire nation.

In parallel with the process taking place in the parent movement, Poaley Zion, it is possible to view the transition from Bar Giora to Hashomer and the ensuing years from 1909 to 1914 as a process of clarification, strengthening and development of national characteristic features. The independent structural framework that the Hashomer people jealously preserved throughout the years of its existence was intended to allow elements of every shade in the Yishuv, not only members of Poaley Zion or other worker groups, to join Hashomer. The declared intuitive position was that the ideological tie to the Palestinian labor movement was one thing and organizational independence, which ensured the all-national character, was another. This was the essence of Hashomer and the central factor in its refusal to submit to the authority of the Poaley Zion party at the time of the *Second Aliya*, or to be swallowed by the Ahdut Ha'avoda party following its establishment in 1919.

The fatal error that determined the future of the former Hashomer people and condemned them to elimination from the public scene was made when they made the Labor Battalion their home and in practice adopted the ideology that regarded the Labor Battalion as the alternative to the Histadrut, the *avant-garde* body that in the future, when the time came, would assume the place of the Histadrut. The decisive step was taken when the Hashomer group established Hakibbutz within the Battalion, a defensive organizational framework parallel to the Hagana; the latter had succeeded Hashomer as the defensive framework possessing national goals, even though it was in fact subject to the authority of the Histadrut. The mistake was ideological and political: ideological, because

by this act they denied their own historic path and assumed the framework of a political and class body; politically, because they cast their lot
and their public future with a body that was defeated in the political arena
and disintegrated within a few years. The splitting and liquidation of the
Labor Battalion in the second half of the 1920s destroyed the social,
economic and political framework that sustained and provided a basis for
the existence of Hakibbutz. The end of the Battalion was also the end of
Hakibbutz, and the former Hashomer people were driven into the political wilderness.

Hakibbutz was not a "seceding" group of the type of such groups in
the 1930s and 1940s, that is, Etzel and Lehi, for several reasons:

1   The Hakibbutz members had no overall ideology different from that
     of Ahdut Ha'avoda, although they held radical activist views in the
     political and socioeconomic fields. In the political area Hakibbutz
     was the first to maintain the view that Britain no less than the Arabs
     was the enemy of Zionism and therefore it was necessary to plan for
     the struggle against it. In the years of its existence Hakibbutz put these
     ideas into practice. In the socioeconomic area Hakibbutz identified
     with the socio-communard ideas of the Battalion. Still, among the
     members and leaders of Ahdut Ha'avoda not a few could be found
     adhering to similar ideas in all these areas. Politically Ahdut
     Ha'avoda stood for cooperation with Britain, but it nevertheless
     contained activist political and certainly social elements that identi-
     fied with the views of Hakibbutz.
2   Hakibbutz did not consider itself a party or an organization owing
     fealty and support to any particular party, including the Labor
     Battalion when the latter entered the political arena in the Yishuv
     with its independent list. It saw itself as an entity possessing national
     goals, albeit linked to the workers' class. Hakibbutz submitted
     entirely to only one concern, defense, which it saw as its exclusive and
     unique domain. In this sphere it considered itself an arm of the
     national movement in the struggle to win Jewish independence in
     Palestine.
3   As stated, Hakibbutz considered itself an organic part of the overall
     and consolidating class frame, that is, a part of the Histadrut.
4   Hakibbutz did not conceive of itself as an organization working
     against the Hagana, but as a catalyst for the Hagana and engaged in
     complementary operations to those of the Hagana.

In retrospect it may be stated that the essence of the defensive-military
concept of the Hashomer people and their successors was correct; it was
before its time in the Yishuv and in Zionism, but it is applied today in the

state of Israel. Their concept was founded on two basic assumptions:

1 The necessity of the existence of a restricted and small nucleus, a sort of regular professional idealistic underground army, dedicated and aware, of commanders, instructors and fighters, which would undertake the three tasks of the Yishuv: current security, training the broad masses, and acquistion of arms.
2 The necessity to create a kind of people's reserve army that would encompass the broader circles of the nation. The popular peripheral circles would be trained for defense activity and would be instructed by that hard and permanent core of professionals, and would be mobilized at times of general emergency.

At the beginning of the 1920s Yisrael Shohat and his comrades found reinforcement and vindication of their ideology in the actual circumstances they witnessed in Germany. The German army rehabilitated by the Versailles treaties and subject to the limitations imposed by the Allies built itself exactly according to the plan envisaged and dreamed of by the Hashomer people and their successors. The Germans established a small regular professional army of commanders and instructors, which trained a reserve echelon and so constructed it that it might be integrated, in a very short time, into a far larger military framework. The process was practicable because the skeletal framework, the commands and the commanders, were in place. The arms for the large army were bought, stored and available, and the reserves were trained by a uniform method and were allocated in advance to the specific units of the skeleton army. This structure, which the Germans produced solely through lack of alternative and the constraints of Versailles, proved itself in Germany in the 1930s. As stated, the concept that was put into practice in Germany remarkably matched the outlook of the Hashomer people and their successors regarding the desirable structure of the Hagana. The pattern developed by the Germans heralded the modern military concept and was tailored to the needs of societies with limited means, particularly to depressed societies in difficult political conditions like the Jewish Yishuv in Palestine. Eventually the Hagana adopted this model.

Furthermore, the concept of the Hashomer people and their sucessors was that the commanders of the defense organization must accept their appointments from people active in the defense body and not from elements external to it. At the same time, they proposed that the sovereignty, authority and control by civilian elements over the defense arm would be ensured by (a) the creation of a civilian supervisory committee that would oversee the defense organization; and (b) the appointment of a representative of the civilian elements who would take part in meetings of the defense organization command and would be the liaison between the civilian institutions and the Hagana command.

This, in fact, was the line of development of the Hagana from the 1930s on. The civilian parity committee served as a civilian supervisory body over the operational command of the Hagana, which in the future was to become the general staff of the Israel Defense Forces (IDF).

Indeed, the defense ideology of the Hashomer and its successors was not backward, suited merely to the limited and primitive situation of the Ottoman period alone, but the opposite. Theirs was a modern military concept, whose essence may be found in the practice of the armies of other nations, the Hagana of the 1930s and the IDF. The Hashomer people and their successors were in advance of their time and of their opponents, and in theory and practice they laid the foundations for the Hagana and the Israel Defense Forces.

Notes

Introduction

1   See *Ha-entsyklopediya ha-'ivrit* (The Hebrew Encyclopedia), "Nationalism," Vol. 21, 66; "Zionism," Vol. 28, 592) (Hebrew). Also Hans Kohn, *The Idea of Nationalism* (New York: Macmillan, 1944); *Nationalism, Its Meaning and History* (Princeton, New Jersey: Van Nostrand, 1965); Carlton J. H. Hayes, *The Historical Evolution of Modern Nationalism* (New York: Macmillan, 1951); Elie Kedourie, *Nationalism* (London: Hutchinson University Library, 1960).
2   Yitzhak Greenbaum, *The Development of the Zionist Movement*, Youth Affairs Dept. of the World Zionist Organization and Reuben Mass, Jerusalem (Hebrew); Arthur Hertzberg, The *Zionist Idea* (Jerusalem: Keter, 1970) (Hebrew).

Chapter 1   Defense and Guarding in the *First Aliya*

1   Israel Klausner, *The Zionist Writings of Rabbi Zvi Kalisher* (Jerusalem: Rav Kook Institute, 1946, 36) (Hebrew); *Ha-'olam* (The World), 5 November 1944; Yehuda Slutsky, "First to guard and to protect," special reprint from *History of the Hagana*, Vol. I (Tel Aviv: Ma'arakhot, 1963), 22 (Hebrew).
2   Rabbi Yehuda Ch. Alkalai, *Writings*, Book 1, Vol. I (Jerusalem: Rav Kook Institute, 1944) (Hebrew). See especially *Minhat Yehuda* (Judah's Offering). On sending Jewish soldiers, see his essay, "Encouraging humility," 1864; also Slutsky, "First to guard."
3   Zvi Hirsch Kalischer, *Derishat Tsiyyon* (Zion's Demand), edition I, 17b (Hebrew).
4   Slutsky, "First to guard," 23.
5   David Gordon, *Selected Articles* (Tel Aviv: Sifriyat Shorashim of Mizpeh Publishers, 1942) (Hebrew), especially the articles on 83–7 and 99–101.
6   Yehiel Schlesinger, *Torat Yehiel, sefer bereshit* (Yehiel's Law, Book of Genesis) (Jerusalem: Committee for Publishing the Books of the Gaon Rabbi Akiva Yosef, 1971), 22–3 (Hebrew); see also Slutsky, "First to guard."
7   Kressel, *Petah Tikva, Mother of Colonies, 1878–1953*, Petah Tikva Municipality, 1953 (Hebrew); Ya'ari (Polskin) and M. Harizman, *Jubilee Book on the Fiftieth Anniversary of the Founding of Petah Tikva (1878–1928)* (Tel Aviv, 1928), 112 (Hebrew); Ya'akov Harozen, *Metulla* (Jerusalem: Sifriyat Ha-Yishuv, 1978) (Hebrew).
8   Slutsky, "First to guard," 70–1, 84, 85; Zalman David Levontin, *To the*

Land of Our Fathers (Tel Aviv: Eytan Press, 1924) (Hebrew); Yisrael Belkind, *The First Step in the Land of Israel* (New York: Hameir, 1917) (Yiddish); Arye Samsonov, *Anonymous Pioneers* (Tel Aviv: Sifriyat Rishonim, 1944) (Hebrew); Moshe Smilansky, *Chapters in the History of the Jewish Community of Palestine* (Tel Aviv: Dvir, 1959) (Hebrew), Vol. I, Book One, is replete with the heroic deeds of *moshava* residents; Ya'ari and Harizman, *Jubilee Book*, 22–3, 111.

9   Slutsky, "First to guard," 69; Moshe Smilansky, *Family of the Earth* (Tel Aviv: Am Oved, 1954) (Hebrew), Book Two, 26–9, 88–92.

10 Ya'ari and Harizman, *Jubilee Book*, 111–12, write that Stamper did not hesitate to defend the colony even on the Sabbath and so served as an example to others. Once, on the Sabbath, Arabs from the village of Umlabash trespassed on *moshava* land, claimed it as theirs, and were about to plow it. Several of the younger Jewish villagers started to fight them; the others were in the synagogue. Stamper, who was very orthodox, immediately removed his *tallit* (prayer shawl) when he heard the first shots, and ran to his house for his rifle. He then ran back to the synagogue and called out to the worshipers to do as he had done; leading them, he repelled the Arabs' attack. In other instances, too, Stamper taught the settlers "to defend themselves and their property with weapon in hand, to defend the honor of the young settlement and the honor of the people as a whole in the eyes of the Arabs."

11 Slutsky, "First to guard," 79–80, describes the exceptional activity of Baron Rothschild's official in Zikhron Ya'akov, who set up the "Maccabi Society of Guardians of the Tranquility of the Colony." In Rishon le-Tsiyyon the farmers guarded their colony but Arabs guarded the fields. Under the influence of the Baron's officials, the independent colonies also adopted this method. Even personalities like Hillel Yaffe and Y. M. Pines accepted the system, arguing that it was enough for the farmers to defend only their homes.

12 Ya'ari and Harizman, *Jubilee Book*, 424.

13 Smilansky, *Chapters,* Vol. I, Book One, 84–5; Slutsky, "First to guard," 90.

14 Slutsky, "First to guard," 80, 91. In effect, bribing local Arab chiefs and officials did not cease, although its scope declined markedly; in other words, the Baron's method continued, albeit greatly reduced.

15 Smilansky, *Chapters,* Vol. I, Book Three, 38.

16 *Poems of Shaul Tchernichovsky* (Tel Aviv: Dvir, 1973), 167, "Lullaby" (Odessa, 1896).

17 *Poems of Ya'akov Cohen* (Tel Aviv: Dvir), 86–7.

18 Moshe Braslavsky, *The Palestinian Labor Movement* (Hakibbutz Hameuhad, 1967) (Hebrew); see "The Bilu constitution," 293–6.

19 Alter Droianov, *Writings on the History of the 'Lovers of Zion' Movement and the Settlement of the Land of Israel* (Odessa: Council for the Settlement of the Land of Israel, 1919).

20 Smilansky, *Family of the Earth,* Book Two, 57ff.; Mordechai Eliav, *The Land of Israel and Its Settlement in the Nineteenth Century, 1777–1917* (Jerusalem: Keter, 1978), 383 (Hebrew); *History of the Hagana* (Ma'arachot, 1954), Part One, Book 2, 194–7; Yitshak Ben Zvi, *Poaley Tsiyyon in the Second Aliya* (Tel Aviv: Mapai, 1950), 28 (Hebrew); *Hashomer Anthology – Memoirs of Alexander Zayd* (Tel Aviv: Labor Archives, 1938), 86ff. (Hebrew); *Alexander Zayd, Before Dawn – A Diary* (Tel-Aviv: Am-Oved, 1975), 19–21 (Hebrew).

21 Slutsky, "First to guard," 123.
22 Smilansky, *Chapters*, Vol. I, Book One, 138ff.

Chapter 2   The *Second Aliya*: Ideology and Organization

1 Mordechai Eliav, *Palestine and the Yishuv in the Nineteenth Century* (Jerusalem: Keter, 1978), 335 (Hebrew). The figures given are as follows: In the period 1904–14 the Yishuv was augmented by 33,000 people, rising from 55,000 to 88,000. Over 40,000 immigrants reached Palestine, but about half of them later left. One-third of the enlargement of the Yishuv was from natural increase. The latter therefore contributed about 11,000 people to the Yishuv, the *Second Aliya* 22,000. See also Yehuda Slutsky, *Introduction to the History of the Israeli Labor Movement* (Tel Aviv: Sifria Universitait, Am Oved, 1973), 146 (Hebrew).

2 According to Eliav, 335, this influx numbered about 3000 people; but Zvi Rosenstein (Even-Shoshan) in his *History of the Workers' Movement in Palestine* (Tel Aviv: Am Oved, 1956), Book One, 226–67 (Hebrew), asserts that the total number of workers in the *moshavot* in 1914 was about 1500–1600. This figure included about 300 Yemeni workers and about 200 more workers from the eastern communities, so that the number of Ashkenazi workers of the *Second Aliya* was no more than one thousand. By his calculation about 10,000 young pioneers immigrated to Palestine in the *Second Aliya*, meaning that only 10 percent of them were absorbed in work on the *moshavot*. The remaining 90 percent either left the country or were absorbed in towns. David Ben-Gurion, "At the Half-Jubilee Celebration," in *Second Aliya Volume*, ed. Brakha Habas (Tel Aviv: Am Oved, 1947), 17 (Hebrew), writes that only about 10 percent of the young workers who came to Palestine remained; Yehuda Slutzky, *Introduction*, 162, presents different figures. He also bases himself on the 1922 census conducted by the Histadrut (General Federation of Labor).

3 Israel Klausner, *The Movement to Zion in Russia: I. With the Awakening of the People* (Jerusalem: Hasifria Hazionit, 1962): see ch. 2, and 93 (Hebrew); Yaacov Goldstein, "The Idea of Settlement in the National Ethos" *Lecture Series in Zionist Study*, No. 8 (University of Haifa, Dr Reuben Hecht Chair in Zionism, 1983) (Hebrew).

4 Slutzky, *Introduction*, 147. He gives the following figures on the size of the population at several large *moshavot* on the eve of the First World War: Petah Tikva, 3300; Rishon Lezion, 1500; Rehovot, 1200; Zikhron Ya'akov, 1000.

5 Yisrael Kollat maintains that a distinction should be made between guarding property and protecting lives on the *moshavot* of the *First* and *Second Aliya*. While the former was placed in the hands of non-Jews, he implies that the latter remained in the hands of the moshava residents. This distinction is correct and important, but must be modified. It holds in respect of some of the large *moshavot* such as Rehovot, Petah Tikva and Rishon Lezion, and also in times of emergency. But in normal times and in most of the *moshavot* the border between non-Jewish guarding of moshava property and safeguarding life was very thin. In many cases non-Jewish guarding extended to include overall protection. See Kollat's lecture at the study day at Yad Tabenkin on 4 May 1983, Yad Tabenkin, Institute for the Study of the Defending Force: *The Roots of Self-Defense*, No. 37, November 1983.

6   For the influence of Michael Halperin on the founders of Bar Giora see
    Yitzhak Ben Zvi, *Poaley Zion in the Second Aliya*, 28 (Hebrew); *Hashomer
    Anthology*, "The Memoirs of Alexander Zayd," 86ff.; Alexander Zayd,
    Toward Morning: Chapters from a Diary, 19–21 (Hebrew).

7   The Circassians fled from their homeland in the Caucasus to Bulgaria after
    their country was conquered by the Russians. After the Russo-Turkish war
    of 1876 they fled from Bulgaria too, and in the spring of 1878 reached Acre
    exhausted and starving. The Turkish authorities settled them on the eastern
    side of the Jordan, in the Golan and in western Palestine in the villages of
    Rehaniya and Kafer Kama in the Galilee and at Hirbet Cherkess (near Pardes
    Hanna). The last-named did not survive long. The Jewish settlements in
    Lower Galilee were established later: Sejera farm, 1900; Sejera moshava,
    1901; Kefar Tabor, 1902; Yavneel-Beit Gan, 1904. See Arie Beitan,
    Settlement Changes in Eastern Lower Galilee, 1800–1978 (Jerusalem: Ben
    Zvi Institute, 1982), 37–9, 53, 83 (Hebrew).

8   *History of the Hagana*, Part One, Book 2, 197; *Hashomer Volume*, 7
    (Hebrew).

9   The *Second Aliya* began with the arrival of the self-defense group from the
    town of Homel on 5 December 1903, during the Hannuka festival. See
    Slutzky, *Introduction*, 160. In contrast to him, from the memoirs of Chaia
    Sara Hankin, *Second Aliya Volume* (Hebrew), 149, it seems that they arrived
    in January 1904. Zvi Rosenstein (Even Shoshan), *History* 72, follows
    Hankin's memoirs. Slutzky (ibid.) writes that "this group fulfilled an impor-
    tant task in the founding of Hashomer." This statement is incorrect. The
    group of 12–14 people disappeared into the country, and apparently broke
    up shortly after their immigration. They had no significance or influence for
    future development in Palestine either as a group or as individuals. Even
    Yehezkel Hankin, the only one of the group to be among the founders of Bar
    Giora and Hashomer, played no major role in these two organizations.

10 Shemuel Ettinger, Lecture delivered at a study day at Efal on 4 May 1983,
    Yad Tabenkin, Institute for the Study of the Defensive Force: *The Roots of
    Self Defense*, No. 37, November 1983, 12ff. Also Yisrael Kollat's lecture,
    ibid., 32ff. See also *History of the Hagana*, Part One, Book 2, 155ff.;
    Hashomer Volume, Yisrael Shohat, "The mission and the way," 3.

11 Shabtai Tevet, *David's Sling* (Hebrew) (Jerusalem–Tel Aviv: Shocken, 1976),
    Vol. I, 97–9. The Poaley Zion conference convened on 4–6 October 1906 in
    Jaffa, at the Spector Hotel. David Ben-Gurion chaired the meeting, and was
    also made chairman of the platform committee elected by the conference.
    The platform committee met at a hostelry in Ramla, where it secreted itself
    on 8–11 October 1906 and composed the first party platform, with its
    Marxist-Borochovist character and which is known as the Ramla
    Programme. The Poaley Zion committee, which met on 5 January 1907,
    confirmed the Ramla Programme. This, as well as the Poaley Zion confer-
    ence, followed the minimum Poltava program of Poaley Zion SD in Russia.

12 Kollat's lecture (n. 10); Yitzhak Ben Zvi, *Poaley Zion*, 55, 57. Ben Zvi
    assumed the role of ideologist of the organization and its interpreter to the
    outside world, including the party. His task was also to win new adherents
    to Bar Giora. In Ben Zvi's opinion there was both an ideological and a
    personal connection between the party and Bar Giora.

13 Yosef Gorney, *The Arab Question and the Jewish Problem* (Tel Aviv: Sifriyat
    Ofakim, Am Oved, 1985), 39–44 and 79ff.; Ben Zvi, *Poaley Zion*, 76–7.

The ambition was to achieve home rule in Palestine, that is, autonomy; and see B. Borochov, *Writings*, ed. L. Levite, D. Ben Nahum (Hakibbutz Hameuhad and Sifriat Hapoalim, Hakibbutz Haarzi–Hashomer Hatzair, 1955) (Hebrew). Chiefly "Our Platform" and also 358, conclusion of resolutions of the regional conference of Poaley Zion in the Poltava region, 19–21 December 1905, and also 385, clauses c3 and c6 of the "Proposed Programme of the Jewish Social Deomcratic Workers' Party Poaley Zion in Russia."

14 Matityahu Mintz, *Friend and Rival* (Yad Tabenkin–Hakibbutz Hameuhad, 1986), 112 (Hebrew). Also 166, n. 27, where he claims that "the Bar Giora organization was intended to serve as the directing core of the military unit of Poaley Zion in Palestine."

15 Gorney, *The Arab Question*, 79, 80–1, bases himself on the article by "Avner," i.e., Yitzhak Ben Zvi, "Our work in Palestine", *Der Idisher Arbeiter*, 19, 4 July 1908 (Yiddish). Gorney asserts that by virtue of the Borochovist thesis that the Arabs would be assimilated among the Jews. Until 1908 Poaley Zion held back from the struggle against the Arab worker and the goal of "conquest of labor"; but after the Young Turk revolution they reached a different conclusion about the likelihood of Arab assimilation and about class solidarity, which they discarded in the special setting of Palestine. Only then did they conclude that Arab labor on the *moshavot* would exacerbate the national conflict. Consequently they adopted the slogan "Jewish labor." Henceforward they supported the demand that the workers place themselves in the first line of the national conflict because a Jewish Palestine would be built only through the leadership of the workers. Shabtai Tevet, *David's Sling*, 100–1, presents a different perception of Poaley Zion ideology then. He is mistaken in his statement that the Poltava minimum program, on the establishment of an independent Jewish state in Palestine, "was the only and last time that a Jewish state was set forth as an overt goal. Later, actually after the Young Turk revolution of 1908, this goal was made secret and hidden." See Borochov, *Writings*, Vol. I, 383ff.

16 *History of the Hagana*, Part One, Book 2, 202. According to this book, Bar Giora was established on 29 September 1907. According to Tevet, *David's Sling*, Vol. I, 109, and also Shohat, "The mission and the way," *Hashomer Volume*, 18, the organization was founded on 28 September 1907.

17 *Hashomer Volume*, 8.

18 Ibid.

19 *Second Aliya Volume*, 165ff.

20 *History of the Hagana*, Part One, Book 2, 198.

21 Mendel Portugali was a member of the Poaley Zion party, and sentenced by the authorities to exile in Siberia, whence he escaped and made his way to Palestine. See *Hashomer Volume*, 9.

22 In his memoirs he appears under various names: Moshe Goldstein, Moshe Giv'oni and Yozover. His name was Moshe Goldstein, which he Hebraized to Giv'oni. He came from the town of Yozovka in the Ukraine, where he was active in self-defense, and from that name he sometimes called himself Yozover. Zvi Nadav, *This Is How We Began* (Hakibbutz Hameuhad, 1957), 218 (Hebrew), writes that Goldstein came from Yozovka, which was a substantial mining town in the Ukraine. In his youth he worked there in the iron mines and therefore was used to working bent over, and so quickly became accustomed to working with the hoe.

23 *History of the Hagana,* Part One, Book 2, 198. This man left Palestine for the United States, and therefore is not mentioned further; Sa'adia Paz, *Memoirs* (published by his family, Haifa, 1983), 19–24, states that Meir'ke Hazanovich was also a member of the "intimate group" at Shefaya.

24 *History of the Hagana,* ibid., 198–9; *Hashomer Volume,* 9–13.

25 Ben Zvi, *Poaley Zion,* 47; Tevet, *David's Sling,* Vol. I, 127. Shohat's journey to the congress was made possible only at the last moment owing to the financial support received from Judah Magnes, who was then visiting Palestine. Ben Zvi went to the congress as part of the Russian quota and traveled from Cracow. Shohat went as the delegate of Poaley Zion in Palestine.

26 *Hashomer Volume,* 13.

27 Ibid., 13–15; Tevet, *David's Sling,* Vol. I, 128.

28 *Hashomer Volume,* 15; Tevet, *David's Sling,* ibid.

29 *Hashomer Volume,* ibid.

30 *History of the Hagana,* Part One, Book 2, 202. The organization was founded on the night of the Simhat Tora festival, 29 September 1907.

31 Ibid., 202–3; *Second Aliya Volume,* "Memoirs of Alexander Zayd," 171; Zayd, *Toward Morning,* 34, omits Yehezkel Hankin. This seems to be a slip, because Hankin appears in the memoirs of all the founders; moreover, Zayd and Hankin were very close friends so no personal reason should be sought for the omission.

32 *Hashomer Volume,* 34.

33 Ben Zvi, *Poaley Zion,* 55; *Hashomer Anthology,* 61–2, he omits Moshe Goldstein-Giv'oni-Yozover; in ibid., 531, in the recollections of Moshe Goldstein-Giv'oni, in addition to Shohat, Ben Zvi, Gil'adi, Beker, Nisanov, Zayd and Hankin, he as well as Komarov appear as founders.

34 Paz, *Memoirs,* 19–24.

35 *Hashomer Anthology,* Moshe Giv'oni, 531: At the founding assembly of Bar Giora two proposals were on the agenda: the founding of a movement of guards and the founding of a movement of herdsmen. The second proposal won a majority. In fact, the outcome was the reverse, and the first proposal was adopted. The reasons for this are not clear.

36 *History of the Hagana,* Part One, Book 2, 203; *Hashomer Volume,* 16; Ben Zvi, *Poaley Zion,* 56–7, 91.

37 The most comprehensive and detailed account is in Shohat's "The mission and the way," which opens *Hashomer Volume.* Remember that the book appeared many years after Hashomer had ceased to exist, and most of its veterans, including the Shohat couple, had been pushed out of public life as a result of their long dispute with the leaders of Ahdut Ha'avoda and the founders of the Hagana. Shohat's article is an attempt to justify his historic path and also the path of Hashomer. It is, therefore, replete with apologetics, historical implications, and factual inaccuracies.

38 *Hashomer Anthology; Hashomer Volume; Paz, Memoirs;* Ben Zvi, *Poaley Zion; Second Aliya Volume;* Nadav, *This Is How We Began* and *From the Days of the Guarding and the Defense* etc. Also *History of the Hagana;* Slutzky, *Introduction;* Tevet, *David's Sling,* Vol. I.

39 *Hashomer Volume,* 13.

40 *History of the Hagana,* Part One, Book 2, 202. The account given in the book is important as a background to the establishment of Bar Giora: "and the leadership of the Zionist movement decided finally to begin settlement activity in Palestine. Both decided that the time for action had come."

41　*Hashomer Volume*, 15.

Chapter 3　From Bar Giora to Hashomer

1　*Hashomer Volume*, Moshe Giv'oni's memoirs, 117; Zayd, *Toward Morning*, 36; *Hashomer Anthology*, 5. From Gil'adi's notes it seems that the request was to the Zikhron Ya'akov farmers to allow the group to guard at Burj (Shuni, near Binyamina). The farmers refused, being afraid and not trusting Jewish guarding.

2　*Hashomer Volume*, recollections of Sa'adia Paz, 106–7; and Paz, *Memoirs*, 30–1.

3　*Hashomer Volume*, recollections of Manya Shohat, 385ff. The tour of the country was financed by a bequest left to her by her brother Benjamin, who died childless in the United States in 1902.

4　Rahel Yanait-Ben Zvi, *Manya Shohat*, 44, 54–62. Yanait relates that Manya returned to Palestine early in 1907; according to *History of the Hagana*, Part One, Book 2, 199–202, she returned in August 1907. Yanait's version is not to be relied on as the book is full of inaccuracies. Also Tevet, *David's Sling*, Vol. I, 135, states that Manya returned after the Eighth Zionist Congress at The Hague, meaning late August or early September 1907.

5　*Hashomer Anthology*, notes of Yisrael Gil'adi, 5–6; *History of the Hagana*, Part One, Book 2, 202.

6　*Hashomer Volume*, 16. According to Yisrael Shohat's account it seems that his group was the initiator of the connection with Manya Vilboshevich. In contrast to Manya's recollections in the *Hashomer Volume*, Tevet (*David's Sling*, Vol. I, 135–6) believes that Manya already knew of the existence of Bar Giora when she came to terms with Yisrael Shohat on the transfer of his group to Sejera. In his view, Manya agreed that the collective would be camouflage for the Bar Giora group. As stated, in her recollections Manya avers the opposite; see *Hashomer Volume*, 386–8.

7　Shlomo Zemah, "Conquest of Labor," *Haaretz* calendar for 1950–1 (Tel Aviv: Haim Publications, 200–17). Zemah relates that one evening in the Hebrew month of Heshvan (October) two carts drove into the Sejera farmyard loaded with iron bedframes, mattresses, and kitchen utensils, together with nine members of the collective: "The local dimly-lit hall filled up with strange and noisy men, their faces and manner like a troop of conquerors and likewise their behavior. They stamped their feet when walking, threw out their chests, held their throats jutting out, they showed off their brown leather pouches on their thighs and flicked their whips, which they struck against their boots for their pleasure. The hands of their watchful and stormy leader held a whip of a special kind, slender and short, the Circassian type, its upper half worked in silver and decorated with elaborations of turrets and mosques." And later, "I arose in the dead of night and fled for my life in the darkness, making for Tiberias."

8　According to Paz, *Memoirs*, 32–33, the collective at first consisted of Ben Zur, Gefen, Pik, Dov Ben Galil, Yisrael Gil'adi, Yehuda Zladin, Moshe Goldstein-Giv'oni, David Yisraeli, Yosef Shapira, and Paz himself. Manya Shohat was the book-keeper of the farm, and it is not certain if she was included in the collective. Yisrael Shohat served as the book-keeper of the farm's flour mill, and it is not clear if he belonged to the collective. Mendel Portugali, Zvi Beker, Ben-Zion Mashevich and Yehuda Proskorovsky (Pross) came to Sejera, but at first found no work there. According to Paz it emerges that initially the collective included people who did not belong to Bar Giora at all, and it is possible that the Bar Giora members were actually a minority. It seems that only in the course of the year did the workers, who did not belong to Bar Giora, leave the collective in various ways, and were replaced by Bar Giora members until the association and the collective were identical. Yisrael Shohat, *Hashomer Volume*, 16, also admits that not all members of the collective were Bar Giora people, but he asserts that his men, including himself, were the majority in the collective.

9   How far the memory may be deceptive is seen in David Ben-Gurion, *Memoirs* I, 324. He writes that the collective was operated by members of Hashomer in 1908–9, for two years. In fact the collective was run by Bar Giora people, and it lasted only one year, from the end of 1907 to the summer of 1908.

10 *Hashomer Anthology*, Gil'adi's notes, 6. According to the latter, Manya was the collective's book-keeper. This still does not prove that she was a member of the collective, because she might have done the work as the farm book-keeper. Gil'adi too attests that the convergence of the Bar Giora people at Sejera was an evolutionary process; their move from Judea to the Galilee went on throughout the year, until "their number at last reached fifteen, after seven new members joined us." This means that originally Bar Giora had only eight members. A description of the farm in 1907–8 and of the collective there is in the memoirs of Kayle (Beker) Gil'adi. See "In the Galilee," in *Women Members in the Kibbutz* (Hebrew), first collection (Ein Harod: Hakibbutz Hameuhad, 1944). Material collected by Lilia Basevich and Yokheved Bat Rahel, ed. M. Poznansky and M. Shehori. According to Kayle Gil'adi, during her time at the farm in addition to the Shturman sisters, the two Beker sisters and Manya Shohat, there was also Rivka Nisanov. Krause paid the Jewish girls who worked at farming five grush a day instead of three grush that the Arab girls got. Kayle Gil'adi affirms that at the end of the 1908 working year the members of the collective and Hashomer left the farm: "After the collective completed the year's work, 1908, successfully and with a profit, almost all the men, the members of Hashomer, left Sejera [a chronological error – Y.G.] and went to set up the guarding that we obtained at Mesha and Kinneret. Most of the farm workers also dispersed, to be replaced by newcomers. We, the girls, remained as 'senior' workers at the farm."

11 *Hashomer Volume*, 17.

12 Ibid., 17–19; *History of the Hagana*, Part One, Book 2, 206; Krause's liking for the young people is attested by Ben-Gurion, *Memoirs* I, 36.

13 Ben-Gurion, ibid., 37.

14 *Hashomer Anthology*, Ben-Gurion, "In Judea and in the Galilee," 330.

15 Paz, *Memoirs*, 34.

16 Ben-Gurion, *Memoirs* I, 37; Yanait-Ben Zvi, *Manya Shohat*, 65.

17 Paz, *Memoirs*, 33.

18 Ben-Gurion, *Memoirs* I, 36.

19 Tevet, *David's Sling*, Vol. I, 143.

20 Nadav, *From the Days of the Guarding and the Defense*, 73, states that a year after the takeover of Arab guarding and work at the farm, these were restored to the farm "as if nothing had been achieved."

21 *Hashomer Volume*, 19.

22 Ibid., 18.

23 Ibid., 19.

24 *History of the Hagana*, Part One, Book 2, 206.
25 *Hashomer Volume*, 19; *History of the Hagana*, Part One, Book 2, 209ff.; in Zayd, *Toward Morning*, 47–51, there is the full story, in a slightly different version, of what occurred at Kefar Tabor. According to this, the incident occurred on the Sabbath in the morning, when the farmers gathered in the street and discussed the theft that had been committed on the Sabbath eve. Just then some Mughrabi guards of the moshava passed by them. The farmers stopped them, and berated them over the occurrence, which was apparently their fault. A Mughrabi on horseback lost his temper and fired into the cluster of men. The round struck the calf of a farmer named Cohen, passed through it, richocheted off a rock and seriously wounded one of the Mughrabi foot guards. The enraged farmers fell on the Mughrabi guards and disarmed them.
26 It is not certain if this took place in July or August 1908. According to Yisrael Shohat, *Hashomer Volume*, 19, the Hebrew date Av (August) 1908 was when the Kefar Tabor farmers offered the contract for guarding, meaning that the incident itself occurred before that month.
27 *Hashomer Volume*, 19–20; *History of the Hagana*, Part One, Book 2, 209–10; another version of the acquisition of the guarding at Kefar Tabor is in Paz, *Memoirs*, 37. He relates that Kefar Tabor had just then replaced the Zbehi tribe guards with Mughrabis, and on this account a quarrel broke out between them. One day, as a result of the strife between the Zbehis and the Mughrabis, one of the latter was wounded in the foot while at the moshava. The injured man died and Mughrabis blamed his death on the moshava, in whose confines the injury had occurred, even though they knew that the attacker was a Zbehi. On this incident see also *Hashomer* collection, recollections of Sa'adia Paz, 516ff.
28 *Hashomer Anthology*, notes of Yisrael Gil'adi, 9. He asserts that the collective broke up because "the comrades were not yet ready for the cooperative life." Then they decided to devote themselves to guarding.
29 *Hashomer Volume*, 20.
30 Ben Zvi, *Poaley Zion*, 73; Rahel Yanait-Ben Zvi, "We Are Coming," 68–71, tells of the great surprise they had, and that the revolution came as a "bolt from the blue."
31 George Antonius, *The Arab Awakening* (New York: Capricorn Books, 1965); Yehoshu'a Porat, *The Emergence of the Palestinian National Movement 1918–1929* (Tel Aviv: Sifria Universitait-Am Oved, 1976) (Hebrew). And *The Palestinian Arab National Movement 1929–1939* (Tel Aviv: Sifria Universitait-Am Oved, 1978) (Hebrew); Michael Asaf, "Relations between Arabs and Jews in Palestine 1860–1948" (Tel Aviv: Tarbut Vehinukh, 1970) (Hebrew); "The Awakening of the Arabs in Palestine and Their Flight" (Tel Aviv: Tarbut Vehinukh, 1967) (Hebrew).
32 Gorney, *The Arab Question*, 92–100; Ben Zvi, *Poaley Zion*, 117, notes that the clarification of the party's political program in light of the 1908 revolution began at the council held in the autumn of 1909. The final formulation was elaborated at the sixth party conference in the spring of 1910.
33 Gorney, ibid., 80–92.
34 Antonius, *The Arab Awakening*; Porat, ibid.; *Hashomer Volume*, 28–9. Shohat relates that Najib Nasar was a Christian Arab employed by Baron Rothschild and dismissed.
35 Ben-Gurion, *Memoirs I*, 44; Eliav, *Palestine*, 384. The revolution created a

sense of throwing off the yoke among the fallahs and the Bedouin. The *moshavot* came under constant threat of attack by their neighbors, hence the need for the creation of a strong guards' organization. Similar accounts are found in *History of the Hagana*, Part One, Book 2, 212; Yanait-Ben Zvi, "We Are Coming," 114–15.

36 *History of the Hagana*, Part One, Book 2, 212; Tevet, *David's Sling*, Vol. I, 154–8.

37 *Hapoel Hatzair*, 12 Tammuz 5669 (July) 1909, No. 17.

38 Ibid.

39 *Hashomer Volume*, 20; Nadav, *This Is How We Began*, 199: The author was then working at Kefar Tabor and was already a member of Bar Giora. He took part in the founding of Hashomer and he writes that they all concurred that the goal of the association was "to establish a Jewish military force in the country, a workers' military force." *History of the Hagana*, Part One, Book 2, 214.

40 *Hashomer Anthology*, 568. Yisrael Shohat compared Bar Giora to other liberation movements, such as the Russian SR and the Polish Sokol, that is, a small and secret group, "which goes as a pioneer before the movement of the masses"; *History of the Hagana*, Part One, Book 2, 215; Nadav, *This Is How We Began*, 201, tells that the founding assembly of Hashomer was preceded by a gathering of the members of Bar Giora, in which Nadav participated. Shohat, who chaired the meeting, explained that the purpose of the creation of Hashomer was the formation of an official association of guards, while Bar Giora would continue to exist as a clandestine organization that would direct the operation of the legal Hashomer. It was also decided at this meeting to continue to work toward settlement. At the time the site under consideration was Bint al-Jabal (now Beit Keshet). The meeting also considered the establishment of a society of herdsmen. On the same day, after the Bar Giora meeting was over, the founding assembly of Hashomer took place. Nadav, *From the Days*, 32, writes of the meeting at Atlit in 1911 when only members of Bar Giora were present, noting that "the ordinary members of Hashomer did not know of the existence of Bar Giora." Nadav writes that the Hashomer members were sometimes aware of consultations among the seniors, but they understood this to be the privilege of the founders, not suspecting the existence of the secret Bar Giora organization. "For many years afterwards, until about the time of the deportation of Yisrael and Manya to Turkey, we still preserved the Bar Giora organization. All that time we managed to keep it a complete secret." This testimony contradicts that of Yisrael Shohat, who states that Bar Giora disbanded in 1912 (*Hashomer Volume*, 24), while Nadav claims that this occurred at the end of 1914 or the beginning of 1915, when the Shohats were deported. Different evidence is found in Yanait-Ben Zvi, *Manya Shohat*, 73–4. Yanait was accepted as a member of Hashomer already at the founding assembly at Kefar Tabor in 1909. According to her, Shohat did tell the founding assembly about Bar Giora. Her account must be treated with great circumspection.

41 Nadav, *From the Days*, 84.

42 Pinhas Shneorson, *In the First Line*, "Behind the Wall," 10–15; *Hashomer Volume*, 127–9. Yehuda Zladin, who was one of the first members of Bar Giora and the collective, tells of Shohat's harsh attitude toward him. When working at Sejera as a member of the collective, Zladin requested Shohat for leave to go and work at Hadera for a while. Zladin wanted to earn money

to send to his parents in the diaspora who were in serious financial straits. Shohat refused, and Zladin was thus forced to leave Bar Giora and the collective, and he went to work in Hadera; *Hashomer Anthology*, 459–60, recollections of Zvi Nadav; *Hashomer Volume*, 24; Mordechai Yigael, *In the Saddle*, 57ff., tells of the small number of members of the association. The paid guards were not interested in learning the profession because they had no wish to join the association. Yigael and Mendel Portugali were in favor of restricting the missions of the association.

43   *Hashomer Anthology*, 10, from the notes of Yisrael Gil'adi.
44   Ibid., 252, from the recollections of Eli'ezer Kroll; David Tsalevich, *From My Diary That Remains as a Remnant*, Hagana Historical Archives (HHA), 277. From his account in HHA 2276 it seems that Zvi Beker did in fact obtain partial guarding at Zikhron Ya'akov together with Tsalevich in 1910, but what happened with the guarding at Giv'at 'Ada is not clear.
45   Yigael, *In the Saddle*, 35–9. He relates that before Hashomer obtained the guarding at Hadera it was watched by the men of Shaykh 'Abd el-Latif Abu Hantash of Kakun. The head of these guards was a tyrannical black called Nimr el-Mahush ("the Terrifying Tiger"); see also *Hashomer Anthology*, Meir Spector, 215–26; ibid., Yissachar Sitkov, 246–7; *Hashomer Volume*, 22–3; *History of the Hagana*, Part One, Book 2, 228–31. In his diary David Tsalevich tells of the "ten commandments" of guarding that he learned from Mendel Portugali in Hadera when he set out with him for his first night of guarding at the moshava. Tsalevich, who was among the first guards at Hadera after the task had been assigned to Hashomer in 1910, writes of the good relations that prevailed between the farmers and the guards in that year of guarding: "What helped me was the friendly attitude between people. Also the incomparably good relations between the people of the moshava and the guards. I recall the Simhat Tora festival, how we celebrated when all the worshipers left the synagogue after the prayer with a long cord. The participants held onto it and went through the streets dancing from house to house and brought out everyone to get hold of the cord, until they came to the guards' house, and we were obliged to get out of bed in a hurry and join onto the cord. In this manner we came to the Feinberg house at the edge of the village, and only when it grew dark did we leave them and go off to guard. We were overjoyed that the villagers considered us to be of use to them." See Tsalevich, *From My Diary*, HHA 2277.
46   *History of the Hagana*, Part One, Book 2, 233–4, states that the lack of manpower caused Hashomer to turn down the guarding at Nes Tsiyona, Gedera, Ruhama farm, and Metulla.
47   *Hashomer Anthology*, 19, notes of Yisrael Gil'adi. When they left the guarding at Hadera they took it on at Ben Shemen; ibid., 178–80, recollections of Zalman Assuchkin. In *Hashomer Volume*, 24, Shohat asserts that the guarding at Hadera was given up because of the wish of the people there to introduce mixed guarding. In adopting this stance the Hadera residents were influenced by the people from Petah Tikva who worked in Hadera and were hostile to Jewish guarding. In *Hashomer Volume*, 29–30, Shohat describes the typical circumstances of obtaining guarding at the *moshavot* by Hashomer: Usually a given moshava reached a crisis in its relations with its non-Jewish guards, and only then did it turn to Hashomer. This was the background to obtaining the guarding at Rehovot. Here, after Hashomer had restored order, the wages of the guards were raised from 18,000 francs to

21,500 francs a year. This sum was for 15 foot guards and five mounted guards. In the fruit-harvesting season one more mounted guard and four more foot guards were added. The guarding at Rishon Lezion too was won only after David Sakharov, the guard there, was murdered. According to Shohat, after Rishon Lezion, Hashomer obtained the guarding at Gedera, Beer Ya'akov, Beer Tuvia, and Ben Shemen, and only Petah Tikva remained with the contract guarding of Avraham Shapira. Shohat states that Hashomer tried to penetrate Petah Tikva also, but failed owing to the vigorous opposition of Avraham Shapira to Jewish guarding, in which he had no faith. Shohat asserts that Shapira was the chief cause of the failure to "conquer" Petah Tikva; *History of the Hagana*, Part One, Book 2, 231–2.

48   *History of the Hagana*, Book One, Part 2, 237–44; Nadav, *From the Days*, 74. Nadav explains that the farmers wanted to treat them as paid employees but they saw themselves as bearers of a national mission. Nor did the farmers have any understanding of the Arab mentality and customs. Nadav, *This Is How We Began*, 188, describes the hatred that Zayd developed for the farmers in 1910 at Kefar Tabor, on account of his socialist consciousness: "The class hatred that had seeped into him in the years of the revolution in Russia found expression in everything." On 199 Nadav depicts his fellow founders of Bar Giora, most of whom were members of *Poaley Zion* still in Russia, as revolutionaries who had soaked up the spirit of the socialist revolution: "They were imbued with hatred for the parasitic exploiting bourgeoisie. And here, in the land, this was expressed in hatred for the citrus grove owner." Nadav lays particular stress on Zayd and Portugali, in whom the use of class terminology was prolific, but the others too, who were the majority, also had reservations about the employers: "Even the Galilee farmers did not win our trust, we did not rely on them and we did not believe that the resurrection of the nation would grow out of them. How much less did we believe in the citrus grove owners in the *moshavot* of Judea or in the city merchants."

49   *History of the Hagana*, Book One, Part 2, 221–3.

50   *Hashomer Volume*, 22; *History of the Hagana*, Part One, Book 2, 223, cites the resolution of the *Poaley Zion* party of the meeting held in the Galilee at the Shavuot festival in spring, 1910. At the meeting fierce criticism was leveled at Avoda, and the resolution adopted was as follows: "We recognize that the goals of Avoda do not contradict our principles, but secrecy and concealment generate mistrust of its work." Here the reason for the objections is different from that given by Shohat. It appears that *Poaley Zion* was not opposed on ideological grounds but negated the secrecy of the organization. One of the greatest opponents of Avoda was David Ben-Gurion, who attacked it forcefully at the sixth conference of *Poaley Zion*, held in Jaffa in April 1910. He mainly rejected the principle of discipline, which harmed the development of the worker's consciousness. He held that there was justification for discipline in Hashomer, but not in Avoda, which engaged in peaceful activities. Ben-Gurion demanded that the party center supervise over what took place in Avoda. He called for such supervision over Hashomer also. See Tevet, *David's Sling*, Vol. I, 170.

51   *Hashomer Volume*, 22.

52   *Hashomer Anthology*, 11–12: from the notes of Yisrael Gil'adi it is clear that there were two companies, one formed in Hadera in the fall of 1909, the other in Sejera. Gil'adi also explains the replacement of the name *Legion*

Ha'avoda by Avoda alone. He states that by spreading out to undertake the two missions, Hashomer became unable to accept new assignments. According to him the Sejera company did not succeed in developing. M. Krigser (Ami'ad), Hashomer Anthology, 131–2, was a member of Avoda and he relates that the members planned to live a collective life. He too attests that the organization was active at Hadera and Sejera. In the latter place the company was put in charge of field crops, but under the supervision of the JCA officials. The work of the Sejera company ended in mid-1910. Krigser gives the following reasons for this: Supervision by the JCA ran counter to their ambitions and was not acceptable to them; social problems stemming from the fact that both Hashomer and Avoda wanted to expand; in time the Hashomer members became a minority in Avoda, but they wished to maintain their own framework, while the majority objected to the making of an organization within an organization. See also Krigser's evidence in the Second Aliya Volume, 432. There he adds an interesting feature explaining the fate of the Sejera group and clarifying the nature of the relations between it and the Galilee workers. This was that Avoda's undertaking the field crop work on the farm caused a dispute with the workers who were already at work there and who saw the Avoda action as a means to expel them. Those affected were important figures among the Second Aliya workers – Ben-Zion Yisraeli, Noah Naftulsky, Meir Rothberg and their comrades. The entire incident gave rise to a very unpleasant episode, which cast its shadow on relations between the Hashomer and Avoda people and the Galilee workers. A partisan note entered into it also, because some of the dismissed workers belonged to Hapoel Hatzair or were non-party. See also Tzalel, Hashomer Anthology, 194ff. He too was a member of Avoda. According to his account the uniform was a broad red belt on which was a leather pouch full of bullets, but instead of the Circassian kolpak he notes that the head was covered by a kafiya and aqal, and a weapon was holstered at the side. Sa'adia Paz, Memoirs, 45–9, confirms that there was a branch of Avoda at Sejera. Later he complains about the other workers who were then at the farm: "These workers wanted to break the Avoda organization for both personal and party reasons, and there were many quarrels, especially at Sejera. Once, matters almost reached the point of a general strike." According to Paz, the Avoda group at Sejera numbered ten youths and five girls, the latter being Esther and Sarah Shturman, Miriam Orlov, Batia Mittelman and Gittl Linevsky. Of the young men he lists Shmuel Hefter, M. Krigser, Natan Haruvi, Yitzhak Nadav, Zvi Rothenberg, Zvi Nadav, H. Shturman, himself, and two more. By his account the strike at Sejera in 1910 was not justified. Paz unleashes withering criticism against those he terms "temporary workers," who were the majority at the farm and it was they who decided on the strike, against the opinion of the senior workers, the main part of whom were Avoda people. By a majority of the "temporaries" it was decided to leave the farm after a strike lasting over a week. Avoda could not remain, otherwise they would be condemned as blacklegs. On this subject see also Nadav, This Is How We Began, 215–23, who relates that after the decision to establish Avoda five members of Hashomer were sent to Hadera to raise a company there. The five were M. Portugali, M. Hazanovich, Moshe Yozover, Zvi Beker, and Nadav himself, who for that purpose left his work at Kefar Tabor with the farmer Zalman Cohen. The five were active in Hadera and slowly gathered around them more workers, out of whom they formed the Avoda

company. On 257 Nadav also attests to the existence of another company at
Sejera, which left the farm because of the strike there. On the debate over the
expansion, see David Tsalevich, *From My Diary*, HHA 2277. On 8,
Tsalevich asserts that the opponents were right. He reached this conclusion
in the summer of 1912, when he went to guard at Rehovot. There he became
acquainted with the group of guards, "and I came to the conclusion that the
comrades had been right in their oppostion at the Hadera meeting to
spreading our forces and taking on the guarding at Rehovot. For most of the
new guards were drawn to it not from ideals but to get away from the back-
breaking work with the hoe, which also was hard to find. Clearly, with such
guards we will not enlarge our forces, as the supporters of taking on the
guarding argued." According to Tsalevich, at the annual assembly of
Hashomer in 1912 [the fourth annual assembly held on 14 September 1912
at Rehovot] there was also a minority that opposed accepting guarding at
Rishon Lezion and Beer Ya'akov: Yisrael Gil'adi, "Notes from a Legacy," in
the *Hashomer Anthology*, 19–20; *History of the Hagana*, Part One, Book 2,
248–52.

53   *Hashomer Volume*, 26; Nadav, *From the Days*, 29–35; a completely
different account of Nisanov's murder is present in the diary of Yitzhak Hoz,
a member of Hashomer. In his entry for 13 September 1914, Hoz notes that
at the time of Nisanov's killing on 13 February 1911 he was at Merhavia.
After news of the murder reached them "we sat in the stable . . . Finally David
aroused himself and called us all together to a spot far within the stable. We
called in the comrades who had remained in the village and who had not
been with us in the fields, and we considered how and what to do. There was
not much argument at that meeting. We were all too depressed and almost
all of us were of a single mind and we felt as one, so the meeting did not last
long . . . We shed no tears, but each one of us swore an oath in his heart that
he would fulfill and execute the decision that all the comrades there had made
just then. We sat at great length in the stable not speaking . . . in the silence
of death." Gershon Gera, *A House in Tel Aviv* (Hebrew), Ministry of
Defense, Tel Aviv 1987, 29–30, writes that Hoz deleted the following
sentence in his diary, crossing it out heavily with a pencil, but he managed
to make out what was written: "Late, at midnight, we sent —— to carry out
one of the decisions . . . " The remainder of the entry is not deleted, and Hoz
had written: "and the same night we executed one of the decisions; at twelve
midnight, ten armed horsemen left the village heading for
Sharona-Yamama." From Hoz's diary it appears that the Hashomer men did
avenge Yehezkel Nisanov's death. If so, this alters all the existing historiography, according to which they did not. There is a reference in David
Tsalevich's diary to the opposition's protest against the official line of
restraint over blood vengeance. He relates that after the physical pressure
that his group applied to Kantarovich, the manager of the Sejera farm on
behalf of the Neta'im society, he and Zvi Beker were called to Tiberias to
meet with Yisrael Shohat, who had then returned from Istanbul. In the argument that broke out they attacked him too on this question and asked, "Why
are we being interrogated about the Sejera affair and the method of revenge
in general, which previously you imbued into the comrades and which you
now wish to uproot, having taken a different view of life? In any event, we
do not agree with you." Tsalevich, HHA 2256, 3.

54   *History of the Hagana*, Part One, Book 2, 248–52. The statement here that

Zvi Beker and his group demanded, that the 1911 decision on the blood vengeance be executed, is inexact. That decision spoke of selective punishment. See also *Hashomer Anthology*, 19–20, notes of Yisrael Gil'adi. Tsalevich, *From My Diary*, HHA 2277, 4–5, attests to the support of Meir Hazanovich in the blood vengeance. "Until such time as we begin to follow their ways, our end will not be good, exactly as it was with the Circassians when they first came to the country . . . But we leave the most vital things on paper and hold back in everything only because we are rags [*nor weil mir zennen shmates*]."

55 Nadav, *This Is How We Began*, 201–4.
56 Paz, *Memoirs*, 23.
57 Zayd, *Toward Morning*, 54–5. According to him, Michael Halperin was the first to dream of a "frontier farm" that would guard the borders of the country from El-Arish to the Horan. See also *Hashomer Anthology*, Alexander Zayd, 86.
58 *Hashomer Anthology*, 25–9, Mendel Portugali, letters to his wife, letter of 4 Iyar (May) 1912 from Rehovot. Some argument between the two orientations broke out at the third assembly of Hashomer at Hadera on 23 September 1911. In the debate over whether to expand and accept the guarding at Rehovot the opponents argued: "It would be more correct to think of improving our position by creating a guards' village, so that we would not remain dependent on the goodwill of the farmers. One year they take us on and another year they have no use for us. What is more, our forces are weakening as a result of our living conditions. (All the things intended here were mostly said by the member Gad Avigdorov, who did not manage to finish, being interrupted by Alexander Zayd, who addressed him in his own language – Yiddish (*Was wilsdu shoin? Haindele, balabesele farzich weren? Shemen zolstdu, yunger mentsch*): 'So what do you want? Chickens? To become a householder? Shame on you, young man'). In short, Comrade Zayd stressed that it was still too soon for us to worry about our personal affairs, as long as we were young and strong we had to continue in our path as we had been doing so far." See Tsalevich, *From My Diary*, HHA 2277. In the following years Zayd apparently changed his position.
59 *Hashomer Anthology*, 29–34.
60 Ibid., 35–6.
61 Ibid. Nadav, 435–6.
62 *History of the Hagana*, Part One, Book 2, 246–8, is based on the memorandum sent by Yisrael Shohat from Istanbul to the Zionist Executive Committee.
63 *Hashomer Anthology*, Zvi Nadav, 436ff.; ibid., Mendel Portugali, 36.
64 Zayd, *Toward Morning*, 102–3.
65 *Hashomer Anthology*, Yisrael Gil'adi, 19–20. He tells of the storm that erupted in the association at the end of 1913 and beginning of 1914. Gil'adi stresses, with a note of exasperation, that on their return Yisrael and Manya Shohat were of the opinion "that the comrades at the head of the association are to blame for the division of views and lack of discipline that has befallen Hashomer. They thought that by changing the people, order would be restored." These few terse sentences show how hurt Gil'adi was, not only by the situation that had arisen but also by the stance of the Shohats, who had spent several years in Istanbul, far from the harsh daily reality with which the association had to contend, but who on their return were capable of

putting the blame on him and his fellow committee members, who had carried the heavy burden. Yisrael Shohat's journey to study law in Istanbul was approved by the third annual assembly of Hashomer at Hadera on 23 September 1911. Some members opposed it. Those who supported it gave as their reason Hashomer's need for its own advocates who would be able to appear in court to defend it. This was because Ottoman law allowed only those who had completed law studies in Istanbul to plead in the Turkish courts. The supporters based themselves on the precedent of the trial of the Merhavia people. The opponents argued that Shohat was the only one who could represent the affairs of Hashomer to the outside. Similarly, he had great influence over members of the association. Moreover, it was important that there be Jewish lawyers, but not necessarily from Hashomer. As stated, the supporters won the day. Tsalevich, *From My Diary*, HHA 2277, 4. The Hashomer calendar in *Hashomer Volume*, 477, notes that Shohat returned from Istanbul on 10 February 1914; Labor Party Archives, section IV-104, Yisrael Gil'adi, file 76. In his notebook Gil'adi remarks on 31 January 1914 that Manya Shohat was in Haifa. On 10 March 1914 he wrote that he was traveling to Haifa to see Yisrael and Manya Shohat, "a couple with his mare."

66   Atara Shturman, "Years in the Land," 7–8, in *Women Members in the Kibbutz*, first collection, ibid.
67   Ibid. Kayle Gil'adi, *In the Galilee*, 26.
68   Ibid. Atara Shturman, "Years in the Land," 13.
69   Labor Party Archives, IV-104, Yisrael Gil'adi, file 78.

Chapter 4   Hashomer and the Yishuv

1   Gorney, *The Arab Question*, 99–104; *Hashomer Volume*, Rahel Yanait-Ben Zvi, 192.
2   Ben Zvi, *Poaley Zion*, 266. From the evidence of Moshe Levit, a Hashomer activist and a founder of Ayelet Hashahar, a consultation took place at Yavneel among several leaders of Hashomer about the money sent by Bloch-Blumenfeld and about Lishansky. The consultation was called by Yosef Nahmani, who told the gathering about the money. On his way back to the Galilee, Gil'adi stopped at Nijmat el-Subah, and told Levit, in whom he confided, about the meeting and the money. Gil'adi said that he opposed Hashomer's retaining the money and that he was not involved in the business of the money at all. This story is important against the background of events and the limited council meeting of Poaley Zion at Mahanayim in which about 20 people participated, most of them from Judea who had drifted to the Galilee because of the war but were not up on developments there. Levit states that there was a display of unjustified malice at the meeting, and his feeling was that they wanted to place the guard on summary trial. Most of those present were men who had been rejected by the association or who were opposed to it, and now they wanted to settle accounts. After a blistering attack on Hashomer, the majority demanded that Gil'adi inform them where the money was. The outburst was against Gil'adi, despite his not then being on the Hashomer committee and despite his claim that the entire affair concerned the Tel Adashim group and the Lower Galilee people; he and his group had had nothing to do with it, and until recently had actually been ignorant of the matter. Levit and his friends called for the decision on

the subject to be postponed until the full council that was to convene in the future. Nothing helped; the majority resolved to expel Gil'adi and Zayd from the party – precisely they who were not involved with the affair of the funds at all. See Shaul Dagan, *Between Tel 'Adas and Hamara, The Memoirs of Moshe Levit, Member of Hashomer*, Society for the Protection of Nature Publication, 1988, 110–14.

3   *Hashomer Volume*, Yisrael Shohat, 33–4.
4   *History of the Hagana*, Part One, Book 2, 287–8; Shneorson, "In the First Line," ibid., 87; *Hashomer Volume*, Yisrael Shohat, 34; Nadav, *From the Days*, 238; Shneorson, ibid., "Who Are We? What Were We?" 21–5.
5   Menahem Ussishkin, *Ussishkin Volume for his 70th Birthday*, Committee for the publication of the book, Jerusalem 1934, "Third Journey to Palestine," 136–7. On the support of the Odessa Committee for the Palestine Yishuv see also the newspaper *Ha'olam* 12 February 1913 (meeting of the Committee of 22 January 1913); 26 February 1913 (meeting of the Committee of 28 January 1913); 24 June 1913 (meeting of the Committee of 3 June 1913); 11 December 1913 (meeting of the Committee of 10 November 1913).
6   *Hashomer Volume*, Yisrael Shohat, 36–7; *Hashomer Anthology*, Sa'adia Paz, 516–20; Slutzky, *Introduction*, 219–20; *History of the Hagana*, Part One, Book 2, 252, and 301–4; Paz, *Memoirs*, 40–2, mentions 7000 francs that the association received from the Zionists of Russia through Ussishkin to the guarantee fund. Paz ascribes this achievement to Manya Shohat. Paz also claims that in 1909 Hashomer got arms from the Defense Committee in Odessa – arms still preserved from the time of the self-defense that had been operative there several years before; Paz attributes this too to Manya Shohat, who, he states, knew those concerned in Odessa.
7   *History of the Hagana*, Part One, Book 2, 275–97.
8   Ibid., 409–12; *Hashomer Anthology*, Zvi Nadav. 460–6: according to Nadav, the committee of the Judea Workers' Union proposed, during the dispute with Hamagen, a compromise, whereby it would not officially recognize the new organization, which Nadav terms "Hanoter," not "Hamagen," but nor would it boycott it. Finally it was agreed that the committee would not support Hamagen in obtaining guarding at more settlements nor would it supply it any longer with manpower – these measures in addition to its official non-recognition of the group. On Hanoter see Zayd's letter against M. Rothberg in *Hahdut*, 3 Heshvan (October) 1912. Tsalevich, HHA 2276, 7, asserts that Hanoter was a group that organized in the vicinity of Petah Tikva in 1915–16, before Hamagen. It had no connection with the Gideonites. The group operated for a short time. In the Labor Party Archives, IV-120, file 5, 64, there is interesting evidence on the Hamagen organization. In a letter of August–September 1916 representatives of the Haro'im (The Herdsmen) group denied any connection with the organization. The text of the letter is as follows:

> Galilee. Tishri, Taraz [?September 1916 – Y.G.] To the central committee in Judea. We hereby announce that our association has no affinity or connection with the Hamagen association. Please note this so as to prevent any misunderstanding that may arise. David Tsalevich, Moshe Shapira

To remove the slightest suspicion or trace of suspicion, the main suspect, David Tsalevich, added a personal letter of his own:

As for me, that word has got about that I am already a member of
Hamagen, I hereby deny this and admit that I did in fact talk of tempo-
rary work with them, *but not as a member*. David Tsalevich. (emphasis
in the original)
Further testimony from Tsalevich about his relations with Hamagen is
present in HHA 2276, 2. Here he attests that "in light of these consideration
I gave Yosef [Lishansky] a positive answer and joined Hamagen." Similar
evidence is found in HHA 2287, 2: "Finally I agreed to join [Hamagen], and
I began to guard as a sole horseman at Ruhama and then at Ekron and
Gedera." Some of the members of Hamagen were recruited among embit-
tered Hashomer applicants who had not been accepted to the latter even after
many years of probation. "I must point out that most of the boys were
disgruntled that after a lengthy time of two years or even three at guarding
they were still out of the picture and were not accepted as members of
Hashomer. And that is what brought them to this pass." Ibid. Evidence of
Tsalevich.

Chapter 5   The Organization and Ideology of Hashomer

1   David Ben-Gurion, *Memoirs* I (Tel Aviv: Am Oved, 1971), 66 (Hebrew),
    wrote that the Ottomanization was organized by himself and by Yitzhak Ben
    Zvi with a group of long-standing residents of Jerusalem: David Yellin,
    Albert Antabi, Yosef Meyuhas, etc. See also Rahel Yanait-Ben Zvi, *Manya
    Shohat* (Jerusalem: Ben Zvi Institute, 1976), 85 (Hebrew); Yitzhak Ben Zvi,
    Poaley Zion in the Second Aliya (publication of the Mapai Party and the
    World Union of Poaley Zion (Z.S) Hitahdut, 1950), 154 (Hebrew); Yisrael
    Shohat, "The mission and the way", in *Hashomer Volume*, 39 (Hebrew).
2   Yisrael Shohat, ibid., 36, 39; Y. Harit, Hagana Historical Archives (HHA),
    961.
3   Ben Zvi, *Poaley Zion*, 154; the journal *Haahdut*, No. 11–12, 30 December
    1914; Ben-Gurion, *Memoirs*, I, 66; Isaiah Friedman, *Germany, Turkey and
    Zionism, 1897–1918* (Oxford: Clarendon Press, 1977), 197 (hereafter,
    Friedman).
4   Shohat, "The mission and the way," *Hashomer Volume*, 39–40.
5   Ibid.
6   Yanait-Ben Zvi, *Manya Shohat*, 85–6.
7   Friedman, 197–9, 219; Yitzhak Ben Zvi, *The Jewish Battalions* (Jerusalem:
    Ben Zvi Institute, 1968), 20–1 (Hebrew); Mordechai Ben Hillel Hacohen,
    The War of the Nations, Vol. I (Jerusalem: Ben Zvi Institute, 1981), 15, 19,
    20, 22, 24, 30, 35 (Hebrew); Hillel Yaffe, *A Generation of Immigrants* (Tel
    Aviv: Dvir, 1939), 493–4 (Hebrew); Shohat, "The mission and the way,"
    Hashomer Volume, 39.
8   Friedman, 211–22; Mordechai Ben Hillel Hacohen, *The War of the Nations*,
    Vol. I, 55, 64–5; Shohat, 39; Zvi Nadav, "From my recollections" *Hashomer
    Anthology*, 443–4 (Hebrew); Rahel Yanait-Ben Zvi, *Our Way to the Land*
    (Tel Aviv: Am Oved, 1962), 199–200 (Hebrew); Yanait-Ben Zvi, *Manya
    Shohat*, 86.
9   Yisrael Shohat, *Hashomer Volume*, 40; Ben-Hillel Hacohen, *The War of the
    Nations*, Vol. I, 64.
10 Shohat, ibid., 41.
11 Yanait-Ben Zvi, *Our Way to the Land*, 205, and also in *Hashomer Volume*,

155–60; Ben Zvi, *Poaley Zion*, 156.

12 Zvi Nadav, in *Hashomer Anthology*, 448–51.

13 Arye Abramson, in *Hashomer Anthology*, 267–74; Moshe Zaludin, ibid., 281–3; Yosef Harit, ibid., 284–6. On the depression in the party see Labor Archives, file 403/IV/13, minutes of the meetings of the council, speech by Bloch-Blumenfeld.

14 Zvi Nadav, in *Hashomer Anthology*, 453–4; Rahel Yanait-Ben Zvi, in *Hashomer Volume*, 177–8. On the Jaffa Group see Avraham Krinitzi, *By Virtue of the Deed* (Tel Aviv: Masada, 1950), 59–62, 146 (Hebrew). According to him the group formed in 1914. Also A. Ramba, *Krinitzi* (Ramat Gan: Masada, 1968), 53–8 (Hebrew).

15 Zvi Nadav, *From the Days of the Guarding and the Defense*, 130; Yanait-Ben Zvi, in *Hashomer Volume*, 177; Nadav, in *Hashomer Anthology*, 462–9. According to Zvi Nadav, they won the guarding through the backing they got from M. Smilansky, Gorodinsky, and Miller, who were supporters of Hashomer on the moshava committee. He appointed Ya'akov Kavashneh as coordinator of the guarding. From the memoirs of Yitzhak Nadav it seems that he won the guarding at Rehovot and was responsible for it, not Zvi Nadav. See Yitzhak Nadav, *Memoirs of a Hashomer Man* (Tel Aviv: Israel Ministry of Defense Publication, 1986) (Hebrew).

16 Yanait-Ben Zvi, *Our Way to the Land*, 234, and also in *Hashomer Volume*, 181; Ya'akov Pat, in *Hashomer Volume*, 206ff. Pat received the guarding at Ruhama in winter 1916. On Pat, see also Eliezer Lubrani, ed., *The Way of a Man, A Collection in Memory of Ya'akov Pat*, published by the Committee to Memorialize Ya'akov Pat, 1958 (Hebrew).

17 Zvi Nadav, in *Hashomer Anthology*, 460–6.

18 Pinhas Shneorson, *In the Front Line* (Tel Aviv: Sifriat Hapoalim, 1978), chapter on the war and the expulsion, 26–60 (Hebrew); Kayle Gila'adi, in *Hashomer Anthology*, 141ff.; Moshe Zaludin, ibid., 283 ff. Nehama Zitzer, ibid., 289–91; memoirs of Zalman Alon (Assushkin), Tova Portugali and Kayle Gil'adi, in *Hashomer Volume*, 339–54; Arye Hetzroni, *Herdsman and Fighter, The Story of Gershon Fleisher, the First of the Sheep-Breeders, Hashomer Man* (Jerusalem: M. Neumann, 1975) (Hebrew); Alexander Zayd, *Toward Morning, Chapters of a Diary* (Tel Aviv: Am Oved, 1975), 120–7 (Hebrew). On the ambivalent attitude of Poaley Zion to the settlement of the Gil'adi group at Hamara see Labor Archives and Museum, file 403/IV/29, minutes of the twelfth conference of Poaley Zion in Merhavia in 6 September 1917, Tzifroni's report. Likewise the complaints of Pinhas Shneorson, 7 and 11–12, against the attitude of the party to his group. On the attempt by the Haro'im group to establish a hold at Tel Hai see also Central Zionist Archives, file J15–6479; file L2, 103, II, file J15–6478. Similarly Labor Archives, Gil'adi file, 104/IV/3. See also Nakdimon Rogel, *The Travellers to the Land of the North* (Jerusalem: Ben Zvi Institute, 1987) (Hebrew).

19 On 4 September 1917 a carrier pigeon was caught in Caesarea, and this supplied the Turks with the first solid evidence of the existence of a spy ring. On 17 September the capture of Na'aman Belkind became known, and this raised tension in the Yishuv to a peak. See also Ben Hillel Hacohen, *War of the Nations*, Vol. I, 498: since April–May the Turks had known of the existence of the network; 504: resolutions of Hapoel Hatzair against the espionage; 512: the meeting of elements in the Yishuv to oppose the espi-

onage; 513: the author's harsh criticism of the network, whose existence was apparently already known in March 1917; Pinhas Shneorson, *In the Front Line*, 31, claims that Belkind's capture was known to them immediately after the Merhavia conference; see also 34; *History of the Hagana*, A3, 369–71.

20   Shneorson, ibid., 35, 37ff.; Zvi Nadav, "From my recollections," *Hashomer Anthology*, 476ff.; also idem, *From the Days*; Yanait-Ben Zvi, *Our Way to the Land*, 243ff.; Shmuel Hefter, in *Hashomer Volume*, 217–20; Shneorson, ibid., 220–3; Yaffe, *A Generation of Immigrants*, 586; Ben Hillel Hacohen, *The War of the Nations*, Vol. II (Jerusalem, 1985), 720ff.

21   At the Sharona meeting it was also decided to try those who attempted to assassinate Lishansky for their failure. The decision was also taken to revive the Political Committee of the Yishuv, but on democratic foundations.

22   Shneorson, *In the Front Line*, the articles "In war and in expulsion," and "Fire in the Galilee"; Yisrael Shohat, in *Hashomer Volume*, 49; Zvi Nadav, *In the Days*, 206.

23   Ben Zvi, *Poaley Zion*, 55, 57.

24   Borochov, *Writings* (Hebrew), Vol. I, L. Levite and D. Ben-Nahum (eds), (Hakibbutz Hameuhad and Sifriat Hapoalim, 1955). See especially the article "Our platform." See also 358, conclusions of the decisions of the regional conference of Poaley Zion in the Poltava district. Also 385, clauses c3 and c6 of "Draft Program of the Jewish Social-Democratic Workers' Party Poaley Zion in Russia." See also Yosef Gorney, *The Arab Question and the Jewish Problem* (Tel Aviv: Sifriat Ofakim–Am Oved, 1985), 39–44 and 79ff. (Hebrew); Ben Zvi, *Poaley Zion*, 76–7; Matityahu Mintz, *Comrade and Enemy* (Yad Tabenkin–Hakibbutz Hameuhad, 1986), 112, 166, n. 27 (Hebrew).

25   Ben Zvi, *Poaley Zion*, 117; Yisrael Shohat, in *Hashomer Volume*, 28–9; Yanait-Ben Zvi, *Our Way to the Land*, 114–15; Ben-Gurion, *Memoirs* I, 44; Yehoshu'a Porat, *The Emergence of the Palestine National Movement 1918–1929* (Tel Aviv: Sifria Universitait-Am Oved, 1976) (Hebrew).

26   Ben Zvi, ibid., 159–61.

27   Ben-Gurion, ibid., 75.

28   Ben Zvi, ibid., 161.

29   Ibid., 157–9. Also Central Zionist Archives, Z3/73.

30   Shabtai Tevet, *David's Sling,* I (Jerusalem–Tel Aviv: Shocken, 1976), 374–5 (Hebrew).

31   Mordechai Eliav, *Palestine and Its Settlement in the Nineteenth Century, 1777–1917* (Jerusalem: Keter, 1978), 443 (Hebrew); Yigal Elam, *The Jewish Battalions in the First World War* (Tel Aviv: Maarakhot, 1973), 171, 181 (Hebrew).

32   Tevet, *David's Sling*, I, 274, 319ff.; Ya'ari-Polskin, *Pinhas Ruthenberg, The Man and His Deeds* (Tel Aviv: Hatekufa Co., 1939) (Hebrew).

33   Tevet, ibid., 319–20, 327.

34   Ibid. Ben Zvi, *Poaley Zion*, 194, and also his *The Jewish Battalions*, 25; Ben-Gurion, *Memoirs*, I, 91–2, includes H. Zhitlovsly among the supporters of Ruthenberg's ideas, while Borochov was opposed. According to Elam, *The Jewish Battalions in the First World War*, 180–3, Professor N. Slushatz was also a supporter of the idea of the battalions. The Poaley Zion party in the United States adopted a neutral position on the war, in accordance with its eighth conference at Rochester in December 1914. The ninth conference of the party, held in Cleveland, in 1915, and the tenth conference in Boston in

1916, reaffirmed the resolution on neutrality. Most party members were satisfied with this line, which was identical with that of the Second International. However, a minority of members, headed by Nahman Sirkin, supported the *Entente* and was in favor of American entry into the war on its side. When this in fact occurred on 6 April 1917 it obviously strengthened this minority. See Tevet, *David's Sling*, I, 373–4.

35   Labor Archives and Museum, file 403/IV/13, minutes of the council meetings. Statement by Bloch-Blumenfeld, 2. Also the council of members, July 1917 (end of file) and the statements of Hempfel and Neta (Harpaz).

36   Field-marshal A. Wavell, *The Palestine Campaigns* (Hebrew translation), Ma'arakhot 1951, 50–1, 56–60.

37   Labor Archives, file 403/IV/37 (1916). See also Ben Hillel Hacohen, *The War of the Nations*, I, 43, the statement by Hacohen of 7 December 1914: "The two workers' weeklies published in Palestine, *Haahdut* in Jerusalem and *Hapoel Hatza'ir* in Jaffa, are divided in their opinions on the war also." Later Hacohen notes the vigorous anti-German position of *Haahdut* as compared with the loyalist position *Hapoel Hatza'ir* adopted toward the Ottoman empire. See also M. Cherkasi, *Second Aliya Volume* (Tel Aviv: Am Oved, 1947), 648ff. He claims that *Haahdut* was closed at the beginning of January 1915 because of an article by N. Sirkin, "When Germany is defeated," in which he described the regime of enslavement and evil that then prevailed in the world. The fact that the paper published the article speaks for itself.

38   Yanait-Ben Zvi, *Manya Shohat*, 85–6.

39   Yisrael Shohat, in *Hashomer Volume*, 39–40.

40   Ibid., 41. In a footnote Shohat writes that present at the meeting were also Yisrael Gil'adi and Mendel Portugali. Yanait-Ben Zvi, *Our Way to the Land*, 205, gives the date of the meeting as 5 March 1915, the day when the memorandum of Ben Zvi and Ben-Gurion was submitted to Jamal Pasha. She asserts that at the meeting were all the members of the Poaley Zion center and all the members of the Hashomer committee. By contrast, according to her recollections in *Hashomer Volume*, 159, the discussion at the Amdursky Hotel was on 11 March, because she writes that on the day of the meeting Ben Zvi and Ben-Gurion were taken to Jaffa. As far as is known, this occurred on 11 March 1915. Contrary to all the other recollections, Ben-Gurion, *Memoirs*, I, 71, writes that the meeting was held in the prison, and the members of Poaley Zion center took part. He does not mention members of Hashomer.

41   Yanait-Ben Zvi, in *Hashomer Volume*, 159, states that the proposal, that she join the Hashomer committee, was made to her by the Shohat couple on board the train carrying them from Haifa to Damascus.

42   Ben Zvi, *Poaley Zion*, 156. Also *Memoirs and Notes*, 220.

43   Ibid.; idem, *The Jewish Battalions*, 22.

44   Yanait-Ben Zvi, *Our Way to the Land*, 205; *Hashomer Anthology*, 538; *Manya Shohat*, 88; also her article in the *Jewish Battalions Volume*, 34.

45   Ben-Gurion, *Memoirs*, I, 71.

46   *The Ben-Gurion Letters* I (1904–1919), compiled and annotated by Yehuda Erez (Tel Aviv: Am Oved and Tel Aviv University, 1971), 442–6. Ben-Gurion, unlike the others, notes that the "historic" meeting was in Jaffa.

47   Ben Zvi, *Poaley Zion*, 166–9; Tevet, *David's Sling*, I, 589–90.

48   Tevet, ibid., 288. For some reason Tevet believed that the two men were indeed charged with the task of establishing battalions in the United States,

but these were to fight on the side of Turkey. I have found no sources to support his interpretation.

49 Ben-Gurion, *Memoirs*, I, 75; *The Ben-Gurion Letters*, I, 443; Ben Zvi, *Poaley Zion*, 161; idem, *Memoirs and Notes*, 222; idem, *The Jewish Battalions*, 22; Michael Bar Zohar, *Ben-Gurion*, I (Tel Aviv: Am Oved, 1975), 100, cites a conversation between himself and Ben-Gurion on the initiative of Jabotinsky and Trumpeldor in Egypt, in which Ben-Gurion said: "Perhaps I was wrong in my evaluation, but if history were to repeat itself I would take the same position."

50 Ben-Gurion, *Memoirs*, I, 91–2.

51 Ibid., 86, 97; Ben Zvi, *The Jewish Battalions*, 26. Ben Zvi claims that the movement for the Jewish Battalion in the United States began some time before the entry of the country into the war. See *Memoirs and Notes*, 238: "The American battalion was created on the eve of the entry of the United States into the war." See also Elias Gilner, *War and Hope* (New York: Herzl Press, 1969), 150; Tevet, *David' Sling*, I, 374–5.

52 Zvi Nadav, "From my recollections," in *Hashomer Anthology*, 458.

53 Labor Archives, file 403/IV/29, the twelfth conference of Poaley Zion at Merhavia, September 1917, minutes of discussions, a version. See especially the speeches of Bloch-Blumenfeld (17ff.) and the speech of Dr Waldstein, who represented the activist line in the party (23ff.), and also the speeches of Rahel Yanait-Ben Zvi and of others (25–6ff.).

Chapter 6   The Status of Women in Hashomer

1 Dvora Bernstein, *A Woman in Palestine* (Hakibbutz Hameuhad, 1987), ch. 1, 16–27 (Hebrew). Sara Malkin, "My Path in the Land" in *Second Aliya Volume*, 488–500, ed. Bracha Habas (Tel Aviv: Am Oved, 1947) (Hebrew).

2 Haya Kroll, "The woman and Hashomer" (Hebrew), *Hashomer Volume*, 363.

3 Sara Malkin, *The Women Workers at Kinneret, Chapters of Hapoel Hatzair*. (Tel Aviv: Tverski Publishers, 1935), Vol. 3, 202–6 (Hebrew).
   Sara Malkin (1885–1949): Among the earliest of the *Second Aliya* and one of its first women workers. Born in Russian, emigrated to Palestine in 1905. Worked at Petah Tikva and Rehovot, and struggled for the right to work. Was the only woman who worked with the first group of workers at the Kinneret farm (Delayka). Member of the "Hadera Commune" and a founder of Degania. A founder of the women workers' movement in 1914 and a member of its first central committee. Active in the women workers' movement and in the Hapoel Hatzair party. Founder and director of the women workers' farm at Afula. See Malkin, "My path in the land."

4 *Chapters of Hapoel Hatzair*, ibid. On the misunderstanding and even the hostility on the part of the male workers, who at times regarded the women workers as competitors for a place to work, see Kayle Gil'adi, "In the Galilee" (Hebrew), *Women of the Kibbutz* (Ein Harod: Hakibbutz Hameuhad, 1944), first collection, 27. Describing her days at Sejera, when the collective had already broken up, she writes of the women of Bar Giora who remained at the farm and who were by then experienced workers of long standing. Krause relied on them and was proud of them. He sent the new male workers to them for instruction: "Occasionally this stance of ours annoyed the boys, and more than once there was some unpleasantness

between us. Upset, one of them would complain, 'You women have taken the livelihood from the men; we'll force you out.'" The same kind of problems is described in Atara Shturman's recollections of the period when she worked, with a group of women, at the Ben Shemen farm, apparently at the end of 1911 and 1912: "Some of us learned how to milk the cows, and the men called us *die milkerkers* – Yiddish for 'dairymaids'. We worked in the henhouse too. We tried to get into every corner where there was work and wanted to learn all kinds of agriculture. Wilenski was proud of our group, and when people from the settlement organizations came to visit the farm he brought them to our work area and told them of our energy and the hard work we put into that vegetable garden. But the male workers at the farm did not behave that way. They showed no liking for our enterprise. Some of them regarded us as competitors, as if we had come to deprive them of their share in Ben Shemen. After our experience at Kinneret, where the girls' farm won warm support from the workers of the Galilee, we suffered from this limited vision. The local community made jokes about us and in the comic paper there they called us 'the girls of the green convent' (because we worked at growing vegetables). But we were proud of ourselves, and after a few months we began to sell the fruits of our labors." See Atara Shturman, "Years in the land", in *Women of the Kibbutz*, first collection, 11 (Hebrew).

5   Margalit Shilo, "The women workers' farm at Kinneret 1911–1917," *Cathedra* 14, 81–112 (Jerusalem: Ben Zvi Institute, 1980) (Hebrew).

6   Lola Porat, "The woman worker in the *Second Aliya*" (Hebrew), *Basha'ar*, Nos 5–6, Sept.–Dec. 1972, 336–9; Esther Beker, "From the life of a Hashomer family", *Second Aliya Volume*, 517 (Hebrew).

7   Kayle Gil'adi, "In the Galilee," in *Women of the Kibbutz*, first collection, 25–6, recounts that she was called from Jerusalem "for kitchen work at the collective that had been founded." The call was from Yisrael Shohat. After some time the farm manager, Eliahu Krause, permitted the girls "to learn all the farming jobs and he made an effort to pay us a wage that would be enough to live on." The Arab women workers earned three grush a day, but the Jewish women began at five grush and very soon reached eight grush a day. Kayle Gil'adi stresses that Krause was the exception in his attitude to the young women: "In those days there was no chance for girls 'of our kind' to find any work at all. Not even as a servant in a private home. Krause was the first and the only one to help us learn farming. He recognized clearly that no agricultural settlement could succeed if the woman was not trained for it also. In fact, we joined in all the work together with the men. We ploughed, harvested, picked, lugged heavy sacks of grain on our backs, we loaded crops and hay onto carts, etc., etc. Only we did not sow."

8   Ibid. Rivka Mahnaimit, "Diary," 38, dated 8 February 1912, tells of her work at the Poria farm. After the workers had got to know her well, and she had been working for a few months in the kitchen, they let her work in the field: "From the start the management objected to women being given work in the field. After requests, demands and arguments with the manager I went out to the field with the men. The manager warned me that I would not get paid even for food . . . On the first day they set me a rate of nine grush (the boys got 2 francs, worth 11.5 Turkish grush). After a few days I was earning no less than the men."

9   Labor Archives, 120/IV/A, file 3b (edited).
     Ya'el Gordon (1879–1958). One of the first women workers of the *Second*

Aliya. A founder of the women workers' movement at Merhavia in 1914, and member of its first central committee. Member of Hapoel Hatzair, the Histadrut and Mapai. Daughter of A. D. Gordon. Born in Podolia, Russia. Emigrated to Palestine in 1905 and accompanied her father for many years. Worked as a laborer at Ein Ganim, at Hanna Maisel's training farm at Kinneret, at the Migdal farm, in the kitchen of the "60 group" at Kinneret, etc. After her father's death she joined Degania.

Hanna Maisel (Shohat) (1888–1972). Born in Grodno, Russia. Acquired agricultural and pedagogical education at universities in Switzerland and France. Active from her youth in the Poaley Zion movement. Emigrated to Palestine in 1908. In 1911 she established the women workers' farm at Kinneret. One of the most oustanding personalities among the women of the *Second Aliya* and the founders of the women workers' movement. From 1920 a member of the world directorate of Wizo. A founder of Nahalal, where she made her home with her husband Eli'ezer Shohat. From 1929 to 1960 she was principal of the Agricultural High School for Girls at Nahalal established by Wizo.

10 At the start of the *Second Aliya* there were very few women workers in Palestine – several dozens in all. Most of the increase in their numbers occurred in the period 1912–14. A census conducted in 1913 by the Palestine Office covering 971 workers in the *moshavot* and the farms of the Jewish National Fund included 194 women, that is, 19 percent of the total. The origins of the women workers' movement were at Kinneret, where the first assembly of women workers was held in April 1911, with the participation of 17 women. The women workers' movement as an overall framework was set up three years later at Merhavia on 30 May–4 June 1914. The first central committee to be elected consisted of Sara Malkin, Yael Gordon, Hanna Maisel and Leah Meron. See Zvi Rosenstein (Even-Shoshan), *History of the Workers' Movement in Palestine*, Book One (Tel Aviv: Am Oved, 1955), ch. 22, 208–20 (Hebrew). See also Ada (Fishman) Maimon, *Fifty Years of the Women Workers' Movement, 1904–1954* (Tel Aviv: Aianot, 1955) (Hebrew).

11 In *Hashomer Volume*, 474–5, there is a list of members of Bar Giora and Hashomer in the period 1907–20. Of the 105 names, 23 are of women.

12 Kayle Gil'adi, "In the Galilee," 25.

13 Ibid., 28.

14 Atara Shturman, "Years in the land," 5.

15 Ibid., 6.

16 Haya Kroll, "The woman and Hashomer," *Hashomer Volume*, 365; Hava Alon (Assushkin), "Wife of a guard," ibid., 356, on her work at Hadera and Rehovot; Yisrael Shohat, "The mission and the way," *Hashomer Volume*, 33; Esther Beker, "The story of a guard's family," *Hashomer Volume*, 143–4.

17 Tzipora Zayd, "With Hashomer," *Second Aliya Volume*, 532–3; Esther Beker, "The story of a guard's family," *Hashomer Volume*, 140.

18 Alexander Zayd, *Toward Morning* (Tel Aviv: Am Oved, 1975), 61; Esther Beker, ibid., 139.

19 Ibid., 56. Tzipora Zayd, "With Hashomer," *Second Aliya Volume*, 531–2. On the fact that the girls of Bar Giora did not have weapons like the boys, see Rahel Yanait-Ben Zvi, *Manya Shohat*, 70. In her book *Our Way to the Land*, 98, there is a slightly different account.

20 Uri Brenner, "The place of the woman in Hashomer", *Shorashim* II
    (Tabenkin Institute for Research and Study of the Kibbutz, Hakibbutz
    Hameuhad, 1980) (Hebrew). Rahel Yanait, "In the First World War,"
    Hashomer Volume, 168. Manya Shohat, in her memoirs, supports this state-
    ment: "In Hashomer there were two types of women: members of Hashomer
    and wives of guards. We, the women members of Hashomer, were few. Most
    of the women were simply wives of men who were members. Our attitude
    to family life was highly constructive. Almost every one of us gave birth every
    two years. We women members of Hashomer learnt how to control our grief.
    We derived great satisfaction from our lives. We enjoyed the romance of life
    and the surroundings no less than the men. We knew what we were suffering
    for. It was not so with the wives of the guards. Only the suffering fell to their
    lot. Their husbands revealed nothing to them. They required only absolute
    passivity from them. When the children began to die, the primal instinct of
    every mother arose in them. Sometimes we women members were ashamed
    to look them in the face: 'Why are things good for us and bad for them?'"
    See Manya Shohat, "The woman in Hashomer" (Hebrew), *Devar Hapoelet*,
    4th year, 11 March 1937, supplement to the newspaper *Davar*.
21 Aviva Opaz, "Letters from Palestine: The guard Mendel Portugali to his wife
    Tova" (Hebrew), *Hadarim* 3–4, winter 1982–3, ed. Hilit Yeshurun, Gordon
    Gallery publication (no date). First letter in the article (undated). Concerning
    Tova Portugali, Uri Brenner cites Rahel Yanait-Ben Zvi, who wrote that
    Tova Portugali believed that women should not be accepted into the associ-
    ation because they did not go out to guard. Therefore, she did not consider
    herself a member of the association and did not attend its meetings. Brenner's
    reference, namely, Yanait's book *Our Way to the Land*, 394, is mistaken.
    The incident is mentioned in Yanait, "In the days of the First World War,"
    Hashomer Volume, 169. There she notes that "Tova does not participate in
    the meeting. Yet she would be accepted, except that she herself denies her
    right to be accepted into Hashomer, as the woman member does not go out
    armed to guard.".
22 Esther Beker, "The story of a guard's family," *Hashomer Volume*, 139;
    Kayle Gil'adi, "In the Galilee," 29, claims that the woman in Hashomer was
    necessarily involved in everything that went on in the association. She was
    unable "to stand apart from the political life all around. This was intense
    and stormy to such a degree that the woman was bound to be caught up in
    it . . . The woman's independence, the need to be involved in all that was
    taking place, was evident in Hashomer as in all the other liberation move-
    ments." But later she herself attests that all this was true for the pristine days
    of the organization, almost certainly meaning the Sejera period, but not
    subsequently: "When the movement grew and various elements were
    attached to it, it became necessary to fight for rights and duties." See also
    Rahel Yanait, "In the days of the First World War," *Hashomer Volume*, 169,
    who writes of the struggle of the senior women Kayle Gil'adi and Haya Sara
    Hankin for equal rights. Rahel Yanait cites Kayle Gil'adi's reasons for the
    need for equal rights: "We, the senior women of Hashomer, know how to
    hold a weapon in the hour of need, although we know that our strength will
    be primarily in the farm we establish, where we shall enjoy equal rights in
    all branches, like the men." It sounds as if even for the speaker only in the
    future would there be full, equal rights. It is certainly possible to infer from
    her words that (a) even the senior women lacked full rights, and (b) Kayle

demanded full rights only for the senior women. See also Alexander Zayd, *Toward Morning*, 60–1. From his words it seems that even in the "glorious" days of the Sejera collective the girls did not have full rights. Yisrael Shohat, "The mission and the way," *Hashomer Volume*, 32; Kayle Gil'adi, "From Sejera to Kefar Gil'adi," *Hashomer Anthology*, 136; Tzipora Zayd, "With Hashomer," *Second Aliya Volume*, 530–1; Ruth Kroll, "Lights and Shadows," *Hashomer Volume*, 360–1.

23 Zayd, ibid. On the ideology that negated giving women equal rights see Yisrael Shohat, "The mission and the way," *Hashomer Volume*, 32, who admits that full equality was given to women only at the Tiberias assembly. By his account the tenth assembly was held at Tiberias on 9 September 1918, while in *History of the Hagana*, Vol. I, Part One, 421, the date is given as 17 October 1918; likewise in *Hashomer Volume*, 478. On Zayd's being in the minority in his attitude to the status of women, see *Toward Morning*, 60.

24 Rahel Yanait, "In the days of the First World War," *Hashomer Volume*, 168. Yanait is mistaken regarding the date of the assembly at Yavneel. As noted, the seventh Hashomer assembly was held at Yavneel on 9 September 1915, and not, as she writes, in August 1915.

25 Haya Kroll, "Numbered moments", *Hashomer Anthology*, 264–7 (Hebrew). On the bitterness of the Hashomer women see also the memoirs of Hava Alon (Assushkin): "All the time I was in Hashomer I felt deprived. This feeling was shared by most of our women comrades, the wives of members of Hashomer, and also by the girls who worked with us. We could not be reconciled with fulfilling a passive role only, like embellishments beside our male comrades. Keeping secrets from us the way they did was certainly not justified; for the fact of the matter is that we knew everything that was happening with Hashomer, but anything we found out was as if by theft, and there was great sadness." Hava Alon (Assishkin), "Wife of a guard," *Hashomer Volume*, 358. See also Rahel Yanait, "In the days of the First World War," *Hashomer Volume*, 161; Tova Portugali, "On the paths" (Hebrew), *Hashomer Anthology*, 259: "In those days the woman would win herself status in work only after great efforts, and if she became attached to a guard she would lose even the little status that she had managed to garner. We talked a great deal on this with Portugali, because he was one of those who understood the position of the woman very well in Hashomer. He used to say: 'My work is hard and sometimes not pleasant, the few moments of peace and quiet come to me from you and this should satisfy you too to some extent.' But I always had the feeling that I was imprisoned and my hands were tied within the creative movement going on around me." See also Haya Yigael, "Behind the front", *Hashomer Anthology*, 256 (Hebrew). "Participation in a meeting was allowed only to the active male members of Hashomer, while we, the women, could enjoy the radiated glory only from afar."

26 Rahel Yanait-Ben Zvi, *Our Way to the Land* (Tel Aviv: Am Oved, Sifriat Yalkut, Haifa Workers' Council, Culture and Education Department, 1962), 218.

27 Labor Archives, 112/IV, file 2 (according to Eli'ezer Kroll); Rahel Yanait, "In the days of the First World War," *Hashomer Volume*, 167–9; Rahel Yanait-Ben Zvi, ibid. The resolutions are cited also in idem, *Manya Shohat* (Jerusalem: Ben Zvi Institute, 1976), 173. Moshe Levit, who took part in the Yavneel assembly, affirms that the subject of rights of women members came

up and Zayd favored granting them equal rights. Levit also states that the assembly decided on equality of rights. See Yisrael Dagan, *Between Tel 'Adas and Hamara, Memoirs of Moshe Levit, a Member of Hashomer, 95* (Hebrew).

28   Labor Archives, 112/IV, file 9. The document also appears in *Hashomer Volume*, 463, and in Yanait-Ben Zvi, *Manya Shohat*, 182. In Uri Brenner, *Shorashim*, 181, the date of the Tiberias assembly is given as 9 September 1918.

29   Haya Kroll, "The woman and Hashomer", *Hashomer Volume*, 366; Ruth Kroll, "Lights and Shadows," ibid., 360–1, tells of the actual situation at Kefar Gil'adi, in which the men took part in security work, but the women did not. The men did not even see fit "to allow us to be told of the deeds they were doing. We felt a burning insult at this attitude to us, we considered it a slight . . . ". On the discrimination preserved at Kefar Gil'adi Manya Shohat writes too, explaining that the woman in Hashomer hoped that at the kibbutz-agricultural settlement inequality would disappear altogether. As for Tel Adashim , equality was achieved in the area of work but not in defense, and this deeply wounded the women at the settlement. Regarding Kefar Gil'adi, "I recall a certain moment. This was in Kefar Gil'adi after the death of Trumpeldor. Once, the men left the place in connection with a transport of arms, when suddenly news came that a search was going to be made. The women called a meeting, decided what to do, how to get organized, what to say and how to remain silent. Without any help they organized everything in exemplary fashion. I was really amazed. When it was all over the women rebelled: 'How long will this go on? Why are we *shtiff kinder* [Yiddish for "step-children"]?' But it did not help, because Hashomer had a tradition of silence that has remained in our blood until this very day. For that reason we have not written and we have not spoken. It was a part of us, like a natural law." See Manya Shohat, "The woman in Hashomer," *Devar Hapoelet*, 4th year, 11 March 1937, supplement to the newspaper *Davar*. See also *Manya Shohat and Yisrael Shohat, Letters and Memoirs, Ten Years after their Deaths* (publication of Hashomer House, IDF Museum and Kibbutz Kefar Gil'adi, 14 March 1971), 27. Letter from Manya to Yisrael Shohat and Yosef Harit of Kefar Gil'adi dated 27 February 1938, in which she writes that she was amazed to hear that at the course they were arranging on the theme of "Neighborly Relations" between the Jews and the Arabs they were not accepting women. Manya threatened that if they did not change their decision she would leave the League for Friendship with the Arabs. This shows that as late as 1938, and on a political matter, Shohat and Harit tended to exclude women.

Chapter 7   The Attitude toward the Arabs

1   Yitzhak Ben Zvi, *Poaley Zion in the Second Aliya*, 210. Draft program, formulated at the first delegates' conference at Jaffa, end of 1906. Clause 2 states: "2. The national question (maximal definition): Regarding the question of the Jews, the party strives for political autonomy for the Jewish people in this country."

2   Ibid., 212–13. Circular No. 6 of the party central committee of 4 September 1908. It admits that the Young Turk revolution came as a total surprise to the party: "Comrades, the *hurriya*, the constitution, came as a complete

surprise to them, to all the citizens of Turkey. Like an earthquake these events have seriously shaken a very old structure to the foundations. The entire edifice trembles." And later, "None of us was prepared hardly at all for this moment . . . " Circular No. 7 of the party central committee, a document declared secret, of September 1908, is more explicit. Again it is stated that the revolution was an unexpected surprise. "The Turkish revolution took on forms that we never imagined, and hence we must conclude, comrades, that we may not base the tactics of our party on a theory that is still a matter for conjecture . . . ". And later, "The answer to the question, How should we act? obliges us, first, to know what we want and what our capability is. In this maximal program of Zionism, it is not a question of national autonomy . . . ". See ibid., 214.

3   Ibid., 214–15, secret circular No. 7 of the Poaley Zion central committee of September 1908. The circular stresses that "We Jews are weak in Palestine as citizens of Turkey." Therefore, there was no chance of directly influencing the elections to the parliament. The ability of the Jews was limited "and obviously, we must act cautiously in our concrete demands in the parliament. On the other hand, we may not, as a matter of principle, concede our right to Palestine in the Turkish parliament." In the given situation the Jews had no real power and there was no chance of making gains through the Turkish parliament. It is important to note that in the resolutions of the fifth conference of 10 October 1908, there is no mention of the demand for national autonomy. See ibid., 215–17. Moreover, the sixth conference, held in Jaffa in April 1910, resolved in clause 2: "Our wide national goal: To build in Palestine a Jewish settlement centered in its land, and independent in the economic sense." The concept of national autonomy had disappeared. See ibid., 219.

4   Avner (Yitzhak Ben Zvi), "Self-defense and proletarian outlook," *Haahdut* No. 16 (January 1913), and also No. 17 (February 1913).

5   *Haahdut*, 4th year, 1913, Issue 27–28. Also cited in Ben Zvi, *Poaley Zion in the Second Aliya*, 228–31.

6   Zvi Nadav, "From my recollections," *Hashomer Anthology*, 435.

7   Ibid., 440.

8   The document is reprinted in *Hashomer Volume*, 455–6.

9   Letter from Yisrael Shohat to Shlomo Kaplansky from Stockholm, dated 15 October 1918, *Hashomer Volume*, 462–3.

10   Minutes of the executive committee of the general workers' federation (Histadrut), Vol. 1, 1920–1. Meeting of the executive committee of 30 December 1920, 1–2. Cited in Yosef Gorney, *The Arab Question and the Jewish Problem*, 169–70.

11   Yisrael Shohat to Nahum Hurwitz (copy), Hashomer Archives at Kefar Gil'adi, container 5, sign *dalet*, file 22. See also: Manya Shohat, *Chapters of Genesis*, offprint from *Mihayeinu*, journal of the Labor Battalion (gedud ha'avoda), No. 93, June 1929 (Hebrew); Shmuel Hefter, "How I joined Bar Giora and how I understood Bar Giora," container 3 (memoirs and evaluations of Hashomer matters by members) sign *dalet*.

12   Yosef Harit, "The Haro'im group," *Hashomer Volume*, 208.

13   Ibid. In his memoirs Harit confused Yisrael Shohat's attempt to form a Jewish volunteer battalion during the Balkan war with his attempt to form a Jewish militia in the Galilee near the time of the outbreak of the First World War.

14   Zvi Nadav, "From my recollections," *Hashomer Anthology*, 446.
15   Moshe Eliovich, "Efforts at good neighborliness," *Hashomer Volume*, 369.
16   Pinhas Shneorson, "Behind the wall," ibid., 87.
17   Yisrael Shohat, "The mission and the way," ibid., 17.
18   Ibid., 21.
19   Ibid., 26.
20   Zvi Nadav, *From the Days of the Guarding and the Defense*, 74.
21   Idem, "From my recollections," *Hashomer Anthology*, 437–40. The Arab
      maydan is a kind of sport in which group military maneuvers are conducted.
      Similarly, the skills of individual horsemen are highlighted for their control
      of the weapon and riding as well as the quality of the weapon and the horses.
22   Yitzhak Hoz, "The conquest of Merhavia," *Hashomer Anthology*, 165.
23   Zvi Nadav, "From my recollections," ibid., 495.
24   Mordechai Yigael, "In the saddle," ibid., 153.
25   Yisrael Shohat, "The mission and the way," *Hashomer Volume*, 27.
26   Yisrael Gil'adi, "Notes from a legacy," *Hashomer Anthology*, 12. Gil'adi
      describes the "conquest" of a tract of land that belonged to Kefar Tabor in
      1908 from members of the Bedouin Zbeh tribe. This was at the request of
      Yehoshu'a Hankin. "At our meeting which was called for this purpose the
      'chief' asked if we were strong enough to go out and plough the land without
      using arms, and if we would not abandon the plough even if the Bedouin
      attacked us. The step required much consideration, because the results might
      affect the relations between the Jews and their neighbors in Lower Galilee
      . . . .".

Chapter 8   The Disbanding of Hashomer

1   Some of the sources for members of Hashomer in the period reviewed are
     found in Pinhas Shneorson's descriptions in the book *In the First Line*,
     wherein his articles are collected. See the articles "Fire in the Galilee," 60ff.,
     and "In the war and the deportation," 26ff. See also *Hashomer Volume*:
     Yisrael Shohat, 49; Zvi Nadav, *From the Days of the Guarding and the
     Defense*, 206.
2   *History of the Hagana*, Part 1, Book 2, 421.
3   Yisrael Shohat in *Hashomer Volume*, 49. There is divergence over the date
     of the assembly between *History of the Hagana* and Yisrael Shohat: the date
     given in the text accords with the former, while the latter, in *Hashomer
     Volume*, 56, states that the assemble convened in 1920.
4   *Hashomer Volume*, 54ff. Also *History of the Hagana*, Part 1, Book 5,
     639–52.
5   Ibid., 653.
6   Ibid.
7   Yosef Gorney, *Ahdut Ha'avoda 1919–30* (Tel Aviv University–Hakibbutz
     Hameuhad, 1973), 388, n. 21 (Hebrew). Yigal Elam, *The Zionist Path to
     Power* (Tel Aviv: Zmora-Bitan- Modan, 1979), 22–3 (Hebrew). David Niv,
     The Battles of the Irgun Tzvai Leumi (Tel Aviv: Klausner Institute, 1965),
     41–7, 91 (Hebrew).
8   Ya'akov Talmon, *Political Messianism, the Romantic Stage* (Tel Aviv: Am
     Oved, 1964) (Hebrew). Idem, *The Beginning of Totalitarian Democracy* (Tel
     Aviv: Dvir, 1955) (Hebrew). Franco Venturi, *Roots of Revolution: A History
     of the Populist and Socialist Movements in Nineteenth-Century Russia* (New

York: Grosset & Dunlap 1966).

9 *History of the Hagana*, Vol. 1, Book 2, 234–6; Yisrael Shohat in *Hashomer Volume*, 37, also 51–2.
10 Ibid., 54.
11 *History of the Hagana*, Vol. 2, Part 3, 1269.
12 Ibid. (n. 10), 56.
13 Ibid., Vol. 2, Part 1, 125.
14 Eliahu Golomb, *Latent Force* I (Tel Aviv: Mapai publication, 1950), 137 (Hebrew).
15 Ibid., 7.
16 *History of the Hagana*, Vol. 2, Part 3, 1269.
17 Ibid. (n. 14), 253. Letter to Berl Katznelson of 9 February 1922.
18 Ibid., 244. Letter to David Hacohen of 19 January 1922.
19 Ibid. (n. 17).
20 Ibid. (n. 18).
21 Eliahu Golomb, "On the battalion," *Kuntres*, 19 September 1924.
22 Yisrael Shohat in *Hashomer Volume*, 37.
23 Ibid., 52.
24 Zvi Nadav, *From the Days of the Guarding and the Defense*, 297–8.
25 Ibid. (n. 17).
26 Ibid. (n. 18).
27 Ibid. (n. 24).
28 Gorney, *Ahdut Ha'avoda 1919–1930*, 179.
29 *History of the Hagana*, Vol. 2, Part 2, 65–6.

Chapter 9   From Unity to Dissolution, 1920–1927

1 Yosef Shechtman, *Zev Jabotinsky, The Story of His Life*, Book 1 (Tel Aviv: Karny, 1956), 399 (Hebrew). The call for the Zionist Organization to cover the cost of maintaining the battalions was rejected by the Zionist leadership. Even staunch supporters of the battalion idea such as Yosef Kovan and Dr M. Eder turned it down.
2 Zev Jabotinsky, *Speeches 1905–1926* (Jerusalem: Jabotinsky publication, 1947–1948), 191ff. (Hebrew). From the speech at the Zionist Executive Committee in Prague in July 1921.
3 *Sprinzak Letters*, Vol. I, Letter 163 (Tel Aviv: Ayanot, 1965), 227 of 17 July 1921 (Hebrew). The Twelfth Congress convened in Carlsbad 1–14 September 1921.
4 Binyamin Lubotzky (Eliav), *The Revisionist Zionists and Betar* (Jerusalem: Institute for Zionist Education), 8 (Hebrew).
5 The delegation consisted of Nahman Sirkin, Haim Fineman, Nahum Nir-Refalkes, Avraham Rivotzky, Avraham Efrati, Pinchuk.
6 The report of the delegation is in *Haadama*, No. 9, 304. On the decisions of Ahdut Ha'avoda see David Ben-Gurion, *The Workers' Movement and Revisionism* (Tel Aviv: The World League for Labor Palestine, League Leadership, 1933), 125–7 (Hebrew).
7 Shechtman, *Jabotinsky*, Book 1, 401, 402–3, 407, 408–9; *The Letters of Berl Katznelson* (1919–1922), Letter 128 (Tel Aviv: Am Oved, 1970), 279. In a letter from London, dated 10 August 1925, Katznelson wrote to the Ahdut Ha'avoda Executive Committee: "The promise of money for the H [Hagana – Y.G.] by Jabotinsky has proved spurious. Do you know this? The campaign

has to begin afresh"; Eliahu Golomb, *Latent Power*, I (Tel Aviv: Mapai Publication, 1946); 242 (Hebrew); Golomb's letter to Dov Hoz of late August 1921.

8 Shlomo Lev-Ami, *In Struggle and in Revolt* (Tel Aviv: Ministry of Defense Publication, n.d.) (Hebrew). The author maintains that the Hagana grew out of this body.

9 *History of the Hagana*, B, 65–6; Hashomer archives, Hashomer actions in the Battalion, box 6, sign Bet, file 35. In the document Shmuel Hefter denied absolutely the conjecture implicit in *History of the Hagana* that the dissolution of Hashomer in May 1920 was merely a trick to escape the pressures applied by Golomb and Ahdut Ha'avoda: "I was among those who declared the dissolution of Hashomer. Not quarrels with anyone motivated me, but entirely different considerations . . . "

10 *History of the Hagana*, B, 1263, Appendix A.

11 Ibid., 74–5 and 1265–6, Appendix B. Passages from the discussion on guarding and defense at the first Histadrut council in Jaffa on 13 March 1921.

12 Zvi Nadav, *From the Days of the Guarding and the Defense* (Tel Aviv: Ma'arachot, 1954), 286. On the friction between the sides see also Yisrael Shohat, *Hashomer Volume*, 59. Shohat claims that at the time the Defense Committee had two tasks: to establish an organizational framework and to acquire arms. Neither was achieved: "Nor was the general Hagana organization established, owing to differences of opinion. Several members of the committee did not trust those who had once been members of Hashomer. They feared their great influence on the activities of the Hagana. But clearly, they alone did not have the strength to establish this organization."

13 *History of the Hagana*, B, 75; Yisrael Shohat, *Hashomer Volume*, 60. Shohat maintains that in fact both the Ahdut Ha'avoda Executive Committee and the Defense Committee approved Fleisher's mission and even instructed Dov Hoz to join Fleisher in Vienna.

14 *History of the Hagana*, B, 73.

15 Hashomer archives at Kefar Gil'adi, file 4, sign Gimmel, Yosef Harit, Memoirs of Hashomer members. See also note 9 for quite different testimony from Shmuel Hefter.

16 Ibid., file 35, sign Bet, Yisrael Shohat, Testimony and evaluations of the work of defense.

17 Elkanah Margalit, *Commune, Society and Politics*, 27, Research Papers, Institute for the Study of Labor and Society (Tel Aviv: Am Oved–Sifria Universitait, 1980). Margalit asserts that in a questionnaire distributed among about 50 former Battalion members it transpired that most were refugees who wanted to flee Russia and its terrors.

18 *History of the Hagana*, B, 68–9.

19 Ibid., 71–2.

20 Ibid., 68; Zvi Nadav, *From the Days of the Guarding and the Defense*, 281; Yisrael Shohat, *Hashomer Volume*, 58. Shohat states that the idea of establishing the Battalion on the basis of the program of the Labor Legion arose in Hashomer circles already at the end of 1919. He says that he even proposed the idea to Trumpeldor himself before the latter departed for Upper Galilee. In this conversation differences of opinion emerged between the two men over the nature of the future Battalion. After Trumpeldor's death, "with renewed vigor I resumed my connections with the group from the Crimea in

order to form the Labor Battalion, which the Hashomer members regarded
as the first and important step toward defending the land." Later Shohat
states that the Crimean group accepted his proposals and for that reason too
a commission was elected to formulate the statutes of the proposed Battalion.
Shohat submitted to this commission the statutes of the Labor Legion. The
Battalion was established on the basis of these, with minor amendments.

21   Zvi Nadav, *From the Days of the Guarding and the Defense*, 281. He notes
that he joined the Crimea group, which was building the Tiberias–Tzemah
road, by the decision of his comrades. "The other Hashomer members too
who had been demobilized from the Jewish Battalion joined them. They
became friendly with the young people and even before the official declaration at the time of the Sukkot festival [autumn] the kernel of the Labor
Battalion had been formed." See also Shaul Dagan, *Between Tel 'Adas and
Hamara, Recollections of Moshe Levit, Member of Hashomer* (Tel Aviv:
Society for the Protection of Nature Publication, 1988), 143; *History of the
Hagana*, B, 70–1.

22   Margalit, *Commune, Society and Politics*, 103–6.

23   Ibid., 180–1. See also Shabtai Tevet, *David's Sling*, B, 145–9, 167. Tevet
notes that Ben-Gurion returned to Palestine from his duties in the offices of
the World Union only at the end of summer 1921. On 8 November he was
elected by the Histadrut Council to the Histadrut Executive Committee and
also to the secretariat of that Committee. Ben-Gurion, according to Tevet,
was never elected to the post of Secretary of the Histadrut. On his return to
Palestine Ben-Gurion worked for renewed discussions between Golomb and
Yisrael Shohat. It is important to note that while the former Hashomer
members took the mis-step of abandoning the Histadrut-controlled Hagana
and withdrawing into the Battalion, Golomb exploited the situation well.
The objective, general progress of events was working to his advantage, he
being ensconced in the party and Histadrut apparatus. Therefore, a triple
identity arose of Golomb's interests, the Ahdut Ha'avoda Party and the
Histadrut, where his party played a dominant role. The defense of the interests and powers of the Histadrut was the defense of his own interests.
Henceforward Golomb represented the general interest, while Hashomer
members could only represent a particular interest; Golomb represented the
general authority, the sovereignty of the whole, namely, the democratic
dimension, while the Hashomer people represented separatism, sectarianism,
and anti-democracy. Golomb gave some expression to his conception in a
letter to Manya Shohat from Vienna dated 13 February 1921, when she was
a member of the Histadrut delegation to the United States. (According to her
evidence she did not receive the letter, which is in the legacy of Berl
Katznelson.) In his letter Golomb attempted to explain the reasons for his
poor relationship with the Hashomer people. He accepted their criticism of
the general situation in Palestine and in the Histadrut, "but this does still not
give the right to fragment the Histadrut or to remove very important functions from it. Absence of organization has to be countered by the
establishment of labor battalions and groups under common discipline,
which the Histadrut lacks. But they too must always remember that their
strength depends on the existence of a strong Histadrut, and their work will
be possible and fruitful only with the strengthening of the worker in general.
They should not isolate themselves from the Histadrut, but work to reinforce
and shore up institutions. For only through this strengthening of the

Histadrut, which will make the workers' community a force capable of fulfilling tasks it is not ready to fulfill at present, does any of our striving have any value whatever . . . ". See Eliahu Golomb, *Latent Power*, A, 255ff. It is noteworthy that in these years Golomb speaks of the Histadrut and workers' interest and not of the national interest or national authority. Only in the 1930s, with the establishment of the Mapai party and the latter's attainment of hegemony over the Yishuv and the Zionist movement did his and his party's interests coincide with the national interests.

24   *History of the Hagana*, B, 223.

25   Ibid. See also a letter apparently from Kefar Gil'adi, from an unidentified writer to Meir Spector, who was then in the United States. The letter, dated 24 August 1926, explicitly notes the name "Hakibbutz." Hagana archives, private archive of Meir Spector, box 113/1, file 12; also Labor archives 112/IV, file 1A, founding platform of Hakibbutz.

26   *History of the Hagana*, B, 219.

27   Ibid., 136; and also the article by Moshe Braslavsky, "The founding that was not forgotten," in the newspaper *Lamerhav*, 24 May 1957, 3, 8. According to Braslavsky most of the material on Hakibbutz that he saw "was lost in the Rafiah days, when the destroyer came upon many of the documentary sources of the defense in Palestine, and only a few remnants of them have I found so far." It seems therefore that the material was lost in mid-1946 in the struggle against the British, especially on the "Black Sabbath" of 29 June 1946.

28   See the diary of Yosef Harit in the Yad Tabenkin archives at Ef'al, private archive of Yosef Harit. The second notebook of the diary covers 1919–35, and it contains several passages on the activity of Hakibbutz, but the material is very sparse considering the central role the diarist played in the organization.

29   Labor archives 112/IV, file 13. Letter of Yosef Nahmani to the Histadrut Executive Committee. According to Nahmani the meeting was on 7 August 1921, not 6 August 1921 as noted in *History of the Hagana*.

30   Ibid., 112/IV file 1D, minutes of the assembly in Tiberias.

31   Ibid., file 13.

32   Yaacov Goldstein, *The Histadrut and the Workers of the United States* (Tel Aviv: Am Oved Tarbut Vehinukh – Pinhas Lavon Research Institute of the Labor Movement, 1984), 19, 48 (Hebrew). See also Sprinzak Letters, Vol. A. (Tel Aviv: Ayanot, 1965), 222, letter to Hanna Sprinzak of 29 June 1921. Sprinzak writes that aboard the ship on which he sailed from Alexandria there were also representatives of the Histadrut, Manya Shohat and Yosef Baratz, who were traveling in the fourth class. See also *Letters of Berl Katznelson 1919–1922*, 258, 261, 266, 270.

33   Labor Archives, 112/IV, file 1A. On the other hand it may be inferred from the lecture attributed to Meir Spector, "A lecture on Hakibbutz," that Hakibbutz was founded some time during 1921. The conjectured date of the lecture is in 1926 and the lecturer spoke of the "five years of existence of Hakibbutz." This is an indirect inference, which does not stand up against the other evidence. See Hagana archives, private archive of Meir Spector, box 113/1, file 4. There is no doubt that the Tiberias assembly was a landmark, as it was the first organized public protest against the failings of the Hagana. This is also indicated by Zvi Nadav's testimony. Hashomer archives at Kefar Gil'adi, box 6, sign Bet, file 35.

34   This is based on a letter I received from Shaul Dagan dated 6 May 1990, in which he gave me this information deriving from personal conversations with the four.

35   Shaul Dagan, *Between Tel Adas and Hamara,* 151–3. See also Shaul Dagan's letter, which attests to the clarity of mind and precision of Moshe Levit, except for the dates, when he recorded the words he spoke.

36   Ibid. Manya Shohat's words may intimate that the meeting was held before the assassination of Tawfiq Bey, i.e., before the end of January 1923.

37   Zvi Nadav, *In the Days of the Guarding and the Defense,* 288; *History of the Hagana,* B, 225: "Hakibbutz arose following disappointment with England after the 1921 riots . . . ".

38   Yad Tabenkin archives, Ef'al, private archive of Yosef Harit, 54 in the first notebook and also 4–11 in the second notebook. See also: (a) Pinhas Shneorson, *In the First Line,* 93–4. According to Shneorson, it is almost certain that the incident with Remez described by Harit took place at the Purim festival of 1921. Shneorson tells of a delegation appointed by the Hashomer people who were in the Migdal company of the Battalion. The gathering that selected the delegation empowered it to demand that the Ahdut Ha'avoda center revive the Hagana. The delegation consisted of Yisrael Shohat, Pinhas Shneorson himself and Yehuda Wolfson. The three met for a long discussion with David Remez as representative of the party center. Remez rejected their demands, arguing that matters of immigration and settlement took precedence over matters of defense, and in the latter area it was possible to rely on Herbert Samuel. Shneorson himself, being a member of the Ahdut Ha'avoda center, attempted to raise the subject of defense at meetings of the center, as requested by his comrades. All his requests and demands were rejected. The members of the center did not consider the subject of any importance, and he gave up in despair.

     (b) Yisrael Shohat, Hashomer archives at Kefar Gil'adi, box 5, sign Dalet, file 22. Shohat describes the renewed organization of the Hashomer veterans against the background of the weakness of the Hagana. Therefore, "the former Hashomer members could not and did not wish to come to terms with such a situation. After many appeals to the Ahdut Ha'avod Executive Committee, which came to naught, they decided to begin operating on their own accord. They believed that deeds would force the Defense Committee to begin taking action. The members of the former Hashomer organized and took in members, and set to work." Later Shohat adds: "Our organization was the continuation of Hashomer." Incidentally, according to Shohat the organization of former Hashomer members operated from 1920 to 1932. It is noteworthy that the two central figures in the recollections of Zvi Nadav, Yosef Harit and Pinhas Shneorson, namely, Shmuel Yavnieli and David Remez, belonged at the time of the *Second Aliya* to the "non-party" people, for whom, in contrast to the members of Poaley Zion, the subject of security was not central. In Ahdut Ha'avoda the non-party people were the predominant group, and this very likely contributed to the fact that the party establishment, in theory and in practice, did not ascribe to defense the same significance as did the Hashomer veterans and a small group of veterans of the First World War battalions who formed around Golomb.

39   In *Hashomer Volume,* 475, there is a list of 57 names under the heading "Association of Former Members of Hashomer." The figure of 60–70 members is given in *History of the Hagana,* 224. On 1136 it is stated that

the list in the *Hashomer Volume* is inaccurate, omitting names of more
people who were active in the Hakibbutz framework; this is how *History of
the Hagana* arrives at its estimate of 60–70 members. It is quite certain that
the author of *History of the Hagana* is right about the imprecision of the list
in the *Hashomer Volume*, where not only are people who were members of
Hakibbutz omitted, but, according to *History of the Hagana*, people who
were not members are included, such as Yosef Nahmani and Yitzhak
Landoberg. Among those excluded *History of the Hagana* notes the group
that migrated to Russia: M. Elkind, Landman, Emanuel Rainin (Emek),
Vitka Rainin, Sasha Rainish, Isaac Altshuler, Baruch Lichthaus, and others.
There are also others, such as A. Zayd, David Fish, Meir Kozlovsky and
Yehoshu'a Isaac. Regarding Haim Shturman, there is no doubt that he was
among the founders of Hakibbutz, and in the minutes of the founding
assembly his name appears among the participants in the discussion. This is
so even though Zvi Nadav, *In the Days of the Guarding and the Defense*,
299, makes an interesting charge against Shturman, that he allegedly
remained aloof from the central group of former Hashomer members
because of resentments left over from the time of the split at Tel Adas and
the creation, and subsequent restoration, of Kefar Gil'adi. On the number of
members of Hakibbutz see also: (a) The Prof. Yehuda Slutzki Center for Oral
Documentation, Labor Archives, testimony of Nahaum Horwitz of
September 1973; the interview was conducted by Moshe Tabenkin.
According to the Horwitz's testimony, there were 120 members in
Hakibbutz, of whom about 57 were former Hashomer members. The
remainder were from the Labor Battalion people and others. (b) Pinhas
Shneorson, *In the First Line*, 27. He supports Horwitz's version. (c)
Hashomer archives at Kefar Gil'adi, box 6, sign Bet, file 35. In a conversa-
tion between Yisrael Shohat and Yehuda Slutzki held on 23 June 1953,
Conversation No. 3, Shohat attested to 130 members. In a letter from Shohat
to Slutzki, dated 15 February 1957, he rejects Slutzki's list and states that he
did not tell Slutzki what the latter attributed to him regarding the composition of the lists.

40   Among the former Hashomer members were: the Shohat couple, Shmuel
      Hefter, Zvi Nadav, Pinhas Shneorson, Nahum Horwitz, Eli'ezer and Zvi
      Kroll, Meir Spector, Meir Kozlovsky and others. Among the former young
      members of Hashomer were: Yosef Harit ("Kash"), Moshe Eliovitz, Moshe
      Alexandrovski, Zelig Shturman, Shim'on Druker, Yosef Malmud, Avraham
      (Avrehemel) Dubnov. Among the Herzlia Gymnasia graduates may be indi-
      cated: Yerahmiel Lukacher (Luka), Shmuel Giv'oni, Yehoshua Isaac,
      Binyamin Bichman, Yitzhak Moldavi, Yisrael Simkin, Binyamin Sheinbaum.
      Among the group of *Third Aliya* people were: the brothers Emanuel (Emek),
      Vitka Reinin, Isaac Altshuler, Zvi Levitin ("Pashchera"), Yitzhak
      ("Isachke") Ratner, Yitzhak Vishnevsky, Yasha Kharolov, Baruch
      Lichthaus, and others. See *History of the Hagana*, B, 1136.

41   Margalit, *Commune, Society and Politics*, 98. Margalit bases himself on an
      article by Menahem Elkind entitled "The Labor Battalion and its goals,"
      published in *Hasolel*, No. 4 (Hebrew). In it Elkind states among other things:
      "d. Defense functions without outside help." Margalit asserts that this defi-
      nition meant entirely independent security activity, which was bound to lead
      to a tense relationship with the Histadrut, which took responsibility and
      authority for the Hagana upon itself.

42   Hashomer archives at Kefar Gil'adi, Activity of Hashomer in the Battalion, box 6, sign Bet, file 35. Testimony of Hanokh Rokhel, recorded by Yehuda Slutzki at Tel Yosef on 29 January 1953.
43   Hagana archives, archive of Meir Spector, box 113/1, file 12. Letter to Meir Spector, who was in the United States, dated 24 August 1926 from Kefar Gil'adi, unsigned. The writer reports to Spector on happenings in the Battalion and in Hakibbutz: "Meanwhile Emek [Emanuel Reinin – Y.G.] succeeded in persuading B to come to Haifa for the days of the meeting of the Battalion center (after the return of the delegation), where also present were Yis., El., Har. and Shm. (and although Har. and Shm. resisted and will not sit in the same meeting with B., Yisr. influenced them), and the decision was reached to convene the Hakibbutz council on Rosh Hashana in Haifa (if the Battalion council is not held then) to conduct a formal clarification of the lame affairs of Hakibbutz. I call this council 'liquidating' because before it there is no other task than dissolution and closure and disposing of the property. Delegates will be elected, as has been usual recently, from the two main currents: right and left. 'Manya's view is that we must totally stop everything (what is everything?) for six months or a year, and then begin anew. Anyway, we'll talk of that again'." See also Labor archives, 112/IV, file 1A, minutes of the founding meeting of Hakibbutz. There was a committee of five members and permanent committees for various subjects appointed by the elected directing committee, and a general meeting convened once a year.
44   *History of the Hagana*, B, 224–5, describes the structure of Hakibbutz.
45   Labor archives, 112/IV, file 1A.
46   Hagana archives, private archive of Meir Spector, box 113/1, file 4.
47   Labor archives, 112/IV, file 1A.
48   Yosef Gorney, *Ahdut Ha'avoda* (Ramat Gan: Tel Aviv University, Hakibbutz Hameuhad Publication, 1973), ch. 7: "The Nature of the Democratic Concept," 169–81 (Hebrew).
49   Labor archives, 112/IV, file 1A.
50   Hagana archives, Meir Spector archive, 113/1, file 4.
51   *History of the Hagana*, B, 163–4.
52   Meir Pa'il, *From the Hagana to the Defense Forces* (Tel Aviv: Zmora Bitan Modan, 1979), 19 (Hebrew).
53   *History of the Hagana*, B, 260.
54   Ibid., 164.
55   Ibid., 219.
56   Ibid., 226. See also Zvi Nadav, *In the Days of the Guarding and the Defense*, 288, 302; Yisrael Shohat, Hashomer archives, box 5, sign Dalet, file 22. In his comments on *History of the Hagana*, Shohat states that owing to the difficult relations in the Hagana the Hashomer people decided "to leave the ranks of the Hagana" and to let Golomb act alone, and that this was in about 1922. Shohat does not mean formally breaking away, but in practice ceasing to be active in the Hagana. That there was a genuine desire on the part of the Hashomer people to cooperate in the Hagana and with the Hagana may be ascertained from letters sent by Manya Shohat, during her mission as member of the first Histadrut delegation to the workers of America in 1921–2, to Rahel Yanait-Ben Zvi. In a letter of late 1921 she writes: "What is going to happen with Yisrael and Eliahu – is it impossible to make peace? It will ruin everything. What is to be done?" This letter too is proof that at

the end of 1921, i.e., after the Tiberias assembly, Hakibbutz did not exist. Such a letter could not have been written if Hakibbutz already existed. See Yitzhak Ben Zvi Institute archives, file 2-6/1/32.

57 *History of the Hagana*, B, 226.
58 Ibid., 75.
59 Ibid., 1282. 1 April 1921.
60 Arye Hetzroni, *Shepherd and Fighter*, 127. See also Zvi Nadav, *From the Days of the Guarding and the Defense*, 285–6.
61 Hetzroni, ibid., 129–31. On Fleisher's mission see also *Hashomer Volume*, 60. Yisrael Shohat states that Fleisher's mission with the defined purpose of arms acquisition was at his and his comrades' initiative, but it received approval by the Ahdut Ha'avoda Executive Committee. *History of the Hagana*, B, 75, admits that "Fleisher took with him to Vienna a letter of recommendation from the Histadrut Executive Committee to people of the Zionist movement in the city . . . ". If so, how can that source claim, in the same breath, that the mission was conducted behind Golomb's back, and on this basis make conclusions casting suspicion on and vilifying the Hashomer people? This is simply a part of the protracted and consistent effort to delegitimize the Hashomer people. See also *History of the Hagana*, B, 1282, Minutes of the meeting in January 1922 of those engaged in arms acquisitions in Vienna. The minutes indicate the degree to which arms acquisitions in Vienna had become an issue under public supervision. On this subject there is also testimony of Shmuel Hefter located in the Hashomer archives, Activities of Hashomer in the Battalion, box 6, sign Bet, file 35. Hefter completely denies the assumption that Fleisher's mission was not with the agreement of the Defense Committee: "At the time I was in Poland on an Ahdut Ha'avoda mission to the Palestine Office on matters of immigration. I took the opportunity of attending the Zionist Congress in Carlsbad. I returned via Vienna, and there I met Fleisher and Moshe Levit, who were handling consignments of arms being sent in refrigerators to the Defense Committee. I helped to arrange the despatch, which Moshe Levit accompanied. I knew that they were working in Vienna on behalf of the Defense Committee. They received the money to buy and ship the arms from Dr Boehm, who was certainly not a member of Hashomer. The arms were addressed to the Defense Committee . . . ".
62 David Horwitz, *My Yesterday* (Jerusalem and Tel Aviv: Shocken, 1970), 117. Horwitz describes Vienna in those years as an ideal place for arms acquisition. He himself, who was there in 1921, obtained several weapons when he was about to return to Palestine and succeeded in carrying them in.
63 *History of the Hagana*, B, 130.
64 Golomb, *Latent Power*, A, 230–6. Letter to Moshe Shertok (Sharett) from Vienna dated 1 January 1922, meaning that Golomb was then already there. Golomb admits in his letter that in Vienna he found diligent and gifted men, and they should not be charged with any real guilt. Even if there had been an error they had had no ill intent. "Fleisher worked here loyally and without politics. He is also devoted, talented, and has gained much experience and many connections." Golomb also wrote that he was withdrawing his accusations against Fleisher and Shohat in a letter to Berl Katznelson dated 12 January 1922. He reported the episode to Katznelson. See ibid., 236ff. In addition, see: (a) Hetzroni, *Shepherd and Fighter*, 131–3. (b) Shmuel Hefter, Hashomer archives, sign Bet, file 14. (c) Golomb, *Latent Power* A, 220.

Letter to Fleisher in Vienna dated 14 June 1921. (d) Ibid., 226–30. Golomb
relates in his letter to Dov Hoz in Vienna dated 26 September 1921 that with
the influence of David Ben-Gurion peace was achieved between the
conflicting groups. A meeting was called of the Defense Committee and "it
was decided to continue the work together."

65   Hetzroni, ibid.
66   *History of the Hagana*, B, 143–6.
67   Ibid., 144–5, 148. See also Shmuel Hefter, Network for purchasing and shipping the arms from Vienna, Hashomer archives at Kefar Gil'adi, sign Bet, file
14. Likewise, Mendel Baranowksy, "A journey and its hardships,"
Hashomer Volume, 336–9. Hagana archives, file 2390: Notes at sessions of
the commission on T.H. (Tel Hai – Y.G.) affairs, 16 September 1926. The
commission concluded that the millstone had been stolen by the Kefar Gil'adi
people. At the same time the commission did not consider the act of great
importance, and ruled that "the deed should not be ascribed to village
members as members of 'The Circle' since the act was directed against other
members who presumably belong to the same 'Circle' . . . ".
68   *History of the Hagana*, B, 1282.
69   Ibid.
70   Tevet, *David's Sling*, B, 192.
71   Ibid., 193; *History of the Hagana*, B, 152–3; IDF archives, Ben-Gurion's
diary, file 2049. Ben-Gurion notes in his diary that there was a meeting of
the Executive Committee on the subject of Eliahu. Only four members participated, and therefore no decision was taken. According to Yisrael Shohat
too, Hashomer people left the Hagana, in effect, at the end of 1922:
Hashomer archives at Kefar Gil'adi, Yisrael Shohat archive, box 5, sign
Dalet, file 22. Comments of Yisrael Shohat on *History of the Hagana*.
72   *History of the Hagana*, B, 153.
73   Ibid., 226–7, and 1137. In *Hashomer Volume*, 292, Pinhas Shneorson states
that the initiative to assassinate Tawfiq Bey was from Yosef Hecht himself.
Shneorson repeats this assertion in his book *In the First Line*, 95. Shneorson's
version is also affirmed by Yisrael Shohat in *Hashomer Volume*, 64. Yosef
Hecht himself wrote a letter, dated 10 May 1958, to the editors of *History
of the Hagana* in which he denied the claim by Shneorson and Shohat.
However, he admitted that a day before the action he received a visit at his
house in the Borochov quarter of Giv'atayim by Lukacher and Bichman, who
informed him of the Hashomer decision. Hecht admits that he did not seek
to prevent them from implementing the decision, and hence the two might
assume that he approved, albeit silently, of the planned act. Shneorson,
Hashomer Volume, 292, relates that at a meeting of Hashomer members
soon after the May 1921 disturbances Manya Shohat declared that she had
sworn to take revenge on Tawfiq Bey and kill him. On the same occasion the
Hashomer members undertook before Manya to carry out the act, but this
was not implemented. On Manya's return from her mission to the workers
of America in summer 1922 she was full of anger that the promise given her
had not been kept. Therefore, so Shneorson explains, for this reason too they
were eager to seize upon Hecht's suggestion that Tawfiq Bay be assassinated.
On the incident see also Yisrael Shohat, Evidence and evaluation of security
activity in the Battalion and in the Hagana, Hashomer archives, sign Bet, file
35. Shmuel Hefter's testimony is of special importance, reinforcing the
evidence of Shneorson and Shohat. Hefter states that the account given in

History of the Hagana on the Tawfiq Bey affair is not precise. "I found out about the matter with all its details from Hecht. He told me of it in a tone of admiration and praise for the courage and skill in the execution." Therefore he does not accept the version that Hecht allegedly was only apprised of it. Shmuel Hefter, Hashomer archives, Activities of Hashomer in the Battalion, box 6, sign Bet, file 35.

74 *History of the Hagana*, B, 227–8.

75 Ibid., 228, and also 1137, where it is related that Haikind left Palestine after the operation. In 1926 he returned, and demanded some of the money that had been stolen then. Haikind even approached the Hagana on this. Then he returned to Poland, where he changed him name to Avraham Lyobes. In 1930 in Warsaw he published memoirs on the battalions. All trace of him is lost in the Second World War. His son Arye enlisted in the British Army and the Palmah and fell in the War of Independence in the battle for Katamon in Jerusalem. On the traditional approach to actions of this kind it is interesting the read Yithak Ben Zvi's testimony before the Clarification Commission on 17 October 1926: "Concerning expropriation . . . he considers it a moral act if it is done by an organized group, he does not see why the state is licensed to collected taxes from him and for its part carry out acts of expropriation, and why another group is not licensed to do so." Hagana history archives, file 2390, "Notes during meeting of the Clarification C., session of 17 October 1926. Yisrael Shohat, Hashomer archives, Evidence and evaluation on security activity in the Battalion and the Hagana, sign Bet, file 35. He relates that the watch on the smugglers lasted about six months. Shohat attributes the planning to himself, but to prevent suspicion he left the country a week before the robbery. In 1926 Haikind returned to Palestine and tried to extort money from Shohat. Shohat claims that he gave Haikind an additional sum so that he would leave the country. It was Manya Shohat who found the engineer Avraham Haikind, who was a member of a Battalion company in Jerusalem. Apart from Haikind, accomplices to the robbery were Lukacher, Bichman and Zvi Kroll; their driver was Zvi Nadav. Other sources on the affair are located in: (a) Shneorson and Y. Harit, Recollections of members about Hashomer, Hashomer archives, sign Gimmal, file 4. (b) Tevet, *David's Sling*, B, 281, and also 654, note to p.281. (c) Yisrael Shohat, Evidence and evaluation of security activity in the Battalion and the Hagana, sign Bet, file 35. Shohat states that he handed over some of the money taken to Kefar Gil'adi, as compensation of sorts for the heavy burden that security activity imposed on the settlement. Most of the money went to buying arms; some of it was invested in Lukacher's journey to Berlin in 1925 and his military education there. (d) Other, negative, evidence on how the money was spent is given by Tzipora Zayd: her evidence before the Clarification Commission, Hashomer archives, unmarked file. (e) Manya Shohat, *Hashomer Volume*, 391.

76 *History of the Hagana*, B, 228–30, 1137; Yisrael Shohat, *Hashomer Volume*, 64–5; Mordechai Teitelman, ibid., 332, "About the arms acquisition activities." Teitelman states that the name of one of the diggers was Brillman and not Brinman; Zvi Kroll, ibid., 333ff., "The store at Kefar Gil'adi," mentions the help of the engineer Gedaliahu Vilbushevich. Kroll writes (p. 335) that the name of one of the diggers was Brinman.

77 *History of the Hagana*, B, 230, 1137; Yisrael Shohat, *Hashomer Volume*, 66–7; Diary of Yosef Harit, Yad Tabenkin, Ef'al, notebook 2, 24, states that

the factory at Afula, Haroshet Ha'emek (Valley Industry) was run by three
men: David Fish, Naftali Shneorson and the engineer Weill from Germany.
In Harit's view, the factory collapsed because the three could not work
together.

78   *History of the Hagana*, B, 230–1.
79   Ibid., 233, 1138.
80   Ibid., 233–4, 1139; Yisrael Shohat, *Hashomer Volume*, 66. Elsewhere
      Shohat admits that Lukacher returned from Germany a communist: "Here
      a serious mishap occurred because I let it. He fell under the influence of the
      communists and became a communist. I told him, 'Lukacher, we have
      invested a lot of money in you, you have to come back to us.' I already knew
      that we had lost him, and so I wanted to save something." See Hashomer
      archives, sign Bet, file 35.
81   Yisrael Shohat, *Hashomer Volume*, 67–9; *History of the Hagana*, B231,
      1138. Shohat mentions that the committee included the Chief Rabbi Tzadok
      Cohen, but he had died in 1905 and the Chief Rabbi in 1924 was Yisrael
      Levi.
82   Zvi Even-Shoshan (Rosenstein), *History of the Workers' Movement in
      Palestine* A (Tel Aviv: Am Oved, 1955), 431–2. The core of the Jewish
      Socialist Workers' Party was members of Poaley Zion who refused to join
      Ahdut Ha'avoda when it was founded in 1919. They formed a new party,
      which they called the Socialist Workers' Party. This party joined the left after
      the split in the World Union of Poaley Zion at the Vienna conference in
      July–August 1920. The SWP was the embryo of the Communist Party in
      Palestine. To win a wider response among the Jewish community in Palestine,
      the party added the word "Jewish" to its name. Therefore it appeared under
      its new title, Jewish Socialist Workers' Party, at the elections to the founding
      conference of the Histadrut.
83   Ibid.
84   Ibid., B (Tel Aviv: Am Oved-Tarbut Vehinukh, 1966), 82–3.
85   Margalit, *Commune, Society and Politics*, 257–8; Anita Shapira, "The Left
      in the Labor Battalion and the Palestine Communist Party until 1928,"
      Hatzionut, B (Tel Aviv: Tel Aviv University Institute for the Research of
      Zionism, Hakibbutz Hameuhad, 1971), 149ff. (Hebrew). Shapira states that
      until 1924 the PCP showed no interest in the Battalion. The split between
      Tel Yosef and Ein Harod in 1923 necessitated the creation of an indepen-
      dent political body. The peak in the trend to the left, Shapira believes, was
      in 1925; Tevet, *David's Sling*, B, 280, maintains that the Ein Harod affair
      forced the Battalion into the arms of the former Hashomer people among its
      members, who tended to the left. Tevet names Zvi Nadav, David Fish and
      Pinhas Shneorson as those with a leftward tendency, and states that they had
      a soft romantic spot for communist Russia, which they traversed in 1919 on
      their way to Palestine. Tevet's assertions are in no way attested, and the
      outcome proves the opposite. The fact is that the great majority of the former
      Hashomer people did not go with the left after the split, and this includes the
      settlements of Kefar Gil'adi and Tel Hai, the fortress of Hashomer.
      Hakibbutz was non-party and the split into left and right in the Battalion in
      1925 harmed it, and so they fought against the politicization of the Battalion,
      and ultimately against the left. The Hakibbutz people had no alliance with
      the left in the Battalion (p. 284). Most of them belonged to the center, which
      in the split went with the right. In the years under review, the early 1920s,

David Ben-Gurion, Tevet's hero, himself had a weakness for Russia and in this he was not unique in his party.

86 Zev Tzahor, *The Roots of Israeli Politics* (Tel Aviv: Hakibbutz Hameuhad–Ben-Gurion University of the Negev, 1987), ch. 3: "The encounter between the *Second Aliya* and the *Third Aliya*," 37ff. (Hebrew).

87 Anita Shapira, *Going to the Horizon* (Tel Aviv: Ofakim Library–Am Oved, 1988); on the break-up of one dream: The Joseph Trumpeldor Labor Battalion, 157ff.

88 Margalit, *Commune, Society and Politics*, 299.

89 Zev Isserzon (On), "Survey of development of events at Tel Hai," Labor archives, 113/IV, file 7; A. M. Koller, "The Kefar Gil'adi–Tel Hai affair" (Hebrew), 24 September 1951, Kefar Gil'adi archive; Hanokh Rokhel, Historical review of the episode, Kefar Gil'adi archives. Kibbutz Kefar Gil'adi joined the Battalion on 14 September 1921; its status was dissimilar from that of the other companies in that it enjoyed autonomy. This is explained by the fact that the kibbutz had many debts and it did not wish to impose the burden of these on the companies, as this would harm its self-respect. Its special status of Kefar Gil'adi made it possible for Hakibbutz to maintain its central base there without the close supervision of the Battalion leadership and institutions. The geographical remoteness also helped in preserving autonomy. Unlike Kefar Gil'adi, the Tel Hai kibbutz joined the Battalion quite late, only in July 1924. See Zev Tzahor, "The break-up of Tel Hai," *Hameasef*, Giv'at Haviva, Vol. 12, 1990 (Hebrew); Tevet, *David's Sling*, B, 287, writes that the union of the two settlements was fully justified economically and the PICA favored it.

90 Margalit, *Commune, Society and Politics*, 300.

91 Memorandum of Alexander Zayd on behalf of the members of the minority of February 1926, Kefar Gil'adi archives.

92 Margalit, *Commune, Society and Politics*, 301, states that the focus of the minority opposition at Tel Hai to unification arose from the poor personal relationships between themselves and their erstwhile comrades at Kefar Gil'adi. This applies particularly to the Zayd family.

93 Margalit, ibid., 301–3.

94 Tevet, *David's Sling*, B, 196, agrees that the expulsion of members of the two settlements from the Histadrut was an arbitrary act: "Ben-Gurion took advantage of the storm to settle accounts generally, and in particular to strike at the left in the Battalion and the 'Circle.'" On p. 299 he states that those expelled from the Histadrut were right in their claim that no trial had found them guilty. Following the affair, Hapoel Hatzair announced that in future it would object to administrative expulsions from the Histadrut. At the third Histadrut conference in 1927 an amendment in this spirit was inserted into the Histadrut constitution; Zev Tzahor, "Sad victory: Ben-Gurion and the Labor Battalion," *Cathedra* 43 (Jerusalem: Ben Zvi Institute, March 1987), 44 (Hebrew). He also accepts the usual version that "Ben-Gurion regarded the affair as an opportunity to strike a decisive blow at the Labor Battalion and to expose the occasions on which the 'clandestine Hakibbutz' had acted as an element dangerous to the Histadrut."

95 Ben-Naftali (pseudonym of Eliahu Golomb), "On the Tel Hai matter," *Kuntras*, 275 (Hebrew).

96 Tzahor, "Sad victory: Ben-Gurion and the Labor Battalion," 33ff. Tevet, *David's Sling*, B, 280, states that the Ein Harod conflict forced the battalion

into the arms of the Hashomer people, who "tended to the left." In my opinion, the leftward tendency in the Battalion was more comprehensive and fundamental, and the Ein Harod affair was only one factor. Likewise the factors causing the clash between the Battalion and the Histadrut were comprehensive and fundamental. As for the Hashomer people, it was clearly not they who caused the leftward swing in the Battalion, nor did most of them tend to the left, but they even tried to fight against the tendency. This is well demonstrated in the speech attributed to Spector, who dealt with this episode. In the opinion of Margalit, *Commune, Society and Politics*, 353ff., at the "split" council of the Battalion on 16–17 December 1926 the forces were divided as follows: The right was the minority but became the majority after the people from the center and Poaley Zion Left joined it. The relationship of forces that arose was 282 on the right and 187 on the left. Margalit stresses that the "Hashomer members were prominent in the struggle they conducted against the left" (p. 355): Nahum Horwitz and Pinhas Shneorson were already prominent at the June 1926 council of the Battalion, when the left abandoned it and did not join the new central committee, to which were elected people of the center and the right almost entirely. And Margalit again: "It may be assumed that the members of the settlements, including the Hashomer people, had decisive influence in consolidating the right and the center in the Battalion."

97 Tevet, *David's Sling*, B, 226, bases himself on Golomb's *Latent Power*: Golomb's letter to David Hacohen dated 19 January 1922 and also his letter to Manya Shohat dated 13 February 1922.

98 Tevet, ibid., 627; Golomb, *Latent Power* A, 280ff., letter of 7 November 1922.

99 IDF archives, Giv'atayim, Ben-Gurion's diary, file 2051, 91; Tevet, *David's Sling*, B, 281. It is not clear to me on what grounds Tevet bases his statement that the initiative to cancel the meeting came from the Hashomer people. Tevet brings no proof for this conjecture, explaining that the cancellation was a result of the bitterness felt by the Battalion toward the Histadrut generally and Ben-Gurion in particular.

100 *History of the Hagana*, B, 232–3; Tevet, *David's Sling*, B, 284, 646; IDF archives, Giv'atayim, Ben-Gurion's diary, file 2052, 63–4, 75; Hagana archives, file 2390, "Notes at the time of the sessions of the Commission on Tel Hai affairs," meeting of 16 September 1926. Ben-Gurion notes in his diary entry for 11 July 1925 (p. 102) that he traveled by rail from Kalkilya to Haifa, and Rahel (Yanait – Y.G.) was with him. She complained bitterly about the decision of the party's Executive Committee on this matter. "The counter-committee. She sees in the decision a move against the 'group' of BZ, herself, Manya and Yisrael." Ben-Gurion did not record in his diary his reply to Rahel Yanait-Ben Zvi's words.

101 Ibid. (diary), 147–8.

102 Ibid., 156, 159.

103 Ibid., 163.

104 Ibid., Diary for 1926, 41; Hashomer archives, box 6, sign Bet, file 35, Comments of Shmuel Hefter on *History of the Hagana*. Hefter relates that there was cooperation between Hakibbutz and the Hagana in 1925 also. For example, according to Hefter, the guard unit of the Labor Battalion company in Jerusalem accepted the authority of Zakhar (Zekharia Urieli), the Hagana commander of the town. Another example, by Hefter, was the approach by

Shaul Meirov (Avigur) in 1925 to Yehoshu'a Isaac that the latter organize the defense of Safed.

105 Ibid., Diary for 1926, 49.

106 Ibid., 91, 93.

107 Yad Tabenkin archives, Ef'al, Yosef Harit's diary, notebook 2, 25. Harit states that the former Hashomer people did not join any political faction in the Battalion and therefore were considered outcasts by all. Yisrael Shohat, *Hashomer Volume*, 76, also attests to the difficult situation in the Battalion which he found on his return from Russia in the summer of 1926: "I was dismayed when I witnessed the destruction that had penetrated the Battalion, causing the loss of years of work. We had seen the continuation of Hashomer in the Battalion, and now it was in collapse, disintegrating before our eyes. The ground was swept from under my feet, but I had no power to prevent it. True, we got rid of the traitors and doubters within our midst, and only loyal and devoted comrades remained in the organization of Hashomer members. But our strength was depleted, the area of our activity was reduced . . . ". *History of the Hagana*, B, 240, asserts that a third of those who emigrated to Russia with Elkind were members of Hakibbutz. It gives no names or exact evidence of this. But it admits that the leaders of Hakibbutz fought against the leftward trend, and then the tendency to leave the country together with Elkind, and they even succeeded in influencing those who had grown up in the country to remain. *History of the Hagana* also admits that the Hakibbutz people among the emigrants were only the young people of the *Third Aliya*, except for Shim'on Druker. Yisrael Shohat, Evidence and evaluation of the work of the Hagana, Hashomer archives, sign Bet, file 35, states that, "Elkind took with him about ninety-five people, of whom all were from the Battalion. Apart from Druker of the jahush (a nickname for the Hashomer youngsters). I was able to persuade about twenty people who were about to leave to remain in the country. The whole affair shocked us deeply. But the core was preserved. We continued to gather arms and men around us. Our appearance in August 1929 is well known." Here we have clear evidence that indeed the life of Hakibbutz ceased with the crumbling of the Battalion, but the nucleus of Hashomer veterans continued to maintain links among themselves and to engage in arms acquistion on a small scale.

108 *Davar*, 1 September 1926.

109 Ben-Gurion's diary, entry for 31 January 1927, 33. On the threats against Ben-Gurion in 1926, including allegedly one of murder, see *Letters of David Ben-Gurion*, Vol. 2, 1921–1928 (Tel Aviv: Am Oved and Tel Aviv University, 1972), 333ff.

110 *History of the Hagana*, B, 238–41, 1140; Tevet, *David's Sling*, B, 287–99, 648. On the original commision there were seven men: Yosef Aharonovich, Moshe Beilinson, Yisrael Betzer, Meir Ya'ari, Ben-Zion Yisraeli, Eli'ezer Shein, and Levi Eshkol. See Margalit, *Commune, Society and Politics*, 304ff.; Shapira, "The left in the Labor Battalion and the Palestine Communist Party until 1928," *Hatzionut*, B, 161–6. As stated, the split in the Battalion occurred at the Tel Yosef council held on 16–17 December 1926. Thereafter, the companies at Tel Hai, Kefar Gil'adi and Tel Yosef went to the right, while the majority of the companies in the towns went to the left. Elkind's decision to emigrate was known several days after the third conference of the Histadrut held in August 1927. According to Shapira, there were 235 members in the "left" Battalion, but the group that emigrated to Russia, and

most of them left only in 1929, consisted of only 50–60 people. This shows the loyalty of the left in the Battalion and also the loyalty of the "left" Battalion to Zionism.

Chapter 10   The Hapoel Association, 1930–1935

1   Yehuda Slutzky, *Introduction to the History of the Israeli Labor Movement* (Tel Aviv: Sifria Universitait–Am Oved, 1973) (Hebrew). See ch. 18. Yosef Shapira, *Hapoel Hatzair, the Idea and the Deed* (Tel Aviv: Ayanot, 1964) (Hebrew).

2   Yisrael Kollat, "Hapoel Hatzair, from the Conquest of Labor to the sanctification of labor," *Baderekh* I (Giva'at Haviva: Studies on the Jewish Workers' Movement, The Baruch Linn Institute for Research on the Jewish Workers' Movement, September 1967) (Hebrew). Yosef Gorny, "Hapoel Hatzair and its attitude to socialism," *Baderekh* VI, December 1970 (Hebrew).

3   Yitzhak Lufban, "The High Commissioner," *Hapoel Hatzair*, 21, 27 February 1925 (Hebrew).

4   Shlomo Shiller, "The Jewish State and the Jewish National Home," *Hapoel Hatzair* 35, 12 June 1925 (Hebrew).

5   Tzioni (Yitzhak Wilkansky, i.e., El'ezri-Vulcani), "The face of the opposition" (Hebrew), *Hapoel Hatzair* 38–39, 10 July 1925.

6   *Sprinzak Letters,* I, 227, Letter 163 of 17 July 1921 (Tel Aviv: Ayanot, 1965), ed. Yosef Shapira (Hebrew). At the Zionist Executive, which preceded the Twelfth Zionist Congress at Carlsbad, Sprinzak and Eli'ezer Kaplan voted against Jabotinsky's proposal, which was accepted by the majority, on the formation of the Jewish Battalions in Palestine. See also Yitzhak Lufban's article "Our stance at the congress," *Hapoel Hatzair* 40, 17 July 1925 (Hebrew). In the article the author negated Revisionism completely, which for him was built "entirely on deliberate demagoguy, from the Supreme Commander, Jabotinsky, down to the last of the workers in the Revisionist Fraction in Tel Aviv."

7   *Sprinzak Letters,* I, 294, Letter 26 of 23 August 1925.

8   Joseph B. Schechtmann, *Zeev Jabotinsky, the Story of His Life.* Book 2, 40; Shlomo Avineri, *The Zionist Idea in Its Varieties* (Tel Aviv: Ofakim–Am Oved, 1980), ch. 16 (Hebrew).

9   Ibid. (Schechtmann), I, 317.

10   Moshe Beilinson, "The Revisionists' conference in Paris," *Kuntres,* Vol. 11, No. 220, 12 June 1925 (Hebrew); Eliahu Golomb, "The Revisionists," ibid., No. 222, 3 July 1925 (Hebrew); also *Kuntres,* Vol. 17, No. 343, 12 July 1928, the Ahdut Ha'avoda council on the conclusions of the Mead Committee. See Eliahu Golomb's statements on p. 21.

11   Zeev Jabotinsky, "We the bourgeois," *Hatzafon,* 8 May 1927 (Hebrew). See also Beilinson and Golomb (n. 10); Zalman Rubashov (Shazar), "Lecture at the seventh conference of the Poaley Zion Union in Vienna in August 1925 on the subject of the Fourteenth Zionist Congress," *Kuntres,* No. 231, 4 September 1925 (Hebrew); David Remez, "From his speech at the Fourteenth Zionist Congress in 1925," *Kuntres,* No. 232, 11 September 1925 (Hebrew).

12   Schechtmann, Book 2, 63.

13   Ibid., 67.

14 Ibid., 114–15.

15 Weizmann Archive, letter from Chaim Weizmann to Maurice Ruthenberg of 2 February 1931; ibid., letter from Weizmann to Dr George Halpern, same date; Mapai Archive, file 23/31 copy D, Meetings of the center and the secretariat in 1931, meeting of the center with the participation of Weizmann on 29 March 1931, 5.

16 Schechtmann, Book 2, 197–8.

17 Mapai Archives, file 23/31, copy D, meeting of Mapai center on 17 March 1931.

18 Ibid., Division 601, no. 602/17, Elections to the Seventeenth Zionist Congress 1931, "Platform of the Palestine Workers' Party (Mapai) for the Seventeenth Zionist Congress: Strengthening of the Histadrut" (Hebrew), paragraph B. See also the speech by Berl Katznelson at Beit Ha'am in Tel Aviv, which was published in *Davar* on 2 February 1931 under the title "In the battle" (Hebrew). Katznelson used the term "Zionist Hitlerism" in reference to Revisionism.

19 David Ben-Gurion, *Letters to Paula and the Children* (Tel Aviv: Am Oved, 1968), 78–9, letter from Basel of 20 July 1931 (Hebrew).

20 Haim Arlozoroff, *Selection of Letters and Life Episodes* (Tel Aviv: Hasifria Hatzionit and Ayanot, Am Oved), 317–19, letter from Basel of 16 July 1931 (Hebrew).

21 David Ben-Gurion, "The Seventeenth Congress and our way in the future" (Hebrew), *Hapoel Hatzair*, No. 40, 21 August 1931. See also Arlozoroff (n. 20 above).

22 Schechtmann, *Zeev Jabotinsky*, Book 2, 305, the article "Basta"; Jabotinsky, "We the bourgeois" (n. 11 above); articles, Zeev Jabotinsky, *Speeches 1927–1940* (Hebrew), 152ff., from Jabotinsky's speech in reply at the fifth conference of the Revisionists in Vienna in August 1932, when he said: "The class conflict is an abomination. I am ready to sit down and negotiate with anyone, but to sit together with those who stand for the class conflict . . . this is repulsive to me. In my eyes, good or bad my class is no less than any other class . . . ". Zeev Jabotinsky, "Working Palestine" (Hebrew), *Doar Hayom*, 5 December 1932; idem, "The First of May" (Hebrew) (from a diary), *Hayarden*, 14 May 1934; idem, "The socialist redemption" (conversation) (Hebrew), Jabotinsky Institute, album 2, 25 November 1934.

23 These were secessionists from the Hapoel Hatzair party, who organized as a separate body at their council at Nahlat Yehuda on 8–9 January 1926. Under the influence of Jabotinsky they joined the Revisionist party in January 1927. The Menora group consisted of Betar people from Latvia, of whom the first group immigrated to Palestine in November 1925, the second in the summer of 1926.

24 J. B. Schechtmann and Y. Benary, *The History of the Revisionist Movement* (Tel Aviv: Hadar Publishing House, 1970), Vol. I, 1924–30, 192–205. There were 17,183 electors of delegates to the third conference of the Histadrut. The Revisionists won 205 votes, giving them two out of the 201 delegates. The two were Dr Y. Weinshall and D. A. Klagswald. See David Ben-Gurion, "The Revisionist enmity", *Davar*, 16 December 1932 (Hebrew).

25 Ofir, *National Worker Volume* (Tel Aviv: The National Histadrut Executive Committee, 1959), 52.

26 Ibid., 75. See also Benyamin Lubotsky (Eliav), *Revisionist Zionism and Betar*, 23ff. (Hebrew).

27 In the newspaper *Rasv'et*, No. 43, 3 October 1932.
28 Zeev Jabotinsky, "Yo brechen" (Yiddish – "Yes, Break"), *Haint*, No. 222, 4 November 1932.
29 Ofir, *National Worker Volume*, 88.
30 Ibid., 94.
31 *History of the Hagana*, B, 417–18; Yosef Avidar, *On the Way to the IDF* (Tel Aviv: Ma'arachot, 1970), 47 (Hebrew).
32 *History of the Hagana*, B, 426ff.
33 Ibid., 426–32; Avidar, ibid., ch. 3.
34 Meir Pa'il, *From the Hagana to the Defense Forces*, 19–20 (Hebrew).
35 Ibid., 21–3.
36 On Yosef Hecht's subordination to the Histadrut organs see the Ben-Gurion diaries, IDF Archives, file 2052, 147, entry for 3 November 1925. Hecht then submitted a report to Ben-Gurion on the state of the Hagana. The report continues on 148, entry for 5 November 1925.
37 *History of the Hagana*, B, 420–1; Pa'il (n. 34 above), 21–2.
38 Ben-Gurion diaries, IDF Archives, 89, entry for 13 September 1929. On 82 Ben-Gurion notes that Hecht had informed Ben-Gurion of his objection to the proposed center on 7 September 1929.
39 Ibid., 91ff., entry for 21 September 1929.
40 *History of the Hagana*, B, 421.
41 Ibid., 422–3.
42 Ibid., 424–6.
43 Ibid., 423.
44 Ibid., 432–4; Pa'il (n. 34 above), 24–5.
45 Yaacov Goldstein, *The Palestine Workers' Party and the Causes of Its Establishment*, chs 1 and 2.
46 Shabtai Tevet, *David's Sling*, Vol. 3, 12.
47 Ibid., Vol. 2, 316–23. The labor movement had only one representative on the Zionist Executives in 1921–1927, and this was Yosef Sprinzak, the representative of the pro-Weizmann Hapoel Hatzair party. The Ahdut Ha'avoda party did not participate in the Weizmannist Executives until 1929, and therefore Shlomo Kaplansky was active in the 1920s only as a special adviser and not as a member of the Zionist Executive. On this see Yaacov Goldstein, "When did Shlomo Kaplansky's membership of the Zionist Executive begin?" in *Riv'on lemehkar hevrati*, Nos 7–8, Haifa Workers' Council 1974, 131–9.
48 Yaacov Goldstein, *On the Way to Hegemony*, 128, based on the Mapai Archives at Beit Berl, file 23/31, meeting of the center on 29 May 1931.
49 Tevet, ibid., Vol. 3, 13–25; Michael Bar-Zohar, *Ben-Gurion*, Vol. A (Tel Aviv: Am Oved, 1975), 229–46; *Ben-Gurion Letters*, Vol. 2, compiled and annotated by Yehuda Erez (Tel Aviv: Am Oved–Tel Aviv University, 1972), 364–72: letter from Ben-Gurion to Baruch Zuckerman of 30 March 1928; *Ben-Gurion Letters*, Vol. 3 (Tel Aviv, 1974), 169–70, letter to Melech Noy-Neustadt of 26 November 1930.
50 *Years of Hapoel* (Hebrew), booklet published by the Histadrut and the Hapoel Assocation, April 1952, 2; Labor archives, 244/IV; Uri Zamir, *Physical Education and Sport in Palestine 1917–1927*, ch. 10 (Wingate Institute, 1971) (Hebrew); Emanuel Gil, *The Story of Hapoel* (Hakibbutz Hameuhad [place and year not given]), 10–11 (Hebrew).
51 Gil, ibid., 16–23. Gil relies on the evidence of Avraham Ashni, holder of

membership card no. 2 of the Hapoel Association in Tel Aviv. The card, according to Gil, bore the date 3 October 1923, from which Gil infers that an association called Hapoel existed in Tel Aviv before it did in Haifa.

52 *Years of Hapoel*, 2–7; Gil, ibid., 23–35. According to Gil the founding council convened in Tel Aviv and not in Petah Tikva. A provisional committee was elected in Tel Aviv, with offices there also.

53 Gil, ibid., 36.

54 The Fraction, the name of the communist faction in the Histadrut.

55 IDF Archives, Ben-Gurion's diaries, file 2055, 81.

56 Ibid., 99–100.

57 Ibid., 99–100, 136, 145. Ben-Gurion promised the members of Hapoel center a half-time post for the work of the secretariat and also additional financial support. In his diary he notes: "Apparently Abba Hushi will come here." On p. 198 he notes that Yair Elbinger asked that Abba Hushi be given three workdays a week in Tel Aviv. Further on he writes that they might be able to arrange for Yair Elbinger himself to work in Tel Aviv, "and then the whole secretariat of Hapoel will be here. I promised to look into it and check the budgets of the Histadrut institutions for Hapoel."

58 Ibid., 6, entry for 1 October 1929. Soon after the disturbances Ben-Gurion held a meeting with the Hapoel people and he recorded in his diary the data the latter gave him on the size of the organization. Hapoel had 19 branches and 5 more in the process of formation, with a total membership of 2590; of these 25 percent were women. The financial turnover of the organization was 120 Palestine pounds a year.

59 Gil, ibid., 138.

60 Labor Archives, 244/IV, Report for 1930–1931, Report of the central committee of Hapoel for the period January 1930–November 1931, in preparation for the first national conference, Tel Aviv, December 1931. On p. 11 it is written that at a joint meeting of members of Hapoel center with members of the Histadrut Executive Committee in March 1930, "comrade Yisrael Shohat was attached to the center on behalf of the Executive Committee." His joining took place at the meeting on 10 March 1930. See Labor Archives, minutes of the Histuadrut Executive Committee, 52–5.

61 Hashomer Archives, Kefar Gil'adi, Yisrael Shohat archive, container 5, sign Dalet, file 22, Shohat's comments on *History of the Hagana*, comments to pp. 3, 4, 5, 6, 7 of the fourth book, ch. 7, 6 of the notes; ibid., container 6, sign Bet, file 35, Hapoel, and in the same file under the title Conversation A, recorded by Yehuda Slutzki on 11 June 1953, first page.

62 Ibid., container 6, sign Bet, file 35, Conversation A.

63 Ibid., container 5, sign Dalet, file 22, pp. 6 and 12 in Yisrael Shohat's notes to ch. 7 of the fourth book of *History of the Hagana*. The emphases in the quotation are mine.

64 IDF Archives, Ben-Gurion diaries, 6, 1 October 1929.

65 Hashomer Archives, Kefar Gil'adi, Yisrael Shohat archive, container 5, sign Dalet, file 23, conversation at the home of Yosef Harit on 29 October 1962 (after the deaths of Yisrael and Manya Shohat). Present were Yosef Harit, Pinhas Shneorson, Efraim Perlstein, Baruch Bag, Tzvia H, Mendel Baranovsky and Yitshak Avineri (Rasner).

66 Gil, ibid., 72–95.

67 Ibid., 70–2.

68 IDF Archives, Ben-Gurion diaries, file 2055, 99–100, entry for 26 January

1928.
69   Ibid., file 2066, 20–1, at a meeting with activists on 12 May 1932.
70   Ben-Gurion's speech before the third national assembly of Hapoel, held in Tel Aviv in October 1932. See IDF Archives, 3342 and *Davar*, 23 October 1932.
71   Labor Archives, division 244/IV, file 167, envelope B, Abba Hushi's speech at a general meeting of Hapoel members in Haifa, 6 January 1933. My emphasis.
72   IDF Archives, Ben-Gurion diaries, file 2066, 21. At the meeting on 12 May 1932, according to Ben-Gurion's entry, David Remez said that the role of Hapoel was essential and it "has to educate toward sport."
73   Labor Archives, division 244/IV, report 30–31, Palestine Worker's Party (Mapai), central committee, on the question of Hapoel. Speech by Abba Hushi at a meeting of Mapai members active in Hapoel. The meeting was on 24–25 May 1935 in Tel Aviv.
74   Ibid.
75   Abba Hushi archive at the University of Haifa, file 27. Similarly Labor Archives, division 244/IV, file 44. Speech of Abba Hushi at the second Hapoel conference in Haifa, in 1936.
76   Ibid. (n. 73 above).
77   *Davar*, 2 May 1928; Moshe Beilinson, *Davar*, 3 May 1928.
78   Ibid., 7 October 1928.
79   Ibid., 3 May 1933.
80   Ibid., 1, 2 and 4 June 1933. On the festival of *Shavuoth* two gatherings were held in Haifa – a Hapoel assembly and a Betar assembly. The Histadrut heads in Haifa considered the latter a planned provocation and warned of what was liable to develop. And indeed, on 31 May 1935 a parade of Betarists marched along Herzl street, dressed in brown uniforms, reminiscent of the Nazi uniform in Germany. They were led by Abba Ahimeir, his hand raised in the fascist salute. The workers attacked them and dispersed the parade. A different version was given by Abba Hushi at the meeting of Mapai center on 31 January 1934: see Mapai Archives, Beit Berl, file 23/34. Yet another version is found in Ofir, *The National Worker Volume*, 116.
81   Mapai Archives, Beit Berl, file 24/34. Meetings of Mapai center.
82   Ibid.; likewise David Ben-Gurion, *Memoirs*, B (Tel Aviv: Am Oved, 1972), 17–20 (Hebrew).
83   Mapai Archives, ibid. Statements at the meeting of Mapai center on 21 February 1934, 2–28.
84   Mapai Archives, Beit Berl, file 23/34, meeting of the center on 31 January 1934.
85   Ibid. Meetings of Mapai center on 31 January, 5 February, 14 February 1934.
86   Ibid.
87   *Years of Hapoel*, 8, Labor Archives, 244/IV. The first commander of the Haifa company was Moshe Asterik.
88   Gil, 74, claims that at the end of 1929 and beginning of 1930 there was such a company in Rehovot. On a similar company in Tel Aviv in 1931 see Labor Archives, division 244/IV, file 227, Hapoel Tel Aviv, minutes notebook, meetings and assemblies of the company.
89   IDF Archives, Ben-Gurion diaries, file 2055, 100, entry for 26 January 1928.
90   Labor Archives, minutes of the Histadrut Executive Committee, 52–5.

Discussion on 10 March 1930.

91 Ibid., division 244/IV, file 227, Hapoel center, years 1931–2, Hasadran company of Hapoel Tel Aviv, minutes notebook of meetings and assemblies of the company, 25–39.

92 IDF Archives, file 600. The document is undated.

93 Ibid., file 2556 and also *Davar*, 23 October 1932.

94 IDF Archives, ibid., file 3342. The document is undated and bears comments which Shabtai Tevet ascribes to Ben-Gurion. See Tevet, *David's Sling*, B, 565.

95 *Letters of David Ben-Gurion*, C (Tel Aviv: Am Oved and Tel Aviv University, 1974), 225.

96 Labor Archives, 244/IV, file 221, Tel Aviv branch, volunteering questionnaires, registration for Hasadran Association; Gil, 110.

97 Labor Archives, ibid. Answers in questionnaires of those registering on 1 September 1933.

98 Ibid., file 220, Petah Tikva branch, answer of Moshe Duvdevani, emphasis in original.

99 Ibid., file 222.

100 Ibid., file 220.

101 Ibid. Reports for 1931, 1932, 1933. Report on activities of the committee of the Hapoel branch in Tel Aviv in preparation for the general assembly of the branch on the period July 1932–December 1933. The emphasis is mine. At the head of the Hasadran company in Tel Aviv were Arie Ben Gad, Shabtai Brenner, Yosef Harit, Efraim Perlstein, Yosef Krasner, Yosef Rokhel (Avidar) and Mordechai Shanfer. See also ibid., file 186c. The letter from Haifa was recorded in the file of the Hapoel center secretariat on 15 July 1933.

102 Ibid., file 63. The last document in the file, handwritten, apparently from 1933.

103 *Ben-Gurion Letters*, C (Tel Aviv: Am Oved–Tel Aviv University, 1974), 323ff. Emphasis in the original.

104 Labor Archives, 244/IV, file 226, Regulations of the Hasadran company (approved by the branch committee on 21 July 1931).

105 Ibid., file 80.

106 Ibid., file 226, circular of the central committee of the Hapoel Association, Hasadran Association, chief directorship, circular No. 1 of 27 August 1933. Concerning: Organization of the Hasadran company.

107 Ibid. Report for 1931–1932, from the report to the second national conference, Haifa 20–23 March 1936, 47–8.

108 Ibid.

109 Mapai Archives, Beit Berl, file 23/34, discussion in Mapai center on 24 February 1934.

110 Yosef Avidar, *On the Way to the IDF* (Tel Aviv: Ma'arachot, 1970), 67 (Hebrew). Likewise interview by the author with Yosef Avidar at his home in Jerusalem on 14 February 1989 and also interview by the author with Moshe Carmel (Zalitzky) at his home in Tel Aviv on 7 February 1989.

111 Mapai Archives, Beit Berl, file 23/34, meeting of Mapai center on 21 October 1934.

112 Echoes of this are also found in the Report to the second conference of Hapoel: see n. 107, 48 in the Report.

113 Goldstein, *On the Way to Hegemony*, 128.

114 David Ben-Gurion, *Memoirs*, A (Tel Aviv: Am Oved, 1971), 511–19.

115 Ibid., 542.
116 Goldstein, *On the Way to Hegemony*, 147.
117 Mapai Archives, Beit Berl, file 22/7, seventh session of Mapai council, Tel Aviv, 21–24 March 1934.
118 Ibid., file 23/34, meetings of the center and political commission in 1934, meeting of Mapai center on 2 August 1934.
119 Goldstein, *On the Way to Hegemony*, 194–5. On 31 July 1934 the World Revisionist Zionism center sent a letter from Paris to Mapai center containing a proposal for direct negotiations between the two parties to find a basis for peaceful co-existence in the Yishuv and in the Zionist movement. Mapai center discussed the proposal at four meetings, on 8, 14, 16 and 21 August 1934, and also at the eighth session of the Mapai council on 24–25 August 1934. See also Yaacov Goldstein and Ya'akov Shavit, *Without Compromise* (Hebrew) (Tel Aviv: Yariv-Hadar, 1979), 40–2.
120 Goldstein and Shavit, ibid., ch. 8, 131–40.
121 Ibid., 55–8.
122 *Hashomer Volume*, 413.
123 Ibid. "We knew that if the Hagana committee found out that we, members of Hashomer, had joined Hapoel as members they would watch us very closely, and at every step it would seem to them that we were breaking into their area of authority and a major quarrel could erupt again."
124 IDF Archives, Ben-Gurion diaries, 82, entry for 7 September 1929.
125 Ibid., 89, entry for 13 September 1929.
126 Labor Archives, minutes of the Histadrut Executive Committee. Discussion on 10 February 1930, 29.
127 Ibid., division 104/IV, file 1052–8. Letter from Manya Shohat to Ben-Gurion dated 5 November 1932. Ben-Gurion had a very low opinion of Manya's political understanding and stability. He told her so on several occasions, without choosing his words. On 6 November 1929, when she had tried to persuade him to support a political step initiated by her close colleagues in Brit Shalom, he records his response to her: "In my opinion, although I believe in her honesty and Zionist loyalty I had to tell her clearly that she is doing now what she did once in the Zubatov business. With good intentions she was caught up by a provocation and got involved in something whose gravity and danger she did not understand. This time the matter was worse than the Zubatov affair. You don't understand the subject, or Magnes." See IDF Archives, Ben-Gurion diaries, 124, entry on his conversation with Manya on 6 November 1929. Also in a discussion in the Histadrut Executive Committee on 10 February 1930, when Manya sought approval for her mission to the US, Ben-Gurion said, "Manya is not stable and she is not a political person." See Labor Archives, minutes of the Histadrut Executive Committee, 26. At another meeting between them on 5 May 1930 Manya approached Ben-Gurion on behalf of an ad hoc committee on the subject of Arab workers, and then too he writes, "I informed her that I could not discuss any political matter with her, because despite her good intentions she is totally devoid of responsibility on any political question, and she is more likely to cause harm than good in anything she gets mixed up with." See IDF Archives, Ben-Gurion diaries, file 2060, 17. On this attitude Manya responded in her letter to Ben-Gurion two years later: "I too have changed greatly. I, taught by experience, have come to the absolute recognition that any separatist *enterprise*, even the highest, within the Histadrut, is a curse,

while the separatist *outlook* may be a blessing. And I am no longer capable of making any separatist step, even if I knew that I would thereby save the entire Jewish nation." This was complete contrition over the historic path by Manya, possibly the most extreme figure among the Hashomer people regarding non-submissionn to authority. See Labor Archive, 104/IV, file 1052–8, letter from Manya Shohat to Ben-Gurion from Kefar Gil'adi dated 5 November 1932.

128 Hashomer Archives, Kefar Gil'adi, Hashomer activity in the Labor Battalion, container 6, sign Bet, file 35. Also ibid., conversation with Yisrael Shohat on 11 June 1956; and ibid., container 5, sign Dalet, file 22, comments by Yisrael Shohat to pages 3, 4, 5, 6, 7 in the fourth chapter of *History of the Hagana*, 6; ibid., 12. See also Gil, 75ff., who basis himself on an interview with Yosef Harit conducted by Eli'ezer Roi for *Yarhon Hasport* No. 4, 1961, on the occasion of the seventh assembly of Hapoel.

129 Labor Achives, 244/IV, file 150, letter from the secretariat of the Hapoel Haifa branch dated 19 June 1934. The writer complains that the Hasadran company has been removed from the authority of the branch and this will harm the other sections as well as Hasadran itself. "I too believe that the best members occupied with sporting activity will not come to terms with being turned into people toying with sport. Not for this do they expend their energy, time and resources. And the reverse: the Hasadran company will lose its vitality through being detached from the club. Instead of a cultural and educational factor and also a fighting one, it will become a regressive force."

130 Ibid. Report 30–31. Minutes of Hapoel council at Kiriat Haim on 21–22 June 1935, 5. In the report to the council Yisrael Carmi referred to the crisis that erupted in Hapoel center over the Hasadran problem: "The essence of the argument on the Hasadran question centered on who should have control of it. Should supreme authority for it be given to the Hapoel organs with the usual supervision of the Histadrut Executive Committee, or to the organization as an autonomous division which coordinates all its work with the Hapoel organs and its sections, but is under the direct authority of the Executive Committee?" See also ibid., file 80, discussion at the Hapoel Hadera branch on 20 November 1935, statements of Eliahu Golomb in the discussion.

131 Ibid. Report submitted to the second national conference of Hapoel, held in Haifa on 20–23 March 1936, 8.

132 Ibid. Report submitted to the fourth national convention of Hapoel, held in Tel Aviv on 19–22 April 1935, 34.

133 Rahel Yanait-Ben Zvi, *Manya Shohat*, 127; Labor Archives, 244/IV, file 186b, letter from Hapoel center to the Haifa branch committee dated 15 October 1931; ibid., another letter to the same address dated 15 November 1931; ibid., file 150, letter from Simik in Haifa to Manya Shohat dated 2 May 1933; Hashomer Archives, Kefar Gil'adi, Manya Shohat archive, container 1, file 4, letter (in English) to the famous Jewish boxer Barry Leonard dated 21 July 1931. Manya wanted to recruit him for activities on bahalf of Hapoel; ibid., letter to Hapoel center from London dated 26 November 1930.

134 Labor Archives, division 104/IV, file 1052–8, letter from Manya Shohat in Kefar Gil'adi to Ben-Gurion dated 5 November 1932.

135 Ibid., division 244/IV, file 150. The letter from Kefar Gil'adi is dated 2 June 1933. Manya Shohat's letter to Hapoel center is in the same source.

136 Hashomer Archives, Kefar Gil'adi, Manya Shohat archive, container 5, file 29.
137 Ibid.
138 Labor Archives, division 104/IV, file 1052–8, letter from Manya Shohat at Kefar Gil'adi to Dov Hoz dated 21 June 1934.
139 Ibid., 244/IV, file 80. Emphasis is mine.
140 Ibid. Minutes of the Hapoel council at Kiriat Haim. Report by Yisrael Carmi, 4.
141 Ibid.; and Hashomer Archives, Kefar Gil'adi, Activities of Hashomer in the Labor Battalion, container 6, sign Bet, file 35.
142 Labor Archives, 244/IV, file 80, minutes of the Hapoel council at Kiriat Haim.
143 Ibid., file 44, from the report to the second conference of Hapoel, in Haifa on 20–23 March 1936.
144 Ibid., minutes (handwritten) from the second conference of Hapoel, closing session, 2–4.
145 Yosef Almogi, *At the Heart of the Matter* (Jerusalem: Yediot Aharonot Books, Edanim, 1980), 22–5; Labor Archives, division 244/IV, file 76, minutes of the Hapoel center of 1936; ibid., file 61, from the diary of Zeev Sherf, entry for 8 April 1937; ibid., file 226, Regulations of the companies, December 1938, with the explicit name "Hapoel Companies"; ibid., expanded session of the executive of the companies on 30 September 1937, 2. Yosef Carlenbaum (Almogi) says "after 15 months of organization of the Companies . . . after 15 months since recruitment was announced," meaning that recruiting for the Hapoel companies began several months after the second conference of Hapoel in Haifa. On 3 see the statement of Bunim Shamir: "We need to learn much from the Hasadran affair" – meaning that they were not Hasadran. At the end of the document there is a circular sent by the Hapoel center to the workers' councils. It is undated. It opens as follows: "As you know, Hapoel center has for more than a year been engaged on the organization of Hapoel companies at various points in the country . . . "; Labor Archives, 244/IV, file 227a, expanded session of the central companies Executive on 25 August 1937; ibid., file 167, envelope C. A document of September 1937 signed by Yisrael Alter explains why the Hapoel companies were established – because "Hasadran is now no longer suitable in its restricted composition . . . "; ibid., file 227a, meeting of the central companies Executive on 28 March 1939, 2. According to Mordechai Nemirovsky (Namir) the Hapoel companies were established in Tel Aviv "with the closing of Jaffa port and the issue of a licence to Tel Aviv port."

Bibliography

Archives
Labor Archives, Lavon Institute, Tel Aviv.
Hashomer Archives, Kefar Gil'adi.
Hagana Archives, Tel Aviv.
IDF Archives, Giv'ataim.
Weizmann Archive, Rehovot.
Mapai Archives, Beit Berl.
Abba Hushi Archives, University of Haifa.
Haifa Archives, Haifa.
Central Zionist Archives, Jerusalem.
Yad Tabenkin Archives, Ef'al.

Newspapers
Davar.
Hapoel Hatzair.
Kuntres.
Doar Hayom.
Hatzafon.
Hayarden.
Haint.
Heahdut.
Ha'olam.
Lamerhav.

Encyclopaedias and Academic Journals (Hebrew)
The Hebrew Encyclopaedia.
Lexicon of Personalities of Palestine, 1799–1948 (ed. Y. Shavit, Y. Goldstein, and H. Bar), Tel Aviv: Am Oved, 1983.
Cathedra, Ben Zvi Institute, Jerusalem.
Basha'ar.
Shorashim, Kibbutz Movement publication (Takam).
Measef, Giv'at Haviva.
Hariv'on lemehkar hevrati, Histadrut, Haifa Workers' Council.
Hatzionut, Collection, Tel Aviv University.

Interviews
With Moshe Carmel, 7 February 1989.
With Yosef Avidar, 14 February 1989.

Books in Hebrew
Alkalai, Yehuda Hai. *The Writings of Rabbi Yehuda Alkelai*, Book 1, Vol. 1, Jerusalem: Harav Kook Institute, 1944.
Almogi, Yosef. *At the Heart of the Matter*, Jerusalem: Edanim, 1980.
Arlozoroff, Haim. *Selection of Writings and Chapters in His Life*, Tel Aviv: Hasifria Hatzionit and Ayanot, Am Oved.
Assaf, Michael. *The Awakening of the Arabs in Palestine and Their Flight*, Culture and Education, Tel Aviv: Am Oved, 1967.
——. *Relations between Arabs and Jews in Palestine 1860–1948*, Tel Aviv: Culture and Education, Am Oved, 1970.
Avidar, Yosef. *On the Way to the IDF*, Tel Aviv: Ma'arachot, 1970.
Avitsur, Shmuel. *Daily Life in Palestine in the Nineteenth Century*, Tel Aviv: Am Hasefer, 1972.
Avneri, Shlomo. *The Zionist Idea in Its Various Forms*, Tel Aviv: Am Oved, 1980.
Bar Zohar, Michael. *Ben-Gurion*, Vol. A, Tel Aviv: Am Oved, 1975. Vols. B, C, 1977.
Beitan, Arie. *Changes in the Yishuv in Eastern Lower Galilee 1800–1978*, Jerusalem: Ben Zvi Institute, 1982.
Belkind, Yisrael. *The First Step in the Settlement of Palestine*, New York: Hameir, 1917.
Ben-Gurion Letters, Vol. A, compiled and annotated by Yehuda Erez, Tel Aviv: Am Oved and Tel Aviv University, 1971.
Ben-Gurion Letters, Vol. B, compiled and annotated by Yehuda Erez, Tel Aviv: Am Oved and Tel Aviv University, 1972.
Ben-Gurion Letters, Vol. C, compiled and annotated by Yehuda Erez, Tel Aviv: Am Oved and Tel Aviv University, 1974.
Ben-Gurion, David. *Letters to Paula and the Children*, Tel Aviv: Am Oved, 1969.
——. *The Workers' Movement and Revisionism*, Tel Aviv: World League for Working Palestine, League Directorate, 1933.
——. *Memoirs*, Vol. A, 1971; Vol. B, 1972; Vol. C, 1973; Vol. D, 1974, Tel Aviv: Am Oved.
Ben Zvi, Yitzhak. *Poaley Zion in the Second Aliya*, Mapai and Ihud Olami, 1950.
——. *Recollections and Notes*, Jerusalem: Ben Zvi Institute, 1967.
——. *The Jewish Battalions*, Jerusalem: Ben Zvi Institute, 1968.
Bernstein, Devora. *A Woman in Palestine*, Hakibbutz Hameuhad, 1987.
Borochov, Ber. *Writings*, Vol. 1, Levite, L. and Ben Nahum, D. (eds), Hakibbutz Hameuhad-Sifriat Poalim, Hakibbutz Haartzi-Hashomer Hatzair, 1955.
Braslavski, Moshe. *Workers and Their Organizations in the First Aliya*, Hakibbutz Hameuhad, 1961.
——. *The Palestinian Workers' Movement*, Hakibbutz Hameuhad, 1966.
Carmel, Alex, *Haifa in the Time of the Turks*, Haifa, 1969.
Chapters of Hapoel Hatzair, Tel Aviv: N. Tverski, 1935.
Dagan, Shaul. *Between Tel Adas and Hamara, Memoirs of Moshe Levit, Member of Hashomer*, Nature Protection Society Publication, 1988.
Dinur, Ben Zion (editor-in-chief). *History of the Hagana*, Hasifria Hatzionit and Ma'arachot, 1954, Am Oved edition.
Droyanov, Alter. *Writings and History of Hibbat Zion and the Settlement of Palestine*, Odessa Committee for the Settlement of Palestine, 1909.
Elam, Yigael. *The Jewish Battalions in the First World War*, Tel Aviv, 1973.
——. *The Hagana: The Zionist Way to Power*, Tel Aviv: Zmora, Bitan, Modan, 1979.

Eshel, Tzadok. *The Hagana Battles in Haifa*, Tel Aviv, 1978.

Gera, Gershon. *A House in Tel Aviv*, Tel Aviv: Ministry of Defense, 1987.

Gil, Emanuel. *The Story of Hapoel*, Hakibbutz Hameuhad (place and year not indicated).

Goldstein, Yaacov. *The Palestine Workers' Party (Mapai), Factors in Its Establishment*, Tel Aviv: Am Oved, Education and Culture, 1975.

——. *On the Way to Hegemony*, Tel Aviv: Am Oved, Culture and Education, 1980.

——. *The Histadrut and the Workers of the United States*, Tel Aviv: Am Oved, Culture and Education, The Pinhas Lavon Research Institute of the Labor Movement, 1984.

——. and Shavit, Ya'akov. *Without Compromise*, Tel Aviv: Yariv- Hadar, 1979.

Golomb, Eliahu. *Latent Force*, Tel Aviv: Mapai publication, 1950.

Gordon, David. *Selected Articles*, Sifriat Shorashim, Tel Aviv: Mitzpe publication, 1942.

Gorny, Yosef. *Ahdut Ha'avoda 1919–1930*, Tel Aviv University and Hakibbutz Hameuhad, 1973.

——. *From Rosh Pina and Degania to Dimona, Talks on the Zionist Building Endeavor*, Tel Aviv: University on the Air, Ministry of Defense publication, 1983.

——. *The Arab Question and the Jewish Problem*, Tel Aviv: Sifriat Ofakim, Am Oved, 1985.

Grinbaum, Yitzhak. *The Zionist Movement in Its Development*, Youth Department of the Zionist Organization, Jerusalem: Reuvan Mass (no year indicated).

Habas, Bracha (ed.). *Second Aliya Volume*, Tel Aviv: Am Oved, 1947.

Hacohen, David. *Time to Tell*, Tel Aviv: Am Oved, 1974.

Hacohen, Mordechai Ben Hillel. *The War of the Nations*, Vol. 1, Jerusalem: Ben Zvi Institute, 1981. Vol. 2, 1985.

Harozen, Ya'akov. *The Vision of Settlement in the Galilee*, Jerusalem: Harav Kook Institute, 1971.

Hashomer Collection. Tel Aviv: Labor Archives publication, 1933.

Hashomer Volume, special edition for the IDF, Ma'arachot, Tel Aviv: Dvir, Ministry of Defense, edition A, 1957, reprinted 1962.

Hertzberg, Arthur. *The Zionist Idea*, Jerusalem: Keter, 1970.

Hetzroni, Arie. *Herdsman and Fighter, The Story of Gershon Fleisher, the First of the Shepherds, Hashomer Man*, Jerusalem: M. Neumann, 1978.

Jabotinsky, Zeev. *Writings, Speeches 1927–1940*, Jerusalem, 1948.

Kalisher, Zvi. "Yearning for Zion", in Klausner, Yisrael. *The Zionist Writings of Rabbi Zvi Kalisher*, Jerusalem: Harav Kook Institute, 1947.

Katznelson, Berl. *Letters 1919–1922*, Tel Aviv: Am Oved, 1970.

Kish, P. H. *Palestine Diary*, translated from English by A. Abadi, Jerusalem: Ahiasaf, 1939.

Klausner, Yisrael. *The Zionist Movement in Russia*, Vol. A, *The Awakening of the People*, Jerusalem: Hasifria Hatzionit, 1962.

Kollat, Yisrael. *Ideology and Reality in the Poaley Zion Movement 1905–1919*, dissertation submitted for the degree of Ph.D. to the Hebrew University, Jerusalem, 1964.

Kostitzki, Avraham. *Before First Light*, Tel Aviv: Ministry of Defense publication, 1983.

Kressel, Gideon. *Petah Tikva, Mother of the Moshavot, 1878–1953*, Petah Tikva:

Petah Tikva Municipality, 1953.
Krinitzi, Avraham. *By Virtue of the Deed*, Tel Aviv: Masada, 1954.
Lacquer, Zeev. *A History of Zionism*, Jerusalem and Tel Aviv: Shocken, 1974.
Lev-Ami, Shlomo. *In Struggle and in Revolt*, Tel Aviv: Ministry of Defense publi-
cation (year not indicated).
Levontin, Zalman David. *To the Land of Our Fathers*, Tel Aviv: Eitan Press,
1924.
Lubovski, Benyamin (Eliav). *Revisionist Zionism and Betar*, Jerusalem: Institute
for Zionist Education, 1946.
Lubrani, Eli'ezer (ed.). *The Way of a Man, Anthology in Memory of Ya'akov Pat*,
Council to Memorialize Ya'akov Pat, 1958.
Maimon, Ada. *Fifty Years of the Women Workers' Movement 1904–1954*, Tel
Aviv: Ayanot, 1955.
Margalit, Elkana. *Commune, Society and Politics*, Research Notebooks, Institute
for Labor and Social Research, Tel Aviv: Sifria Universitait-Am Oved, 1980.
Meirovich, Meir. *Pangs of Rebirth*, Tel Aviv: Commerce and Industry publica-
tion, 1931.
Michael, Ben Zion. *Sejera*, Tel Aviv, 1973.
Mintz, Matityiahu. *Friend and Rival*, Yad Tabenkin–Hakibbutz Hameuhad,
1986.
Nadav, Yitzhak. *Recollections of a Hashomer Man*, Tel Aviv: Ministry of Defense
publication, 1986.
Nadav, Zvi. *From the Days of the Guarding and the Defense*, Tel Aviv:
Ma'arachot, 1954.
——. *This Is How We Began*, Hakibbutz Hameuhad, 1957.
Naor, Mordechai (ed.). *Idan 4, The Second Aliya, 1903–1914*, Jerusalem: Ben Zvi
Institute, 1985.
Niv, David. *Battles of the Irgun Tzvai Leumi*, Tel Aviv: Klausner Institute, 1965.
Ofir, Yeruham. *National Worker Volume*, Tel Aviv: Histadrut Executive
Committee publication, 1959.
Pa'il, Meir. *From the Hagana to the Israel Defense Forces*, Zmora, Bitan, Modan,
1979.
Paz, Sa'adia. *Memoirs*, published by his family, Haifa, 1963.
Porath, Yehoshu'a. *The Growth of the Palestinian Arab National Movement
1918–1929*, Tel Aviv: Sifria Universitait-Am Oved, 1976.
——. *From Disturbances to Rebellion: The Palestinian Arab National Movement
1929–1939*, Tel Aviv: Sifria Universitait-Am Oved, 1976.
Ramba, A. *Krinitzi*. Ramat Gan: Masada, 1968.
Repetor, Berl. *Without Ceasing*, Tel Aviv: Hakibbutz Hameuhad, 1973.
Rogel, Nakdimon. *Tel Hai – A Front Without Rear*, Tel Aviv: Yariv-Hadar, 1979.
——. *Those who Went Northbound*, Jerusalem: Ben Zvi Institute, 1987.
Rosenstein (Even-Shoshan), Zvi. *A History of the Workers' Movement in
Palestine*, Tel Aviv: Am Oved, 1955.
Samsonov, Arie. *Zikhron Ya'akov*, Tel Aviv: Amanot, 1942.
——. *Zikhron Ya'akov, its History 1882–1942*, Moshava Committee through the
Book Committee, 1943.
——. *Anonymous Pioneers*, Tel Aviv: Sifriat Rishonim, 1944.
Schechtmann, Joseph B. *Zeev Jabotinsky, The Story of His Life*, Vols A–C, Tel
Aviv: Carni, 1956.
Schlezinger, Yehiel. *The Teaching of Yehiel*, Book of Genesis, Jerusalem:
Committee for the Publication of the Works of the Gaon Rabbi Akiva Yosef,

of Blessed Memory, 1971.

Shalem, M. and Zamir, D. (eds). *The Jewish Herdsman's Volume*, Merhavia, 1957.

Shapira, Anita. *To the Horizon*, Sifriat Ofakim, Tel Aviv: Am Oved, 1988.

Shapira, Yosef. *Hapoel Hatzair, The Idea and the Deed*, Tel Aviv: Ayanot, 1967.

Shneorson, Pinhas. *In the First Rank* (compiled and edited by Shlomo Shva), Sifriat Hapoalim, 1978.

Shohat, Manya and Shohat, Yisrael. *Letters and Recollections, Ten Years after Their Deaths*, Beit Hashomer, IDF Museum and Kibbutz Kefar Gil'adi, 1971.

Slutzki, Yehuda. *The First to Guarding and Defense*, special reprint from *History of the Hagana*, Vol. A, Ma'arachot, Tel Aviv 1963.

——. *Introduction to the History of the Israeli Labor Movement*, Tel Aviv: Sifria Universitait-Am Oved, 1973.

Smilansky, Moshe. *Family of the Earth*, Tel Aviv: Am Oved, 1954.

——. *Chapters in the History of the Yishuv*, Tel Aviv: Dvir, 1959.

Soffer, A. and Kipnis, B. (eds). *Atlas of Haifa and the Carmel*, Haifa, 1980.

Sprinzak (Yosef) Letters, Vols A, B, C, compiled, edited and annotated by Yosef Shapira, Tel Aviv: Ayanot, 1965.

Talmon, Ya'akov. *The Beginnings of Totalitarian Democracy*, Tel Aviv: Dvir, 1955.

——. *Political Messianism – The Romantic Stage*, Tel Aviv: Am Oved, 1964.

Tamir, Nahman (ed.). *People of the Second Aliya*, Vol. 6, Tel Aviv: Center for Culture and Education, 1974.

Tevet, Shabtai. *David's Sling*, Vols A (1976), B (1980), C (1987), Jerusalem: Shocken.

Twenty-Five Years of Hapoel, Histadrut and Hapoel Association publication, April 1952.

Tzahor Zeev. *On the Way to the Leadership of the Yishuv*, Jerusalem: Ben Zvi Institute, 1982.

——. *The Roots of Israeli Politics*, Tel Aviv: Hakibbutz Hameuhad-Ben-Gurion University of the Negev, 1987.

Ussishkin, Menahem. *The Ussishkin Volume on His Seventieth Birthday*, Jerusalem: Committee for the Publication of the Book, 1934.

Wavell, Field-Marshal A. F. *The Palestine Campaigns*, Tel Aviv: Ma'arachot, 1953.

Weitz, Yosef. *First Pages*, Tel Aviv, 1958.

Women in the Kibbutz, first collection, Hakibbutz Hameuhad, 1944, compiled by Lilia Basevich and Yocheved Bat Rahel. M. Poznansky and M. Shehori, eds.

Ya'ari, Avraham. *Memoirs of Palestine*, Jerusalem, 1947.

Ya'ari-Polskin, Y. and Harizman, M. *Jubilee Volume Fifty Years since the Founding of Petah Tiakva, 1878–1928*, Tel Aviv: Jubilee Committee of the Local Council, 1929.

——. *Pinhas Ruthenberg, The Man and His Work*, Tel Aviv: Hatekufa Ba'am, 1939.

Yad Tabenkin, Institute for the Study of the Defensive Force. Paper No. 37, "Roots of Self Defense," November 1983.

Yaffe, Hillel. *A Generation of Illegal Immigrants*, Tel Aviv: Dvir, 1939.

Yanait-Ben Zvi, Rahel. *We Are Coming*, Tel Aviv: Sifriat Yalkut, Haifa Workers' Council–Am Oved, 1962.

——. *Manya Shohat*, Jerusalem: Ben Zvi Institute, 1976.

Yigael, Mordechai. *In the Saddle*, second edition, amended and expanded, Tel

Aviv: Ma'arachot (no year indicated).

Zamir, Uri. *Physical Education and Sport in Palestine 1917–1927*, Wingate Insitute, 1971.

Zayd, Alexander. *Toward Morning, Chapters in a Diary*, Tel Aviv: Am Oved, 1975.

Books in English

Antonius, George. *The Arab Awakening*, New York: Capricorn Books, 1965.

Duff, D.W. *Sword for Hire*, London: John Murray, 1934.

Friedman, Isaiah. *Germany, Turkey and Zionism 1897–1919*, Oxford: Clarendon Press, 1977.

Gilner, Elias. *War and Hope*, New York: Herzl Press, 1951.

Hayes, Carlton J. H. *The Historical Evolution of Modern Nationalism*, New York: Macmillan, 1951.

Kedourie, Elie. *Nationalism*, London: Hutchinson University Library, 1960.

Kohn, Hans. *The Idea of Nationalism*, New York: Macmillan, 1944.

——. *Nationalism, Its Meaning and History*, Princeton, New Jersey: D. Van Nostrand, 1965.

Palestine: A Study of Jewish, Arab and British Policies, Yale University Press and Oxford University Press, 1947; New York: Kraus Reprint Co., 1970.

Schechtman, J. B. and Benary, Y. *The History of the Revisionist Movement*, Tel Aviv: Hadar Publishing House, 1970, Vol. I.

Venturi, Franco. *Roots of Revolution: A History of the Populist and Socialist Movements in Nineteenth Century Russia*, New York: Grosset & Dunlap, 1966.

Articles and Other Publications (Hebrew)

Brenner, Uri. "The place of the woman in Hashomer," *Shorashim* B, Tabenkin Insitute for Research and Study of the Kibbutz, Hakibbutz Hameuhad, 1980.

Goldstein, Yaacov. "When did Shlomo Kaplanski's membership of the Zionist leadership begin?" in *Hariv'on lemehkar hevrati*, Nos 7–8, Haifa: Haifa Workers' Council, 1974.

——. "The idea of settlement in the national ethos," lecture series in Zionism studies, No. 8, University of Haifa publication, Reuben Hecht Chair in Zionism, 1983.

Gorny, Yosef. "Hapoel Hatzair and its attitude to socialism," *Baderekh*, Giv'at Haviva, December 1970.

Kollat, Yisrael. "Hapoel Hatzair from Conquest of Labor to sanctification of labor," *Badereckh*, A, September 1967, Giv'at Haviva.

Opaz, Aviva. "Letters from Palestine, the Hashomer man Mendel Portugali to his wife Tova," *Hadarim* 3–4, winter 1982–1983, Gordon Gallery publication (undated).

Porat, Lola. "The woman worker in the Second Aliya," *Basha'ar*, Nos 5–6, September–December 1972.

Shiloh, Margalit. "The women workers' farm at Kinneret 1911–1917," *Cathedra* 14, Jerusalem: Ben Zvi Institute, 1980.

Tzahor, Zeev. "The disbanding of Tel Hai (1926): The last link in the struggle between the Histadrut and the Labor Battalion," *Measef*, 12, 1980–1981, Giv'at Haviva.

——. "Sad victory: Ben-Gurion and the Labor Battalion," *Cathedra*, No. 43, Jerusalem: Ben Zvi Institute, spring 1987.

Tzemah, Shlomo. *Conquest of Labor Calendar for 1950–1951*, Tel Aviv: Haim Publications.

Index